BARRON'S

1100 WORDS You Need to Know

EIGHTH EDITION

RICH CARRIERO, MURRAY BROMBERG, AND MELVIN GORDON

Published by Kaplan, Inc., d/b/a Barron's Educational Series
1515 W. Cypress Creek Road
Fort Lauderdale, FL 33309
www.barronseduc.com

ISBN: 978-1-5062-7118-7

10 9 8 7 6 5 4 3 2 1

CONTENTS

How to Use This Book v
Full Pronunciation Key vi
Week 1: Wisdom 1
Week 2: Folly 8
Week 3: Success 15
Week 4: Failure 22
Week 5: Dishonesty 30
Week 6: Wealth 37
Week 7: Poverty 44
Week 8: Youth 51
Week 9: Age 59
Week 10: Horror 66
Week 11: Drama 73
Week 12: Skilled 80
Week 13: Cause and Effect 87
Week 14: Courage 94
Week 15: Crime 101
Week 16: Work 107
Week 17: Persuasion 114
Week 18: Expression 121
Week 19: Power 127
Week 20: Insults 134
Week 21: Indefinite 141
Week 22: Sloth 147
Week 23: Uncertainty 153
Week 24: Belief 160
Week 25: Conflict 167
Week 26: Writing 173
Week 27: Beauty 180
Week 28: Geography 186

Week 29: Speed 193
Week 30: Happiness 199
Week 31: Conformity 205
Week 32: Size 212
Week 33: Scarcity/Weakness 219
Week 34: Sadness 226
Week 35: Speech 232
Week 36: Bizarre 238
Week 37: Anger 245
Week 38: Law 252
Week 39: Strength 258
Week 40: Time 264
Week 41: Health 271
Week 42: Information 277
Week 43: Quantity 283
Week 44: Chaos 289
Week 45: Cooperation 295
Week 46: Virtue 301

Appendix

Answer Key 310
Index 343

HOW TO USE THIS BOOK

This book is designed around a simple principle: information is more easily assimilated when you have context.

Words Organized by Theme

Rather than studying random or alphabetized lists of words (which are quite arbitrary when it comes to how words are related), in this edition the words are organized into lists based on common concepts or themes. Themes are noted on the top right of the page. This should, on its own, make the words easier to retain. For example, if you forget what *languid* means but remember that it belongs to the list of words related to *sloth*, you'll know that it probably has something to do with laziness or lacking energy.

This way of organizing words affords a few study options. For example, you can study related groups of words like *speech*, *expression*, and *writing* or opposite pairs of words like *success* and *failure* to build ever larger frameworks of context.

A natural consequence of organizing words by common meaning is that you will encounter many words with similar or identical meanings. So, while working through exercises, do not be disturbed by the fact that while you used one word to answer a question, a synonymous word is listed as the answer. **If your answer is synonymous with the correct answer, both answers are correct!**

Notable Roots

Another feature of this book is the list of *notable roots* that follows each day's words. This includes roots, prefixes, and suffixes found in your vocabulary words that can also be found in other words. This gives you yet another context for study: groups of words that share common roots.

Weekly Study Program

The book is organized into 46 weeks of study, each containing four lists of six words to be studied during the week and a series of review exercises for the fifth day (or weekend if you prefer). Review exercises not only cover that week's words, but also periodically review words learned on previous weeks. This brings up an important point—success with vocabulary study comes through repetition. Each day's words should be reviewed a few times throughout the day, and past words need to be studied and used in order for them to stick.

FULL PRONUNCIATION KEY

a	**a**pple, b**a**t
ā	**a**ge, l**a**ce
ä	**a**lms, f**a**ther
är	**ar**m, j**ar**
b	**b**ag, so**b**
ch	**ch**ill, su**ch**
d	**d**one, sai**d**
ə	**a**round, wak**e**n, pencil, dem**o**n
e	**e**lk, m**e**t
ē	**e**ase, s**ee**
er	**air**, w**ear**
ėr	**ur**n, w**or**th
f	**f**eel, sti**ff**
g	**g**one, bi**g**
h	**h**im, be**h**ind
hw	**wh**ich, **wh**ale
i	**i**nch, p**i**n
ir	**ear**, ch**eer**
ī	**i**vy, h**i**de
j	**j**ust, en**j**oy
k	**k**in, tal**k**
l	**l**ose, hur**l**
m	**m**ice, cra**m**
n	**n**ot, i**n**to
ŋ	so**ng**, ri**ng**
o	**o**x, r**o**t
ō	**o**pen, bl**ow**
ô	**a**ll, b**ough**t
ôi	**oi**l, b**oy**
ôr	**ore**, c**or**d
ou	**ow**l, m**ou**se
p	**p**est, ca**p**
r	**r**ed, t**r**ee
s	**s**pell, be**s**t
sh	**sh**rug, cra**sh**
t	**t**ime, ac**t**
th	**th**ink, tee**th**
TH	**th**is, brea**the**
u	b**u**ll, f**oo**t
ur	s**ure**, p**ure**
ū	**oo**ze, c**u**te
û	**u**p, m**o**nth
v	**v**ast, ha**v**e
w	**w**ish, sq**u**eak
y	**y**outh, f**ew**
z	**z**oo, bu**zz**
zh	**g**enre, plea**s**ure
-	denotes separate syllables

READING WISELY

An *astute* reader can *surmise* the logic and general meaning of a text without necessarily being influenced by it. She has the mental *acuity* to separate fact from opinion. She does not shun the latter but instead weighs *proffered* insights according to the *probity* of the writer as well as the degree to which subjective views conform with her experience, values, and *prudence*.

NEW WORDS

astute
ə - stût

surmise
sur - mīz

acuity
ə - kyū - i - tē

proffer
pro - fėr

probity
prō - bi - tē

prudence
prū - dins

Notable Roots: mis = send out; ac = sharpness; prob = worth, goodness

Sample Sentences: Use your new words in the following sentences. Occasionally, it may be necessary to change the ending of a word (e.g., *indiscriminate* to *indiscriminately*).

1. The mayor's business dealings left his ________________ open to question.
2. To receive a driver's license you must demonstrate your visual ________________.
3. ________________ is the hallmark of a sound investment strategy.
4. Above all, a hiring manager must be a(n) ______________ judge of character.
5. The professor ________________ the following advice: choose a well-researched topic.
6. From his demeanor, Beth _______________ that her brother wished to be left alone.

Definitions: Now that you have seen and used the new words in sentences and have the definitions "on the tip of your tongue," try to pair the words with their meanings.

7. astute	_________		**a.**	to determine by observation and deduction
8. surmise	_________		**b.**	to present in a helpful manner
9. acuity	_________		**c.**	upright moral character
10. proffer	_________		**d.**	caution; good sense
11. probity	_________		**e.**	clever; keenly observant
12. prudence	_________		**f.**	sharpness; perceptiveness

INFORMATION OVERLOAD

Though information technology has put a glut of it at our fingertips, knowledge is not always power. A healthy democracy does depend on a citizenry *cognizant* of facts and *apprised* of current events. To be truly *circumspect* about it, however, we *concoct* so many studies, "news" articles, and angry screeds for *perusal* that readers can become numb, while the *pedantic* merely use facts and talking points to impress.

Sample Sentences: Now that you've seen the words used in context and have an idea of their meanings, try to use them in the following sentences. Remember that a word ending may have to be changed.

1. The teacher easily saw through the excuse her student had ________________.
2. An array of intelligence services keeps the president ________________ of foreign and domestic threats to national security.
3. ________________ of what the pitcher was about to throw, the center fielder confidently swung the bat.
4. Einstein was modest and never ________________ toward those who lacked his brilliance.
5. While the young are prone to rashness, the old are more ________________.
6. The young couple had their attorney ________________ the contract before they would sign it.

NEW WORDS

cognizant
kog - ni - zent

apprise
ə - prīz

circumspect
ser - kûm - spekt

concoct
kun - kokt

peruse
pə - rūz

pedantic
pə - dan - tik

Notable Roots: cog = thought, knowledge; circum = circle; spec = sight; ped = teaching, child

Definitions: Test yourself by matching the new words with the definitions.

7.	cognizant	________	a.	to review with care
8.	apprise	________	b.	thoughtful; cautious
9.	circumspect	________	c.	showing off one's knowledge
10.	concoct	________	d.	to be aware of specific information
11.	peruse	________	e.	to create or prepare
12.	pedantic	________	f.	to provide information

LEND FEW THY TONGUE

Sylvia was a *canny* survivor. For months one decree after another came down from the new management team without any input from the workforce. Accustomed to a more open corporate culture, griping colleagues found themselves victims of "restructuring." Sylvia had found that a *politic* approach gave her a better chance at keeping her post. Thus, she maintained an *introspective* silence. When the atmosphere finally became too toxic, she crafted a corporate memo offering a *cogent* analysis of company failings with many *incisive* critiques. After *ruminating* over whether to send it, however, she chose instead to polish her resume and begin the search for an employer that deserved her skills and loyalty.

NEW WORDS

canny
kan - nē

politic
pol - i - tik

introspective
in - trō - spek - tiv

cogent
kō - jent

incisive
in - sī - siv

ruminate
rū - min - āt

Notable Roots: polis = city; intro = inward; spec = sight; cis = cut; rumen = chew on

Sample Sentences: Try your hand at using your new words by writing them in their correct form (change the endings if necessary) in these sentences:

1. Luddendorf's ________________, feverish mind was steadied by Hindenberg's pragmatism and calmness; together they formed a highly effective leadership team.
2. Dole and Clinton were ________________ in their eulogies of the polarizing Nixon, choosing to focus on his many foreign policy achievements while glossing over the Watergate scandal.
3. The quiet of nature allows us a chance to ________________, finding insights into and solutions for the vexations of everyday life.
4. A ________________ argument will always win more people over than a convoluted one.
5. Malik is naturally more ________________, often apologizing for breaches of etiquette that are barely noticed, if at all.
6. Lincoln's kindly, story-telling persona belied what a ________________ politician he was.

Definitions: If you are having trouble picking the right definitions, it may be best *not* to do them in the order given, but to do the ones you are surest of first.

7. canny	________	a.	inward looking; self-aware
8. politic	________	b.	expressed clearly and forcefully
9. introspective	________	c.	careful to avoid giving offense; shrewd
10. cogent	________	d.	to consider carefully
11. incisive	________	e.	perceptive; astute*; cautious
12. ruminate	________	f.	clear and penetrating; harsh

*astute—studied previously, see page 1. *Each review word studied previously will be followed by an asterisk—you will find the first use of the word by consulting the index at the back of the book.*

NERVOUS NELLY

Contract signing always made Chris feel *pensive*. He had done his job well, bringing buyers and sellers together. This was the moment when he would earn his commission, but past experience had taught him to take a *pragmatic* view: so many things could still go wrong. *Perspicacious* first-time homebuyers asked many questions, some reasonable and *trenchant*, others quibbling and paranoid. To assuage their fears as much as possible, he felt it best to be transparent. "The contract *stipulates* $20,000 in earnest money," he pointed out, then added, *pedagogically*, "That's a down payment the sellers keep in case you back out before closing."

NEW WORDS

pensive
pen - siv

pragmatic
prag - ma - tik

perspicacious
pėr - spik - ā - shəs

trenchant
tren - chent

stipulate
stip - ū - lāt

pedagogue
ped - ə - gog

Notable Roots: pens = thinking; spec = sight; trench = depth; ped = teaching, children

Sample Sentences: Getting the hang of it? Now go on to use the six new words in the following sentences—remember, past tenses may be required.

1. Few modern satirists are as ________________ as H. L. Mencken, whose wit was devastating.
2. Elle's ________________ expression stood out in the sea of smiling faces in the class photo.
3. As a natural ________________, Malini was a font of both useful information and trivia.
4. The visionary Root designed buildings of sublime beauty for the clients secured by the charming and ________________ Burnham.
5. The ________________ general manager, "Stick" Michael, assembled the Yankee dynasty of the late 1990s by recognizing the latent potential of unsung prospects and free agents.
6. The terms ________________ in the labor agreement are so clear that management and the workforce rarely have serious disagreements.

Definitions: Pick the letter of the definition that matches your new word and write it in the answer space.

7. pensive	________	a.	to set as a condition for an agreement
8. pragmatic	________	b.	teacher; one who offers unsolicited information
9. perspicacious	________	c.	observant; sarcastically witty
10. trenchant	________	d.	thoughtful; nervous
11. stipulate	________	e.	perceptive; discerning
12. pedagogue	________	f.	having a practical point of view

GROUP REVIEW

You have accomplished something worthwhile this week. In learning 24 useful words, you have taken a step toward a greater mastery of the English language. In studying a single group of related words, you are more likely to retain this mastery. As a result of today's lesson, you will become aware of those words that require greater study on your part for complete success in these first lessons.

Matching

Directions: Take the following quiz by matching the best possible definition with the words you have studied. Write the letter that stands for that definition in the appropriate answer space.

	REVIEW WORDS	DEFINITIONS
______	**1.** acuity	**a.** to be aware of specific information
______	**2.** apprise	**b.** having a practical point of view
______	**3.** astute	**c.** to consider carefully
______	**4.** canny	**d.** thoughtful; nervous
______	**5.** circumspect	**e.** perceptive; astute*; cautious
______	**6.** cogent	**f.** upright moral character
______	**7.** cognizant	**g.** perceptive; discerning
______	**8.** concoct	**h.** expressed clearly and forcefully
______	**9.** incisive	**i.** to determine by observation and deduction
______	**10.** introspective	**j.** teacher; one who offers unsolicited information
______	**11.** pedagogue	**k.** clear and penetrating; harsh
______	**12.** pedantic	**l.** thoughtful; cautious
______	**13.** pensive	**m.** observant; sarcastically witty
______	**14.** perspicacious	**n.** showing off one's knowledge
______	**15.** peruse	**o.** to set as a condition for an agreement
______	**16.** politic	**p.** caution; good sense
______	**17.** pragmatic	**q.** careful to avoid giving offense; shrewd
______	**18.** probity	**r.** clever; keenly observant
______	**19.** proffer	**s.** to review with care
______	**20.** prudence	**t.** sharpness; perceptiveness
______	**21.** ruminate	**u.** to provide information
______	**22.** stipulate	**v.** to present in a helpful manner
______	**23.** surmise	**w.** to create or prepare
______	**24.** trenchant	**x.** inward looking; self-aware

Exploring Roots

As the most common roots are to be found in many different words, knowledge of them is an important tool for breaking down new and unfamiliar vocabulary. Whether you recognize a word's etymology or its similarity to a foreign language word, improving your knowledge of these building blocks will improve your mastery of vocabulary.

Directions: Match the root definition with the sentence containing an italicized word using the same root.

________	**1.** teaching, child	**a.** *Ruminants* are the principle source of milk production.
________	**2.** sight	**b.** The modern *metropolis* offers much for tourists to admire.
________	**3.** depth	**c.** Judges often sentence first-time offenders to *probation*.
________	**4.** circle	**d.** Some personality disorders can be treated with *cognitive* behavioral therapy.
________	**5.** thought	**e.** *Entrenched* attitudes are the hardest to eradicate.
________	**6.** chew on	**f.** Magellan died before he could complete the *circumnavigation* of the world.
________	**7.** city	**g.** The daredevil amazed the *spectators*.
________	**8.** worth	**h.** Vaccination is a contentious subject among parents and *pediatricians*.

Wordsearch

Directions: Using the clues listed below, fill in each blank in the following story with one of the new words you learned this week.

Clues

3rd Day

2nd Day

1st Day

4th Day

1st Day

Reggie the Con Man

In the annals of crime, there are few scoundrels who could match the exploits of Reggie Hayes, who also used the names of Reginald Haven, Ricardo Hermosa, Father Harris, and dozens of other aliases. Reggie's police record, principally in Chicago and Baltimore, demonstrates his ________ knack for exploiting the gullible.

Dressed as a priest ("Father Harris"), he __________ his most daring ruse. An ________ judge of character, he would carefully select his mark, then "find" a wallet stuffed with hundred-dollar bills (but lacking identification) outside a supermarket and invite his victim to share his good fortune. But first, to establish her credibility, he ___________ that his victim had to put up a sum of money as a testimonial to her _________. Mrs. Emma Schultz, age 72, tearfully told the police that she had withdrawn $14,000 from her bank and placed it in a shopping bag supplied by the helpful priest. He told her to hold onto the bag while he went next door to a lawyer's office to make the sharing of their good fortune legal.

After a seemingly interminable wait, Mrs. Schultz discovered to her chagrin that the heartless thief had skipped out the back way, leaving her "holding the bag"—a switched bag containing shredded newspaper—while he made his getaway with her life savings.

WEEK 2 DAY 1

Folly

TO THE POINT

Calvin Coolidge was one of the most *dilatory* presidents in history. Elevated to the Oval Office by the unexpected death of his predecessor, Warren Harding, Coolidge presided over the boom economy of the Roaring Twenties. While an improvement over the *unsavory* scandals of the Harding days, the benign neglect of the Coolidge administration allowed the *iniquities* of the era to thrive. Believing government should do as little possible, Coolidge was no *egotist*; he avoided grand gestures and was *infamous* for his laconic speech. One Sunday, after Mr. Coolidge had listened to an interminable sermon, a throng of newsmen gathered around him. An intrepid reporter asked: "Mr. President, we know that the sermon was on the topic of sin. What did the minister say?" Coolidge replied, somewhat *impishly*, "He was against it."

NEW WORDS

dilatory
dil - ə - tôr - ē

unsavory
un - sāv - or - ē

iniquity
in - i - kwi – tē

egotist
ē - gō - tist

infamous
in - fə - mus

impish
imp - ish

Notable Roots: dil = delay; equi = equal; ego = self; fam = fame, celebration

Sample Sentences: Use the new words in the following sentences.

1. The 1919 White Sox are _______________ for accepting bribes to throw the World Series.
2. The _______________ behavior of their two-year-old made the Antonuccis miss their flight.
3. The kitten had an _______________ streak, often pouncing on unsuspecting passersby.
4. The _______________ details of his dishonesty ruined the ambassador's public image.
5. Prior to the Fair Housing Act of 1968, minority renters faced entrenched _______________ in their search for quality homes and apartments.
6. An unrepentant _______________, Walter White is as reckless as he is arrogant, rising and falling spectacularly during his brief criminal career.

Definitions: Match the new words with their definitions.

7. dilatory	________	a.	well known for negative reasons; notorious
8. unsavory	________	b.	slow; tending to cause delay
9. egotist	________	c.	mischievous
10. iniquity	________	d.	conceited; boastful
11. infamous	________	e.	wickedness; unfairness
12. impish	________	f.	distasteful; morally questionable

IF I HAD THE WINGS OF AN ANGEL

Casting a furtive glance over his shoulder, the *miscreant* slipped out the main prison gate, his *slovenly* appearance unnoticed in the British fog. Though few, if any, figures in mainstream media made *untoward* remarks about the penal system, the plethora of escapes from supposedly secure prisons embarrassed the *asinine* wardens. To compound their problems, irate citizens spread *scurrilous* rumors that some guards were accepting bribes from *brigands* and thieves whose motto was: "Stone walls do not a prison make, nor iron bars a cage."

NEW WORDS

miscreant
mis - crē - ent

slovenly
slov - ən - lē

untoward
un - tôrd

asinine
as - i - nīn

scurrilous
scur - ə - ləs

brigand
brig - ənd

Notable Roots:
mis = evil; crea = create; sloven = careless; ward = direction

Sample Sentences: Use the new words in the following sentences.

1. ________________ dress and grooming belies the impressiveness of any resume.
2. The presence of ________________ on the plains during the nineteenth century was a natural consequence of the failure to develop adequate law enforcement.
3. Many, but by no means all, ________________ grow up without proper parental guidance.
4. In the minds of many voters, the arcane details of public policy are no match for the ________________ details of scandal.
5. Hannibal defeated well-disciplined Roman legions led by ________________ commanders.
6. The politician, rather than apologize for the ________________ comments he had made, claimed that they were taken out of context.

Definitions: Match the new words with their meanings.

7.	miscreant	________	a.	inappropriate
8.	slovenly	________	b.	robber
9.	untoward	________	c.	vulgar
10.	asinine	________	d.	immoral person
11.	scurrilous	________	e.	foolish
12.	brigand	________	f.	sloppy in appearance

UNEARNED RESPECT

The young can be forgiven the *callow* conviction that they are the center of the universe. After all, the constant validation of early childhood makes each of us feel talented and special. While there's nothing *sinister* about parents seeking to instill confidence in their children, some grow up to be adults with a *pathological* need for praise, often coupled with an inability to acknowledge criticism or to persevere in the face of failure. A hallmark of such *megalomania* is to consider oneself a master of any skill, refusing to accept that without hard work one remains a *dilettante* in all endeavors. Such individuals who attain positions of power surround themselves with *obsequious* "yes men" who spare them such hard truths.

NEW WORDS

callow
cal - ō

sinister
sin - i - stėr

pathological
path - ə - loj - ik - əl

megalomania
meg - ə - lō - mā - nē - ə

dilettante
dil - ə - tont

obsequious
ob - sē - kwē - us

Notable Roots:
path = feeling, suffering; mega = great; mania = madness; dil = delay

Sample Sentences: Use the new words in the following sentences.

1. The cardiologist politely withheld comment as the ________________ lectured her about the latest heart-healthy fad diet.
2. Iago's ________________ demeanor gives Othello no reason to suspect him of treachery.
3. A ________________ speaker, Wilfred's use of impressive vocabulary cannot conceal the vapidness of his discourse.
4. While a runner on second base stealing a catcher's signs is a time-honored tradition, there's something ________________ about using long-range photographic equipment.
5. A ________________ liar will make false statements about easily verifiable facts.
6. Germany began to lose the Second World War when Hitler's ________________ caused him to ignore or overrule his general staff.

Definitions: Pick the letter of the definition that matches your new word and write it in the answer space.

7. callow	________	a. caused by disease; abnormal
8. sinister	________	b. one who has superficial knowledge of a subject
9. pathological	________	c. excessively flattering
10. megalomania	________	d. immature; inexperienced
11. dilettante	________	e. delusions of greatness
12. obsequious	________	f. threatening; foreboding

CASTLES OF AIR

No form of securities fraud is as *sordid* as the Ponzi Scheme. In 1920, Charles Ponzi, a charming Italian immigrant whose name was soon to become *nefarious*, set up a company to take advantage of a loophole that made it possible to purchase postage in Italy and redeem it for more valuable U.S. stamps. He promised investors a 50% profit within three months and attracted $1,800 in startup capital. Ponzi met his initial target and, thanks to the economic *bias* known as "fear of missing out," within months he had amassed millions in new investment capital. Unfortunately, when Ponzi's postage idea didn't work, he *callously* began paying out "profits" to older investors with newly invested money. As long as *servile* reverence for Ponzi's supposed financial acumen* persisted, he was safe as most simply reinvested their profits. By July of 1920, however, investigators realized that no legitimate firm could consistently offer such large returns. Ponzi's exposure was more than a *lurid* national scandal: his investors had been cheated out of $20 million (roughly $200 million today), and his name became a byword for corruption.

NEW WORDS

sordid
sôr - did

nefarious
nə - fer - ē - us

bias
bī - us

callous
cal - us

servile
sėr - vīl

lurid
lėr - id

Notable Roots:
ne = not, bad; far/fer = make, do; call = skin; serv = servant, slave

Sample Sentences: Use the new words in the following sentences. You may have to change the ending of a word.

1. Predatory animals have an instinctive _______________ toward hunting easier prey.
2. The _______________ aversion of his eyes betrays how much Theon has suffered at his captor's hands.
3. High-speed chases, while captivating news, show a _______________ disregard for public safety and should be avoided.
4. George Remus left the _______________ business of distributing bribes to underlings.
5. All of suspects were, in fact, guilty, but the victim was such a _______________ blackmailer that the inspector chose to report that an unknown assailant was responsible.
6. Sensationalist newspapers devote color photographs and banner headlines to the most _______________ stories.

Definitions: Match the new words with their meanings.

7.	sordid	________	a.	villainous; notorious
8.	nefarious	________	b.	insensitive
9.	bias	________	c.	slavish
10.	callous	________	d.	distasteful
11.	servile	________	e.	repulsive; horrifying
12.	lurid	________	f.	favoritism

GROUP REVIEW

Keep adding to your vocabulary, as it is one of the most useful tools you can possess. Let's go over the 24 new words you studied during this week.

Matching

Directions: In the following quiz, match the best possible definition with the words you have studied. Write the letter that stands for that definition in the appropriate answer space.

REVIEW WORDS		DEFINITIONS	
________	**1.** asinine	**a.**	repulsive; horrifying
________	**2.** bias	**b.**	delusions of greatness
________	**3.** brigand	**c.**	slavish
________	**4.** callous	**d.**	evil person
________	**5.** callow	**e.**	robber
________	**6.** dilatory	**f.**	sloppy in appearance
________	**7.** dilettante	**g.**	foolish
________	**8.** egotist	**h.**	vulgar
________	**9.** impish	**i.**	insensitive
________	**10.** infamous	**j.**	inappropriate
________	**11.** iniquity	**k.**	one who has superficial knowledge of a subject
________	**12.** lurid	**l.**	well known for negative reasons
________	**13.** megalomania	**m.**	threatening; foreboding
________	**14.** miscreant	**n.**	excessively flattering
________	**15.** nefarious	**o.**	favoritism
________	**16.** obsequious	**p.**	mischievous
________	**17.** pathological	**q.**	slow; tending to cause delay
________	**18.** scurrilous	**r.**	villainous; notorious
________	**19.** servile	**s.**	distasteful
________	**20.** sinister	**t.**	wickedness; unfairness
________	**21.** slovenly	**u.**	morally questionable
________	**22.** sordid	**v.**	caused by disease; abnormal
________	**23.** unsavory	**w.**	conceited; boastful
________	**24.** untoward	**x.**	immature; inexperienced

Exploring Roots

As the most common roots are to be found in many different words, knowledge of them is an important tool for breaking down new and unfamiliar vocabulary. Whether you recognize a word's etymology or its similarity to a foreign language word, improving your knowledge of these building blocks will improve your mastery of vocabulary.

Direction: Match the root definition with the sentence containing an italicized word with the same root.

______	**1.** feeling	**a.** By *dallying* too long, Ron was unable to make the last ferry.
______	**2.** creation	**b.** It's actually quite normal for toddlers to exhibit *egocentric* behavior.
______	**3.** delay	**c.** The 13th Amendment prohibits involuntary *servitude*.
______	**4.** not	**d.** The arson investigator recognized the signature techniques of the notorious *pyromaniac*.
______	**5.** slave	**e.** A bad reputation can fade, but *infamy* endures.
______	**6.** madness	**f.** Too much food is wasted because of public *apathy*.
______	**7.** self	**g.** The impression of brilliance is too often *negated* by arrogance.
______	**8.** fame	**h.** The title *Frankenstein* refers to the doctor, not his unnatural *creature*.

Wordsearch

Directions: Using the clues listed below, fill in each blank in the following story with one of the new words you learned this week.

Clues

3rd Day

2nd Day

4th Day

3rd Day

2nd Day

The Best Laid Plans

Gloria Rogers overslept and then had to sprint to catch the same Greyhound Bus that she boarded on the last Thursday of every month. After a three-hour uneventful ride, she finally arrived at the bus terminal where a courtesy van was ready to transport bus passengers to Visitors Day at the State Penitentiary.

Although Gloria tried to act casually, she was more than a little nervous. Her boyfriend, Art, a convicted felon and ___________ liar, had managed to gain admittance to the prison's hospital on the pretense of having a gall bladder attack. Fortunately, no one had noticed her ___________ manner of dress: under her own pants and bulky sweater, Gloria had been wearing an extra set of clothes that she removed in the hospital bathroom and passed on to Art. He planned to use them after making his escape in the back of the prison ambulance that was parked outside his ward.

Art had spelled out his escape plan during Gloria's last visit. He disguised his ___________ lack of concern by making the plan seem foolproof. All that she had to do was appear to have a seizure. Then she would fabricate a story about her epilepsy while Art, with the smuggled clothes concealed under his prison bathrobe, would slip out of the ward during the excitement. As a naturally ___________ girlfriend, she agreed. Unfortunately for the ___________ schemers, when they set their plan in motion, an astute* hospital guard spotted Art climbing into the rear of the ambulance and quickly foiled the escape attempt. The result was that Art had three years added to his sentence, and Gloria was imprisoned for her role in the misadventure.

THE PEP TALK

A *prestigious* team, defending champs and *prolific* scorers, we were undefeated. But spending so much time at the *zenith* of our sport, we had become complacent, buying into the *acclaim* dished out in the newspapers. Now we were losing 45–20 at halftime to our crosstown rivals. "If there's one thing I hate," the coach said, "it's a quitter." Just as coach's caustic remarks had us fired up, he changed tone, reminding us that a comeback was still *feasible*. Thus, with renewed confidence, we *sallied* forth, determined to wrest control of the game from our rivals.

NEW WORDS

prestigious
pres - tē - jus

prolific
prō - lif - ik

zenith
zē - nith

acclaim
ə - klām

feasible
fē - zə - bəl

sally
sal - ē

Notable Roots:
pre = before;
pro = forward;
clamo = announce

Sample Sentences: Use the new words in the following sentences.

1. After presenting a business idea that was both ________________ and profitable, Ashanti acquired the business loan.
2. While today an underdog and crowd favorite, at the ________________ of his powers, Tiger Woods dominated professional golf.
3. Attending a ________________ college not only promises an excellent education, but it can provide valuable social connections to those in the most competitive fields.
4. Before the overloaded *Eastland* could ________________ out onto Lake Michigan on a pleasure cruise, the ship rolled over at dockside.
5. Picasso was a ________________ painter, producing hundreds of works during his long career.
6. *Casablanca* more than lives up to the ________________ of critics; it's a timeless masterpiece.

Definitions: Match the new words with their definitions.

7.	prestigious	________	a.	public recognition
8.	prolific	________	b.	highest point of trajectory
9.	zenith	________	c.	to charge; set out
10.	acclaim	________	d.	realistic
11.	feasible	________	e.	highly regarded; exclusive
12.	sally	________	f.	productive

ALL GLORY IS FLEETING

As the Bombers took the field for the first game of the series, the young players were *ebullient*, anticipating their success. Jeffries, however, the Bombers' captain and veteran catcher, was circumspect.* Waiting to be announced, he took in the light show of countless camera flashes and the din of 50,000 fans roaring in unison. He dwelled on how fleeting such moments can be. When the Bombers last won it all, he was a rookie: a *prodigy* with the bat looking ahead to the future of the franchise. He had naively believed the *plaudits* of his adoring fans and had taken reaching the *acme* of his sport for granted. In the ensuing 15 years, he had never been back. Now, at the *pinnacle* of his profession once more, he appreciated all it had taken to reach this moment, how *fortuitous* that he had stayed healthy and played well for long enough to earn this chance.

NEW WORDS

ebullient
eb - ul - ē - ənt

prodigy
pro - di - jē

plaudits
plô - ditz

acme
ak - mē

pinnacle
pin - ik - əl

fortuitous
fôr - tū - it - tus

Notable Roots: pro = forward; laud = praise; fortui = luck, fortune

Sample Sentences: Can you put the new words in the right sentences?

1. Setting foot on the _______________ of Mount Everest is widely considered the zenith* of mountaineering.
2. Theodore Roosevelt is remembered for his _______________ smile.
3. At the _______________ of her career, Marilyn Monroe was considered an icon, more famous for her persona than her achievements.
4. A musical _______________, Mozart began composing at age five.
5. A _______________ turn of phrase can be the result of tireless writing practice or a gift of unpredictable inspiration.
6. The effusive _______________ that marked her introduction left the brilliant historian blushing as she stepped up to the lectern.

Definitions: Match the new words with their meanings.

7. ebullient	________	a.	highest point; summit
8. prodigy	________	b.	statements of praise
9. plaudits	________	c.	accidentally favorable
10. acme	________	d.	highest level of achievement
11. pinnacle	________	e.	lively; cheerful
12. fortuitous	________	f.	person possessing great talent

CAUTIOUS OPTIMISM

The polls had been predicting a landslide for weeks, but you'd never know it from the pensive* mood at campaign headquarters. Public statements and press interviews were appropriately *sanguine*, but seared into everyone's mind was the gut punch four years ago when the pollsters and pundits had practically *anointed* Gwen Martinez the next governor of North Carolina before a flurry of returns from rural districts put Brad Olsen ahead at the wire. This time around, the party took nothing for granted. Olsen campaigned as the most *viable* candidate. A platform of policies of known *efficacy* was drafted. A relentless ground game was unleashed upon the state. Only when the TV showed a weary, slump-shouldered Governor Olsen *ascend* the stage did a sense of relief spread through the crowd, followed swiftly by *nirvana*.

NEW WORDS

sanguine
seng - gwin

anoint
ə - noint

viable
vī - ə - bəl

efficacy
ef - ik - ə - sē

ascend
ə - send

nirvana
nėr - vo - nə

Notable Roots: sangre = blood; via = way; able = able; scend = move

Sample Sentences: Fill in the blanks with the new words you learned.

1. Bluffing is only a ________________ poker strategy if you can remain impassive.
2. After the pressure of executing a large wedding, a honeymoon can be a period of blissful ________________.
3. Bronze Age kings were often ________________ through a ceremony during which oil was poured on their heads.
4. A West Point education will give you an advantage if you wish to ________________ to a higher rank in the U.S. Army.
5. Despite the onset of gangrene, President Garfield's doctor remained ________________ that his patient would recover and refused all professional assistance.
6. The ________________ of vaccines is embraced by doctors but sometimes doubted by a skeptical public.

Definitions: Match the new words with their meanings.

7. sanguine	________	a. offering a prospect of success
8. anoint	________	b. optimistic
9. viable	________	c. a carefree and joyous state of mind
10. efficacy	________	d. to rise
11. ascend	________	e. to proclaim; to sanctify
12. nirvana	________	f. effectiveness

CALL ME BY MY RIGHT NAME

In the *halcyon* days of the Roman Republic, priests spent much of their time interpreting signs in nature to determine which public endeavors were *auspicious*. Luck was not considered a matter of cold probability but a manifestation of the will of the gods. Fortuna, the Roman goddess of luck, was depicted with veiled eyes, a fact that calls to mind the *felicitous* expression that "luck is blind." The lucky were considered more industrious, honest, and pious. The gods tended to reward such *laudable* qualities with *propitious* outcomes in civil life. In war, generals often invoked Alexander the Great's maxim "fortune favors the bold" to justify swift action and the *burgeoning* of Roman power.

NEW WORDS

halcyon
hal - sē - on

auspicious
ô - spi - shəs

felicitous
fə - lis - it - əs

laudable
lô - də - bəl

propitious
prō- pish - əs

burgeon
ber - jən

Notable Roots: auspice = good omen; felix = happy, lucky; laud = praise; pit = strive

Sample Sentences: Fill in the blanks with the new words you learned.

1. Wei's _______________ network of contacts allowed easy recruitment of new talent.
2. F. Scott and Zelda Fitzgerald's portraits give the misleading impression of a power couple living a _______________ existence.
3. Ned Stark embodies _______________ ideals that become a liability in corrupt times.
4. Antoninus Pius presided over such a _______________ era that few dramatic events occurred during his reign to attract the attention of historians.
5. McClellan, with his trim good looks and martial bearing, at first seemed a _______________ commander when he took command of the Army of the Potomac.
6. To be the target of bird droppings is, oddly enough, considered _______________ by some.

Definitions: Match the new words with their meanings.

7. halcyon	________	a.	predictive of good fortune
8. auspicious	________	b.	praiseworthy
9. felicitous	________	c.	favorable to success
10. laudable	________	d.	to expand
11. propitious	________	e.	happy; well suited
12. burgeon	________	f.	characterized by success and prosperity

GROUP REVIEW

The word *review* means "to view again," and that is the purpose of our weekly review. You will have noticed, of course, that many of the words that appear as new words are repeated in subsequent lessons. Sometimes they are in the paragraph, sometimes in the sample sentences, and occasionally in the definitions or directions. This continued emphasis on "viewing again" will help you to become familiar with the vocabulary.

Matching

Directions: In the following quiz, match the best possible definition with the words you have studied. Write the letter that stands for that definition in the appropriate answer space.

	REVIEW WORDS		DEFINITIONS
________	**1.** acclaim	**a.**	to rise
________	**2.** acme	**b.**	happy; well suited
________	**3.** anoint	**c.**	highest point of trajectory
________	**4.** ascend	**d.**	favorable to success
________	**5.** auspicious	**e.**	predictive of good fortune
________	**6.** burgeon	**f.**	person possessing great talent
________	**7.** ebullient	**g.**	highly regarded; exclusive
________	**8.** efficacy	**h.**	characterized by success and prosperity
________	**9.** feasible	**i.**	to proclaim; to sanctify
________	**10.** felicitous	**j.**	realistic
________	**11.** fortuitous	**k.**	offering a prospect of success
________	**12.** halcyon	**l.**	praiseworthy
________	**13.** laudable	**m.**	optimistic
________	**14.** nirvana	**n.**	effectiveness
________	**15.** pinnacle	**o.**	productive
________	**16.** plaudits	**p.**	accidentally favorable
________	**17.** prestigious	**q.**	lively; cheerful
________	**18.** prodigy	**r.**	to charge; set out
________	**19.** prolific	**s.**	to expand
________	**20.** propitious	**t.**	highest level of achievement
________	**21.** sally	**u.**	public recognition
________	**22.** sanguine	**v.**	a carefree and joyous state of mind
________	**23.** viable	**w.**	statements of praise
________	**24.** zenith	**x.**	highest point; summit

Wordsearch

Directions: Using the clues listed below, fill in each blank in the following story with one of the new words you learned this week.

Clues

1st Day

1st Day

3rd Day

2nd Day

3rd Day

Desert Storm Decision

The 1991 Persian Gulf War, where the United Nations forces, led by Americans, ousted the invading Iraqi army from Kuwait's soil, met with much popular ___________. The United States won the gratitude of Kuwait and the admiration of world in part because the conflict was a master class in the overwhelming technical superiority of an elite military at the ___________ of its powers. The Gulf War is also remembered, however, as a mercifully short conflict thanks to the setting of specific, ___________ objectives.

When asked by the media why he hadn't pursued the enemy all the way to Baghdad, General H. Norman Schwarzkopf, the U.S. field commander, explained:

"It would have been foolhardy for us to try to occupy that capital city and pile up American casualties from sniper attacks by Iraq's guerillas. That may be hard for you Monday morning quarterbacks to understand, but I thoroughly agreed with the president who was convinced that such an action would have sent a bad message to the world and would have splintered the Allied partnership." This proved a ___________ decision in light of the bloody insurgency that would follow the Iraq War 12 years later.

Schwarzkopf added "that dictator's days are numbered, but I expect his end is likely to come at the hands of his own people." This ___________ prediction turned out to be quite accurate: after his capture by American forces in December 2003, Saddam was tried and later executed by the new Iraqi government.

Synonym Shout-Out

Since the words in each group are related to a common concept, some are naturally going to be exact or very close synonyms. Match each word with the choices most similar in meaning. As indicated by the number in parentheses, some words will have more than one match.

1. acclaim ____________
2. servile ____________
3. nefarious ____________
4. prudent ____________
5. fortuitous (3) ____________
6. pensive ____________
7. acme (2) ____________
8. incisive (4) ____________
9. viable ____________
10. sanguine ____________
11. miscreant ____________
12. untoward (3) ____________

a. ebullient
b. propitious
c. sordid
d. feasible
e. felicitous
f. canny
g. infamous
h. zenith
i. circumspect
j. unsavory
k. astute
l. plaudits
m. perspicacious
n. pinnacle
o. obsequious
p. auspicious
q. trenchant
r. lurid
s. introspective
t. brigand

WEEK 4 DAY 1

MULLINS, A K.O. VICTIM

In every press conference and interview, K.O. Mullins promised *carnage*. In *ominous* tones, he declared himself the *harbinger* of the champion's downfall, that his foe would be *incapacitated* by stinging jabs and *succumb* to a hail of body blows within five rounds. The result was a pure *debacle*. When the bell sounded, Mullins sprang from his stool and charged across the ring, showing disdain for the champion. Although his belligerence seemed impressive, it failed to intimidate the champ, who laid the hapless Mullins low with an adroit feint and an uppercut.

NEW WORDS

carnage
kär - nej

ominous
om - in - us

harbinger
här - bin - jer

incapacitate
in - kə - pas - i - tāt

succumb
sə - kûm

debacle
də - bok - əl

Notable Roots: carn = flesh; omen = bad sign; capit = head

Sample Sentences: Use the new words in the following sentences.

1. Before Mt. Pelée's catastrophic eruption, many ________________ signs were observed.
2. The Army of the Potomac lost many hard-fought encounters with the Confederates, but the Battle of Fredericksburg was a true ________________.
3. Ninety-degree weather in Alaska could be a ________________ of long-term climate disruption.
4. The 2004 tsunami caused ______________ on all coasts of the Indian Ocean.
5. When a stroke ________________ Woodrow Wilson, his wife, Edith, helped him execute the duties of his office.
6. Ruth did not ________________ to her desire to retaliate against the player who tripped her.

Definitions: Match the new words with their meanings.

7.	carnage	________	a.	portending doom
8.	ominous	________	b.	to disable
9.	harbinger	________	c.	to give in; to die
10.	incapacitate	________	d.	bloodshed
11.	succumb	________	e.	an abject disaster
12.	debacle	________	f.	a sign of bad luck

MULLINS THROWS DOWN THE GAUNTLET

His *abortive* challenge for the title proved to be the *nadir* of K.O. Mullins's career. Ignoring the *ramifications* of the loss on his ranking and reputation, the pugnacious Mullins demanded a rematch. To *forestall* any attempt to ignore him, he took out a full-page ad in the newspaper calling out the champ. When the champ's manager saw the ad, he accosted Mullins, who was surrounded by a throng of reporters. The manager belittled his antics as a pathetic attempt to resurrect a *moribund* career. Mullins, never one to *balk* at such barbs, punched the manager, knocking them both off their feet.

NEW WORDS

abortive
ə - bôr - tiv

nadir
nā - dēr

ramifications
ram - ə - fik - ā - shuns

forestall
fôr - stäl

moribund
môr - i - bund

balk
bälk

Notable Roots: fic/fac = make/do; fore = before; mori = death; bund = bound

Sample Sentences: Use the new words in the following sentences.

1. After the scandal broke, a confession and apology might have ________________ demands for the prime minister's resignation.
2. Three ________________ empires did not survive the Great War: the Austrian, Ottoman, and Russian.
3. The investors who ________________ at the opportunity to purchase shares in the new software company would come to regret it within a decade.
4. When Alaric sacked Rome in 410, it was the ________________ of the empire's long history.
5. Given the complexity of Earth's natural cycles, the ________________ of human activities can take decades to reveal themselves.
6. Attempts to create a universal language have proven ________________ from the start.

Definitions: Match the new words with their meanings.

7.	abortive	________	a.	to head off
8.	nadir	________	b.	consequences
9.	ramifications	________	c.	dying
10.	forestall	________	d.	doomed from the start
11.	moribund	________	e.	to hesitate; to refuse
12.	balk	________	f.	the low point of one's fortunes

MULLINS FORCED TO EAT HUMBLE PIE

The consequences of K.O. Mullins's foolish actions proved to be *catastrophic*. The irate 80-year-old manager pressed charges against Mullins, suing him for assault. Any attempt to deny such a public act was *fruitless*: dozens of reporters had witnessed the event, and the manager carried a deep laceration over his eyebrow. When the case was brought before the court, the *besieged* defense team *capitulated*. The judge castigated Mullins for the sordid* incident and *repulsed* his plea for leniency. In addition to a costly financial settlement, Mullins was required to make a public apology to the octogenarian. The *fiasco* marked the ignominious end of Mullins's career.

NEW WORDS

catastrophic
cat - ə - strof - ik

fruitless
frūt - les

besiege
bē - sēj

capitulate
kə - pit - ū - lāt

repulse
rē - püls

fiasco
fē - a - skō

Notable Roots:
fruit = product; capit = head; pulse = push

Sample Sentences: Use the new words in the following sentences.

1. Team USA was able to ________________ every Soviet rush and hold on for a 4–3 win.
2. Failure to freeze the cookie dough proved a ________________ error.
3. During the nine months that Petersburg was ________________, much of Lee's army deserted.
4. After the first fall, the rest of the skater's routine turned into a ________________.
5. Swatting away the cloud of mosquitoes proved to be a ________________ endeavor.
6. Rather than ________________, Richard III became the last English king to die in battle.

Definitions: Match the new words with their meanings.

7. catastrophic	________	a.	to attack relentlessly
8. fruitless	________	b.	embarrassing performance
9. besiege	________	c.	disastrous
10. capitulate	________	d.	to fend off
11. repulse	________	e.	to surrender
12. fiasco	________	f.	futile

THE DECLINE OF MULLINS

After the trial, K.O. Mullins found his bid for a rematch at an *impasse*. He attempted to rebuild his image by hiring a publicist to set up appearances on talk shows during which he would profess to be a "changed man." In the end, however, this campaign *faltered*, *stymied* by Mullins's impulsivity and proclivity for misbehavior. Only genuine remorse and meaningful change could have rescued him from his *quandary*. Rather than accepting that his actions had brought about his *plight*, however, Mullins blamed the champ and his old manager. In a frenzy of self-pity, he would often trumpet scurrilous* attacks on the champ, the old manager, and the judge, whom he blamed for *thwarting* his dreams.

NEW WORDS

impasse
im - pas

falter
fäl - tėr

stymie
stī - mē

quandary
kwon - drē

plight
plīt

thwart
thwärt

Notable Roots: pass = way; falt = defect, mistake; quand = when

Sample Sentences: Use the new words in the following sentences.

1. The Joker is always ________________ in his plans by the timely arrival of Batman.
2. In 1922, a young Hemingway chronicled the ________________ of Greeks fleeing Anatolia.
3. Cracking the Enigma codes presented Bletchley Park with a ________________: how to use the intelligence without tipping off the Germans that they'd been hacked.
4. Dreams ________________ for many reasons: laziness, doubt, and distraction among them.
5. Sultan Mehmet II broke the ________________ by having his ships dragged overland to harass the Byzantines from within their secure harbor.
6. The gale-force winds ________________ all attempts to fight the forest fire from the air.

Definitions: Match the new words with their meanings.

7.	impasse	________	a.	to lose strength; to fail
8.	falter	________	b.	to defeat another's plans
9.	stymie	________	c.	hardship
10.	quandary	________	d.	stalemate
11.	plight	________	e.	to block another's success
12.	thwart	________	f.	dilemma

GROUP REVIEW

Let's see how many of the new words studied during the course of this week you remember. Incidentally, try to keep a record of the many times you find your new words in magazines, newspapers, and books. Before you knew the meanings of those words, you probably skipped right over them.

Matching

Directions: In the following quiz, match the best possible definition with the word you have studied. Write the correct letter in the appropriate answer space.

REVIEW WORDS		DEFINITIONS	
______	**1.** abortive	**a.**	futile
______	**2.** balk	**b.**	to head off
______	**3.** besiege	**c.**	dilemma
______	**4.** capitulate	**d.**	to disable
______	**5.** carnage	**e.**	to fend off
______	**6.** catastrophic	**f.**	the low point of one's fortunes
______	**7.** debacle	**g.**	to defeat another's plans
______	**8.** falter	**h.**	an abject disaster
______	**9.** fiasco	**i.**	dying
______	**10.** forestall	**j.**	portending doom
______	**11.** fruitless	**k.**	to lose strength; to fail
______	**12.** harbinger	**l.**	disastrous
______	**13.** impasse	**m.**	consequences
______	**14.** incapacitate	**n.**	hardship
______	**15.** moribund	**o.**	to hesitate; to refuse
______	**16.** nadir	**p.**	to block another's success
______	**17.** ominous	**q.**	to give in; to die
______	**18.** plight	**r.**	stalemate
______	**19.** quandary	**s.**	embarrassing performance
______	**20.** ramifications	**t.**	bloodshed
______	**21.** repulse	**u.**	doomed from the start
______	**22.** stymie	**v.**	to surrender
______	**23.** succumb	**w.**	a sign of bad luck
______	**24.** thwart	**x.**	to attack relentlessly

Sensible Sentences?

(From Week 4)

Underline the word that makes sense in each of the sentences below.

1. The linebacker was *(forestalled, incapacitated)* by a broken tibia.
2. The riots that followed Caesar's assassination proved a *(harbinger, quandary)* of the civil wars to come.
3. The *(plight, impasse)* of the polar bear is symbolic of the dangers of climate change.
4. Hudson's voyage up the river that bears his name in search of a Northwest Passage to India proved both *(catastrophic, fruitless)* and time-consuming.
5. With the advent of online shopping, once great retail chains have become *(moribund, ominous)*—if not defunct—enterprises.
6. His first professional defeat, a loss to reigning champion, Joe Frazier, proved to be the *(debacle, nadir)* of Ali's storied career.
7. The destruction of the Baltic Fleet at Tsushima completed the *(impasse, fiasco)* of the Russo-Japanese War.
8. George Bailey's plan to see the world before heading to college was *(faltered, thwarted)* by his father's untimely death.
9. Most *(abortive, moribund)* attempts to open a restaurant are the brainchildren of dilettantes* ignorant of the demands of the food service industry.
10. Despite the intense scrutiny of the media, Jackie Robinson never *(faltered, besieged)*, sparking the Dodgers to a decade of success while never giving in or reacting to bigotry.

Antonyms Attract

Directions: Another way to get vocabulary to stick in your memory is to develop an awareness of antonyms. If you can remember a word's opposite, you can remember the word. Match the following words with their antonyms. Multiple antonyms indicated by parentheses.

1. ominous (2) ____________
2. nadir (2) ____________
3. prestigious ____________
4. iniquity ____________
5. callow (2) ____________
6. introspective ____________
7. fruitless (2) ____________
8. falter ____________
9. laudable (3) ____________
10. asinine ____________
11. repulse (2) ____________
12. ebullient ____________

a. probity
b. propitious
c. callous
d. viable
e. infamous
f. scurrilous
g. politic
h. auspicious
i. capitulate
j. astute
k. zenith
l. feasible
m. pragmatic
n. sally
o. acme
p. succumb
q. lurid
r. moribund
s. sordid

Wordsearch

Directions: Using the clues listed below, fill in each blank in the following story with one of the new words you learned this week.

Clues

4th Day

4th Day

1st Day

1st Day

2nd Day

Want to Run for Office?

In these hyper-partisan years, as all cooperation between parties is at an ___________, we have seen the phenomenon of incumbent politicians retiring in record numbers. When interviewed, many of them admitted that they had lost their taste for the job because of the abuse to which a candidate for office is subjected.

"My last campaign was a sordid* affair in which my opponents did everything to sully my record and air scurrilous* charges about my private life," said one congressman, bemoaning his ___________. "I won't stand still for such treatment," he added, "which was terribly embarrassing to me and my entire family."

Citizen groups, appalled by the candidates' mudslinging, have sought to do something about the ___________. Committees have been formed in a number of states to study ways to elevate the tone of the process to intelligent discourse on the issues instead of the ___________ of all-out war.

"Unless we clean up this mess," said the chairman of an Illinois caucus, "the best and the brightest will ___________ at entering a career in politics. After all, who but a masochist wants to be a punching bag?"

WEEK 5 DAY 1

CHEATING

Because of my code of ethics, I have always considered the *duplicity* of cheating to be dishonorable. Apparently, some students are not above such *chicanery*. Recently, I read an article in which, under the *subterfuge* of learning disabilities that they did not possess, a group of friends visited unscrupulous learning specialists whose recommendations gain them extra time to take exams. By *duping* the system, these students gain an unfair advantage over others while abusing accommodations reserved for those who honestly need them. Another *perfidious* scheme involves students *absconding* with their phones to the bathroom to look up answers to test questions.

NEW WORDS

duplicity
dū - pli - si - tē

chicanery
shi - kon - ə - rē

subterfuge
sub - ter - fūzh

dupe (v.)
dūp

perfidious
per - fid - ē - us

abscond
ab - skond

Notable Roots:
dup = two; plac = please; sub = below; fide = belief; ab = away

Sample Sentences: Use the new words in the following sentences.

1. Lies and ________________ are necessary skills for successful espionage.
2. The perpetrator of the Ponzi Scheme ________________ with a sizable stash of his clients' investments but was recognized abroad and apprehended.
3. While the workmanship might fool the untrained eye, a $50 price tag for a Rolex isn't going to ________________ anyone.
4. The ________________ of bogus medicine, once the purview of nineteenth-century snake oil salesmen, has made a resurgence thanks to cheap online advertising.
5. Honesty will get you out of some speeding tickets; ________________ will always increase the fines.
6. The queen was so pathologically* ________________ that none in the North expected the reinforcements she had promised to materialize.

Definitions: Match the new words with their meanings.

7. duplicity	________	a.	to trick
8. chicanery	________	b.	to sneak away
9. subterfuge	________	c.	falseness of character
10. dupe	________	d.	faithless to one's word
11. perfidious	________	e.	scheming; trickery
12. abscond	________	f.	trick to gain advantage

CRACKING DOWN

Mr. Dorsey, our new principal, was determined to do something about the rash of *mendacious* academic behavior. He issued bulletins and began to admonish those teachers who did not proctor alertly. Though they did not appreciate the responsibility *foisted* upon them, under *duress* the faculty reported the worst *cabals* of habitual cheaters. Though their possessors claimed that they were *fabricated*, several cheat sheets were turned in as tangible evidence of the offense. Mr. Dorsey's inexorable campaign against academic *charlatans* seemed to be paying off.

NEW WORDS

mendacious
men - dā - shəs

foist
fôi - st

duress
dur - es

cabal
kə - bäl

fabricate
fab - ri - kāt

charlatan
shär - lə - tin

Notable Roots: mend/ment = lie; dur = hard; fabric = create

Sample Sentences: Into which sentences do the new words fit best?

1. A ________________ of aristocrats initiated the assassination plot against Julius Caesar.
2. Confessions given under ________________ are rarely admissible in court.
3. Because the criminals did not ________________ their stories together, questioning them separately quickly brought out the truth.
4. A ________________ story repeated enough can become nearly impossible to debunk.
5. It is a historical irony that most people will reject a democracy ________________ upon them.
6. Always a ________________, the con man became a magician using tricks to entertain.

Definitions: Match the new words with their meanings.

7.	mendacious	________	a.	to lie; to make up
8.	foist	________	b.	trickster
9.	duress	________	c.	a secret group
10.	cabal	________	d.	to place an unwelcome burden
11.	fabricate	________	e.	characterized by dishonesty
12.	charlatan	________	f.	force or threats to obtain compliance

STAR PLAYER IS CAUGHT

The cheating scandal came to a head when Art Krause, our football captain, was caught cheating on a midterm exam. An all-conference quarterback, Art was used to *fawning* fans, *fulsome* press clippings, and a certain leniency from his teachers. His ghostwritten term papers were explained away by the *artifice* of having a "writing tutor." Art was happy to *usurp* the grades that other students worked hard to earn. With such an attitude, it's unsurprising he would put little *guile* into his cheating and was easily caught by the first teacher to keep an eye on him. If Art were suspended, however, our chances for winning the city championship would evaporate, so the coach asked the principal to overlook Art's *prevarication.* Mr. Dorsey replied that the players "needed coaching in morality."

NEW WORDS

fawning
fô - niŋ

fulsome
ful - sûm

artifice
är- tə - fis

usurp
ū - sėrp

guile
gīl

prevarication
prē - var - i - kā - shun

Notable Roots:
artific = created by man; pre = before; vari/veri = truth

Sample Sentences: Use the new words in the following sentences.

1. Dillinger's ________________, rather than his capacity for violence, made him Public Enemy #1 for federal law enforcement.
2. Since he had been caught on film, no amount of ________________ could explain his actions.
3. By collecting funds for the army, Bismarck ________________ the power of Parliament.
4. The ________________ manner of the sycophant repulses* true leaders.
5. Returning to play an encore after a prolonged ovation is an ________________ lovingly enacted by musicians and audiences alike.
6. Queen Margaret warns the Yorkist nobles that Richard's ________________ often precedes his most egregious crimes.

Definitions: Match the new words with their meanings.

7.	fawning	________	a.	to seize unlawfully or by force
8.	fulsome	________	b.	dishonest or evasive statements
9.	artifice	________	c.	excessive flattery
10.	usurp	________	d.	cleverness; trickery
11.	guile	________	e.	a lie of convenience
12.	prevarication	________	f.	obnoxious through excessive praise

OUR PYRRHIC VICTORY

Mr. Dorsey summoned a group of teachers and student leaders to his office under the *guise* of gauging their reactions to the suspension. One teacher suggested that rather than "punishing the whole school for one student's transgression," the suspension should be delayed. Mr. Dorsey, however, would not indulge such *fallacious* wishful thinking. He countered that *feinting* discipline would make a *canard* of the school's zero-tolerance policy. He loathed having to discipline Art Krause so severely, but all excuses for the quarterback's activity were completely *factitious*. Unless strict measures were taken, other students would regard the school's honor code as toothless. "We may lose a football game," the principal said, "but we can salvage our self-respect." After the principal's diatribe, all present *repressed* any further dissent.

NEW WORDS

guise
gīz

fallacious
fə - lā - shəs

feint (v.)
fānt

canard
kən - ärd

factitious
fak - tish - shəs

repress
rē - pres

Repress:
falt = defect; fac/fec = create; press = push, convey

Sample Sentences: Use the new words in the following sentences.

1. The normally stoic Jeter could not ________________ his emotions before leaving the field in uniform for the last time.
2. The famed frontier politician never denied the ________________ that he'd killed a notorious outlaw in a duel.
3. Such was Janine's charm that interviewers never seemed to notice the ________________ items of her CV.
4. The Parthians were known for ________________ a mounted retreat before turning in the saddle to fire a fusillade of arrows at their pursuers.
5. The Supreme Court prefers not to reverse precedents unless the justices find the reasoning of the predecessors to be particularly ________________.
6. Dictators maintain the ________________ of popular support by holding rigged elections.

Definitions: Place the letter of the correct definition in the blank next to the new vocabulary word.

7. guise	________	a.	to make a deceptive move
8. fallacious	________	b.	an unproven lie or rumor
9. feint	________	c.	to hold back opinions or emotions
10. canard	________	d.	surface appearance
11. factitious	________	e.	based on faulty reasoning
12. repress	________	f.	artificially created

GROUP REVIEW

Congratulations! You have covered the first 120 words in the book. With the same diligence, you should be able to tackle the remaining work and to master most of the challenging words.

Matching

Directions: Take the following quiz by matching the best possible definition with the word you have studied. Write the letter that stands for that definition in the appropriate answer space.

	REVIEW WORDS	DEFINITIONS
________	**1.** abscond	**a.** excessive flattery
________	**2.** artifice	**b.** dishonest or evasive statements
________	**3.** cabal	**c.** to hold back opinions or emotions
________	**4.** canard	**d.** characterized by dishonesty
________	**5.** charlatan	**e.** a secret group
________	**6.** chicanery	**f.** based on faulty reasoning
________	**7.** dupe	**g.** to sneak away
________	**8.** duplicity	**h.** faithless to one's word
________	**9.** duress	**i.** surface appearance
________	**10.** fabricate	**j.** to seize unlawfully or by force
________	**11.** factitious	**k.** trick to gain advantage
________	**12.** fallacious	**l.** force or threats to obtain compliance
________	**13.** fawning	**m.** cleverness; trickery
________	**14.** feint	**n.** to trick
________	**15.** foist	**o.** artificially created
________	**16.** fulsome	**p.** to make a deceptive move
________	**17.** guile	**q.** to lie; to make up
________	**18.** guise	**r.** obnoxious through excessive praise
________	**19.** mendacious	**s.** scheming; trickery
________	**20.** perfidious	**t.** to place an unwelcome burden
________	**21.** prevarication	**u.** falseness of character
________	**22.** repress	**v.** a lie of convenience
________	**23.** subterfuge	**w.** trickster
________	**24.** usurp	**x.** an unproven lie or rumor

Wordsearch

Directions: Using the clues listed below, fill in each blank in the following story with one of the new words you learned this week.

Clues

4th Day

3rd Day

3rd Day

2nd Day

4th Day

Noncooperation

One of the great ____________ of history is that successful nonviolent movements are passive in nature. Gandhi famously balked* at such a notion, retorting that he had never advocated passivity in anything. Nonviolent movements based on civil disobedience are actually quite active. They require patience, ____________, and the courage to face legal consequences. Henry David Thoreau, Martin Luther King, and Gandhi all spent time in jail cells.

One common ___________ that has been successfully deployed by oppressive societies is that they are civilized and decent. Under __________, however, such as when facing the economic consequences of a strike or disruption of civil services, those in power have a tendency to brutally crack down. When authorities ____________ a marginalized group by force, such as using firehoses against civil rights marchers or jailing suffragettes, average citizens are forced to confront systemic injustice.

Exploring Roots

As the most common roots are to be found in many different words, knowledge of them is an important tool for breaking down new and unfamiliar vocabulary. Whether you recognize a word's etymology or its similarity to a foreign language word, improving your knowledge of these building blocks will improve your mastery of vocabulary.

Directions: Match the root definition with the sentence containing an italicized word with the same root.

______ **1.** defect	**a.**	The Hollywood law firm earned half of its revenue from the *infidelity* of married celebrities.
______ **2.** truth	**b.**	The most powerful emotions are often *inexpressible*.
______ **3.** belief	**c.**	Moriarty is Sherlock Holmes's most *implacable* foe.
______ **4.** hard	**d.**	Whenever you make a mistake, remember that no one is *infallible*.
______ **5.** convey	**e.**	Sears homes, though *prefabricated*, were legendary for their elegance and quality.
______ **6.** please	**f.**	*Abdication* did not ultimately save the life of Tsar Nicholas II or his family.
______ **7.** created	**g.**	Too often, partisans willingly confuse honesty with *verisimilitude*.
______ **8.** away	**h.**	The marathon is a well-known trial of *endurance*.

KEEP IT SIMPLE

Most inventors, although motivated by *mercenary* interests, recognize that the key to success is identifying an unmet need in the lives of potential customers. While a *surfeit* of unusual and ultimately useless products are out there, the most *lucrative* inventions are those that possess a simplicity that makes their utility obvious. During the nineteenth century, a *glut* of overelaborate electronic communication devices failed to catch on until Samuel Morse created a very simple code made of nothing more than simple pulses of energy. Devices that are simple, reliable, and of obvious value like the telegraph are most likely to be *underwritten* by investors and reap the *pecuniary* rewards of a grateful public.

NEW WORDS

mercenary (adj.)
mėr - sen - er - ē

surfeit
sėr - fit

lucrative
lū - krə - tiv

glut
glut

underwrite
un - dər - rīt

pecuniary
pə - kyū - nē - er - ē

Notable Roots: merc = sell/hire; sur = above; pecunia = money

Sample Sentences: Fit the new words into the proper blanks.

1. The most _______________ government contracts attract the fiercest bidding.
2. The team owner gave the coach one more season to improve but made it clear that he would no longer _______________ failure.
3. Despite her excellent work, Ellen's superiors felt she lacked commitment to the company vision and was a purely _______________ worker.
4. Fracking has produced a prolonged _______________ in the natural gas markets, and prices have yet to recover.
5. Despite his reputation with free market capitalists as a _______________ wizard, J. P. Morgan was known in his day for ruthlessly throttling destructive competition.
6. The Covid-19 pandemic has made it clear that a _______________ of medical supplies should be maintained at all times.

Definitions: Match the new words with their meanings.

7. mercenary	________	a.	an oversupply
8. surfeit	________	b.	related to money or finances
9. lucrative	________	c.	motivated solely by money
10. glut	________	d.	an abundance
11. underwrite	________	e.	profitable
12. pecuniary	________	f.	to accept financial responsibility

GOLD IN THE HILLS

A *hoard* of jewels and gold coins worth more than $2 million could be hiding in the Rocky Mountains. It sounds like an Old West legend, but it's very much a twenty-first-century story. In 2010, Forrest Fenn, an *affluent* art dealer from New Mexico, announced that he had hidden a chest filled with *copious* riches somewhere in the Rockies. He published the "treasure map" in his autobiography, a poem containing clues to the casket's whereabouts. He explained that his *largess* was intended to inspire people. Be it by adventure or *avarice*, the Fenn treasure has certainly motivated legions of hunters. Most were *compensated* for their lost time in exercise and fresh air, but an unlucky few have actually died from mishaps in the wilderness.[1]

NEW WORDS

hoard (n.)
hôrd

affluent
af - lū - ent

copious
cō - pē - us

largess
lär - jes

avarice
av - ə - ris

compensation
com - pen - sā - shən

Notable Roots:
flu = flow; copia = plenty; pen = hang

Sample Sentences: Use the clues above to help find the proper words.

1. The ________________ of wealthy benefactors provides considerable support for the arts.
2. The greatest entertainers in the world command levels of ________________ unimaginable even a century ago.
3. Seed banks are ________________ of biological treasure meant to secure our survival in the event of a global catastrophe.
4. Despite the anonymity of a uniform, officers born ________________ can often be distinguished by their speech and mannerisms.
5. The ________________ fruit from this year's tomatoes allowed me to give many away.
6. Kaiser Wilhelm II erroneously believed Britain too motivated by ________________ to go to war to protect Belgian neutrality.

Definitions: Match the new words with their meanings.

7. hoard	________	a.	generosity
8. affluent	________	b.	in great quantity
9. copious	________	c.	payment
10. largess	________	d.	having a significant amount of money
11. avarice	________	e.	a valuable collection
12. compensation	________	f.	greed

[1] In 2020, Fenn announced on social media that the treasure had been found. The identity of its discoverer is as yet unknown.

RENAISSANCE RESEARCHERS

Many of the first scientists were what we would consider today to be amateurs. Some were independently wealthy and pursued what they termed "natural philosophy" from the comfort of their *sumptuous* palaces and mansions. The work they did was simply to indulge their own curiosity and not with any thought of *remuneration*. Brilliant scholars born without means, on the other hand, could hope for a church *sinecure*, a much-*coveted* arrangement, which provided income without responsibility so that they could pursue their scientific inquiries at their leisure. The less fortunate would work enough to meet their *fiscal* needs while conducting research in whatever time they could spare. Prior to the Scientific Revolution, the only truly paid research work was that which benefited European militaries, which *voraciously* consumed innovations that could be used against rival powers in times of war.

NEW WORDS

sumptuous
sŭmp - shū - us

remuneration
rē - myūn - ėr - ā - shun

sinecure
sin - ə - kyur

covet
kuv - it

fiscal
fis - kəl

voracious
vör - ā - shəs

Notable Roots: muni = gift; sine = without; vor = eating

Sample Sentences: Insert the new words in the following sentences.

1. Corrupt politicians often offer ________________ to their most generous supporters.
2. Sound ________________ policy rests on the principle of keeping debt low unless government spending is needed to stave off recession.
3. The Palace of Versailles was intended to be a ________________ cage allowing the French King to keep a close eye on his nobility.
4. Donald Trump is known to be a ________________ consumer of cable television.
5. Native Americans rarely received the ________________ for their land promised by treaties.
6. It is one thing to admire those we find heroic but quite another to ________________ the wealth and status that others have earned through talent and hard work.

Definitions: Match the new words with their meanings.

7. sumptuous	________	a.	a paid position without duties
8. remuneration	________	b.	characterized by great luxury
9. sinecure	________	c.	relating to finance
10. covet	________	d.	having great appetite
11. fiscal	________	e.	compensation; reward
12. voracious	________	f.	to desire immorally; to envy

IS GREED GOOD?

Without a doubt, the profit motive is one of the most powerful creative engines that exists. The *cupidity* of entrepreneurs can bring the dreams of inventors to life if both parties recognize the value a new idea can provide. During the Gilded Age, Andrew Carnegie was pillar of a *bountiful* economy featuring countless innovations that made use of the cheaper and more reliable steel his mills created. Certainly, tycoons like Carnegie lived in *opulence*, constructing *palatial* estates along Manhattan's Fifth Avenue and Long Island's "Gold Coast." They were also *munificent* benefactors of public institutions like the Metropolitan Museum of Art and Carnegie Hall. While there are exceptions—*rapacious* speculators like Jay Gould, who could wreck economies—history teaches that on the balance, the drive for wealth and success benefits society if leavened by social conscience.

NEW WORDS

cupidity
kyū - pi - də - tē

bountiful
boun - tə - ful

opulence
op - yə - ləns

palatial
pə - lā - shul

munificent
myū - ni - fi - sənt

rapacious
rə - pā - shəs

Notable Roots: cupid = desire; bounti = reward; opus = achievement; rapa = grasping

Sample Sentences: Use the new words in the proper blanks.

1. Some of the most ________________ homes are bequeathed as parks and museums.
2. The motivation of past amateur athletes was love of the game rather than mere ________________.
3. Eighteenth century pirates were so ________________ that they would seize ships regardless of flag.
4. Rome's burgeoning* empire relied on ________________ Egyptian grain harvests.
5. The ________________ of Venice is astonishing to those who have never seen Byzantine art.
6. "Golden Parachutes" are ________________ severance packages for business executives whose failures have too often cost shareholders billions.

Definitions: Play the familiar matching game.

7. cupidity	________	a.	extremely generous
8. bountiful	________	b.	fitting for royalty
9. opulence	________	c.	eagerness to possess something
10. palatial	________	d.	overly greedy; willing to take by force
11. munificent	________	e.	plentiful; abundant
12. rapacious	________	f.	impressive wealth

GROUP REVIEW

After reading about these new ideas, you should be inventive enough to handle this review. If there is a necessity for it, you may turn back to the original lesson to check on the meaning of a word. As someone once remarked, "Necessity is the mother of invention."

Matching

Directions: Match the 24 words with their meanings. Write the letter that stands for the definition in the appropriate answer space.

	REVIEW WORDS		DEFINITIONS
________	1. affluent	a.	compensation; reward
________	2. avarice	b.	plentiful; abundant
________	3. bountiful	c.	payment
________	4. compensation	d.	characterized by great luxury
________	5. copious	e.	motivated solely by money
________	6. covet	f.	having great appetite
________	7. cupidity	g.	greed
________	8. fiscal	h.	in great quantity
________	9. glut	i.	profitable
________	10. hoard	j.	impressive wealth
________	11. largess	k.	to accept financial responsibility
________	12. lucrative	l.	a paid position without duties
________	13. mercenary	m.	generosity
________	14. munificent	n.	extremely generous
________	15. opulence	o.	to desire immorally; to envy
________	16. palatial	p.	having a significant amount of money
________	17. pecuniary	q.	an oversupply
________	18. rapacious	r.	an abundance
________	19. remuneration	s.	fitting for royalty
________	20. sinecure	t.	a valuable collection
________	21. sumptuous	u.	relating to finance
________	22. surfeit	v.	related to money or finances
________	23. underwrite	w.	eagerness to possess something
________	24. voracious	x.	overly greedy; willing to take by force

Wordsearch

Directions: Using the clues listed below, fill in each blank in the following story with one of the new words you learned this week.

Clues

1st Day

1st Day

1st Day

3rd Day

4th Day

From Nomads to Subjects

While violence from nature or rival bands were constant hazards, hunter-gatherer societies were characterized by relative equality. After all, without permanent homes, early humans could amass little in the way of wealth. With nothing to fight for, members of each group cooperated with one another to face external threats.

The invention of agriculture changed everything. Cultivation of food crops was arduous work and required settlement. The payoff was a ___________ of calories that allowed human populations to grow as never before. Larger populations and food surpluses led to specialization: people no longer needed for the harvest could become builders, craftsmen, and warriors. Thus, villages grew into towns and towns into cities.

People in cities situated along migration routes or waterways discovered that trading goods could be just as ___________ as producing them. As a city's wealth grew, so too did the demands of urban life. As the needs of buyers and sellers became more specific, ___________ systems became necessary to replace bartering. Judicial systems were also needed to resolve disputes. Sophisticated production and trade enterprises needed to learn the science of ___________ management. Writing was thus invented initially as a means for bookkeeping.

By the Bronze Age, the greatest cities in China, India, and the Near East had become so large and complex that they appointed the most prominent leaders to become kings who would enforce the law and face down military threats. These first monarchs enjoyed great wealth and power. Some became tyrants, styling themselves as gods and committed only to their own pleasures. The wisest, however, like Sargon of Akkad and Hammurabi recognized that ___________ and pageantry were conspicuous ways to advertise their importance and to maintain control over their societies with minimal bloodshed.

Sensible Sentences?

Directions: Underline the word that makes sense in each of the sentences below.

1. Spanish treasure ships that sank in storms left behind submerged *(gluts, hoards)* of gold.
2. The position of customs agents of the seldom-visited port was a desired *(sinecure, surfeit).*
3. During the Thirty Years' War, Italian *(pecuniary, mercenary)* soldiers pillaged at will.
4. Henry VIII was known for his *(rapacious, copious)* appetite.
5. The *(largess, cupidity)* of religious missions is motivated by the desire to win converts.
6. The representatives of the Estates General were adamant in their refusal to *(underwrite, compensate)* the monarchy's financial irresponsibility any further.
7. The *(sumptuous, bountiful)* quality of Chinese silk is renowned throughout the world.
8. Clever accountants help their *(rapacious, affluent)* clients avoid excessive tax exposure.
9. The *(opulence, avarice)* of Gatsby's mansion was intended to impress his lost love.
10. Debasing silver coinage with cheaper metals proved a disastrous *(fiscal, munificent)* policy that sparked rampant inflation.

THE CRASHING TWENTIES

The Roaring Twenties was a time *bereft* of caution. Everyday Americans played the market on credit, paying only a *pittance* up front. One morning in 1929, the investor Bernard Baruch got a stock tip from his shoeshine boy. Recognizing in this that the stock boom had become a bubble, he sold off his shares just before the market collapsed in a welter of panicked selling. Millionaire speculators became *insolvent*. Banks faced *liquidation* of their assets in a *futile* attempt to recover their depositors' money. The savings of millions of Americans were wiped out. Within months credit froze, businesses shuttered, and jobs evaporated, leaving average Americans facing *destitution*.

bereft
bė - reft

pittance
pit - ins

insolvent
in - solv - ent

liquidation
lik - wid - ā - shun

futile
fyūt - tīl

destitution
des - ti - tū - shun

Notable Roots:
reft = robbed;
solv = solution

Sample Sentences: Use the new words in the following sentences.

1. After a ________________ effort to stop the inferno, the crew abandoned the *Morro Castle*.
2. Savvy buyers frequent ________________ sales to get steep discounts.
3. ________________ of wise counsel, the queen consented to the destruction of the rebel city.
4. The ________________ of the Paris slums and the countryside radicalized the French peasantry that took charge of the revolution in 1792.
5. The seizure of his bank accounts left the fugitive embezzler________________.
6. While in prison, convicted felons are paid a ________________ for their work.

Definitions: Match the new words with their meanings.

7. bereft	________	a.	abject poverty
8. pittance	________	b.	unable to pay one's debts
9. insolvent	________	c.	useless
10. liquidation	________	d.	selling of assets (often to pay debts)
11. futile	________	e.	to be completely without something
12. destitution	________	f.	a trivial sum of money

BREAD LINES

By 1933, one in four American workers was unemployed and many were soon *penniless*. Entire manufacturing districts in once-thriving cities were now silent and *barren*. With entire professions out of work, there was a *dearth* of well-paying jobs and too many *supplicants* for each. These conditions left many workers reliant on *alms* to support the *meager* existence of themselves and their children. Soon lengthy bread lines formed to provide sustenance to the poor.

NEW WORDS

penniless
pen - ē - les

barren
bar - in

dearth
dėrth

supplicant
sup - lik - ent

alms
älmz

meager
mē - gėr

Notable Roots: penni = penny; bar = bare; plic/plac = plea

Sample Sentences: Use the new words in the following sentences.

1. No Man's Land was a particularly bleak and ________________ landscape.
2. Those seeking ________________ in the medieval town lined up on the cobblestone bridge.
3. Ebenezer Scrooge's dinner of cold gruel was quite ________________.
4. Faced with a ________________ of public support, the candidate dropped out.
5. To seek favor of a tyrant, a ________________ had best resort to flattery.
6. For those in serious debt, to be literally ________________ would be an improvement.

Definitions: Match the new words with their meanings.

7. penniless ________	**a.**	deficient in quantity or quality
8. barren ________	**b.**	a scarcity
9. dearth ________	**c.**	charity for the poor
10. supplicant ________	**d.**	lacking any money
11. alms ________	**e.**	unproductive; devoid of improvement
12. meager ________	**f.**	one seeking assistance

HOOVERVILLE

One of the most *piteous* sights during the Great Depression was the sudden appearance of shanty towns known as Hoovervilles, after the sitting president, Herbert Hoover. Since many of the newly *indigent* in America were now also homeless, accommodations in public shelters soon became *scanty*. Many of America's *paupers* possessed building skills and began constructing shelters on public lands. One such community in New York's Central Park was constructed from driftwood from the Hudson River. This example in particular shows how *privation* can encourage resourcefulness but also how widespread *penury* had become in the working classes.

piteous
pi - tē - us

indigent
in - di - jint

scanty
skan - tē

pauper
pô - pėr

privation
prī - vā - shun

penury
pen - yur - ē

Notable Roots: piti = pity; dige = desire/consume; priva = necessary

Sample Sentences: In which of the following newspaper headlines do the new words belong?

1. From Prince to _______________: The Fall of a Tycoon
2. Does _______________ Set Students Up for Success?
3. Information About Suspect Still _______________
4. Donated Suits and Showers Help the _______________ Get Work
5. Once Great Hotel Now in _______________ Condition
6. Lack of Health Insurance Drives Many to _______________

Definitions: Match the new words with their meanings.

7. piteous ________ a. the condition of being needy
8. indigent ________ b. the condition of doing without
9. scanty ________ c. extreme poverty
10. pauper ________ d. evoking sympathy
11. privation ________ e. insufficient in quantity or quality
12. penury ________ f. a very poor person

DUST BOWL

The *abjection* of the Great Depression was not limited to cities. Farmers had been suffering ever since the collapse of agricultural pricing that followed World War I. At the same time, small farmers faced mortgage rates that were little better than *extortion*. As the Depression worsened, a *parsimonious* president and his cabinet of *miserly* millionaires were not inclined to offer much relief. To make matters worse, decades of short-sighted farming practices had allowed much of the topsoil in the Midwest to erode away, creating a barren* landscape of windswept fields festooned with clouds of dust. With a *paucity* of options left to them, many farmers abandoned their land in their automobiles to join the *mendicants* in the Hoovervilles on the West Coast.

Sample Sentences: Use the new words in the following sentences.

1. Thriftiness is a virtue but those who act in a ________________ manner are pathologically* greedy or cheap.
2. The ________________ of quality programming on any one television channel may stem from the number of channels now in competition.
3. Odysseus appeared as a ________________ in his own court when he returned from Troy.
4. The line between persuasion and _____________ is crossed when threats come into play.
5. The ________________ of the town became certain when the last factory closed.
6. His ________________ gift-giving matched his harsh manner of speaking with family.

Definitions: Match the new words with their meanings.

7.	abjection	_________	a.	a short supply
8.	extortion	_________	b.	beggar
9.	parsimonious	_________	c.	characterized by cheapness
10.	miserly	_________	d.	the worst degree of a bad situation
11.	paucity	_________	e.	to act in a stingy manner
12.	mendicant	_________	f.	obtaining money or cooperation by threat

NEW WORDS

abjection
ab - jek- shun

extortion
ex - tôr - shun

parsimonious
pâ - sim - ō - nē - us

miserly
mī - zer - lē

paucity
pô - si - tē

mendicant
men - də - kənt

Notable Roots:
ab = away; ject = throw; tort = twist/squeeze; pauca = few

GROUP REVIEW

Pupils want to be individuals these days, and many of them refuse to conform to regulations unless there are good reasons for such rules. In the area of vocabulary study, however, the only rule that makes sense to all is that true mastery derives from continuous practice.

Matching

Directions: Match the 24 words with their meanings. Write the letter that stands for the definition in the appropriate answer spaces. (Which two review words are almost synonymous?)

REVIEW WORDS		DEFINITIONS	
_______	**1.** abjection	**a.**	unproductive; devoid of improvement
_______	**2.** alms	**b.**	abject poverty
_______	**3.** barren	**c.**	deficient in quantity or quality
_______	**4.** bereft	**d.**	insufficient in quantity or quality
_______	**5.** dearth	**e.**	to act in a stingy manner
_______	**6.** destitution	**f.**	to be completely without something
_______	**7.** extortion	**g.**	the condition of being needy
_______	**8.** futile	**h.**	beggar
_______	**9.** indigent	**i.**	extreme poverty
_______	**10.** insolvent	**j.**	evoking sympathy
_______	**11.** liquidation	**k.**	unable to pay one's debts
_______	**12.** meager	**l.**	a very poor person
_______	**13.** mendicant	**m.**	the worst degree of a bad situation
_______	**14.** miserly	**n.**	one seeking assistance
_______	**15.** parsimonious	**o.**	characterized by cheapness
_______	**16.** paucity	**p.**	charity for the poor
_______	**17.** pauper	**q.**	a trivial sum of money
_______	**18.** penniless	**r.**	a short supply
_______	**19.** penury	**s.**	selling of assets (often to pay debts)
_______	**20.** piteous	**t.**	a scarcity
_______	**21.** pittance	**u.**	obtaining money or cooperation by threat
_______	**22.** privation	**v.**	lacking any money
_______	**23.** scanty	**w.**	useless
_______	**24.** supplicant	**x.**	the condition of doing without

Wordsearch

Directions: Using the clues listed below, fill in each blank in the following story with one of the new words you learned this week.

Clues

3rd Day

3rd Day

1st Day

2nd Day

4th Day

Happy Days Are Here Again

Herbert Hoover became a millionaire through a career in mining. Ironically, he entered public life providing relief to the people of Belgium and Northern France who had been reduced to ___________ by German occupation during World War I. After America's entry in 1917, Hoover was named to head the U.S. Food Administration. In this role, he encouraged citizens to voluntarily endure limited___________ though initiatives like "Meatless Monday" and "Wheatless Wednesday," to ensure sufficient supplies for the troops without causing shortages.

In 1921, Hoover became President Harding's Secretary of Commerce. Hoover's stewardship helped new fields like radio and air travel expand with minimal growing pains. As the economy boomed through the 1920s, Hoover seemed destined to succeed President Coolidge. Then, in 1927, he virtually clinched the White House by effectively providing relief to several states following the Mississippi River floods of that year. Hoover's election in 1928 was by landslide with 58% of the popular vote and 40 out of 48 states.

Hoover entered office promising an end to __________ by effective partnership between government and private enterprise. Prior to the stock market crash on October 29th, few had reason to doubt him. As the Great Depression set in, however, Hoover fundamentally misread the crisis. He sought to buoy confidence in business by avoiding government intervention, failing to see that lack of oversight had led to the Crash. He also refused to offer financial relief to everyday Americans, believing such measures would make Americans permanent ___________.

No other president who won election so convincingly has been so soundly defeated when bidding for reelection. In 1932, Franklin Roosevelt became president by promising to bring relief to those who were struggling. His buoyant rhetoric instilled confidence in voters, inviting them to overcome their fears. Herbert Hoover, a man who had made his reputation offering relief in the wake of disaster and war, in the end has gone down, somewhat unfairly, as a___________ and uncaring millionaire who ignored his countrymen's pleas for help.

Synonym Shout-Out

Directions: As you might imagine, studying words that are related by concept will expose you to many pairs and groups of synonyms. In fact, some words are so close that if you mistake one synonym for another in an answer to a question in this book, you still basically got the question right. In the following exercise, match the words from weeks 5–7 with their close synonyms.

1.	pecuniary	________	**a.**	supplicant
2.	avarice	________	**b.**	bountiful
3.	perfidious	________	**c.**	surfeit
4.	chicanery	________	**d.**	penury
5.	copious	________	**e.**	palatial
6.	destitution	________	**f.**	mendacious
7.	meager	________	**g.**	cupidity
8.	sumptuous	________	**h.**	artifice
9.	mendicant	________	**i.**	scanty
10.	glut	________	**j.**	fiscal

ENTER DR. THOMAS A. DOOLEY

In 1956, *Look Magazine* named Thomas Dooley as one of the year's ten most outstanding men. A *neophyte* just under 30 years of age at the time, Dr. Dooley had already distinguished himself by caring for a half-million sick and emaciated Vietnamese refugees. When fighting broke out in the divided country of Vietnam, the northern communist Viet Minh forces surged southward, scattering thousands of refugees before them. The *fledgling* doctor was a lieutenant during the *incipient* war, chafing at the *indolence* of his position at a tranquil naval hospital in Japan. With the *impetuous* confidence of youth, he volunteered for duty on a navy ship that had been chosen to transport the refugees to sanctuary in Saigon. The curtain was beginning to ascend* on Dooley's *nascent* career.

NEW WORDS

neophyte
nē - ō - fīt

fledgling
flej - ling

incipient
in - sip - ē - ənt

indolence
in - dō - ləns

impetuous
im - pech - ū - us

nascent
nā - sənt

Notable Roots:
neo = new; cip = grasp; dol = pain, sadness; nasc/nat = birth

Sample Sentences: Use the new words in the following sentences.

1. Lee's decisions are sometimes regarded as ________________ by critics who fail to see that the general took the initiative as a way to offset his inferior numbers.
2. The ________________ rebellion must be put down before it spreads.
3. As a ________________, Thomas Becket had fresh eyes and was able to recognize King Henry's attempts to seize control over the church.
4. The Battle of Britain served as a major test of the ________________ coalition government.
5. That Jefferson was chosen to write the Declaration of Independence at such a young age clearly showed the promise of his________________ public career.
6. A life of ________________ does little to prepare one for emergencies.

Definitions: Match the new words with their meanings.

7.	impetuous	________	a.	at an early stage
8.	nascent	________	b.	idleness
9.	neophyte	________	c.	rash; showing little forethought
10.	fledgling	________	d.	a newcomer
11.	indolence	________	e.	showing early promise of potential
12.	incipient	________	f.	untested and new

DOOLEY'S MISSION

Aboard the refugee ship, Dooley's destiny took shape. His initial *ingenuous* outlook was quickly dispelled by the level of disease, ignorance, and fear that afflicted the passengers. He discerned that compared with the communists, Americans had been *dabblers* in the propaganda battle: the assumption that American ideals would naturally prevail with the Vietnamese he saw to be hopelessly *quixotic* given the steady drumbeat of Anti-American rhetoric on the ground. Looking to do his part, Dooley chose *artless* but tangible action over *utopian* sentiment as the best way to win over the Vietnamese. Thus, he pitched in to build shelters in Haiphong and to comfort the residents in the besieged* city. For his services, Dooley received the U.S. Navy's Legion of Merit. He told the story of his transformation from *juvenile* idealist to seasoned activist in *Deliver Us from Evil*, a bestseller that alerted America to the plight of the Vietnamese and what Dooley saw as the sinister intentions of Communism.

NEW WORDS

ingenuous
in - jen - ū - əs

dabbler
dab - lėr

quixotic
kwik - sot - ic

artless
ärt - ləs

utopian
ū - tōp - ē - ən

juvenile
jū - ven - īl

Notable Roots: gen = create; art = device, trick; topos = place

Sample Sentences: Use the new words in the following sentences.

1. The Prince was known to be a _______________ in his official duties, preferring to spend his time in luxury.
2. His _______________ behavior betrayed the fact that favoritism, and not merit, had led to the young executive's elevation.
3. The abbot's _______________ manner of speaking concealed a shrewd nature.
4. _______________ communities arise periodically but fail when their ideas of human perfectibility ring hollow.
5. Her _______________ nature convinced the jury that her answers were truthful.
6. While the Hague Conferences to end war were admirable efforts, they ultimately proved _______________ endeavors after the outbreak of World War I.

Definitions: Match the new words with their meanings.

7. ingenuous ________	a.	lacking trickery
8. dabbler ________	b.	immature
9. quixotic ________	c.	based on an ideal of perfectibility
10. artless ________	d.	innocent; authentic
11. utopian ________	e.	a disinterested amateur
12. juvenile ________	f.	overly idealistic

STYMIED* BY PERSONAL SICKNESS

After an extensive lecture tour in 1956, Dr. Dooley, the once *jejune* activist and now *scion* of anticommunism, returned to Laos to set up a mobile medical unit. Because the Geneva Agreement barred the entrance of military personnel to the country, he resigned from the Navy and went to work as a civilian. That story is told in *The Edge of Tomorrow*. The next year, despite a growing illness, the ubiquitous Dooley turned up in the remote village of Muong Sing, attempting to thwart* his traditional enemies—disease, dirt, ignorance, and starvation. He still maintained the increasingly *fatuous* hope of halting the spread of Communism. More optimist than *puerile* dreamer, he failed to recognize the deteriorating situation in the region. But his trained medical eye soon told him that the pain in his chest and back was a harbinger* of a malignant cancer. Recognizing that a *dilatory* attitude toward his condition be *imprudent*, he sought treatment.

NEW WORDS

jejune
zhā - zhūn

scion
sī - on

fatuous
fa - chū - əs

puerile
pwer - īl

dilatory
dil - ə - tôr - ē

imprudent
im - prū - dənt

Notable Roots:
june = young; puer = boy; dil = delay; prude = caution

Sample Sentences: Use the new words in the following sentences.

1. Churchill was a renowned soldier, writer, and _______________ of a noble family.
2. Max's attempts to impress his older cousins only made him look _______________.
3. The _______________ effort to halt the forest fire was woefully inadequate.
4. The critic, while noting the young actor's potential, found his performance to be both _______________ and over the top.
5. It would be _______________ to question your supervisor in front of the whole team.
6. With the expression, "Let them eat cake," Marie Antoinette revealed her _______________ and shallow attitude toward her French subjects.

Definitions: Match the new words with their meanings.

7. jejune	________	a. boyish
8. scion	________	b. unserious
9. fatuous	________	c. late; unhurried
10. puerile	________	d. young; inexperienced
11. dilatory	________	e. unwise
12. imprudent	________	f. son; rising star

BAD IS BAD

Ever since *tyro* pop sensation Ellipsis broke upon the music scene, critics and fans alike have noted his proclivity for flamboyant dress and *infantile* behavior. His "…" clothing line is noted for the heavy use of fringe and rhinestones, and a court recently denied his petition to change his name to the punctuation mark. Ellipsis's career began with the debut album *Profound*, which music guru Jai Delacroix described as "the kind of *pretentious* tripe middle schoolers write in notebooks." Certainly, tracks like "Let My Love Be Your Lily Pad," laden with *mawkish* sentimentality aren't exactly Shakespearean. Yet the catchiness of Ellipsis's songs is undeniable, and they have only grown in popularity with increased air play. He also has a certain *sophomoric* charisma, as can be seen in the video for "Gondola Girl," which depicts the singer on a boat in Venice serenading the object of his affection with a ukulele. Despite the *maudlin* lyrics ("you stole a piazza my heart (!)") the lovesick star wins over his girl with mischievous smiles and silly stunts (like falling into the canal after his attempt to do a jig on a gondola goes wrong).

NEW WORDS

tyro
tī - rō

infantile
in - fən - tīl

pretentious
prē - ten - shəs

mawkish
môw - kish

sophomoric
sof - môr - ik

maudlin
môwd - lin

Notable Roots: infant = child; soph = wise; mor = fool

Sample Sentences: Use the new words in the following sentences.

1. Capote struck an intense, yet casual pose for the portrait on the jacket of his first novel that many considered ________________, if not obscene.
2. My mother can become ________________ when reminiscing about the past.
3. Hacking the Harvard home page on a dare was a ________________ thing to do.
4. When thwarted,* many dictators are prone to ________________ protests, even tantrums.
5. I prefer my own words to the ________________ clichés of most greeting cards.
6. Hannibal and Alexander the Great showed that some military ________________ are still great strategists.

Definitions: Match the new words with their meanings.

7.	tyro	________	a.	attempting to appear significant
8.	infantile	________	b.	excessively sentimental
9.	pretentious	________	c.	sentimental in a sickly way
10.	mawkish	________	d.	exhibiting talent but immaturity
11.	sophomoric	________	e.	babyish
12.	maudlin	________	f.	a newcomer

GROUP REVIEW

Shortly before his death, Dr. Dooley was selected by the U.S. Chamber of Commerce as one of America's ten most outstanding young men. There may be no connection between success of that type and an expanded vocabulary—but one never knows.

Matching

Directions: Match the 24 words with their meanings. Write the letter that stands for the definition in the appropriate answer space. For exact synonyms, either answer is correct.

	REVIEW WORDS		DEFINITIONS
_______	**1.** artless	**a.**	a disinterested amateur
_______	**2.** dabbler	**b.**	immature
_______	**3.** dilatory	**c.**	innocent; authentic
_______	**4.** fatuous	**d.**	exhibiting talent but immaturity
_______	**5.** fledgling	**e.**	unserious
_______	**6.** impetuous	**f.**	untested and new
_______	**7.** imprudent	**g.**	babyish
_______	**8.** incipient	**h.**	a newcomer (1)
_______	**9.** indolent	**i.**	young; inexperienced
_______	**10.** infantile	**j.**	attempting to appear significant
_______	**11.** ingenuous	**k.**	son; rising star
_______	**12.** jejune	**l.**	based on an ideal of perfectibility
_______	**13.** juvenile	**m.**	overly idealistic
_______	**14.** maudlin	**n.**	idleness
_______	**15.** mawkish	**o.**	excessively sentimental
_______	**16.** nascent	**p.**	rash; showing little forethought
_______	**17.** neophyte	**q.**	showing early promise of potential
_______	**18.** pretentious	**r.**	sentimental in a sickly way
_______	**19.** puerile	**s.**	boyish
_______	**20.** quixotic	**t.**	at an early stage
_______	**21.** scion	**u.**	a newcomer (2)
_______	**22.** sophomoric	**v.**	lacking trickery
_______	**23.** tyro	**w.**	unwise
_______	**24.** utopian	**x.**	late; unhurried

Sensible Sentences?

Directions: Underline the word that makes sense in each of the sentences below.

1. Dickens's contemporary critics bemoaned *(mawkish, maudlin)* characters like the afflicted Tiny Tim and the orphan Oliver Twist.
2. Calls for bipartisanship seem increasingly *(puerile, quixotic)*.
3. The *(dilatory, fledgling)* FBI built its public profile hunting famed bank robbers.
4. The great Rivera ended the *(incipient, ingenuous)* rally with two strikeouts.
5. The champ's *(indolent, fatuous)* lifestyle sapped his strength.
6. Octavian exploited his status as *(tyro, scion)* of Julius Caesar's family.
7. A busy woman, Dr. Patil's *(artless, imprudent)* manner of speaking allows her to use an economy of words.
8. The future of Huxley's *Brave New World* seems at first to be a *(utopian, nascent)* paradise.
9. The *(impetuous, pretentious)* troops cleared Missionary Ridge without orders.
10. The *(sophomoric, nascent)* attitude of the tech billionaire angered the senators.
11. At first rather *(infantile, jejune)*, the intern soon adapted to corporate culture.

Parts of Speech

Directions: Choose the noun, verb, or adjective that answers each of the questions and write the corresponding letter in the appropriate answer space.

a. affluent
b. artless
c. avarice
d. bereft
e. burgeon
f. covet
g. debacle
h. duplicity
i. incisive
j. liquidation
k. munificent
l. puerile
m. stipulate
n. viable
o. voracious

_______ **1.** Which noun describes a disaster?
_______ **2.** Which verb means to want what isn't yours?
_______ **3.** Which adjective describes a boyish attitude?
_______ **4.** Which adjective means you're rather rich?
_______ **5.** If a firm branches out into other fields, which verb describes its growth?
_______ **6.** Which adjective means you've been deprived of what you need?
_______ **7.** If you had to name a specific condition of agreement, which verb would be appropriate?
_______ **8.** What noun denotes dishonest dealing?
_______ **9.** A good substitute for *greed* would be which noun?
_______ **10.** Which adjective describes an *insatiable* appetite?
_______ **11.** What noun best describes the sale of one's assets?
_______ **12.** What adjective would fit the act of speaking and acting without guile?
_______ **13.** Which adjective describes that which is feasible?
_______ **14.** One who is very generous might best be described by which adjective?

Wordsearch

Directions: Using the clues listed below, fill in each blank in the following story with one of the new words you learned this week. Change parts of speech if needed.

Clues

3rd Day

1st Day

1st Day

3rd Day

2nd Day

Aftermath of an Earthquake

The Egyptian earthquake in October 1992 killed 600 residents of Cairo and hospitalized thousands of others. ___________ initial rescue efforts meant that many were expected to die as a result of their injuries. Especially hard hit were the people who inhabited the city's slums, who had to seek shelter in those government buildings, schools, and factories that remained standing.

Religious Muslim groups formed ___________ relief organizations to provide aid to the survivors in the form of food, water, blankets, and tents to house the more than 300 families made homeless by the disaster. Believers took the opportunity to spread the message that the earthquake was a harbinger* of worse things to come and that an ___________ population of ___________ sinners must follow God's laws if they expected to appease heaven.

Throughout history, following volcanic eruptions, hurricanes, tidal waves, and other calamities that periodically bedevil mankind, religious leaders have used such occurrences to bring ___________ back to their faith.

Since many Egyptians had expressed unhappiness about their government prior to the earthquake, there was a good chance for religious Muslim groups to win new converts by showing that the answer to recovery was not through man's efforts, but through God's.

JUST SPELL THE NAME CORRECTLY

P. T. Barnum, the *eminent* circus impresario, was once confronted by a woman who showed him a scurrilous* manuscript about himself and said that unless he paid her, she would have the book printed. Barnum, an *inveterate* showman, rejected the extortion* attempt. "Say what you please," he replied, "but make sure that you mention me in some way. Then come to me, and I will estimate the value of your services as a publicity agent." The *seasoned* Barnum obviously felt that adverse criticism was an asset for one who *perennially* seeks fame. *Inured* against insult, he believed a man who seeks the limelight should not care what is written about him but should be concerned only when they stop writing about him. Barnum's philosophy suggests that we might do well to review the plethora of publicity given to bigoted *curmudgeons*.

NEW WORDS

eminent
em - ə - nənt

inveterate
in - vet - er - ət

seasoned
sēz - ənd

perennial
pə - ren - ē - əl

inured
in - urd

curmudgeon
kur - muj - ən

Notable Roots:
vet = experienced; ennial = year; cur = dog

Sample Sentences: Use the new words in the following sentences.

1. Hitler was a(n) ________________ liar who Chamberlain never should have trusted.
2. The ________________ promotor brought headline acts to communities across the country.
3. DiCaprio was a ________________ favorite for Best Actor, but it took several attempts to win the Oscar.
4. Harris's work as a prosecutor had ________________ her against the abuse of politics.
5. Every neighborhood has one ________________ who views everyone with suspicion.
6. A truly ________________ baseball manager knows when to make a change and when to do nothing.

Definitions: Match the new words with their meanings.

7.	eminent	________	a.	skillful through experience
8.	inveterate	________	b.	highly regarded
9.	seasoned	________	c.	a disagreeable person
10.	perennial	________	d.	hardened through use
11.	inured	________	e.	habitual
12.	curmudgeon	________	f.	continually recurring

THE RISE OF THE ECHO CHAMBER

The advent of the Internet seemed to represent an era of greater truth with the power to disseminate information now at the fingertips of average people. Gone are the days when *erudite* journalists clustered in major cities shaped the narratives of the news cycle. The air of superiority of such distant and *urbane* sophists, after all, had long alienated many in rural areas. Consequently, the formerly *revered* edifice of mainstream media quickly became *enfeebled* by the proliferation of websites offering news in real time. However, unlike the *prosaic* neutrality of established media outlets, the contributors to these sites view events through one political perspective. The *sage* elders of the past, like Walter Cronkite, have given way to angry and frequently bigoted pundits who spurn impartiality. Lacking access to alternative points of view, twenty-first-century Americans have increasingly gathered into like-minded tribes.

NEW WORDS

erudite
er - ū - dīt

urbane
ur - bān

revere
rē - vēr

enfeebled
in - fē - bəld

prosaic
prō - zā - ik

sage
sāj

Notable Roots: rud = rough; urban = city; feeble = weak

Sample Sentences: Use the new words in the following sentences.

1. The ________________ Voltaire had refined his philosophies in the salons of Paris.
2. Though ________________ by old age, Thomas Jefferson helped design the layout of the University of Virginia.
3. Some scholars spend their lives in books, becoming ________________ though not wise.
4. A common moral precept is to ________________ one's parents.
5. ________________ advice is most often heeded by those who ask for it.
6. A consummate adventurer, Theodore Roosevelt could not endure the ________________ existence of a quiet retirement.

Definitions: Match the new words with their meanings.

7.	erudite	________	a.	commonplace; ordinary
8.	urbane	________	b.	deeply respect; admire
9.	revere	________	c.	wise
10.	enfeebled	________	d.	learned; well-read
11.	prosaic	________	e.	sophisticated; suave
12.	sage	________	f.	weakened

CRAZY UNCLES

The crazy uncle is a *venerable* trope of American comedy. Part *patriarch* and part curmudgeon,* he is a deliberate throwback to bygone days that are imagined to have been simpler and more innocent. His manner of speech and dress are invariably *unaffected* as he has nothing but contempt for newfangled ways. He reserves particular scorn for urbane,* well-educated, and politically correct younger men who serve as both his foil and nemesis. The pairing of a *decrepit* crazy uncle with a condescending idealist has often made for pure comedy gold. The sparring between Archie Bunker and his liberal son-in-law "Meathead" is perhaps the most famous example. Of course, the dark side of *trite* situation comedy is that the crazy uncle, by virtue of his craziness, has the fool's ability to openly speak his mind without fear or shame. The Archie Bunkers of this world, both real and imagined, revel in this indulgence, spouting off *archaic*, often bigoted opinions. The costars roll their eyes, the audience laughs, and racism is quietly perpetuated.

NEW WORDS

venerable
ven - ėr - ə - bul

patriarch
pā - trē - ärk

unaffected
un - ə - fek - təd

decrepit
dē - krep - it

trite
trīt

archaic
ärk - ā - ik

Notable Roots: ven = love, respect; patri = father; arch = ancient

Sample Sentences: Use the new words in the following sentences.

1. Through a child's eyes, I did not see how Grandpa's charming cabin was actually rather ________________ from years of neglect.
2. Great politicians seem folksy in an ________________ way, a skill few can master.
3. A ________________ movie is one where the entire plot is discernible from the trailer.
4. Vito, the ________________ of the Corleone family, commands both fear and admiration.
5. There's a huge difference between adherence to the text of the Constitution and a slavish devotion to centuries-old and frequently________________ common law.
6. The athletic director, recognizing the fans' devotion to the ________________ old coach, kept him on long past the point when he could be truly effective.

Definitions: Match the new words with their definitions.

7. venerable	________	a.	natural; authentic
8. patriarch	________	b.	overly done; unoriginal
9. unaffected	________	c.	respected and admired
10. decrepit	________	d.	ancient; old-fashioned
11. trite	________	e.	broken-down; decayed
12. archaic	________	f.	male elder

THE BAD OLD DAYS

There's nothing new about curmudgeons* bemoaning the loss of public virtue. Whether a *doddering* bigot or a kindly grandmother, it's natural for the elderly to miss the period of their lives when their bodies were strong, beautiful, and blessedly free of infirmity. Such a *pedestrian* explanation does not fully explain human nostalgia, however. Our minds have a way of editing memory so that our fleeting successes become *immutable* triumphs. Meanwhile, the *stagnant* swaths of time that make up much of everyday life are forgotten because they are simply not memorable, and our failures are little more than *recondite* footnotes because remembering them causes pain. The same distortion occurs when we recall the world in which we grew up. While the music and fashion of the 1950s may be *passé*, that decade is often recalled as an American golden age. What is often forgotten, however, is that while America may have been a superpower, it could not halt the spread of Communism. Fear of nuclear war saw American schoolchildren hiding under their desks and their parents building bomb shelters. Thousands of intellectuals, suspected of communist sympathies, saw their careers cut short. Meanwhile, horrors like the mass murder of the Clutter family (memorialized by Capote's *In Cold Blood*) made for lurid* front-page news.

NEW WORDS

doddering
dod - ėr - ing

pedestrian (adj.)
ped - es - trē - en

immutable
im - mūt - ə - bul

stagnant
stag - nent

recondite
rek - un - dīt

passé
pas - ā

Notable Roots:
ped = foot; mut = change; stag = stand

Sample Sentences: Use the new words in the following sentences.

1. Bill Belichick's knowledge of ________________ football rules has enabled his team to play the game in novel ways.
2. Eliminating sources of ________________ water helps prevent the spread of mosquitoes.
3. His ________________ manner did not save the former Nazi from trial for his crimes.
4. Nothing is more damaging to a social media company than becoming ________________.
5. For the paparazzi, no celebrity errand is too ________________ to not merit a photograph.
6. While they may appear to be ________________, the stars do eventually fade out or explode.

Definitions: Match the new words with their definitions.

7.	doddering	_________	a.	unchanging
8.	pedestrian	_________	b.	out of date
9.	immutable	_________	c.	sluggish; at a standstill
10.	stagnant	_________	d.	obscure; not well known
11.	recondite	_________	e.	mundane; commonplace
12.	passé	_________	f.	unsteady; feeble

GROUP REVIEW

Matching

Directions: Match the 24 words with their meanings. Write the letter that stands for the definition in the appropriate answer space.

REVIEW WORDS		DEFINITIONS	
_______	**1.** eminent	**a.**	sluggish; at a standstill
_______	**2.** inveterate	**b.**	obscure; not well known
_______	**3.** seasoned	**c.**	wise
_______	**4.** perennial	**d.**	highly regarded
_______	**5.** inured	**e.**	ancient; old-fashioned
_______	**6.** curmudgeon	**f.**	male elder
_______	**7.** erudite	**g.**	commonplace, ordinary
_______	**8.** urbane	**h.**	unchanging
_______	**9.** revere	**i.**	recurring
_______	**10.** enfeebled	**j.**	sophisticated; suave
_______	**11.** prosaic	**k.**	habitual
_______	**12.** sage	**l.**	mundane; commonplace
_______	**13.** venerable	**m.**	skillful through experience
_______	**14.** patriarch	**n.**	overly done; unoriginal
_______	**15.** unaffected	**o.**	learned; well-read
_______	**16.** decrepit	**p.**	unsteady; feeble
_______	**17.** trite	**q.**	weakened
_______	**18.** archaic	**r.**	natural; authentic
_______	**19.** doddering	**s.**	hardened through use
_______	**20.** pedestrian	**t.**	respected and admired
_______	**21.** immutable	**u.**	a disagreeable person
_______	**22.** stagnant	**v.**	broken-down; decayed
_______	**23.** recondite	**w.**	deeply respect; admire
_______	**24.** passé	**x.**	out of date

Wordsearch

Directions: Using the clues listed below, fill in each blank in the following story with one of the new words you learned this week.

Clues

4th Day

1st Day

1st Day

4th Day

2nd Day

The Twentieth Century's Deadliest Disease

Most years influenza is a ___________ nuisance, causing widespread illness and loss of productivity but something we are used to. Despite this perception, influenza has been and remains a serious disease, killing 24,000–50,000 people in the United States alone. Victims are typically the very old, the very young, or the immunocompromised. Pandemics occur every 30–50 years when a new strain of the disease jumps from animals (usually pigs or birds) into the human population. During such years, the death toll is higher, but experience has still ___________ us against panic.

The worst influenza outbreak on record occurred in 1918 during the last year of World War I. It is believed to have originated within an army camp in Kansas and circled throughout the world, aided by the movement of soldiers. Strict press censorship, however, kept the epidemic out of the newspapers until it flared up in neutral Spain. For this reason, the 1918 flu has come to be known to history as the Spanish flu.

The Spanish flu was unusually virulent compared with the strains we endure on a ___________ basis. Rather than striking in a single wave, it struck in four successive waves that circled the globe from 1918 to 1919. The second wave, which commenced just as flu season is traditionally winding down, was by far the worst. Estimates are that 30–60 million people died worldwide as a result, including 650,000 Americans.

One clue as to why this particular flu was so deadly can be seen in the pattern of mortality. The Spanish flu killed the old, the young, and the ___________, as would be expected. However, some of the most severe cases occurred among adults between 20 and 40 years of age. Death rates among this population were some of the highest. It is believed that in the strong and healthy, the virus triggered an overreaction of the immune system that had never encountered a similar germ before. Those who were more ___________, but not actually in ill health, tended to fare better.

Sensible Sentences?

Directions: Underline the word that makes sense in each of the sentences below.

1. Cornelius Vanderbilt, the family *(patriarch, curmudgeon)*, made a fortune in land speculation.
2. A *(seasoned, decrepit)* quarterback runs less in order to preserve his health.
3. An orator who flaunts knowledge might seem *(trite, erudite)* but comes across as tiresome.
4. While Prohibition was repealed, the amendments that make up the Bill of Rights are regarded as *(stagnant, immutable)*.
5. The Red Sox championship drought was actually exacerbated by their status as *(perennial, prosaic)* contenders for the pennant.
6. Lord Henry's *(doddering, urbane)* manner rubs off on the impressionable Dorian Gray.
7. Sincere words of comfort are better than *(trite, sage)* aphorisms every time.
8. Nixon gradually morphed from a pariah to a *(venerable, pedestrian)* elder statesman.
9. The rules of papal conclave are as mysterious as they are *(eminent, archaic)*.
10. By the end of his presidency, FDR had become *(passé, enfeebled)* and emaciated.

WEEK 10 DAY 1

JERRY HART'S SIXTH SENSE

An *insidious* feeling had made Jerry Hart miserable all day long. It was difficult to explain, but the similar sensations in the past had been accurate—something *heinous* was about to occur. Just as some people can predict the onset of inclement weather because of a *pernicious* aching in their bones, so could Jerry detect incipient* disaster. He sat at his desk, trying to peruse a company report, but his efforts were ineffectual. The *repugnant* gnawing at his insides, the tinge of uneasiness, the premonition of calamity that besieged* him would not desist. When the phone rang, he *recoiled* with fear—it was his wife and she was hysterical. Something *grotesque* had happened: their son had been bitten by a mad dog!

NEW WORDS

insidious
in - sid - ē - us

heinous
hā - nus

pernicious
per - nish - us

repugnant
re - pug - nənt

recoil
ri - kôil

grotesque
grō - tesk

Notable Roots:
sid/sed = sit;
hein/hain = hate;
nic/nec = kill;
pug = fight

Sample Sentences: Use the new words in the following sentences.

1. Although Belle initially ________________ from the Beast, she comes to recognize his kind nature.
2. Comments sections are often rife with ________________ statements.
3. Picasso's portraits are often ________________ and breathtaking at the same time.
4. Many believe the death penalty is warranted for the most ________________ criminals.
5. Iago's words over the first few acts have an ________________ effect on Othello's psyche.
6. Slavery had a ________________ influence on the growth of the fledgling* United States.

Definitions: Match the new words with their meanings.

7. insidious ________ a. to pull back; to flinch
8. heinous ________ b. secretly causing harm
9. pernicious ________ c. ugly, sometimes in an amusing way
10. repugnant ________ d. distasteful
11. recoil ________ e. having a slow, destructive effect
12. grotesque ________ f. extremely wicked

CRISIS!

Jerry Hart got the pertinent facts from his wife; *appalled*, he dashed out of the office on his way home. Normally a polite, unassuming man with a deep *aversion* to rudeness of any kind, he jostled people in the hallway, implored the elevator operator to hurry, and with flagrant disregard for a *mortified* elderly gentleman, jumped into the cab he had hailed. The 20-minute taxi ride seemed interminable, and all the while *abhorrent* thoughts occurred to Jerry. Visions of a *malevolent* hound with foaming jaws obsessed him. A crowd of people had gathered in front of his house so that in a state of utmost *trepidation*, Jerry had to force his way through them. Little Bobby was on his bed, surrounded by a doctor, a police officer, Jerry's doleful wife, his two daughters, and a half-dozen wan neighbors.

appalled
ə - pawld

aversion
ə - ver - zhun

mortified
mör - tif - īd

abhorrent
ab - hör - int

malevolent
mə - lev - ō - lent

trepidation
trep - i - dā - shun

Notable Roots: pal = pale, shroud; vers = turn; mort = death; hor = horror; mal = bad

Sample Sentences: Use the new words in the following sentences.

1. The ________________ speech drew widespread condemnation.
2. A sly smile hid the general's ________________ nature.
3. Jeanie's mother was ________________ at having to pick her up at the police station.
4. The delegates were ________________ by the king's proclamation of rebellion.
5. All ________________ vanished once the race began.
6. My ________________ to cheesecake often raises eyebrows at parties.

Definitions: Match the new words with their meanings.

7. appalled	________	a.	outraged; deeply embarrassed
8. aversion	________	b.	evil
9. mortified	________	c.	fearful anticipation
10. abhorrent	________	d.	shocked
11. malevolent	________	e.	deep dislike
12. trepidation	________	f.	disgusting; hateful

A TIME FOR DECISION

The doctor explained the situation calmly but avoiding any *unctuous* attempt to sound overly optimistic. They didn't know whether the dog had rabies but had been unable to find him so far. The doctor had a strong *antipathy* for taking unnecessary risks and advised that Bobby undergo the admittedly *odious* vaccination daily for two weeks. Mrs. Hart concurred; she said that a neighbor who had seen the dog had been *repulsed* by its appearance. She claimed that it had been foaming at the mouth, barking, and growling constantly. But the policeman interjected that there hadn't been a case of a mad dog in the county in over 20 years and advocated that they do nothing for at least another day. Dramatic action was *anathema* to Jerry Hart's even-keeled nature, and he was inclined to agree. It was far from an *acrimonious* discussion, but given the stakes Mr. and Mrs. Hart had to think about their next step.

NEW WORDS

unctuous
ûŋk - chū - əs

antipathy
an - tip - ə - thē

odious
ō - dē - əs

repulse
rē - puls

anathema
ən - eth - ə - mə

acrimonious
ac - rə - mōn - ē - əs

Notable Roots: unct = oily; path = feeling; pul/pel = push; acri = bitter

Sample Sentences: Use the new words in the following sentences.

1. The _______________ manner of the sports agent repelled prospective clients.
2. When compromise becomes politically _______________ to the electorate, gridlock results.
3. Debate in Congress was never more _______________ than in the days prior to Civil War.
4. The _______________ Hitler and Stalin felt for one another made their pact shocking.
5. The Minute Men _______________ numerous Redcoat attacks at the Battle of Bunker Hill.
6. Laying off workers is the most _______________ task of a manager.

Definitions: Match the new words with their meanings.

7.	unctuous	________	a.	very unpleasant
8.	antipathy	________	b.	bitter
9.	odious	________	c.	something one bitterly opposes
10.	repulse	________	d.	flattering in an off-putting way
11.	anathema	________	e.	to repel
12.	acrimonious	________	f.	hatred

THE PERTINENT FACTS ABOUT RABIES

"Give me some of the basic information about the disease, Doc," said Jerry, glancing toward the figure of his son. The doctor, who *loathed* this part of his job, took a breath: "Well, it was once one of the most *reviled* of all diseases. It was called 'hydrophobia,' meaning fear of water, because one of the symptoms is an inability to swallow liquids. It is caused when the virus from the saliva of an infected animal gets into a bite wound. The virus travels along the nerves to the spine and brain." "What are the symptoms?" asked Mrs. Hart. "Pain, numbness, difficulty swallowing, headaches, muscle spasms, and convulsions." "And what is the treatment for rabies?" Jerry asked. "Two shots in the abdomen every day for two weeks." Mrs. Hart, like any mother, was *loath* to subject her son to such gruesome regiment. Sensing her *internecine* emotions, the doctor added, "While it is the *antithesis* of the bedside manner I prefer, I feel it my duty to say that once symptoms appear, death is almost inevitable. Before vaccination, people who contracted rabies were chained up before going mad and left to die a *noisome*, agonizing death." "I think we should go ahead with the injections," the distraught Mrs. Hart said. "I've heard enough."

NEW WORDS

loathe
lōTH

revile
rē - vīl

loath
lōth

internecine
in - ter - nes - ēn

antithesis
an - tith - ə - sis

noisome
nôi - sûm

Notable Roots:
vile = repulsive;
inter = between;
nec = kill; thesis = idea

Sample Sentences: Use the new words in the following sentences.

1. ________________ to admit defeat, the Cougars fought on though effectively beaten.
2. After Carthage fell, only ________________ class struggle weakened Ancient Rome.
3. The ointment, while ________________, does help greatly with rashes.
4. Aaron Burr, who rarely discussed political theory, was the ________________ of the other Founding Fathers.
5. Because Tybalt ________________ him, Romeo had little chance to avoid a fight.
6. The fan who interfered with the team's win was so ________________ that he moved away within a year.

Definitions: Match the new words with their meanings.

7.	loathe	_________	a.	destructive internal struggle
8.	revile	_________	b.	harmful; foul smelling
9.	loath	_________	c.	to despise
10.	internecine	_________	d.	reluctant
11.	antithesis	_________	e.	to repudiate; to insult
12.	noisome	_________	f.	opposite belief

GROUP REVIEW

At the end of this week's study, you will have covered 240 words. In addition, you will have seen many of those words used in subsequent lessons. If you have been operating at only 75% efficiency, you have, nevertheless, added substantially to your arsenal of words.

Here's a thought: wouldn't it be wonderful if through genuine attention to the daily dosage you could move up to 80%—or even 90%? Start by matching the 24 words with their meanings.

Matching

Directions: Write the letter that stands for the definition in the appropriate answer space. Did somebody say 100%?

	REVIEW WORDS		DEFINITIONS
______	**1.** abhorrent	**a.**	very unpleasant
______	**2.** acrimonious	**b.**	opposite belief
______	**3.** anathema	**c.**	deep dislike
______	**4.** antipathy	**d.**	bitter
______	**5.** antithesis	**e.**	harmful; foul smelling
______	**6.** appalled	**f.**	fearful anticipation
______	**7.** aversion	**g.**	to repel
______	**8.** grotesque	**h.**	destructive internal struggle
______	**9.** heinous	**i.**	evil
______	**10.** insidious	**j.**	to despise
______	**11.** internecine	**k.**	hatred
______	**12.** loath	**l.**	something one bitterly opposes
______	**13.** loathe	**m.**	secretly causing harm
______	**14.** malevolent	**n.**	to repudiate
______	**15.** mortified	**o.**	ugly, sometimes in an amusing way
______	**16.** noisome	**p.**	reluctant
______	**17.** odious	**q.**	having a slow, destructive effect
______	**18.** pernicious	**r.**	distasteful
______	**19.** recoil	**s.**	extremely wicked
______	**20.** repugnant	**t.**	shocked
______	**21.** repulse	**u.**	to pull back; to flinch
______	**22.** revile	**v.**	disgusting; hateful
______	**23.** trepidation	**w.**	outraged; deeply embarrassed
______	**24.** unctuous	**x.**	flattering in an off-putting way

Wordsearch

Directions: Using the clues listed below, fill in each blank in the following story with one of the new words you learned this week.

Clues

2nd Day

1st Day

2nd Day

2nd Day

4th Day

The Potato That Strangled Idaho

People who are ___________ at the sight of blood or ___________ in horror from most forms of violence would do well to avoid some of the movies now being shown at their local cinemas. Producers have learned that films that scare the patrons out of their seats, ironically, put millions of fans into those seats, keeping them shivering in ___________ at the terrifying spectacles that flash across the screen.

Of course, each movie carries with it a rating that indicates its suitability for certain age groups, either because of its subject matter, language, presentation, or level of violence. Pictures with a "G" rating are approved for all audiences, while, at the other end of the scale, those that are given an "NC–17" rating are for adults only with no children allowed under any circumstance. Getting an "R" rating indicates that the movie is restricted (no one under 18 can be admitted without an adult), but some Hollywood moguls consider the "R" to be the magnet that ensures box office success. And we can be sure that as long as shock films ring up a merry tune on the cash registers, producers will show no ___________ to making them.

A director who specializes in making gory films involving monsters, vampires, and brutal serial killers boasted in a college lecture that his work was in good taste. One student who disagreed was provoked and retorted that, in his opinion, the diet of "shock-schlock" movies was the very ___________ of good taste, worse even than pictures that contained vulgar language and nudity. "At least they're honest," he declared.

First and 10

Directions: Match each word with the group from weeks 1–10 to which it belongs. There are two words for each group.

GROUP		REVIEW WORDS	
1. Dishonesty	______	a. indigent	k. dilatory
2. Failure	______	b. artifice	l. bereft
3. Wealth	______	c. impish	m. nadir
4. Success	______	d. ingenuous	n. loathe
5. Youth	______	e. plaudits	o. cupidity
6. Age	______	f. capitulate	p. probity
7. Wisdom	______	g. surfeit	q. inured
8. Folly	______	h. odious	r. astute
9. Poverty	______	i. subterfuge	s. mawkish
10. Horror	______	j. urbane	t. sanguine

THE SEARCH FOR THE DOG (CONTINUED)

Meanwhile, the Harts had notified the local radio stations to broadcast an appeal for the dog's owner to come forward. The general public was *enthralled*, and the station was soon inundated with phone calls, but all leads were fruitless.* The only eyewitness to the event was Bobby. Naturally, the attack made a *vivid* impression. More from fear than any desire to *embellish*, the boy's story veered into *hyperbole*. In the most *florid* language a six-year-old can muster, he described a gray beast that was taller than him with foam dripping from razor-sharp fangs. All the police could glean from this was that the dog was gray and *adorned* with a metal collar. Despite the lack of tangible evidence, however, the police remained sanguine.*

NEW WORDS

enthralling
in - thräl - ing

vivid
viv - id

embellish
əm - bel - ish

hyperbole
hī - pėr - bō - lē

florid
flôr - id

adorn
ə - dôrn

Notable Roots: thrall = slave; viv = life; hyper = to a great deal; flor = flower

Sample Sentences: Use the new words in the following sentences.

1. The use of _______________ for emphasis is one of the most common rhetorical strategies of persuasion.
2. Every street in Munich was _______________ with garlands of hops for Oktoberfest.
3. The secret of Van Gogh's _______________ paintings was the great master's use of complementary colors in pairs.
4. Marc Antony's _______________ funeral oration turned the masses against Caesar's assassins.
5. Lawyers and judges do not take kindly to witnesses who _______________ their stories.
6. Hemingway's prose is famously lacking in _______________ description.

Definitions: Match the new words with their meanings.

7. enthralling	________	a.	to decorate
8. vivid	________	b.	to add detail; to exaggerate
9. embellish	________	c.	complex and full of detail
10. hyperbole	________	d.	fascinating; demanding attention
11. florid	________	e.	lifelike; vibrant
12. adorn	________	f.	extreme statements, not meant literally

NO RELIEF

The normally phlegmatic Jerry Hart had become the *archetype* of the grieving father. Twenty-four hours had passed under the *pall* of a horrific disease. This would be enough to drive most parents to *histrionics*, but Jerry was determined to see his son receive the vaccine. At the suggestion of some friends, he organized a *panoply* of friends and neighbors to fan out around the supermarket. They knocked on every door, inspected every dog, and came back empty-handed. Although the Harts were sick with worry (they had to be coerced into going to sleep), little Bobby seemed to be in great spirits. The *excruciating* vigil continued without *deliverance*.

NEW WORDS

archetype
ärk - ə - tīp

pall
päl

histrionic
his - trē - on - ik

panoply
pan - ə - plē

excruciating
eks - krūsh - ē - āt - ing

deliverance
də - liv - ėr - əns

Notable Roots: arch = structure; pan = all; cruc = pain

Sample Sentences: Use the new words in the following sentences.

1. It's amazing how ________________ a hangnail can be.
2. The ________________ of warships at Queen Victoria's royal review in 1897 was stunning.
3. Lear's Fool has become the ________________ of the character who can say truth to power.
4. Though the forest fires were far away, a ________________ of smoke hung over town.
5. The ________________ behavior of a demagogue's acolytes should not be mistaken for popular support.
6. The paratroopers asserted that they didn't need ________________ by ground forces.

Definitions: Match the new words with their meanings.

7.	archetype	________	a.	overly dramatic
8.	pall	________	b.	an impressive assembly
9.	histrionic	________	c.	causing great pain
10.	panoply	________	d.	a dark cloud
11.	excruciating	________	e.	relief
12.	deliverance	________	f.	a stereotypical example

THE POLICE FIND THE DOG

Forty hours of police work and the publicity brought the Hart's tragedy to a *climactic* end. Their *rhetoric* had garnered widespread response. By meticulously checking the registrations of every red station wagon in the neighborhood and then cross-checking dog licenses, the police narrowed the search to four owners. After a few calls, the owner was located. She brought her muzzled German shepherd to the Hart domicile. With a *flamboyant* squeal, Bobby identified the dog, and the animal was taken to a veterinarian to have the necessary tests performed. The owner, Mrs. McGraw, at first defended her dog's behavior. *Entranced*, she listened as the police warned her of the severity of the incident. Without further *pageantry*, she admitted that the dog had a sporadic mean streak. In *grandiloquent* terms, she scoffed at the idea of rabies. Jerry Hart noticed for the first time in two days that his uneasy feeling had departed.

NEW WORDS

climactic
clī - mak - tik

rhetoric
ret - ör - ik

flamboyant
flam - bôi - ənt

entrancing
in - trans - ing

pageantry
paj - en - trē

grandiloquent
gran - dil - ō - kwint

Notable Roots:
rhetor = speaker;
flam = flame, shine;
grand = great;
loq = speech

Sample Sentences: Use the new words in the following sentences.

1. The passion of some fascists can have an ________________ effect on angry citizens.
2. Career criminals tend to avoid ________________ displays of wealth.
3. Pickett's Charge was the ________________ moment of the Battle of Gettysburg.
4. The guest speaker's ________________ introduction actually embarrassed her.
5. The ________________ of a royal wedding is a breathtaking spectacle.
6. Whether the new president's actions will match his ________________ remains to be seen.

Definitions: Match the new words with their meanings.

7.	climactic	________	a.	elaborate manner of speaking
8.	rhetoric	________	b.	ostentatious display
9.	flamboyant	________	c.	mesmerizing
10.	entrancing	________	d.	final; conclusive
11.	pageantry	________	e.	showy
12.	grandiloquent	________	f.	speech

ALL'S WELL THAT ENDS WELL

The Harts were greatly relieved by the *resolution* to this crisis, learning that the conjecture about the dog was not true. Because of the *salient* fact that the German shepherd was not rabid, the necessity for the painful treatment was obviated. The police gave the dog's owner a summons for allowing the animal to go unmuzzled. Her *sanctimonious* attitude certainly did not endear her to the authorities, but her eventual cooperation proved to be an *extenuating* circumstance that ensured her penalty was not worse. Little Bobby was treated to a *rousing* compensation for his ordeal: an ice cream sundae and a movie. Following the happy *denouement*, the neighbors searched for other lurid* happenings, and Jerry Hart went back to his office. "What kind of dog was that?" his secretary asked. "Oh, his bark was worse than his bite," quipped Jerry.

NEW WORDS

resolution
rez - ō - lūsh - ən

salient
sāl - ē - int

sanctimonious
sank - tə - mōn - ē - əs

extenuating
eks - ten - ū - āt - ing

rousing
rou - zing

denouement
dā - nū - mən

Notable Roots:
solu = solve; sanct = sacred; mon = warning; ten = stretch

Sample Sentences: Use the new words in the following sentences.

1. After his _______________ keynote speech in 2004, Barack Obama's stature increased.
2. The detectives found few _______________ clues at the crime scene.
3. The _______________ of the international crisis by arbitration was a win for peace.
4. The judge determined that no _______________ facts can excuse murder.
5. Pundits that adopt a _______________ manner often attract more viewers.
6. Authors often include an epilogue to their novels to provide a satisfactory _______________ for their characters.

Definitions: Match the new words with their definitions.

7. resolution	________	a. offsetting; excusing
8. salient	________	b. final settlement
9. sanctimonious	________	c. acting morally superior
10. extenuating	________	d. obvious
11. rousing	________	e. inspiring
12. denouement	________	f. completion

GROUP REVIEW

Many teachers have jested about their students who confused *rabies* with *rabbis*, Jewish clergymen. We know that those who get the message of this book, true vocabulary mastery, will make few such errors.

Matching

Directions: Match the 24 words with their meanings. Write the letter that stands for the definition in the appropriate answer space.

	REVIEW WORDS		DEFINITIONS
______	**1.** adorn	**a.**	extreme statements, not meant literally
______	**2.** archetype	**b.**	offsetting; excusing
______	**3.** climactic	**c.**	completion
______	**4.** deliverance	**d.**	speech
______	**5.** denouement	**e.**	causing great pain
______	**6.** embellish	**f.**	obvious
______	**7.** enthralling	**g.**	elaborate manner of speaking
______	**8.** entrancing	**h.**	a stereotypical example
______	**9.** excruciating	**i.**	complex and full of detail
______	**10.** extenuating	**j.**	inspiring
______	**11.** flamboyant	**k.**	to decorate
______	**12.** florid	**l.**	acting morally superior
______	**13.** grandiloquent	**m.**	fascinating; demanding attention
______	**14.** histrionic	**n.**	lifelike; vibrant
______	**15.** hyperbole	**o.**	mesmerizing
______	**16.** pageantry	**p.**	a dark cloud
______	**17.** pall	**q.**	ostentatious display
______	**18.** panoply	**r.**	an impressive assembly
______	**19.** resolution	**s.**	showy
______	**20.** rhetoric	**t.**	to add detail; to exaggerate
______	**21.** rousing	**u.**	final settlement
______	**22.** salient	**v.**	relief
______	**23.** sanctimonious	**w.**	final; conclusive
______	**24.** vivid	**x.**	overly dramatic

Wordsearch

Directions: Using the clues listed below, fill in each blank in the following story with one of the new words you learned this week.

Clues

1st Day

4th Day

1st Day

3rd Day

3rd Day

Sophomoric Scribes

At some point in their education, all young writers go through a period when they first learn to use challenging language but have not yet learned restraint and good taste. The poetry of teen and young adult writers is often filled with __________ descriptions and melodramatic musings about life and love. Essays on the indignities of everyday life become __________ diatribes about the unfairness of it all. More reasoned arguments are rife with __________, the extreme nature of which often undercuts the point being made.

The __________ nature of youthful prose should be no discouragement from self-expression, however. Like a budding chef, a young writer must experiment with verbal spices and sauces to learn what combinations pair well and best represent their creativity. Above all, the hallmark of mature writing is the sparse use of compelling language to have an __________ effect when flaunting the occasional verbal gem.

Sensible Sentences?

Directions: Underline the word that makes sense in each of the sentences below.

1. A *(panoply, pageantry)* of limousines made up the president's motorcade.
2. A second-degree burn tends to cause one *(extenuating, excruciating)* pain.
3. Delirious with fever, the traveler saw *(vivid, florid)* hallucinations.
4. Contempt for one's spouse is the most *(climactic, salient)* sign of a doomed marriage.
5. The prize-winning photo captured the hostages' elation at their *(deliverance, resolution)*.
6. The general's *(histrionic, rousing)* rant did little to inspire his men.
7. The performer's use of *(flamboyant, sanctimonious)* costumes increased her fame.
8. The Treaty of Westphalia proved a durable *(pall, denouement)* to the Thirty Years' War.
9. The crown is *(adorned, embellished)* with over 500 precious gemstones.
10. Walter Cronkite remains the *(rhetoric, archetype)* of the honest reporter.

Exploring Roots

Directions: Remember that word roots provide you with a second key to remembering vocabulary. This knowledge also helps pick the lock of new words that share the same roots as those you know.

Match the root definition with the sentence containing an italicized word with the same root.

________	**1.** sacred	**a.** There's more to *patriotism* than flag-waving.
________	**2.** speech	**b.** *Philosophy* is a demanding and precise art.
________	**3.** slave	**c.** The *ingenuity* of his design earned the inventor notice.
________	**4.** father	**d.** Celebrities are much too *aggrandized* these days.
________	**5.** wise	**e.** The tribunes of the Roman Senate were considered *sacrosanct* and immune from violence.
________	**6.** create	**f.** A photovoltaic cell *converts* sunlight into electricity.
________	**7.** great	**g.** Too much coffee makes me *loquacious*!
________	**8.** turn	**h.** Involuntary *servitude* is only legal as punishment.

OFF BROADWAY

When Monte Ziltch told his boss, Mr. Foy, that, despite his *aptitude* for the work, he was quitting as an accountant to become an actor, the man was convulsed with laughter. After Mr. Foy realized that Monte was serious, the normally *savvy* manager launched into a diatribe on the importance of responsibility in the younger generation. Monte confessed that he had chosen his profession for its *utilitarian* reputation and that he had been developing ulcers as an accountant. *Aptly* enough, an opportunity to get into show business had arisen, requiring Monte to make an immediate decision. Monte said he considered himself a *versatile* individual and had always harbored a secret ambition to try his hand in the performing arts. Mr. Foy stormed out of the office, muttering incoherently about the *chimerical* nature of millennials.

aptitude
apt - ə - tūd

savvy
sav - ē

utilitarian
ū - til - ə - ter - ē - ən

apt
apt

versatile
vėr - sə - təl

chimerical
chī - mer - ik - əl

Notable Roots:
apt = fitted; sav = wise; util = use, tool; vers = turn

Sample Sentences: Use the new words in the following sentences.

1. ________________ investors see economic downturns as an opportunity to buy.
2. Children are known for ________________ observations that adults are too polite to make.
3. The ________________ musician Trent Reznor plays several different instruments.
4. Joel is talented but possesses a________________ nature, refusing to commit to any vocation.
5. Ana found that her ________________ with multiple languages was one of her greatest assets.
6. ________________ but dependable cars like the Civic and Outback have loyal followings.

Definitions: Match the new words with their meanings.

7. aptitude _________ a. idealistic; flaky
8. savvy _________ b. flexible; multitalented
9. utilitarian _________ c. useful
10. apt _________ d. shrewd; wise
11. versatile _________ e. ability
12. chimerical _________ f. appropriate; well chosen

AN ALL-AROUND MAN

The need for a decision came about when a local theater *impresario* invited an *obliging* Monte to join his prestigious summer stock company. His position as "apprentice" would require him to be *agile*. He would have to take tickets; paint scenery; prepare placards; assist with lighting, costumes, and props; and carry an occasional spear in a walk-on role. Since the company would stage five major plays during the summer, there was a chance that if Monte proved *adept* in the execution of his duties, he might actually get a part before too many weeks had elapsed. In addition, he would increase his acting *acumen* by attending the drama classes that were an integral part of the summer theater. The remuneration* would be nominal, but at last Monte Ziltch would be able fulfill his life-long ambition to become a *proficient* actor.

NEW WORDS

impresario
im - pres - är - ē - ō

obliging
ō - blī - jing

agile
aj - əl

adept
ə - dept

acumen
ak - yū - mən

proficient
prō - fish - ənt

Notable Roots: oblig = commitment; dept = attain; ac = sharp; fic = make/do

Sample Sentences: Use the new words in the following sentences.

1. Despite great speed, an Olympic sprinter is often less _______________ than a soccer player.
2. An _______________ prosecutor, Kamala Harris was well prepared for her debates.
3. Celebrities who are _______________ toward fans are often the most popular.
4. P. T. Barnum came to define the modern circus _______________.
5. My father's culinary _______________ always surprised my friends.
6. Most switch hitters are more _______________ from one side of the plate.

Definitions: Match the new words with their meanings.

7.	impresario	________	a.	able to move or adapt easily
8.	obliging	________	b.	ability; knowledge
9.	agile	________	c.	accomplished
10.	adept	________	d.	helpful; kind
11.	acumen	________	e.	organizer of entertainment
12.	proficient	________	f.	skillful

FROM LEDGERS TO SCRIPTS

During the first weeks of the summer, Monte Ziltch didn't have time to wonder if he had made a mistake typical of *precocious* youth. He had become a *lithe* stagehand, performing a thousand and one odd jobs around the theater. First there was the opening production of *A Chorus Line*, then two weeks of *The Fantasticks*, followed by *The Diary of Anne Frank*, which did excellent business. All through those weeks, Monte painted, carried, nailed, collected, and ran with *dexterity*. He observed his fellow players, *emulating* their techniques. He had expunged all traces of debits and credits from his mind and had become an *aficionado* of the theater. His impromptu career change was proving an *apposite* adjustment to his circumstances.

NEW WORDS

precocious
prē - kōsh - əs

lithe
līTH

dexterity
deks - ter - i - tē

emulate
em - ū - lāt

aficionado
ə - fish - ə - nod - ō

apposite
ap - pō - sit

Notable Roots: cog = aware; pre = before; dext = skillful; ap = fitting

Sample Sentences: Use the new words in the following sentences.

1. Touch typing with speed and _______________ is a function of practice.
2. The _______________ physique of the lead dancer belied her strength.
3. An _______________ is more than expert: such a person shows true passion for a pursuit.
4. One habit of those who become successful is to _______________ those who have made it.
5. Be it a war or moon landing, Cronkite's words were _______________ to every occasion.
6. Veteran teachers often struggle with their most _______________ students.

Definitions: Match the new words with their meanings.

7.	precocious	________	**a.**	skillfulness
8.	lithe	________	**b.**	advanced for one's age
9.	dexterity	________	**c.**	appropriate to a situation
10.	emulate	________	**d.**	flexible; graceful
11.	aficionado	________	**e.**	to copy; to surpass
12.	apposite	________	**f.**	an enthusiastic fan or expert

IRONY FOR MERRYWEATHER

Monte found himself a more *protean* individual than he ever expected and so, when at last, his chance to perform came, he handled it with *aplomb*. He had played the timorous Lion in *The Wizard of Oz*. Now there was an open audition to cast the final show of the season. It was to be a postmodern comedy written by a *maverick* playwright and given a summer tryout prior to a Broadway opening. Monte, who by now had adopted the stage name of Monte Merryweather, read for the producers, hoping to get the part of the hero's fractious landlord. Though he *adroitly* delivered his performance, the competition was too tough—but the director, a *connoisseur* of budding talent, assigned Monte to a less ostentatious part. It seems that fate, the *arbiter* of all outcomes, has a sense of humor and so for the first two weeks in September, the stage-struck accountant had a two-minute, two-line part. What was his role? The hero's accountant!

NEW WORDS

protean
prō - tē - ən

aplomb
ə - pləm

maverick
mav - ėr - ik

adroit
ə - drôit

connoisseur
con - ə - sur

arbiter
är - bit - ər

Notable Roots: plum = balance; droit = right; arbit = judge, witness

Sample Sentences: Use the new words in the following sentences.

1. Paul Ryan possessed remarkable _______________ for such a young speaker.
2. Metternich was the most _______________ diplomat of the early nineteenth century.
3. A wine _______________ knows the best brands and vintages for every occasion.
4. Scott Weiland was known as much for his _______________ appearance as his vocal skill.
5. Scientific _______________ trust their data more than time-honored theories.
6. A Supreme Court justice is an _______________ of the Constitution's "true" meaning.

Definitions: Match the new words with their meanings.

7. protean	_________	a.	judge; decision maker
8. aplomb	_________	b.	graceful
9. maverick	_________	c.	changeable
10. adroit	_________	d.	independent person
11. connoisseur	_________	e.	grace; poise
12. arbiter	_________	f.	expert

GROUP REVIEW

How many of the new words have now become a part of your working vocabulary? At first, their use may be conscious, even studied. However, the squeaks will soon disappear. Try a few this weekend.

Matching

Directions: Match the 24 words with their meanings. Write the letter that stands for the definition in the appropriate answer space.

REVIEW WORDS			DEFINITIONS	
________	**1.**	acumen	**a.**	independent person
________	**2.**	adept	**b.**	advanced for one's age
________	**3.**	adroit	**c.**	judge; decision maker
________	**4.**	aficionado	**d.**	organizer of entertainment
________	**5.**	agile	**e.**	flexible; multitalented
________	**6.**	aplomb	**f.**	expert
________	**7.**	apposite	**g.**	skillfulness
________	**8.**	apt	**h.**	idealistic; flaky
________	**9.**	aptitude	**i.**	appropriate to a situation
________	**10.**	arbiter	**j.**	shrewd; wise
________	**11.**	chimerical	**k.**	to copy; to surpass
________	**12.**	connoisseur	**l.**	able to move or adapt easily
________	**13.**	dexterity	**m.**	accomplished
________	**14.**	emulate	**n.**	skillful
________	**15.**	impresario	**o.**	graceful
________	**16.**	lithe	**p.**	grace; poise
________	**17.**	maverick	**q.**	ability; knowledge
________	**18.**	obliging	**r.**	changeable
________	**19.**	precocious	**s.**	appropriate; well chosen
________	**20.**	proficient	**t.**	helpful; kind
________	**21.**	protean	**u.**	ability
________	**22.**	savvy	**v.**	flexible; graceful
________	**23.**	utilitarian	**w.**	useful
________	**24.**	versatile	**x.**	an enthusiastic fan or expert

Sensible Sentences?

Directions: Underline the word that makes sense in each of the sentences below.

1. A naturally *(savvy, precocious)* child, I tended to repeat facts learned in books.
2. In tennis, tall, big servers tend to lose to more *(apt, lithe)* shot makers.
3. John McCain was famously called a *(maverick, impresario)* for his willingness to vote against his own party.
4. A long-running debate has raged over whether Michelangelo was *(chimerical, utilitarian)* or simply a versatile* artisan with prodigious energy.
5. My brother was promoted to a *(prestigious, flamboyant)* job in his company.
6. Major Andre, knowing he was caught, met his end with *(acumen, aplomb)*.
7. AC/DC has proven to be a *(protean, obliging)* musical act, employing an ever-changing lineup over four decades.
8. The most *(agile, versatile)* runner on the team is typically the tailback.
9. A corrupt leader prefers a crony on the bench to an impartial *(arbiter, aficionado)* of law.
10. Barbara, known for her *(adroit, apt)* speaking, was chosen to give the eulogy.
11. The blackjack dealer's *(aptitude, dexterity)* was so great his hands were a blur.

Wordsearch

Directions: Using the clues listed below, fill in each blank in the following story with one of the new words you learned this week.

Clues

2nd Day

4th Day

3rd Day

3rd Day

1st Day

2nd Day

4th Day

1st Day

The Big Three

Men's tennis was once a wide-open sport where any number of players could attain a higher level of _____________ for a fortnight and win a Grand Slam title. Of course, there have been past eras marked by rivalries, such as the 1990s, when the composed and _____________ Pete Sampras, known for his booming serve, went head-to-head with the _____________ returner, Andre Agassi. In the past, however, other players still had their opportunities.

The early twenty-first century has seen unparalleled dominance by a trio of players. First came the _____________ young Swiss, Roger Federer, who won his first Grand Slam at Wimbledon in 2003 at the age of 21. He would win the next four as well as his first five U.S. Open titles. During these years, he held the #1 ranking for a record 237 weeks.

Rafael Nadal grew up on the sun-washed island of Mallorca in Spain. Where Federer was a _____________ player known for his intelligent play and vast repertoire of shots, Nadal was blessed with size, speed, and the determination to run down any ball. Nadal won the French Open in 2005, when he was 19. He quickly attained fame for his _____________ on clay courts, winning an unprecedented nine French Opens in his first ten appearances. While Nadal amassed a lopsided record against Federer on clay, the Swiss prevailed when the two met on grass and hard courts. That changed in 2008, when, in what many deem the greatest match ever played, Nadal finally outlasted Federer for the Wimbledon crown (in his third attempt).

Something of a _____________ in a normally staid sport, Novak Djokovic was known for his hilarious impressions of other players and on-court displays of emotion. Despite his _____________ personality, the Serb possessed laser-like ground strokes and a superb backhand. In 2011, Djokovic took over tennis. He won his first 41 matches en route to a 70–6 record, three Grand Slam titles, and the most prize money of any season in history. After that year, the Big Three maintained a stranglehold on the sport. During the 2010s, they collectively won 33 of 40 Grand Slam titles and held the #1 ranking for all but 41 weeks.

A VISIT TO THE PRESIDENT

In the winter of 1941, Enrico Fermi and a number of other distinguished scientists lent their voices to an effort to *induce* President Franklin Roosevelt to authorize an all-out effort in atomic energy research. The scientists had been *incited* by incontrovertible evidence of surreptitious German experiments. The Italian-born Fermi was the ideal man to lead the atomic research. Already in 1938, he had won the Nobel Prize for work with radioactive elements and neutron bombardment. Fermi had found a haven from Fascist *reactionaries*, and he knew that if the Germans were the first to develop an atomic bomb, it would be *tantamount* to world dominance for Hitler. Fermi's intent was to *preclude* such a calamity. The international race for atomic supremacy began *forthwith*.

NEW WORDS

induce
in - dūs

incite
in - sīt

reactionary
rē - ak - shən - er - ē

tantamount
tant - ə - mount

preclude
prē - klūd

forthwith
fôrth - with

Notable Roots:
duc = lead; cit = move; clude = close off

Sample Sentences: Use the new words in the following sentences.

1. Today's loss ________________ any chance at a playoff berth.
2. Revolution and reform nearly always spark ________________ movements.
3. The Prince declared that Romeo is banished ________________.
4. While free speech is protected, ________________ a riot is not.
5. Not receiving a response to a job application is ________________ to rejection.
6. By 42 weeks of pregnancy, most obstetricians will ________________ labor.

Definitions: Match the new words with their meanings.

7. induce	________	a.	to avoid or make unnecessary
8. incite	________	b.	equivalent to
9. reactionary	________	c.	to persuade; to bring about
10. tantamount	________	d.	immediately
11. preclude	________	e.	to encourage; to stir up
12. forthwith	________	f.	opposed to new ideas or reform

THE *ULTIMATE* WEAPON TAKES SHAPE

Enrico Fermi designed a device that could *eventuate* in a fission reaction. It consisted of chunks of uranium that emitted neutrons between layers of graphite that slowed them down. Holes were left for long cadmium safety rods. The basic *premise* of the device was simple: withdrawing the control rods acted as a *catalyst* for the production of neutrons that could split uranium atoms. When the rods were withdrawn to a critical point, then the neutrons would be produced so fast that they could not be absorbed. In that manner, a self-*perpetuating* "chain reaction" would result. In a nuclear weapon, the *culmination* of this process would be a cataclysmic explosion. Fermi's device could also be the *precursor* of a new power generation system. Slowly, the first atomic pile began to grow in a subterranean room at Columbia University.

NEW WORDS

eventuate
i - ven - chū - āt

premise
pre - mis

catalyst
cat - ə - list

perpetuate
pėr - pech - ū - āt

culmination
cul - min - ā - shən

precursor
prē - ker - ser

Notable Roots:
event = occur; pre = before; miss = message; cata = change; pet = go; cur = run

Sample Sentences: Use the new words in the following sentences.

1. The fall of Petersburg proved the _______________ of Grant's eastern campaign.
2. The _______________ of a one-ring scam is that the unsuspecting will return missed calls.
3. Diligent preparation often _______________ fortuitous outcomes.
4. Abolitionism proved a _______________ for an organized women's suffrage movement.
5. The telegraph was the humble _______________ of modern telecommunications.
6. Social media companies must work to stop misinformation from _______________ online.

Definitions: Match the new words with their meanings.

7.	eventuate	________	a.	an agent that spurs a change or reaction
8.	premise	________	b.	to keep something going
9.	catalyst	________	c.	a forerunner
10.	perpetuate	________	d.	climax; highest point
11.	culmination	________	e.	to result in
12.	precursor	________	f.	principle upon which an idea is based

THE SQUASH COURT EXPERIMENT

As the pile neared completion, Fermi moved the project to an abandoned squash court at the University of Chicago. The possibility that the Germans were close to *consummating* their own project *fomented* considerable anxiety—there was no *contingency* plan for losing the race. At last, six weeks after the project had been *engendered*, critical mass was achieved. Three brave assistants ascended the pile, ready with liquid cadmium if anything *inadvertently* went wrong. Almost fifty scientists and incredulous observers mounted a balcony to watch. One physicist remained on the floor to extract the final cadmium control rod. Unbearable tension permeated the atmosphere; one physicist described the experiment as *analogous* to "tickling a dragon's tail." Fermi completed his calculations, took a deep breath, and then gave the signal.

NEW WORDS

consummation
con -sū - mā - shən

foment
fō - ment

contingency
cən - tin - jən - sē

engender
ən - jen - dėr

inadvertent
in - ad - vėr - tənt

analogous
ən - al - ə - gəs

Notable Roots: con = together; sum = total; gen = create; ad = toward; vert = turn; log = words

Sample Sentences: Use the new words in the following sentences.

1. Failure in business often results from the ________________ managers fail to see.
2. The actor was discovered ________________ when she accompanied a friend to an audition.
3. For ________________ rebellion, the Founding Fathers faced execution.
4. Honest mistakes by baseball players like Buckner and Snodgrass have frequently ________________ enduring animosity from unreasonable fans.
5. Governor DeWitt Clinton pouring water from Lake Erie into New York Harbor marked the ________________ of the Erie Canal project.
6. The competition of nature can be viewed as ________________ to that of the marketplace.

Definitions: Match the new words with their meanings.

7.	consummation	________	a.	to bring about
8.	foment	________	b.	logically similar
9.	contingency	________	c.	unintentional
10.	engender	________	d.	to stir up a negative reaction
11.	inadvertent	________	e.	unpredictable result or situation
12.	analogous	________	f.	completion; joining

THE ITALIAN NAVIGATOR LANDS

It worked! Enrico Fermi's calculations *extrapolated* perfectly into reality as the team had successfully brought about a chain reaction. After 28 minutes, Fermi gave the signal to replace the control rod. The significance of the moment *obviated* any explanation and *precipitated* a tremendous cheer from the normally reserved scientists. Some of the men, however, remarked soberly that the breakthrough would prove an *antecedent* to much darker discoveries; Fermi's work would be the *substrate* upon which nuclear weapons research would build. For this reason, the achievement could not be widely *promulgated* within the scientific community. On December 2, 1942, the news of Fermi's achievement was relayed in a cryptic telephone message to Washington:

"The Italian Navigator has reached the New World."
"And how did he find the natives?"
"Very friendly."
The Atomic Age was inchoate—but truly here!

extrapolate
ek - strap - ə - lāt

obviate
ob - vē - āt

precipitate (v.)
prē - sip - i - tāt

antecedent
an - tə - sēd - ənt

substrate
sub - strāt

promulgate
prom - ul - gāt

Notable Roots: via = way; ante = before; cede = yield; sub = under; strat = layer

Sample Sentences: Use the new words in the following sentences.

1. Beware of ________________ grand theories from small samples of data.
2. Cratons are the hard, ancient ________________ underlying the continents.
3. The results of today's games have ________________ any tie-breaking matches.
4. The day's riots ________________ a dramatic change in the attitudes of the lawmakers.
5. The Articles of Confederation are the ________________ of the U.S. Constitution.
6. Hitler widely ________________ his intention to seize German lands lost by treaty.

Definitions: Match the new words with their meanings.

7. extrapolate	________	a.	underlying layer
8. obviate	________	b.	to announce; to declare
9. precipitate	________	c.	something that comes before
10. antecedent	________	d.	remove the need for something
11. substrate	________	e.	extend a principle in a new way
12. promulgate	________	f.	to cause or accelerate

GROUP REVIEW

No matter what the theme, no matter what the source, we can expect that important concepts will require a mature vocabulary. This week's topic, scientific and biographical in nature, serves as a vehicle for teaching you 24 worthwhile words. You now have the chance to see whether you remember their definitions. Write the letter that stands for the definition in the appropriate answer space.

REVIEW WORDS		DEFINITIONS	
______	1. analogous	a.	to result in
______	2. antecedent	b.	to cause or accelerate
______	3. catalyst	c.	unintentional
______	4. consummation	d.	remove the need for something
______	5. contingency	e.	underlying layer
______	6. culmination	f.	a forerunner
______	7. engender	g.	to bring about
______	8. eventuate	h.	immediately
______	9. extrapolate	i.	climax; highest point
______	10. foment	j.	an agent that spurs a change or reaction
______	11. forthwith	k.	to avoid or make unnecessary
______	12. inadvertent	l.	completion; joining
______	13. incite	m.	to encourage; to stir up
______	14. induce	n.	to stir up a negative reaction
______	15. obviate	o.	to announce; to declare
______	16. perpetuate	p.	opposed to new ideas or reform
______	17. precipitate	q.	something that comes before
______	18. preclude	r.	logically similar
______	19. precursor	s.	to persuade; to bring about
______	20. premise	t.	to keep something going
______	21. promulgate	u.	equivalent
______	22. reactionary	v.	extend a principle in a new way
______	23. substrate	w.	principle upon which an idea is based
______	24. tantamount	x.	unpredictable result or situation

Wordsearch

Directions: Using the clues listed below, fill in each blank in the following story with one of the new words you learned this week.

Clues

1st Day

4th Day

2nd Day

1st Day

1st Day

Drug Smugglers Beware

The urgent message came to Officer Matt Jagusak: "Drug search tomorrow—bring pig."

Jagusak, with the Union County, New Jersey, Sheriff's Department Search and Rescue Unit, had ___________ his superiors to put Ferris E. Lucas, a super sniffer, to work. Lucas is a Vietnamese pot-bellied pig with a fantastic olfactory sense that is one million times greater than a human's and could be the weapon that ___________ the breaking up of the drug trade.

A trainer who had worked with Lucas's ___________, sniffer dogs, offered the pig to Union City, suggesting that its greater intelligence and superior skill would make Lucas a critical fighter against illegal narcotics. ___________ by this revelation, Jagusak has worked feverishly training Lucas. He has already taught his 55-pound porker-detective how to find cocaine, hashish, and marijuana. While some more ___________ law enforcement officials were hesitant at first, they quickly became believers when they saw the Sherlock Holmes of the sty locate underground drug scents that had eluded trained dogs. Thus, the department resolved to put Lucas to work.

"I don't care if it's a dog, a pig, or an elephant," Jagusak's boss said. "If it benefits the department and our community, we'll try it."

Exploring Roots

Consider a word you learned this week: *obviate*. The prefix *ob* is a Latin preposition that basically means in front of. The root, *via*, is an extremely common one that typically refers to a means or possibility. A *viable* solution has a way forward. Getting to work *via* the subway means using that conveyance. To the Romans, however, *via* was their word for road. The *Via Appia* and *Via Flaminia* referred to roads into the city, named for the city gate through which they passed. Put these parts together and you have a reference to an object in the road ahead of you. Thus, to *obviate* means, in a literal sense, to remove an obstruction from your path.

Directions: Match the root definition with the sentence containing an italicized word with the same root.

________	**1.** head	**a.** Economic development creates social *stratification*.
________	**2.** yield	**b.** The physicist was so *maladroit* that he tripped on the rug.
________	**3.** run	**c.** The quiet girl turned out to be a chess *savant*.
________	**4.** aware	**d.** The Gauls *capitulated* after a long Roman siege.
________	**5.** wise	**e.** Our *cognitive* biases can never be eliminated if we remain unaware of them.
________	**6.** layer	**f.** A loser *conceding* defeat is an important political norm.
________	**7.** right	**g.** The *convertible* sports car attracted police attention.
________	**8.** turn	**h.** The transcontinental railroad was built by two teams working *concurrently* from opposite directions.

SUNDAY MORNING AT PEARL HARBOR

At breakfast time on Sunday morning, December 7, 1941, Dorie Miller was serving coffee aboard the seemingly *indomitable* battleship West Virginia. Dorie was African American, and the highest job to which an *intrepid* African-American sailor could aspire to in the U.S. Navy at the time was that of messman. While Dorie was technically a member of an *imperious* fighting fleet, he was not expected to fight. Due to the *intransigence* of racism in American culture at the time, most Army and Navy officers inveighed against African Americans as fighting men. While he took such overt prejudice as an *affront*, Dorie Miller apparently accepted being relegated to the role of a mess hall servant and did his job with *poise*. Now, as he poured the coffee, Dorie was wondering why the airplanes above were making so much noise on a peaceful Sunday morning.

NEW WORDS

indomitable
in - dom - it - ə - bəl

intrepid
in - tre - pid

imperious
im - pēr - ē - əs

intransigence
in - tran - sij - əns

affront
ə - frûnt

poise
pôiz

Notable Roots:
domi = lord; trep = fear; trans = cross; signa = seal, agreement

Sample Sentences: Use the new words in the proper blanks.

1. The Montagues and Capulets are tragically punished for their ________________.
2. Harding's ________________ gaze belied his timid and retiring nature.
3. The ________________ little terrier stood its ground against the larger hound.
4. The Franco-Prussian war started over an exaggerated diplomatic ________________.
5. A group of ________________ Rangers scaled the Normandy cliffs under German fire.
6. Hemingway described heroism as ________________ in the face of death and loss.

Definitions: Match the new words with their meanings.

7. indomitable	________	a.	offensive act
8. intrepid	________	b.	stubbornness; refusal to back down
9. imperious	________	c.	daring; enterprising
10. intransigence	________	d.	unable to be intimidated or defeated
11. affront	________	e.	calm and dignified manner
12. poise	________	f.	arrogant; fierce

THE INFAMOUS ATTACK

The coffee cups suddenly went spinning as an explosion knocked Dorie Miller flat on his back. Jumping up from his supine position, the *stalwart* messman from Waco, Texas, headed for the deck. Everywhere that Dorie looked, he saw smoke and once-*formidable* warships lying on their sides. Overhead, dozens of Japanese dive bombers controlled the skies without a U.S. plane to repulse* their *brazen* attack. There was no time to decry the *effrontery* of the surprise attack as the Japanese pilots had the *temerity* to make pass after pass, strafing the survivors. Without hesitating, Dorie joined a team that was feeding ammunition to a machine gunner. Unfortunately, the torpedo planes were *undaunted* by this ineffectual attempt to protect their battleship.

NEW WORDS

stalwart
stäl - wərt

formidable
fôr - mid - ə - bəl

brazen
brā - zin

effrontery
ə - frûnt - ə - rē

temerity
tə - mer - it - ē

undaunted
un - dôn - təd

Notable Roots:
fort = strong; front = face; daunt = intimidate

Sample Sentences: Use the new words in the proper blanks.

1. The President's aide castigated the blackmailer for his ________________.
2. A great hockey team needs ________________ defenders to protect its ace scorers.
3. Dr. Shih recognized at once the challenge the ________________ new virus posed.
4. Boss Tweed attracted condemnation not because he was corrupt but because he was so ________________ in his dealings.
5. A great fighter pilot needs intuition and quick reflexes, not ________________.
6. Nadia Comaneci was completely ________________ by pressure, earning the first perfect scores in the history of Olympic gymnastics.

Definitions: Match the new words with their meanings.

7.	stalwart	________	a.	bold
8.	formidable	________	b.	carelessness
9.	brazen	________	c.	durable; powerfully built
10.	effrontery	________	d.	unfazed by adversity
11.	temerity	________	e.	insolence; disrespect
12.	undaunted	________	f.	impressively powerful or tough

THE HEROISM OF DORIE MILLER

Men all around Miller were succumbing to the *obdurate* spray of Japanese bullets. Showing incredible *audacity*, Miller dragged his captain to safety and turned back to see that the machine-gunner had been killed. The *stolid* messman took the big gun and trained it on the incoming bombers. Within the space of ten minutes, he was credited with destroying four bombers while dodging the bullets of their fighter escorts. After demonstrating their *braggadocio* and striking a *brash* but effective blow, the Japanese flew back to their carrier fleet. Amidst the dead bodies and the ruined fleet were the heroes such as Dorie Miller. The Navy had doubted and tried to discourage him, but he hadn't listened. Now Dorie's *recalcitrance* served as a potent example for a nation thrust into the largest conflict in human history.

NEW WORDS

obdurate
ob - dur - it

audacity
ô - das - i - tē

stolid
stol - lid

braggadocio
brag - ə - dōs - ē - ō

brash
brash

recalcitrant
rē - cals - ə - trənt

Notable Roots:
dur = hard; brag = boast; calc = heel, kick

Sample Sentences: Use the new words in the proper blanks.

1. The grim, ________________ face of Joe Torre betrayed neither hope nor despair.
2. After Hannibal's crushing victories, anyone but the ________________ Romans would have sued for peace.
3. Some ________________ is always expected at the beginning of any football game.
4. The ________________ young congresswoman was determined to show her district's contempt for Washington deal-making.
5. Napoleon's speed and ________________ allowed the French to choose the battlefield.
6. Whole neighborhoods could not be saved from the ________________ flow of lava.

Definitions: Match the new words with their meanings.

7.	obdurate	________	a.	boldness; decisiveness
8.	audacity	________	b.	unwilling to change
9.	stolid	________	c.	display of courage or arrogance
10.	braggadocio	________	d.	defiant; uncooperative
11.	brash	________	e.	not showing emotion
12.	recalcitrant	________	f.	assertive; irreverent

"FOR DISTINGUISHED DEVOTION TO DUTY"

Some months later, Dorie Miller was serving on an aircraft carrier when Admiral Chester Nimitz, the commander of the Pacific Fleet, came aboard to preside over a special awards ceremony. In *stentorian* tones, the admiral presented Miller with the prestigious* Navy Cross, commending him for his singular act of valor and "disregard for his own personal safety." Prior to the battle, many of Miller's shipmates, who had treated him with a *haughty* sense of superiority, were also notable for their displays of *bravado*. While some of these same sailors abandoned ship in terror during the attack, Miller had displayed true *pluck* while maintaining an inspiring degree of *gravitas* under fire. Miller's example helped to shatter the previously *intractable* bias against African Americans in the armed forces. Although he could have accepted a sinecure* at a U.S. naval base, Dorie remained in the combat zone and was killed in action in December 1943.

NEW WORDS

stentorian
sten - tô - rē - ən

haughty
hô - tē

bravado
brə - vod - ō

pluck
plûk

gravitas
grô - vē - tôs

intractable
in - trak - tə - bəl

Notable Roots: haut = high; brava = brave, brag; grav = serious; tract = control

Sample Sentences: Use the new words in the proper blanks.

1. Washington's ________________ was so great that he was addressed as "his excellency."
2. A team of expensive all-stars will often lose to a cheaper team with more ________________.
3. A judge with a ________________ voice can command a courtroom.
4. In retrospect, given his quick knockout, the challenger's ________________ was laughable.
5. While it may resemble a horse, the zebra is quite ________________.
6. The new manager's ________________ manner quickly alienated his entire staff.

Definitions: Match the new words with their meanings.

7. stentorian	________	a.	dignity
8. haughty	________	b.	great courage
9. bravado	________	c.	acting superior
10. pluck	________	d.	cannot be managed
11. gravitas	________	e.	showy appearance of courage
12. intractable	________	f.	having a loud voice

GROUP REVIEW

Many people agree that a lawyer should be skillful with words. A trial lawyer, it goes without saying, must have an extensive vocabulary in order to help him or her present a case.

Matching

Directions: Match the 24 words with their meanings. Write the letter that stands for the definition in the appropriate answer space.

REVIEW WORDS		DEFINITIONS
________	**1.** affront	**a.** unwilling to change
________	**2.** audacity	**b.** acting superior
________	**3.** braggadocio	**c.** defiant; uncooperative
________	**4.** brash	**d.** having a loud voice
________	**5.** bravado	**e.** great courage
________	**6.** brazen	**f.** bold
________	**7.** effrontery	**g.** daring; enterprising
________	**8.** formidable	**h.** arrogant; fierce
________	**9.** gravitas	**i.** boldness; decisiveness
________	**10.** haughty	**j.** insolence; disrespect
________	**11.** imperious	**k.** unable to be intimidated or defeated
________	**12.** indomitable	**l.** dignity
________	**13.** intractable	**m.** display of courage or arrogance
________	**14.** intransigence	**n.** unfazed by adversity
________	**15.** intrepid	**o.** cannot be managed
________	**16.** obdurate	**p.** showy appearance of courage
________	**17.** pluck	**q.** carelessness
________	**18.** poise	**r.** offensive act
________	**19.** recalcitrant	**s.** stubbornness; refusal to back down
________	**20.** stalwart	**t.** not showing emotion
________	**21.** stentorian	**u.** durable; powerfully built
________	**22.** stolid	**v.** impressively powerful or tough
________	**23.** temerity	**w.** assertive; irreverent
________	**24.** undaunted	**x.** calm and dignified manner

Wordsearch

Directions: Using the clues listed below, fill in each blank in the following story with one of the new words you learned this week.

Clues

1st Day

2nd Day

1st Day

2nd Day

2nd Day

Sugar and Spice and Everything Nice

Teen Talk Barbie, the best-selling $50 model, has gone a step too far in the opinion of the American Association of University Women. Representatives of that group consider it an ___________ that one of her four preprogrammed phrases is "Math class is tough."

For years, the university professors, as well as members of feminist organizations, have inveighed against the stereotype that portrays girls as weak math and science students. "Because that brainwashing message is conveyed to girls at an early age, they come to accept what we consider to be a ___________ lie," said Dr. Ellen Kaner, a Dallas chemist. "We are just beginning to make progress in our campaign to recruit women with the requisite talent and ___________ for challenging, well-paying careers in math and science," she added, "and were shocked to learn that a toy company has had the ___________ to spread such harmful nonsense."

Facing such ___________ opposition, the executives of the company that manufactures Teen Talk Barbie had to set matters right. They admitted that the phrase in question, one of 270 selected by computer chips, was a mistake. In a press release, their president said, "We didn't fully consider the potentially negative implications of this phrase. Not only will we remove it immediately but will exchange the offending doll for a new one."

We wonder how Ken feels about the matter.

Too Much of a Good Thing?

Directions: As the saying goes, most things are only good in moderation. Taken to excess, virtue becomes vice and the creative, destructive. In the sentences below, the two words are similar but differ by degree. Underline the appropriate choice.

1. The *(pluck, temerity)* of a champion racehorse cannot be taught.
2. A *(tyro, prodigy)*, the new company owner rode the firm into the ground.
3. The 1919 wheat harvest proved a *(bounty, glut)* that led to a crash in prices.
4. The family *(curmudgeon, patriarch)* is the guest of honor at holiday gatherings.
5. The *(intrepid, brash)* George Creel headed the Committee on Public Information at the age of 41 and succeeded at garnering support for the war effort.
6. The Intolerable Acts *(anteceded, fomented)* rebellion in the colonies.
7. Marnie is such a *(grandiloquent, rousing)* speaker that it's hard to listen to her without rolling one's eyes.
8. Hamlet's flaw is that he is too *(cognizant, circumspect)* to avenge his father before arousing the suspicion of his murderous uncle.
9. By means of his *(guile, duplicity)*, Oedipus is able to defeat the Sphinx.
10. Shakespeare depicts the young Henry V as a *(miscreant, dilettante)* who drinks and keeps low company before reaching his full potential.

DANNY ESCOBEDO GOES TO JAIL

In 1960, a young Chicagoan, Danny Escobedo, was given a 20-year jail sentence for an *unconscionable* crime. Danny had confessed to *perpetrating* the murder of his brother-in-law after the police had refused to allow him to see his lawyer. Actually, Danny, the *alleged* killer, was tricked into blaming a friend for the *egregious* crime, thereby establishing himself as an *accomplice*. Despite the fact that Danny later recanted his confession, he was found *culpable* and jailed. Danny had been profiled as a hoodlum, and nobody raised an eyebrow over the hapless felon's troubles.

NEW WORDS

unconscionable
un - kon - shən - ə - bəl

perpetrator
pėr - pe - trā - tėr

alleged
ə - lej - id

egregious
ə - grē - jəs

accomplice
ə - kom - plis

culpable
kûl - pə - bəl

Notable Roots: patra = father; leg = law; greg = flock; culpa = blame, guilt

Sample Sentences: Use the new words in the following sentences.

1. Gavrilo Princip, the killer of Archduke Ferdinand, worked with several ________________.
2. The most ________________ crimes capture the most publicity.
3. The ________________ thief was never convicted due to lack of evidence.
4. A person with no morals is easily capable of the ________________.
5. To be ________________ in a conspiracy to commit a crime, one need only have foreknowledge of the deed and aid it by one overt act.
6. The ________________ of the 1920 Wall Street Bombing was never identified.

Definitions: Match the new words with their meanings. Two of the words are very close in meaning.

7.	unconscionable	________	a.	deserving blame
8.	perpetrator	________	b.	accused of being
9.	alleged	________	c.	associate in crime
10.	egregious	________	d.	without decency
11.	accomplice	________	e.	outrageously bad
12.	culpable	________	f.	one who performs a crime

WEEK 15 DAY 2

ESCOBEDO'S LAWYER APPEALS

Barry Kroll, a Chicago lawyer, took an interest in Danny Escobedo's case. Kroll felt that his client's rights under the Constitution had been *abrogated*. Since Escobedo had *blatantly* been denied access to an attorney, Kroll asked the courts to *expurgate* him forthwith.* He proposed that lawyers be present when the police question someone suspected of an *infraction*, but the Illinois courts rejected that on the grounds that it would result in *rampant* interference with all questioning by legal authorities. If such a law were upheld, the police felt that it would *jeopardize* their ability to conduct criminal investigations.

NEW WORDS

abrogate
a - brō - gāt

blatant
blā - tənt

expurgate
eks - pėr - gāt

infraction
in - frak - shun

rampant
ram - pənt

jeopardize
jep - ėr - dīz

Notable Roots: rog/reg = law; purg = cleanse; fract = break; ramp = climb

Sample Sentences: Use the new words in the following sentences.

1. The police cannot prevent every________________, so they must prioritize serious crimes.
2. The ________________ violence of Chicago during Prohibition is still the subject of movies.
3. Accepting gifts can ________________ a college athlete's eligibility to play sports.
4. Many treaties made between Native Americans and the United States during the nineteenth century were later ________________ at the latter's convenience.
5. The advent of DNA evidence ________________ many who were wrongfully convicted.
6. Fascists often tell ________________ lies as a demonstration of their power.

Definitions: Match the new words with their meanings.

7. abrogate	________	a.	done openly
8. blatant	________	b.	a violation of rules or law
9. expurgate	________	c.	to imperil
10. infraction	________	d.	exonerate
11. rampant	________	e.	to revoke; treat as nonexistent
12. jeopardize	________	f.	widespread

A HISTORIC SUPREME COURT RULING

Lawyer Kroll persevered in his defense of Danny Escobedo. The case was argued before the Supreme Court, and in 1964, in a landmark decision, the Court reversed Danny's conviction. Legal aid, said the judges, must be instantly available to a suspect before *indictment*. "A system of law enforcement that comes to depend on the confession," one justice *reprimanded*, "will, in the long run, become *tainted* and less reliable than one that depends on *empirical* evidence independently secured through skillful investigation." A justice *admonished* against what many considered to be legal *heresy*: "I think the rule is ill-conceived and that it seriously fetters perfectly legitimate methods of criminal enforcement."

NEW WORDS

indict
in - dīt

reprimand
rep - rə - mand

taint
tānt

empirical
em - pēr - ik - əl

admonish
ad - mon - ish

heresy
her - ə - sē

Notable Roots: dic = say; mand = order, summon; mon = warn

Sample Sentences: Use the new words in the following sentences.

1. The judge ________________ the first-time offenders and let them off without punishment.
2. Given the strife caused by competing theologies, the medieval church had no tolerance for ________________.
3. The shipment of ________________ milk led to hundreds of cases of food poisoning.
4. The doctor firmly________________ the ulcer patient against taking aspirin.
5. Despite its popularity among fiscal conservatives, ________________ data for the benefits of supply side economics has proven elusive.
6. After her alibi was shown to be fabricated,* the widow was ________________ for murder.

Definitions: Match the new words with their meanings.

7. indict ________   a. to scold
8. reprimand ________   b. based on experience
9. taint ________   c. to scold; to warn
10. empirical ________   d. ideas contrary to accepted beliefs
11. admonish ________   e. to make impure
12. heresy ________   f. to formally accuse

THE EFFECTS OF THE ESCOBEDO DECISION

After Danny Escobedo's release from prison, hundreds of inmates brought lawsuits to *redress* their alleged* rights violations. Each case was heard on its merits and many who had been convicted of *flagrant* offenses were freed. After getting out, Danny led a nomadic existence, relying on *nepotism* to gain employment without qualifications. The police maintained he was a *culprit* in numerous crimes. Danny was *unrepentant*, *castigating* the justice system for harassment. Although the Escobedo case was controversial, most agree that it inspired better law enforcement procedures and increased scientific crime detection.

NEW WORDS

redress
rē - dres

flagrant
flā - grənt

nepotism
nep - ə - tizm

culprit
kul - prət

unrepentant
un - rē - pen - tənt

castigate
kas - tə - gāt

Notable Roots:
dress = correct, prepare;
flagra = burning;
nepos = nephew;
culp = blame

Sample Sentences: Use the new words in the following sentences.

1. Dictatorships often are marked by rampant* _______________ enriching the leader's family.
2. The First Amendment includes the right to petition for a _______________ of grievances.
3. After a raid revealed _______________ health code violations, the restaurant was shuttered.
4. The intern was _______________ so harshly that he soon quit.
5. The governor vowed that the _______________ of the attack would be brought to justice.
6. By his demeanor, it was clear to the jury that the killer was completely_______________.

Definitions: Match the new words with their meanings.

7. redress	________	a. corrupt favoritism, usually toward family
8. flagrant	________	b. guilty person
9. nepotism	________	c. remedy or compensation
10. culprit	________	d. scold harshly
11. unrepentant	________	e. obvious
12. castigate	________	f. without remorse

GROUP REVIEW

Police who have resorted to wire-tapping have been able to get evidence that was useful in gaining convictions. In a sense, everyone who listens to you is wire-tapping your conversation. Are the "detectives" impressed with the extent of your vocabulary? By the end of this week, you will have gained a greater familiarity with 300 words and 60 idioms—enough to educate a conscientious wire-tapper.

Matching

Directions: Match the 24 words with their meanings. Write the letter that stands for the definition in the appropriate answer space.

	REVIEW WORDS		DEFINITIONS
______	**1.** abrogate	**a.**	to scold; to warn
______	**2.** accomplice	**b.**	remedy or compensation
______	**3.** admonish	**c.**	done openly
______	**4.** alleged	**d.**	to formally accuse
______	**5.** blatant	**e.**	to revoke; treat as nonexistent
______	**6.** castigate	**f.**	without decency
______	**7.** culpable	**g.**	corrupt favoritism, usually toward family
______	**8.** culprit	**h.**	to make impure
______	**9.** egregious	**i.**	a violation of rules or law
______	**10.** empirical	**j.**	scold harshly
______	**11.** expurgate	**k.**	widespread
______	**12.** flagrant	**l.**	without remorse
______	**13.** heresy	**m.**	accused of being
______	**14.** indict	**n.**	obvious
______	**15.** infraction	**o.**	to imperil
______	**16.** jeopardize	**p.**	guilty person
______	**17.** nepotism	**q.**	deserving blame
______	**18.** perpetrator	**r.**	associate in crime
______	**19.** rampant	**s.**	to scold
______	**20.** redress	**t.**	based on experience
______	**21.** reprimand	**u.**	exonerate
______	**22.** taint	**v.**	ideas contrary to accepted beliefs
______	**23.** unconscionable	**w.**	one who performs a crime
______	**24.** unrepentant	**x.**	outrageous

Wordsearch

Directions: Using the clues listed below, fill in each blank in the following story with one of the new words you learned this week.

Clues

2nd Day

4th Day

2nd Day

4th Day

3rd Day

4th Day

1st Day

1st Day

Questionable Advertisements

The Nostalgia Factory, a Boston art gallery, staged an exhibit of ___________ outrageous advertisements. For example, one of the fast-food chains ran a TV commercial that showed school cafeteria workers in hairnets, making that experience less tasty than a visit to Roy Rogers. Another ad, which was ___________ by psychiatrists and groups such as the Alliance for the Mentally Ill, suggested to readers that if they had paid $100 for a dress shirt, they were fit candidates for a straitjacket. Similar sensitivity had restricted ad writers from using terms such as "nuts" or "crazy."

Why such protests and where do they come from? Who is asking companies to ___________ contracts with those agencies that are complicit in creating messages that perpetuate* such ___________ stereotypes? Parents who took exception to the Burger King spot that announced, "Sometimes You Gotta Break the Rules," said no to it because it gave the wrong message to their children. And when a potato chip ad featured a "bandito," angry Mexican Americans used some choice words to ___________ the ad maker for such a stereotype.

The conclusion to be reached is that segments of the population have become increasingly vocal about insensitive ads, demanding that corporations ___________ their complaints by never again commissioning advertisements that are clearly provocative and harmful to good human relationships. The advertising agencies that are ___________ in these offenses should also reform their conduct. Any___________ and habitual offenders could find themselves facing boycotts of their products and services.

MEET THE BEES

One of the most interesting inhabitants of our world is the bee, an *industrious* insect that is indigenous to all parts of the globe except the polar regions. The honeybee is a *resourceful* insect whose habitat is a colony that he shares with as many as 80,000 bees. Although the individual bees are essentially *automatons* that live for only a few days, their colony can *persevere* for several years. A cursory study of the activities of these insects reveals a *punctiliousness* and a social structure that is truly amazing. For example, bees in a particular hive have a distinct odor; therefore, when an intruder seeks access, *vigilant* guard bees can identify him quickly and repulse* his invasion.

NEW WORDS

industrious
in - dus - trē - əs

resourceful
rē - zôrs - ful

automaton
ô - tom - ə - ton

persevere
pėr - sə - vēr

punctilious
punk - til - ē - əs

vigilant
vij - əl - ənt

Notable Roots: struer = build; auto = self; mato = think; severe = serious; punct = point

Sample Sentences: Use the new words in the following sentences.

1. Gandhi taught Indians to _______________ in their fight without using force.
2. The _______________ Lakota derived dozens of uses for the buffalo they hunted.
3. With better pay and benefits, workers tend to be more _______________.
4. Early industrialists wanted workers to be __________, performing repetitive mundane tasks.
5. The foreman was _______________ in his quest to root out unionizing among workers.
6. From cooperative factory work came the need to be _______________ about time.

Definitions: Match the new words with their meanings.

7. industrious ________ a. strict regarding details
8. resourceful ________ b. hardworking
9. automaton ________ c. to struggle through adversity
10. persevere ________ d. skillful at finding solutions
11. punctilious ________ e. carefully watchful
12. vigilant ________ f. machine or person that follows instructions without thinking

WEEK 16 DAY 2

QUEENS, WORKERS, DRONES

Each colony of honeybees consists of three classes: a) the queen who is an *unflagging* layer of eggs, b) the *attentive* worker, and c) the sedentary drone whose only function is to mate with a young queen. The queen lays the eggs that hatch into thousands of female workers; some queens live as long as five years and can *unstintingly* lay up to one million eggs. The *thrifty* worker *meticulously* builds and maintains the nest and frugally collects and stores the honey. The lazy drone, or male honeybee, does not work and has no sting. When the drone is no longer needed, the workers *promptly* let him starve to death. It's a cruel, cruel world!

NEW WORDS

unflagging
un - flag - ing

attentive
ə - ten - tiv

unstinting
un - stin - ting

thrifty
thrif - tē

meticulous
mə - tik - yū - ləs

prompt
prom - pt

Notable Roots:
flag = tire; tent = keep/hold; stint/stunt = limit

Sample Sentences: Use the new words in the following sentences.

1. The team owner was _______________ in his praise of the new coach.
2. Survivors of the Great Depression formed a lifetime habit of being _______________.
3. _______________ service is prized in the restaurant industry.
4. The _______________ building inspector noticed small cracks in the building's foundation.
5. As the ferocity of the 1900 hurricane became apparent, the _______________ telegraph operator stayed at his post and saved lives by stopping rail service into Galveston.
6. Spouses who are _______________ to each other's needs tend to stay together.

Definitions: Match the new words with their meanings.

7.	unflagging	________	a.	keeping a close eye on something
8.	attentive	________	b.	fast and reliable
9.	unstinting	________	c.	careful about spending and waste
10.	meticulous	________	d.	generous
11.	thrifty	________	e.	tireless
12.	prompt	________	f.	particular about details

SPOTLIGHT ON THE WORKER

Let us examine the activities of the *assiduous* workers in greater detail. After the workers have completed the *arduous* task of constructing a hive of waterproof honeycomb (made from beeswax), the queen begins to lay eggs in the first cells. While some workers *scrupulously* tend the hive, others *forage* for nectar and pollen. Once provisioned, they fly back to the hive and then dance around the honeycomb, their movements indicating the direction of the flowers. Meanwhile, other workers have been cleaning cells, caring for the young, and guarding the precious cache of nectar. Another *indefatigable* cohort is entrusted with heating or cooling the hive. Dedicated to the welfare of the entire insect community, all of these workers are not *chary* about working hard.

NEW WORDS

assiduous
ə - si - jū - əs

arduous
âr - jū - əs

scrupulous
skrū - pyū - ləs

forage
fôr - əj

indefatigable
in - də - fat - əg - bəl

chary
châr - ē

Notable Roots: sid/sed = sit; ardor = passion; scruple = principle; fatig = tired

Sample Sentences: Use the new words in the following sentences.

1. Prior to the invention of agriculture, humans ________________ for much of their food.
2. ________________ in his own dealings, Andrew Mellon was one of the few honest brokers in the Harding Administration.
3. Following the Mormon Trail from Nebraska to Utah was an ________________ journey.
4. Unlike the other Founding Fathers, Burr worked________________ for his own interests.
5. Nuclear deterrence made the U.S. and U.S.S.R. ________________ about the prospect of war.
6. The ________________ Fiorello LaGuardia expanded New York's infrastructure and fought both corruption and organized crime during three terms as mayor.

Definitions: Match the new words with their meanings.

7. assiduous	________	a.	tireless
8. arduous	________	b.	wary; averse to risks
9. scrupulous	________	c.	to gather resources
10. forage	________	d.	hardworking
11. indefatigable	________	e.	difficult
12. chary	________	f.	careful about details; ethical

THE SAGA OF THE QUEEN BEE

Although the *laborious* lives of the workers are remarkable, the queen bee is really the main story. Workers *fastidiously* choose a few larvae to be *aspiring* queens, feeding them royal jelly, a substance rich in proteins and vitamins. While the queen is changing from a larva to a pupa, a team of workers builds a special cell for her. Soon the young queen hatches, eats the prepared honey, and grows strong, *resolved* to reign. After she kills any rivals who challenge her, she flies from the hive *soliciting* the drones that can fly highest to mate with her. Then the process of egg laying begins. When her progeny saturate the hive, *tenacious* scouts are dispatched to find a new location, and the bees swarm after their leader to begin the amazing cycle again.

NEW WORDS

laborious
lə - bôr - ē - əs

fastidious
fa - stid - ē - əs

aspire
ə - spīr

resolve (v.)
rē - zâlv

solicit
sə - lis - it

tenacious
tən - ā - shəs

Notable Roots: labor = work; spir = breathe; sol = lone; ten = keep, hold

Sample Sentences: Use the new words in the following sentences; remember, different tenses may be required.

1. It's unwise to _______________ advice from people of unknown character.
2. General MacArthur famously _______________ to retake the Philippines.
3. During the Renaissance, talented _______________ artists were apprenticed to great masters.
4. Many investigators take crime personally and are _______________ in their efforts to bring down perpetrators* who believe they are above the law.
5. It can come off as vanity to be overly _______________ about one's appearance.
6. Coaling a warship was one of the most _______________ tasks a sailor would perform.

Definitions: Match the new words with their meanings.

7. laborious	________	a.	stubborn; unwilling to let go
8. fastidious	________	b.	settle on a course of action
9. aspire	________	c.	requiring considerable hard work
10. resolve	________	d.	to aim for a high position
11. solicit	________	e.	detail oriented; particular
12. tenacious	________	f.	to ask for something from someone

WEEK 16 ☼ DAY 5

GROUP REVIEW

Even if you are as busy as the proverbial bee, you can always manage the 15 to 20 minutes that are required for these daily vocabulary sessions.

Matching

Directions: Match the 24 words with their meanings. Write the letter that stands for the definition in the appropriate answer space.

REVIEW WORDS

_______ 1. arduous
_______ 2. aspire
_______ 3. assiduous
_______ 4. attentive
_______ 5. automaton
_______ 6. chary
_______ 7. fastidious
_______ 8. forage
_______ 9. thrifty
_______ 10. indefatigable
_______ 11. industrious
_______ 12. laborious
_______ 13. meticulous
_______ 14. persevere
_______ 15. prompt
_______ 16. punctilious
_______ 17. resolve
_______ 18. resourceful
_______ 19. scrupulous
_______ 20. solicit
_______ 21. tenacious
_______ 22. unflagging
_______ 23. unstinting
_______ 24. vigilant

DEFINITIONS

a. particular about details
b. wary; averse to risks
c. strict regarding details
d. hardworking (1)
e. fast and reliable
f. skillful at finding solutions
g. carefully watchful
h. settle on a course of action
i. tireless (1)
j. careful about spending and waste
k. difficult
l. to aim for a high position
m. to struggle through adversity
n. to ask for something from someone
o. hardworking (2)
p. requiring considerable hard work
q. keeping a close eye on something
r. careful about details; ethical
s. to gather resources
t. generous
u. tireless (2)
v. stubborn; unwilling to let go
w. detail oriented; particular
x. machine or person that follows instructions without thinking

Wordsearch

Directions: Using the clues listed below, fill in each blank in the following story with one of the new words you learned this week.

Clues

2nd Day

4th Day

4th Day

3rd Day

1st Day

Cheating a Cheater

"Our neighborhood was so tough," the comedian joked, "that two guys held up a bank and were mugged as they ran to their getaway car." Later that evening, as Roy and Timmy were discussing the comic's routine, Roy was reminded of a true (he said) story that went like this:

Mr. D, the gang kingpin in our community, loved money. He was notoriously ___________ , however, preferring to keep his wealth rather than spend it. Mr. D's trove was concealed in a wall safe behind a painting in his office. He was also ___________ about counting it by hand himself. The $50 and $100 bills made his hands dirty as he counted them, but Mr. D didn't mind. The filth of the lucre did not disturb him at all.

One Friday evening, Roy continued, an ___________ young thief looking to make a name for himself had the temerity* to try to steal the ill-gotten gains. Having bought the combination from a less-than-___________ relative who had installed Mr. D's safe, he stuffed his loot into a laundry bag and was halfway out the door when he spied a $10 bill on the floor. His cupidity* made him go back for that small change, and in that moment, Mr. D arrived on the scene.

The quick-thinking thief ___________ and rather than giving himself away blurted out, "I'll have the shirts back on Friday." Hoisting the laundry bag over his shoulder, he was out the door before the confused mobster could figure out what had happened.

Timmy, who had listened patiently, said, "I don't believe a word of that story because it would take a guy with a great deal of *starch* to pull it off!"

Exploring Roots

It's no coincidence that the root word in *attentive* comes from the Latin verb *teneo*, which means to keep or grasp. After all, students are asked to *pay* attention, and teachers struggle to *keep* the attention of their students. *Advertisements* (prefix ad = to; root vert = turn) seek to *turn* your attention *to* their messaging.

Directions: Match the root definition with the sentence containing an italicized word with the same root.

________	**1.** circle	**a.** It's harder than you might think to write clear *instructions*.
________	**2.** keep	**b.** Nadal *punctuated* the magnitude of his win by falling to the ground.
________	**3.** sit	**c.** Diane's client failed to grasp the *severity* of the charges.
________	**4.** build	**d.** Smugglers seek to *circumvent* the duties and tariffs normally assessed on certain goods.
________	**5.** serious	**e.** Excessive *solitude* is often considered psychologically unhealthy.
________	**6.** point	**f.** Golf, as a *spectator* sport, can be an acquired taste.
________	**7.** lone	**g.** The best employers have high *retention* rates for workers.
________	**8.** vision	**h.** The doctor gave the hysterical patient a strong *sedative*.

WEEK 17 ✹ DAY 1 — Persuasion

A PLAN TO FOOL THE NAZIS

In war, misinformation is an important tool to *alleviate* enemy scrutiny of secret operations. One of the truly remarkable stories of World War II concerns a ruse that helped *ameliorate* Allied losses during the most dangerous operation of the war. The simple and ingenious subterfuge, which British officers concocted,* is the subject of Ewen Montagu's classic, *The Man Who Never Was*. In short, the idea was to plant false documents and *credentials* concerning the Allied invasion of Europe upon a dead officer, then have his body recovered by agents who, looking to *ingratiate* themselves with the Nazis, would transmit the lie to Germany. By observing German behavior, the British would then know if the Nazis were *cajoled* into *accommodating* their plan to divert German troops away from the beaches of Normandy.

NEW WORDS

alleviate
ə - lēv - ē - āt

ameliorate
ə - mel - ē - ôr - āt

credentials
krə - densh - əls

ingratiate
in - grā - shē - āt

cajole
kə - jōl

accommodate
ə - kom - ə - dāt

Notable Roots: lev = lift; mel = better; cred = belief; grat = favor; com = together

Sample Sentences: Use the new words in the following sentences.

1. Which ________________ a voter can use has become a matter of bitter political debate.
2. Most standardized test makers now ________________ test takers with special needs.
3. A sluice way helps ________________ pressure on a dam.
4. Lennox knew how to ________________ his parents into heeding his wishes.
5. The chairman would not tolerate subordinates who tried to ________________ themselves through flattery.
6. Nixon's declarations failed to ________________ indignation caused by Watergate.

Definitions: Match the new words with their meanings.

7. alleviate	_______	a. documents that establish one's identity
8. ameliorate	_______	b. to gently or subtly persuade
9. credentials	_______	c. to comply with another's wishes
10. ingratiate	_______	d. to improve a bad situation
11. cajole	_______	e. to gain favor
12. accommodate	_______	f. to lessen the impact of something

"MAJOR MARTIN" GOES TO WAR

After repeated *entreaties*, Commander Montagu and his colleagues *wheedled* official approval for their dangerous escapade from their superiors. First, they needed a body that looked as though it had recently been killed in an airplane disaster. Then, a detailed history of the man had to be invented that would be so impeccable that the enemy would be *propitiated*. Documents, love letters, personal effects, keys, and photographs were needed to *allay* suspicions. Commander Montagu's fears that the ruse would fail were only *assuaged* once every detail had been considered. Failure would mean more sad telegrams to *inconsolable* parents. As a result, in the late spring of 1942, "Major Martin" was prepared to do his part for his country.

NEW WORDS

entreaty
ən - trē - tē

wheedle
wē - dəl

propitiate
prō - pish - ē - āt

allay
ə - lā

assuage
ə - swāj

inconsolable
in - cən - sōl - ə - bəl

Notable Roots: treat = plead; consol = comfort, advise

Sample Sentences: Use the new words in the following sentences.

1. The widow's grief was somewhat ________________ knowing her husband died a hero.
2. Ancient peoples often made blood sacrifices to ________________ their gods.
3. The tyrant was________________ when his orders were disobeyed for any reason.
4. The doctor's cold, clinical manner did little to ________________ his patients' fears.
5. Greta Thunberg has made ________________ to world leaders regarding climate change.
6. The kitten was quickly adept at ________________ extra food from her owner.

Definitions: Match the new words with their meanings.

7. entreaty	_________	a.	to appease
8. wheedle	_________	b.	unable to be comforted
9. propitiate	_________	c.	a plea
10. allay	_________	d.	to lessen pain or grief
11. assuage	_________	e.	to obtain by flattery or persuasion
12. inconsolable	_________	f.	to calm fears, worries, or doubts

THE PLOT THICKENS

A submarine slipped "Major Martin" into the Atlantic waters off the coast of Huelva, Spain. Attached to the courier's coat was a briefcase that contained the components of the hoax. Fascist Spain was technically neutral but had been a *petitioner* for German aid during the recent civil war. Thus, the Spanish were inclined to *placate* the Nazis. Shortly thereafter, the Spanish Embassy notified the British, with their *condolences*, that the body had been recovered. But Commander Montagu learned that the important documents had already been scrutinized and later resealed to *quell* British suspicions. With the usual diplomatic *blandishments*, the Spanish *importuned* the German High Command to evaluate the find. Now, the true test of the months of assiduous* planning would come—would the Germans swallow the bait?

NEW WORDS

petitioner
pə - tish - ən - ėr

placate
plā - kāt

condolence
kən - dōl - əns

quell
kwel

blandishment
blan - dish - mənt

importune
im - pôr - tūn

Notable Roots:
plac = please; dol = sadness; port = gate/door

Sample Sentences: Use the new words in the following sentences.

1. The warlord had learned to disregard the _______________ of those seeking favor.
2. Lloyd George chose to _______________ labor unrest during World War I by giving in.
3. The old friends reconnected when Dr. Lambeau offered his _______________ to Dr. McGwire after his wife's death.
4. The _______________ stood before the Queen with his head bowed low.
5. The reporter repeatedly _______________ the mayor for an exclusive interview.
6. Despite their modest declamations, fascist ambitions are never _______________.

Definitions: Match the new words with their meanings.

7. petitioner	________	a.	words of comfort
8. placate	________	b.	to quiet disorder or rebellion
9. condolence	________	c.	one making a formal request
10. quell	________	d.	to badger someone
11. blandishment	________	e.	to satisfy
12. importune	________	f.	flattery

A PUZZLE FOR HIS MAJESTY

All evidence confirmed that the German High Command, *insatiable* for intelligence into Allied movements, was *pacified* by the ruse. Their defense troops were *deflected* from the true invasion sites to inconsequential areas. Subsequently, when the actual attack took place, Allied losses were *mollified*. The Allied deception campaign was so successful that even after the attack had begun, German commanders had to *implore* their superiors for help. Only after the false attack failed to materialize was the high command *coerced* by events into reinforcing the Normandy sector. After the war, Commander Montagu received a medal from the king of England. At the presentation ceremony, the king politely inquired where the young officer had earned his citation. "At the Admiralty," Montagu replied.

NEW WORDS

insatiable
in - sāsh - ə - bəl

pacify
pas - ə - fī

deflect
dē - flekt

mollify
mol - ə - fī

implore
im - plôr

coerce
kō - ėrs

Notable Roots:
satis = enough; pac = peace; flec = bend; plor = cry out

Sample Sentences: Use the new words in the following sentences.

1. Union officers _______________ their men to fight, but the Bull Run defeat was total.
2. The genuine respect shown by the victorious Devils helped _______________ the frustration the Ducks felt after their Cinderella run came to an end.
3. "What about" arguments are a classic strategy to ____________ attention from an accusation without refuting it.
4. The defense lawyer had the case dropped after proving the confession had been __________.
5. The obstreperous mob's appetite for violence proved to be _______________.
6. Pizza and a movie were enough to _______________ the disappointed children.

Definitions: Match the new words with their meanings.

7. insatiable	_________	a.	to calm; to satisfy
8. pacify	_________	b.	to beg someone
9. deflect	_________	c.	to force compliance by threat
10. mollify	_________	d.	cannot be satisfied
11. implore	_________	e.	to calm; to decrease the severity of something
12. coerce	_________	f.	to redirect something from its path or purpose

GROUP REVIEW

Major Martin, if he had lived, would have used the word *bonnet* to refer to the hood of his auto, and he might have referred to a truck as a *lorry*. As you can see, there are differences between American and British English. But Major Martin, undoubtedly, would have known all the words below—do you?

Matching

Directions: Match the 24 words with their meanings. Write the letter that stands for the definition in the appropriate answer space.

REVIEW WORDS		DEFINITIONS
________	1. accommodate	a. unable to be comforted
________	2. allay	b. flattery
________	3. alleviate	c. documents that establish one's identity
________	4. ameliorate	d. to lessen the impact of something
________	5. assuage	e. to comply with another's wishes
________	6. blandishment	f. to beg someone
________	7. cajole	g. to gain favor
________	8. coerce	h. to gently or subtly persuade
________	9. condolence	i. to satisfy
________	10. credentials	j. to calm; to satisfy
________	11. deflect	k. to appease
________	12. entreaty	l. to improve a bad situation
________	13. implore	m. a plea
________	14. importune	n. cannot be satisfied
________	15. inconsolable	o. to obtain by flattery or persuasion
________	16. ingratiate	p. to calm fears, worries, or doubts
________	17. insatiable	q. to redirect something from its path or purpose
________	18. mollify	r. words of comfort
________	19. pacify	s. to quiet disorder or rebellion
________	20. petitioner	t. one making a formal request
________	21. placate	u. to badger someone
________	22. propitiate	v. to force compliance by threat
________	23. quell	w. to calm; to decrease the severity of something
________	24. wheedle	x. to lessen pain or grief

Wordsearch

Directions: Using the clues listed below, fill in each blank in the following story with one of the new words you learned this week.

Clues

1st Day

3rd Day

2nd Day

4th Day

2nd Day

Brother, Can You Spare a Dime?

The U.S. Department of Health and Human Services, in a probe of Social Security disability payments, focused on Jack Benson, a Seattle panhandler. Mr. Benson had claimed that whatever money he collects on the street can be compared to the funds raised by legitimate charities, and, therefore, his request for a federal tax deduction should be ___________. Government officials disagree. It is their contention that, since Benson's income is unearned, it should be subtracted from his disability payments.

Mr. Benson may not be highly regarded as a street beggar, but that didn't stop him from appearing as a ___________ in the Federal District Court in Oregon to assert that his ___________ for cash are an art form, thereby making him eligible for most of the $472 a month that he had been receiving. Not so, declared the government, quoting from a 1990 ruling that found that "money received through begging is better classified as 'gifts' rather than as 'wages' or 'net earnings from self-employment.'"

Mr. Benson's lawyer will not be ___________ by such a judgment and has not given up. She countered that, if Jack merely sat on a street corner with his hand out, the government had a good case. However, in her words, "Jack Benson is a professional who has elevated begging to a respectable level because of his skill in actively ___________ contributions from passersby."

It may take all of Benson's talent as a salesman to get the government to put some money in his collection basket.

Sensible Sentences?

Directions: Underline the word that makes sense in each of the sentences below.

1. The truant's parents were not *(quelled, placated)* by his obviously false excuses.
2. In a friendly, casual way the salesman *(cajoled, importuned)* his clients.
3. The diplomat's *(entreaties, credentials)* had been stolen.
4. Raising interest rates will help *(coerce, alleviate)* deflation.
5. Mark's manners and good nature *(assuaged, ingratiated)* him with his colleagues.
6. Let this promise in front of witnesses *(allay, deflect)* your fears.
7. The novel *(wheedles, implores)* its readers to take a stand against injustice.
8. The Romans could be *(ameliorated, propitiated)* by gifts paid in gold.
9. The Serbs *(mollified, accommodated)* all but one Austrian demand.
10. The *(inconsolable, insatiable)* Austrians declared war anyway.

TEACHING CHIMPANZEES TO TALK

Two resourceful* psychologists at the University of Nevada have made splendid progress *evoking* complex communication from chimpanzees using human language. Following a number of abortive* attempts to *impart* French, German, or English vocabulary to the gregarious primates, the researchers persevered* until they hit upon the American Sign Language system. This has proven a perfect fit for the physically *demonstrative* animals, whose movements naturally include *hailing* each other in greeting. The researchers have had to modify the language somewhat in order to accommodate* the animals' *gesticulations*. With a *lexicon* of innate movements and learned ones, some chimps now have an extensive vocabulary.

NEW WORDS

evoke
ē - vōk

impart
im - pârt

demonstrative
də - mon - strə - tiv

hail
hāl

gesticulate
jes - tik - yū - lāt

lexicon
leks - ə - kon

Notable Roots: voc = voice, call; greg = together; mon = show, warn; lex = word, law

Sample Sentences: Use the new words in the following sentences.

1. The swimmer ________________ wildly to get the lifeguard's attention.
2. A ________________ umpire enhances the drama of a baseball game.
3. Failure is not in the ________________ of the ebullient CEO.
4. Rush hour is the worst time to ________________ a cab in New York.
5. The former POW's story ________________ sadness and anger in the audience.
6. Parents ________________ all the wisdom they can to their children.

Definitions: Match the new words with their meanings.

7.	evoke	________	a.	visually expressive
8.	impart	________	b.	list of words
9.	hail	________	c.	to elicit
10.	demonstrative	________	d.	to express oneself through movement
11.	gesticulate	________	e.	bestow; offer up
12.	lexicon	________	f.	to signal; to salute

CHIMPANZEES ARE SMART

Washoe the chimpanzee has more than a *veneer* of intelligence; she can signal her desire to eat, go in or out, be covered, or brush her teeth. In addition, she can make signs for *emotive* expressions like "I'm sorry" and "I hurt." Humans convey information through *countenance* and gesture, after all. This *vivacious* animal can *evince* her desire for more dessert by putting her fingers together ("more"), and then placing her index and second fingers on top of her tongue ("sweet"). With hardly a *grimace*, she has mastered her daily assignments.

Sample Sentences: Use the new words in the following sentences.

1. Iago never outwardly ________________ his hatred for Othello.
2. The ________________ young bride captivated all of the wedding guests.
3. Using ________________ language to frame a policy debate can strongly influence voters.
4. Gilded jewelry has a thin ________________ of gold that soon chips away.
5. The dentist could tell by the patient's ________________ that he needed more Novocaine.
6. Throughout the trial, Eichmann wore an impassive ________________ despite the horrors that were related by witnesses and on film.

Definitions: Match the new words with their meanings.

7.	veneer	________	a.	expressing strong feelings
8.	emotive	________	b.	facial expression
9.	vivacious	________	c.	pained expression
10.	evince	________	d.	thin covering
11.	countenance	________	e.	to make a feeling known
12.	grimace	________	f.	lively

NEW WORDS

veneer
və - nir

emotive
ē - mōt - iv

countenance (n.)
koun - tə - nəns

vivacious
vī - vāsh - əs

evince
ē - vins

grimace
grim - əs

Notable Roots: mot = move; contin = contain, control; viv = life; vinc = conquer

EASY TO TRAIN

The chimpanzees are deemed by scientists to be the closest to humans in terms of the *tableau* of abilities they possess. Several years ago, two married researchers *avidly* embarked on an interesting project: they reared and trained a chimp in almost the same manner as they would have raised a child. While some might *wince* at the idea of living with an animal in such a manner, the *diminutive* baby chimp did beautifully, convincing the couple of the *innate* ability of the chimpanzee. Is it really such a surprise? Coming face to face with any great ape, the interplay of emotion and reasoning visible in its *mien* is so analogous to the workings of our own minds.

NEW WORDS

tableau
tab - lō

avid
av - id

wince
wins

diminutive
də - min - yū - tiv

innate
in - āt

mien
mēn

Notable Roots:
table = flat, setting;
min = small;
nate = birth

Sample Sentences: Use the new words in the following sentences.

1. The chief of staff ________________ at his boss's verbal gaffe.
2. Eddie seems to have an ___________ sense of direction: he's never lost.
3. Babies can scrutinize the ________________ of a stranger for threat or security.
4. Raphael's *School of Athens* is a famous ________________ of ancient philosophers.
5. The ________________ Statue of Liberty in Paris was a model for the real one.
6. An ________________ expert of a sport is better described as an aficionado.*

Definitions: Match the new words with their meanings.

7. tableau	________	a.	to flinch slightly
8. avid	________	b.	arising naturally
9. wince	________	c.	collection; assembly
10. diminutive	________	d.	enthusiastic
11. innate	________	e.	revealing facial expression
12. mien	________	f.	very small

WEEK 18 DAY 4

Expression

MORE FACTS ABOUT CHIMPS

Chimpanzees are known for expressing themselves with other individuals in their troop by means of sounds, motion, and *demeanor*. While some vocalizations have obvious meaning, others are more *nondescript*. Like humans, however, the chimp has an expressive *physiognomy*. Socially chimps live in small groups with a dominance hierarchy usually dominated by males. To avoid violence, male chimps prefer to assume a fearsome *facade* to get rivals to back down. Chimps have a *penchant* for forming alliances, which can improve their social standing, often to the *chagrin* of stronger but less "popular" males.

NEW WORDS

demeanor
də - mēn - ər

nondescript
non - də - skript

physiognomy
fiz - ē - og - nō - mē

facade
fə - sod

penchant
pen - chənt

chagrin
shə - grin

Notable Roots:
mean = face, bearing;
script = writing;
gno = knowledge

Sample Sentences: Use the new words in the following sentences.

1. Many nineteenth-century Midwestern buildings have impressive _______________.
2. To my manager's _______________, I have decided to accept the job offer.
3. Dora has a _______________ for lateness so save her a place at dinner.
4. The Secret Service agent quickly noted the _______________ of the menacing heckler.
5. Cato the Elder's cantankerous disposition is clear in the grim, well-lined _______________ of his famous plaster bust.
6. A _______________ appearance is an asset for a covert operative.

Definitions: Match the new words with their meanings.

7.	demeanor	________	a.	lacking notable characteristics
8.	nondescript	________	b.	bearing or behavior
9.	physiognomy	________	c.	distress
10.	facade	________	d.	preference; tendency
11.	penchant	________	e.	outer face or shell
12.	chagrin	________	f.	revealing facial expression or appearance

GROUP REVIEW

While it is true that scientists have had remarkable success in teaching chimpanzees to communicate, we can be certain that even super-monkeys would have difficulty with any of the words below. However, higher animals who apply themselves can master all of them.

Matching

Directions: Match the 24 words with their meanings. Write the letter that stands for the definition in the appropriate answer space.

	REVIEW WORDS		DEFINITIONS
________	**1.** avid	**a.**	visually expressive
________	**2.** chagrin	**b.**	arising naturally
________	**3.** countenance	**c.**	to elicit
________	**4.** demeanor	**d.**	outer face or shell
________	**5.** demonstrative	**e.**	pained expression
________	**6.** diminutive	**f.**	revealing facial expression
________	**7.** emotive	**g.**	facial expression
________	**8.** evince	**h.**	lacking notable characteristics
________	**9.** evoke	**i.**	thin covering
________	**10.** facade	**j.**	bestow; offer up
________	**11.** gesticulate	**k.**	collection; assembly
________	**12.** grimace	**l.**	distress
________	**13.** hail	**m.**	expressing strong feelings
________	**14.** impart	**n.**	to signal; to salute
________	**15.** innate	**o.**	to express oneself through movement
________	**16.** lexicon	**p.**	enthusiastic
________	**17.** mien	**q.**	to make a feeling known
________	**18.** nondescript	**r.**	lively
________	**19.** penchant	**s.**	to flinch slightly
________	**20.** physiognomy	**t.**	revealing facial expression or appearance
________	**21.** tableau	**u.**	bearing or behavior
________	**22.** veneer	**v.**	preference; tendency
________	**23.** vivacious	**w.**	list of words
________	**24.** wince	**x.**	very small

Wordsearch

Directions: Using the clues listed below, fill in each blank in the following story.

Clues

3rd Day

2nd Day

4th Day

2nd Day

3rd Day

3rd Day

2nd Day

3rd Day

4th Day

4th Day

Life Imitating Art

Picture the most awkward portraits of yourself as a teenager. What stands out is the self-consciousness and lack of naturalism. Makes you ___________ just thinking about it, right? Pictures of small children are not typically so awkward. Naturally ___________ and emotional, children are a whirlwind of mercurial sincerity. That is, unless you force them to sit down, look at the camera and smile. Then you get the same ___________ leer of the adolescent.

The salient* feature of a bad portrait is the disconnect between the mouth and eyes that occurs when trying to mimic the facial expressions that come naturally with strong emotions. You get a ___________ like a robot's poor imitation of natural human gestures. Method actors know the secret to authentic posing—experience the feeling that corresponds to the ___________ you want to display. If you want a real smile, then like Peter Pan, think a happy thought.

Facial expressions are one of the most powerful ways for humans to convey emotional content. Babies can read a whole ___________ of facial cues within days of birth and spend much of their time scrutinizing the emotional weather crossing the faces of their caregivers. This partly explains why so many children are afraid of clowns—simply by applying their makeup carelessly, clowns can unintentionally give off ___________ cues that convey fear or danger.

Adults ___________ perceive qualities like confidence, honesty, and empathy (or their opposites) from cues like eye contact, facial tension, as well as mouth and eye shape. In fact, it was commonly believed until quite recently that the ___________ of a person could not help but betray a person's true character. Only a monster, it was held, like Shakespeare's Iago or Richard III, is capable of a perfectly fabricated ___________.

TROUBLE IN RURITANIA

King Andre of Ruritania had come to consider himself, like God, to be *omnipotent* and *infallible*. To the chagrin* of his people, he had become something of a *despot* as a result. After ten years of his *tyranny*, the treasury was bankrupt, unemployment was rampant,* domestic strife was mounting, and the number of the king's opponents was *legion*. Following a bloodless *coup*, his nephew, Prince Schubert, took command of the poor nation.

NEW WORDS

omnipotent
om - nip - ə - tənt

infallible
in - fal - ə - bəl

despot
des - pət

tyranny
tēr - ə - nē

legion (adj.)
lē - jən

coup
kū

Notable Roots: omni = all; poten = power; fall = fail; leg = law

Sample Sentences: Based upon your understanding of the new words, place them in the spaces provided.

1. Paradoxically, ________________ is often practiced by weak, insecure regimes.
2. Fans of celebrity culture are ________________, a fact that has more to do with the power of electronic media than anything else.
3. In nations where the military is politicized, ________________ are all too common.
4. Considered ________________ by his acolytes, the cult leader's orders were not questioned.
5. Despite his association with Voltaire, Frederick the Great was still a ________________.
6. By forcing Henry II to do public penance for Becket's murder, the Pope was asserting that the church alone was ________________ and even kings have to obey.

Definitions: Match the new words with their meanings.

7. omnipotent ________ a. heavy-handed autocratic rule
8. infallible ________ b. undemocratic takeover of government
9. despot ________ c. all-powerful
10. tyranny ________ d. great in number
11. legion ________ e. incapable of error
12. coup ________ f. absolute ruler

PRINCE SCHUBERT IN ACTION

Forgoing an *august* coronation, which was his *prerogative*, Prince Schubert's first move was to *abjure* persecution of political opposition. To that end, he invited home all Ruritanian expatriates. Those who had been jailed on false charges were exonerated by special tribunals. The young leader then announced that he would reform the *officious* bureaucracy. In place of King Andre's cronies, the prince installed industrious,* *disinterested* ministers. In all things, his *paramount* concern was helping the country move forward. Things began to look up temporarily for the citizens who perceived in Prince Schubert sincerity, idealism, and honesty.

august
ô - gust

prerogative
prə - rog - ə - tiv

abjure
ab - jur

officious
ə - fish - əs

disinterested
dis - in - trəs - təd

paramount
par - ə - mount

Notable Roots: rog = ask; ab = away; jure = swear; offic = duty; para = by; mount = above

Sample Sentences: Use the new words in the following sentences.

1. A judge cannot be so _______________ about the letter of the law that she lacks good sense.
2. A _______________ witness of good character can give the most compelling testimony.
3. Fenway Park and Wrigley Field are two of the most _______________ ballparks.
4. The aspiring* senator was forced to _______________ his mentor after the scandal broke.
5. As company president, it is my _______________ to choose our new logo.
6. Of the Manhattan Project's many priorities, secrecy was _______________.

Definitions: Match the new words with their meanings.

7.	august	________	a.	to formally renounce
8.	prerogative	________	b.	uninvolved personally or financially
9.	abjure	________	c.	highest
10.	officious	________	d.	grand; deserving respect
11.	disinterested	________	e.	one's right or privilege
12.	paramount	________	f.	overly concerned with protocol

REFORM MOVEMENT

Ruritania's financial situation was fraught with peril. Though Prince Schubert had installed an able finance minister, the bulwark of *abstruse* rules barring unilateral action and the *puissant* jurists who upheld them seemed an *impregnable* barrier to meaningful reform. At the local level, many of the most corrupt officials were *potentates* unto themselves, refusing all cooperation. To stave off financial collapse, the government needed the will to *subjugate* these unelected bosses who wanted reform to *miscarry* at all costs.

abstruse
ab - strūs

puissant
pwē - sont

impregnable
im - preg - nə - bəl

potentate
pō - tən - tāt

subjugate
sub - jə - gāt

miscarry
mis - ca - rē

Notable Roots: pren = take; poten = power; jug = join

Sample Sentences: Prove that you are not a flash in the pan by using the new words correctly in the following sentences.

1. The walls of Constantinople proved ________________ for a thousand years.
2. The ________________ of the ancient near east were revered as deities.
3. In due course, the Romans ________________ the Latins, Etruscans, and Samnites.
4. Napoleon's reconquest of Europe in 1815 ________________ before it began.
5. The ________________ nobles of England increasingly gained power over the crown.
6. The "fair catch kick," which allows an unobstructed field goal attempt immediately after receiving a punt, is among the most ________________ plays in football.

Definitions: Match the new words with their meanings.

7. abstruse	________	a.	unable to be taken by force
8. puissant	________	b.	to fail during development
9. impregnable	________	c.	to conquer or subdue
10. potentate	________	d.	powerful
11. subjugate	________	e.	obscure
12. miscarry	________	f.	ruler

DISAPPOINTMENT AND DEDICATION

When Prince Schubert asked for additional restrictive measures, the people began to balk.* Preferring cooperation to *peremptory* decrees, the young reformer took to the airwaves to explain why higher taxes and food rationing were *imperative*. Nevertheless, a resistance movement bent on *stymying* the reform began to coalesce. Moreover, though they had once burned him in *effigy*, the people began to feel nostalgia for the *regal* King Andre. They admitted that corruption had been rife under Andre, but at least "everybody got his slice of the pie." Although Prince Schubert was tempted to *abdicate*, he determined that he would help the people in spite of themselves.

NEW WORDS

peremptory
pėr - emp - tə - rē

imperative
im - per - ə - tiv

foil
fȯi -əl

effigy
ef - ə - jē

regal
rē - gəl

abdicate
ab - də - kāt

Notable Roots: imper = command; regis = king; dic = state/command

Sample Sentences: Use the new words in the following sentences.

1. Though often reviled, compromise is _______________ for a republic to function.
2. King Edward VIII famously _______________ after less than a year on the throne.
3. Jay Gatsby's _______________ bearing belies his humble origins.
4. To commemorate the thwarting* of the Gunpowder Plot each November 5th, Britons burn _______________ of captured conspirator Guy Fawkes.
5. President Lincoln replaced McClellan after the Union general continued to stall despite Lincoln's _______________ order to attack the Confederacy.
6. Thomas Jefferson's agenda was repeatedly _______________ by the Supreme Court.

Definitions: Match the new words with their meanings.

7. peremptory	________	a.	to ruin plans
8. imperative	________	b.	having a noble or royal demeanor
9. foil	________	c.	final; allowing no refusal
10. effigy	________	d.	to give up an office or duty
11. regal	________	e.	mandatory
12. abdicate	________	f.	a model of a person made for destruction

GROUP REVIEW

Ruritania is a mythical kingdom, impossible to find on a map or a dictionary. The words that you are about to review, however, are all legitimate, acceptable dictionary words.

Matching

Directions: Match the 24 words with their meanings. Write the letter that stands for the definition in the appropriate answer space.

	REVIEW WORDS	DEFINITIONS
________	**1.** abdicate	**a.** overly concerned with details and protocol
________	**2.** abjure	**b.** heavy-handed autocratic rule
________	**3.** abstruse	**c.** uninvolved personally or financially
________	**4.** august	**d.** all-powerful
________	**5.** coup	**e.** final; allowing no refusal
________	**6.** despot	**f.** incapable of error
________	**7.** disinterested	**g.** absolute ruler
________	**8.** effigy	**h.** undemocratic takeover of government
________	**9.** foil	**i.** to conquer or subdue
________	**10.** imperative	**j.** to formally renounce
________	**11.** impregnable	**k.** to fail during development
________	**12.** infallible	**l.** highest
________	**13.** legion	**m.** grand; deserving respect
________	**14.** miscarry	**n.** mandatory
________	**15.** officious	**o.** obscure
________	**16.** omnipotent	**p.** great in number
________	**17.** paramount	**q.** a model of a person made for destruction
________	**18.** peremptory	**r.** unable to be taken by force
________	**19.** potentate	**s.** having a noble or royal demeanor
________	**20.** prerogative	**t.** one's right or privilege
________	**21.** puissant	**u.** powerful
________	**22.** regal	**v.** to give up an office or duty
________	**23.** subjugate	**w.** to prevent or obstruct
________	**24.** tyranny	**x.** ruler

Wordsearch

Direction: Using the clues listed below, fill in each blank in the following story with one of the new words you learned this week.

Clues

4th Day

4th Day

3rd Day

1st Day

1st Day

2nd Day

2nd Day

2nd Day

3rd Day

3rd Day

Hail to the Queen

Elizabeth II wasn't born to rule. When she was born in 1926, her father was second in line to succeed King George V. Her uncle, Edward, was the heir apparent. What no one could predict is that Edward would _________ in order to marry an American divorcee.

In an instant, Elizabeth's father became King George VI and the ten-year-old princess was heir to the throne. King George led his nation with ___________ tact and fortitude through some of the darkest years in modern history. When Britain declared war on Germany in 1939, King George heroically mastered his stutter to reassure his people via radio address that their island fortress was ___________ and that the nation would resist Nazi ___________, no matter the cost. Princess Elizabeth did her bit, joining the Auxiliary Territorial Service and training to be a truck driver and mechanic to aid the war effort. On the day Germany surrendered, Princess Elizabeth and her sister, Princess Margaret, slipped out to mingle with the rejoicing Londoners, whose numbers were ___________.

After the war, Princess Elizabeth married and became a mother. She also took on more royal ___________ and responsibilities, filling in for her ailing father at public events throughout the Empire. Then, during a visit to Kenya in February 1952, she received word that her father had died. She was now Queen Elizabeth II.

Elizabeth I reigned during an age when Shakespeare was writing his greatest plays. The Elizabethan era saw the defeat of the Spanish Armada and the voyages of Sir Francis Drake. For the people of 1952, the possibility of a second Elizabethan age was understandably exciting, although it would not be easy to live up to the legacy of her ___________ ancestor. Then came a sign: three days before Elizabeth's coronation, Sir Edmund Hillary conquered the summit of the world's ___________ peak, Mount Everest.

Elizabeth II has presided over an era of cooperation, not conquest. Instead of ruling over ___________ peoples, Britain leads a voluntary commonwealth. As ___________, she is the symbol of that commonwealth. Her portrait graces coins from Jamaica to New Zealand. In 2015, Elizabeth II became the longest-reigning monarch in British history. While her reign may not have produced Shakespeare, it did give us the Beatles!

LA CUCARACHA—THE COCKROACH

The poor cockroach has been called the "most *vilified* creature on the face of the earth." Nobody loves him—except, perhaps, another cockroach. Fiction, non-fiction, and poetry are replete with *defamatory* references to these ubiquitous bugs. Public health officials in published *polemics* are quick to *denigrate* the insects as carriers of viruses that cause yellow fever and polio. Recent studies show that an allergy to roaches may contribute significantly to asthma. Little wonder, therefore, that the pesky cockroach has been so *stigmatized* and is the target of universal *opprobrium*.

vilify
vil - ə - fī

defamatory
də - fam - ə - tôr - ē

polemic
pə - lem - ik

denigrate
den - ə- grāt

stigmatize
stig - mə - tīz

opprobrium
ə - prō - brē - um

Notable Roots:
vil = ugly, dishonorable; fam = fame; stigma = mark or stain

Sample Sentences: Use the new words in the following sentences.

1. Written ________________ remarks without evidence can be grounds for a libel suit.
2. While ________________ expose problems, they offer few solutions.
3. A public figure who apologizes for a mistake should not be ________________ for life.
4. Cannabis use was largely ________________ during the 1930s due to its association with countercultural elements in society.
5. Fascism has earned the ________________ heaped on it by historians.
6. Alfred Dreyfus, who was falsely convicted of espionage by the French army, was ________________ by the press and people even after his exoneration.

Definitions: Match the new words with their meanings.

7. vilify	________	a. written or spoken attack
8. defamatory	________	b. to put someone down
9. polemic	________	c. to cast in a negative light
10. denigrate	________	d. disgrace
11. stigmatize	________	e. criticize or condemn
12. opprobrium	________	f. harmful toward one's reputation

WAITER, PLEASE TAKE THIS BOWL OF SOUP BACK

Cockroaches have *besmirched* reputations for a number of reasons. Doctors understandably *excoriate* cockroaches because of the health risks they pose. Those that live with them, however, take *umbrage* with their smell. Upon entering a cellar that is redolent with their aroma, you are not likely to forget the odor. The most intense *calumny* you can level at a place of lodging for its lack of cleanliness is to *deride* it as a "roach motel." Roaches will also *condescend* to feed on literally anything: wallpaper, upholstery, nylon stockings, and beer.

NEW WORDS

besmirch
bē - smėrch

excoriate
eks - kôr - ē - āt

umbrage
um - brəj

calumny
kal - um - nē

deride
də - rīd

condescend
kon - də - send

Notable Roots:
core = heart, center;
umbra = shadow;
rid/ris = laugh

Sample Sentences: The words above fit into the blanks below.

1. Voters are tired of leaders who ________________ to them.
2. ________________ is a fancy word for character assassination.
3. After Lily Bart's name is ________________ by a prominent woman in New York society, she becomes a social outcast.
4. The ______________ felt by supporters of both parties is quite intense.
5. Those who ________________ the young, ambitious Nixon became his lifelong enemies.
6. Peter Stuyvesant was ________________ by his employers for attempting to exclude Jews from New Amsterdam.

Definitions: Match the new words with their meanings.

7. besmirch	________	a.	false insulting remarks
8. excoriate	________	b.	offence
9. umbrage	________	c.	to mock
10. calumny	________	d.	to act superior
11. deride	________	e.	attack someone's character
12. condescend	________	f.	harshly criticize

WEEK 20 ⚙ DAY 3

THE ROACH LIVES ON

Although we *belittle* them, cockroaches are remarkable survivors. They are the oldest extant winged insects, dating back 350 million years. In comparison, our 100,000-year existence is *risible*. In response to human roach-bashing, one writer has *retorted*, "The miraculous survival of the roach is explained by its inherent adaptability." They *scoff* at the dangers of weather, natural disasters, and war. They reside comfortably in caves in South America, in transcontinental airplanes, on mountain tops, in Park Avenue edifices, and in television sets. In fact, many a cynic has *quipped* that cockroaches would be the only thing left after a nuclear war. It's only natural that such an ancient creature is indifferent to our *disdain*.

belittle
bē - lit - əl

risible
rīz - ə - bəl

retort
rē - tôrt

scoff
skôf

quip
kwip

disdain
dis - dān

Notable Roots: rid/ris = laugh; tort = turn; dain = acknowledge

Sample Sentences: Use the new words in the following sentences.

1. Before Einstein, many scientists ________________ at the idea of the atom.
2. Mencken was always ready with a quick ________________ to any jibe.
3. The general public considered the Edsel's design ________________.
4. The French aristocracy's ________________ for the Third Estate helped provoke revolution.
5. It is not socially acceptable to ________________ those who are physically different.
6. Gandhi famously ________________ that Western Civilization is a "nice idea."

Definitions: Match the new words with their meanings.

7. belittle	________	a.	to make a witty remark
8. risible	________	b.	to dismiss scornfully
9. retort	________	c.	to make fun of someone
10. scoff	________	d.	reply to an insult
11. quip	________	e.	contempt or distaste
12. disdain	________	f.	ridiculous

TONGUE IN CHEEK?

An array of products exist that purportedly exterminate roaches. They are often marketed with commercials that *disparage* the insects as *repulsive* and helpless before the might of man-made poisons. Scientists have *repudiated* such claims by pointing out that whenever a new insecticide debuts, it only provides temporary relief. Hardy roaches always survive and breed offspring resistant to the new insecticide. *Contemptuous* of the roach as we may be, any long-term solution seems unlikely. Some sentimental souls even *deprecate* such attempts. A writer *caustically* suggested a crash program of aid for the cockroach, calling him "a victim of his slum environment."

NEW WORDS

disparage
dis - par - əj

repulsive
rē - pul - siv

repudiate
rē - pyū - dē - āt

contemptuous
kon - temp - shū - əs

deprecate
dep- rə - kāt

caustic
kôs - tik

Notable Roots: par = equal; puls = push; prec = ask

Sample Sentences: Use the new words in the following sentences.

1. To occasionally ________________ oneself can be a charming attribute.
2. If Woodrow Wilson had not been so ________________ of compromise, he might have persuaded enough Republicans to ratify the Treaty of Versailles.
3. General Lanrezac helped the French avoid encirclement in 1914, but his ________________ manner led to his dismissal.
4. Scrooge eventually ________________ the merciless predatory lending that made him rich.
5. Dorian Gray's portrait is as ________________ as his character is corrupt.
6. The Brooklyn Dodgers, long ________________ as "Bums," beat the Yankees in 1955.

Definitions: Match the new words with their meanings. Three choices are close enough in meaning to be considered interchangeable.

7.	disparage	________	a.	disgusting
8.	repulsive	________	b.	regarded as worthless
9.	repudiate	________	c.	corrosive; sarcastic
10.	contemptuous	________	d.	to reject
11.	deprecate	________	e.	to disapprove of; to put down
12.	caustic	________	f.	to regard scornfully

GROUP REVIEW

There are many choice epithets for cockroaches, and over the centuries man has been most resourceful* in concocting* adjectives to describe the insects. Whether you are going to rant or rave about the roach, it helps to have a rich vocabulary.

Matching

Directions: Match the 24 words with their meanings. Write the letter that stands for the definition in the appropriate answer space.

REVIEW WORDS		DEFINITIONS
________	**1.** belittle	**a.** harmful toward one's reputation
________	**2.** besmirch	**b.** to dismiss scornfully
________	**3.** calumny	**c.** to put someone down
________	**4.** caustic	**d.** to cast in a negative light
________	**5.** condescend	**e.** to make fun of someone
________	**6.** contemptuous	**f.** criticize or condemn
________	**7.** defamatory	**g.** to attack someone's character
________	**8.** denigrate	**h.** harshly criticize
________	**9.** deprecate	**i.** disgrace
________	**10.** deride	**j.** reply to an insult
________	**11.** disdain	**k.** disgusting
________	**12.** disparage	**l.** ridiculous
________	**13.** excoriate	**m.** to reject
________	**14.** opprobrium	**n.** corrosive; sarcastic
________	**15.** polemic	**o.** to regard scornfully
________	**16.** quip	**p.** false insulting remarks
________	**17.** repudiate	**q.** offence
________	**18.** repulsive	**r.** contempt or distaste
________	**19.** retort	**s.** to act superior
________	**20.** risible	**t.** to disapprove of; to put down
________	**21.** scoff	**u.** to make a witty remark
________	**22.** stigmatize	**v.** regarded as worthless
________	**23.** umbrage	**w.** written or spoken attack
________	**24.** vilify	**x.** to mock

Hapless Headlines

Directions: Restore meaning to the headlines below by inserting the word that the careless typesetter omitted. Instances when multiple choices are possible are indicated by the number of possibilities.

- **a.** belittle
- **b.** besmirch
- **c.** calumny
- **d.** caustic
- **e.** condescend
- **f.** contemptuous
- **g.** defamatory
- **h.** denigrate
- **i.** deprecate
- **j.** deride
- **k.** disdain
- **l.** disparage
- **m.** excoriate
- **n.** opprobrium
- **o.** polemic
- **p.** quip
- **q.** repudiate
- **r.** repulsive
- **s.** retort
- **t.** risible
- **u.** scoff
- **v.** stigmatize
- **w.** umbrage
- **x.** vilify

1. CEO Shows ________________ for Subpoena
2. Manager Takes ________________ with Pitcher's Comments
3. Senate ________________ by Overriding President's Veto
4. Alma Mater ________________ (3) Heisman Winner in Wake of Scandal
5. Owner ________________ at Strikers' Demands
6. ________________ Leveled Against Author Proven False
7. Actress ________________ (7) Former Husband
8. New Film ________________ (5) for Lack of Originality
9. Conditions in Slums Described as "________________" by First Lady
10. Cheating Sprinter Faces Universal ________________

Wordsearch

Directions: Using the clues listed below, fill in each blank in the following story with one of the new words you learned this week.

Clues

1st Day

2nd Day

1st Day

1st Day

1st Day

1st Day

4th Day

3rd Day

1st Day

2nd Day

Chlorine Compounds on Trial

Chances are that the water supply where you live is disinfected by chlorine, one of the elements on the periodic table. Yet, ___________ complaints about chlorine continue, ___________ it as a health and environmental risk.

Greenpeace, the environmental activist group, has published numerous ___________ alleging that chlorinated organic compounds are toxic. The Environmental Protection Agency is reexamining the health hazards that are prevalent when materials containing chlorine are processed at high temperatures. And, worldwide, nations are banning chlorine compounds that destroy the earth's protective ozone layer. It seems harsh to ___________ one of nature's basic elements.

When we enter a pool that is redolent with the aroma of chlorine, we don't associate it with the much ___________ element now being blamed for tumors, reproductive problems, arrested development, destruction of wildlife, and sundry other ills that plague our planet. Without chlorination, public pools would still be sources of water-borne diseases like polio. The use of chlorine gas as a weapon during World War I deserves the ___________ of all mankind—as do all poison gases. Before ___________ the reputation of a faultless element of nature, however, we should recall the far greater ravages of disease that chlorinated antiseptics help keep at bay.

When elements bond together, their natures change. It would be utterly ___________ to fault water for containing hydrogen, a known explosive. Chlorine makes up 50% of table salt, better known as sodium chloride. Shall we ___________ the salt of the earth? Instead, let us avoid sweeping judgements and take ___________ only with specific compounds that cause harm.

LOCKED IN AN IVORY TOWER

Prince Siddhartha Gautama was the scion* of a family of warrior kings in northern India. There was little philosophical *nuance* to his education; he was being indoctrinated for the time when he would assume his father's throne. The cruel realities of the world were *imperceptible* to the young prince. He could only *conjecture* about life outside his father's walls. Despite the army of servants who catered to his every whim and *deluded* him with fulsome* praise, a *latent* spiritual hunger left him *dubious* about the life he was living. It wasn't until the prince was 30 that he took the first step toward becoming the Buddha, one of the world's greatest spiritual leaders.

NEW WORDS

nuance
nū - əns

imperceptible
im - pėr - sept - ə - bəl

conjecture
kon - jek - chėr

delude
də - lūd

latent
lāt - ənt

dubious
dū - bē - əs

Notable Roots: percept = sense; ject = throw; lud = play; dubit = doubt

Sample Sentences: Use the new words in the following sentences. (Which two words are almost synonymous?)

1. One common practice of totalitarian states is ________________ the masses with propaganda.
2. While the need for evidence is crucial, scientists should not be afraid of ________________.
3. A cool object that is warmer than its surroundings has ________________ heat.
4. Impressionists studied the ________________ of light and shadow playing upon a subject.
5. The ________________ prospect of ending poverty was dispelled by the Great Depression.
6. Even at supersonic speeds, the effects of time dilation are practically ________________.

Definitions: Match the new words with their meanings.

7. nuance	________	a.	to mislead
8. imperceptible	________	b.	hidden
9. conjecture	________	c.	skeptical
10. delude	________	d.	subtle detail; subtlety
11. latent	________	e.	a guess or hypothesis
12. dubious	________	f.	undetectable

Indefinite

SIDDHARTHA'S EYES ARE OPENED

One day, Siddhartha expressed his *dormant* desire to ride out among his people. He was profoundly *disabused* by the misery, destitution, and disease with which his people were afflicted. *Inscrutable* in his designs, he retired to his room to ponder over what he had seen. Lost in contemplation, he remained *reticent* for several days until the nature of his existence was no longer *opaque* to him. To Siddhartha, it would be a *euphemism* to say that his life had been privileged. He felt it had been sinfully decadent, and he was determined to make amends.

NEW WORDS

dormant
dôr - mənt

disabused
dis - ə - byūzd

inscrutable
in - scrū - tə - bəl

reticent
ret - ə - sənt

opaque
ō - pāk

euphemism
yū - fem - izm

Notable Roots:
dor = sleep; scru = search; taci/teci = silent; eu = good; pheme = speech

Sample Sentences: Use the new words in the following sentences.

1. As cataracts form, the lenses of the eye become ________________ to light.
2. A great poker player maintains an ________________ face at all time.
3. "Corporate restructuring" is just a ________________ for mass layoffs.
4. Many once ________________ volcanoes have caused the worst destruction.
5. Family members of cult victims find it difficult to ________________ their loved ones.
6. On his deathbed, the gangster, Arnold Rothstein, remained ________________ about the identity of the rival who fatally shot him.

Definitions: Match the new words with their meanings.

7.	dormant	________	a.	immune to understanding
8.	disabused	________	b.	not transparent
9.	inscrutable	________	c.	inactive
10.	reticent	________	d.	a kind phrase that conceals darker truth
11.	opaque	________	e.	to convince someone a belief is false
12.	euphemism	________	f.	quiet

THE ENLIGHTENED ONE

Siddhartha's *ostensible* plan was simple. First, he would exchange his sumptuous* garments for a more *discreet* monk's robe. Then, he would cleanse himself of his previous life by becoming an ascetic. Finally, he would study *esoteric* Hindu wisdom in order to be prepared to help his suffering people. After six years of *circuitous* wandering and attracting only a handful of disciples, Siddhartha came to a huge tree near the Indian city of Gaya. For seven weeks, he sat *furtively* beneath its branches, seeking an answer for his personal torment. Finally, it is said, he underwent a metamorphosis, piercing the *nebulous* veil of common understanding to become the Enlightened One—the Buddha.

NEW WORDS

ostensible
os - tens - ə - bəl

discreet
dis - krēt

esoteric
es - ō - ter - ik

circuitous
sėr - kyū - it - əs

furtive
fėr - tiv

nebulous
neb- yū - ləs

Notable Roots: ten = hold, maintain; crete = grow; circu = circle; nebul = cloud

Sample Sentences: Use the new words in the following sentences.

1. A ______________ glance gave the would-be assassin away.
2. Red dwarf stars, while large, are also ________________ in appearance.
3. A public figure can always benefit from the counsel of a ________________ publicist.
4. The state trooper's ________________ reason for the traffic stop was a taillight violation.
5. Football has a highly ________________ language that only former players really understand.
6. Newton's writing was so dense and ________________ that it required Edmund Halley to translate and publicize the brilliant ideas captured in the *Principia*.

Definitions: Match the new words with their meanings.

7. ostensible	________	a. winding and indirect
8. discreet	________	b. official or overt, often concealing another intent
9. esoteric	________	c. hazy; undefined
10. circuitous	________	d. careful; showing tact
11. furtive	________	e. hidden
12. nebulous	________	f. obscure; technical

LOVE OVER HATRED, GOODNESS OVER EVIL

Buddha rejected the *impenetrable* knowledge and *surreptitious* mysteries favored by many religious cults of the time. His vision was not *ambiguous* or open only to a *clandestine* elect. He outlined three paths that men might travel. The first two—worldly pleasure and self-torment—each had their allure but were of *specious* spiritual value. Only through a middle path between these extremes could man achieve peace and salvation. One had to repudiate* materialism, keep self-control, reject selfish drives, and nurture goodness. Through good deeds and pure thoughts, man may reach nirvana.* Interestingly enough, the man who was *reputed* to object to traditional religious worship was to become idolized by millions throughout the world.

impenetrable
im - pen - ə - trə - bəl

surreptitious
sėr - rep - tish - əs

ambiguous
am - big - yū - əs

clandestine
klan - des - tin

specious
spē - shəs

reputed
rē - pyū - təd

Notable Roots:
sur = on, under;
rap = seize; ambi = two;
specie = real

Sample Sentences: Use the new words in the following sentences.

1. In battle, an ________________ plan is a recipe for disaster.
2. The ________________ activities of Cold War intelligence agencies were fascinating.
3. Although he was often called a "butcher," General Grant was ________________ to hate the sight of blood.
4. The job ad, which only spoke of great perks, seemed highly ________________.
5. ________________ hazing rituals, now exposed, are widely banned.
6. The monks were troves of ________________ knowledge, but they lacked worldly experience.

Definitions: Match the new words with their meanings.

7.	impenetrable	________	a.	hidden to avoid penalty
8.	surreptitious	________	b.	believed to be
9.	ambiguous	________	c.	obscure; not well known
10.	clandestine	________	d.	of questionable authenticity
11.	specious	________	e.	secretive
12.	reputed	________	f.	unclear

GROUP REVIEW

For the past 20 weeks, each of these review exercises has contained a bit of propaganda to point out the need for you to expand your vocabulary. This week is no exception.

Matching

Directions: Match the 24 words with their meanings. Write the letter that stands for the definition in the appropriate answer space.

	REVIEW WORDS		DEFINITIONS
________	**1.** ambiguous	**a.**	a kind phrase that conceals darker truth
________	**2.** circuitous	**b.**	official, often concealing another intent
________	**3.** clandestine	**c.**	subtle detail; subtlety
________	**4.** conjecture	**d.**	careful; showing tact
________	**5.** delude	**e.**	undetectable
________	**6.** disabuse	**f.**	skeptical
________	**7.** discreet	**g.**	immune to understanding
________	**8.** dormant	**h.**	a guess or hypothesis
________	**9.** dubious	**i.**	inactive
________	**10.** esoteric	**j.**	of questionable authenticity
________	**11.** euphemism	**k.**	obscure; not well known
________	**12.** furtive	**l.**	quiet
________	**13.** impenetrable	**m.**	hidden to avoid penalty
________	**14.** imperceptible	**n.**	to convince someone a belief is false
________	**15.** inscrutable	**o.**	secretive
________	**16.** latent	**p.**	winding and indirect
________	**17.** nebulous	**q.**	believed to be
________	**18.** nuance	**r.**	hazy; undefined
________	**19.** opaque	**s.**	unclear
________	**20.** ostensible	**t.**	hidden (1)
________	**21.** reputed	**u.**	obscure; technical
________	**22.** reticent	**v.**	not transparent
________	**23.** specious	**w.**	hidden (2)
________	**24.** surreptitious	**x.**	to mislead

Indefinite

Wordsearch

Directions: Using the clues listed below, fill in each blank in the following story with one of the new words you learned this week.

Clues

2nd Day

1st Day

3rd Day

3rd Day

1st Day

2nd Day

1st Day

1st Day

3rd Day

4th Day

1st Day

History's Most Extraordinary Person?

In a celebrated essay about Joan of Arc, Mark Twain wrote movingly of her brief moment in the spotlight, which left an indelible mark on world history. To say that Joan was inexperienced would be a ___________: at age 16 she was illiterate, had never strayed from her sleepy little village, and knew nothing of military combat. But at age 17, she promised to the ___________ Dauphin to restore him to his throne. Sensing some ___________ quality of fate at work, the deposed French heir named Joan his commander in chief.

Hatred against the usurping* English was hardly ___________. Only the most ___________ English nobles could fail to see that the French were not conquered, and with the charismatic King Henry V dead, the barely ___________ spirit of rebellion was ready to burst forth. Joan proved to be the catalyst.* She attracted many followers and seemed to grasp ___________ of warfare that escaped seasoned commanders. Through her surprising and brilliant victories, she helped rouse the ___________ patriotism of once-demoralized countrymen.

Unfortunately, Joan was brought low by treachery at the French court and captured by the enemy. Although she could neither read nor write, Joan showed a mastery of the ___________ aspects of French law when she defended herself at a court trial. She was also ___________ to have the ability to forecast future events with remarkable accuracy, correctly predicting her own martyrdom. Mark Twain understood how geniuses such as Napoleon and Edison could develop, but could not begin to ___________ how this humble peasant girl could display the qualities of a mature statesman, a learned jurist, and a military wizard. He concluded: "she is easily and by far the most extraordinary person the human race has ever produced."

HIDING IN PLAIN SIGHT

A common screed that seems to garner attention on digital media holds that smart phone usage is to blame for increasing levels of social *apathy*. The general formula goes like this: while work has long been *drudgery*, human beings are uplifted by connecting with strangers on their journeys through public space. We have become increasingly *aloof* now that we can hide behind screens. The socially *lethargic* never have to raise their eyes or ask the time with their *timorous* voices. Call me *cynical*, but I think it's hilarious reading these polemics* on my phone.

NEW WORDS

apathy
ap - ə - thē

drudgery
druj - ə - rē

aloof
ə - lūf

lethargic
le - thär - jik

timorous
tim - ər - əs

cynical
sin - ik - əl

Notable Roots:
path = feeling;
lethe = forgetfulness;
timor = fear

Sample Sentences: Use the new words in the following sentences.

1. Acting superior and ________________ at parties is usually a sign of insecurity.
2. Only a ________________ person would order a veggie burger with bacon.
3. The ________________ of the masses is the greatest barrier to meaningful reform.
4. Mary felt so ________________ that she didn't leave her couch all day.
5. Most soldiers during the Great War preferred the danger of combat to the ________________ of digging fortifications.
6. A ________________ attitude precludes the creativity needed to solve tough problems.

Definitions: Match the new words with their meanings.

7. apathy ________
8. drudgery ________
9. aloof ________
10. lethargic ________
11. timorous ________
12. cynical ________

a. lacking energy
b. skeptical of human nature
c. fearful
d. lack of concern; indifference
e. unapproachable
f. tedious work

DOWN IN A HOLE

Depression is often mischaracterized as an extremity of sadness. Anguish is a healthy response to tragedies like losing a spouse or a terminal diagnosis, however. The depressed tend to experience *stupor*, not sadness, their daily existence is plagued by unrelenting *lassitude*. Once-fulfilling activities are sapped of their pleasure. Sufferers can become *lax* about dressing and hygiene, giving them an *unkempt* appearance, regardless of their past habits. This *inhibition* ultimately worsens to the point that anything but a *sedentary* lifestyle seems impossible.

NEW WORDS

stupor
stū - pər

lassitude
las - ə - tūd

lax
laks

unkempt
un - kempt

inhibition
in - hə - bish - ən

sedentary
sed - ən - ter - ē

Notable Roots:
stup = dull/numb; las/lax = late; sed = sit

Sample Sentences: Use the new words in the following sentences.

1. An ________________ job applicant typically lacks a sense of professionalism.
2. The morphine given to the patient brought about a merciful ________________.
3. A ________________ lifestyle can lead to dangerous blood clotting.
4. The children of ________________ parents often crave structure.
5. After recovering from a stroke, Mr. Chang acquired a certain ________________.
6. Some people's ________________ runs so deep that dancing seems alien and terrifying.

Definitions: Match the new words with their meanings.

7.	stupor	________	**a.**	weariness
8.	lassitude	________	**b.**	internal restraint on action or expression
9.	lax	________	**c.**	characterized by immobility
10.	unkempt	________	**d.**	loosely regulated
11.	inhibition	________	**e.**	a state of numbness or insensibility
12.	sedentary	________	**f.**	messy; uncared for

CATCH-22

Neurotransmitters act on our mood and energy levels. While pleasurable goals, like eating, are self-rewarding, others—like winning, learning, and social bonding—are not. To reinforce behaviors that help us achieve such goals the brain releases dopamine, which causes feelings of arousal—like the *taut* focus of a cat hunting prey. Without dopamine, life can feel unbearably *banal*, but constant arousal leaves one *tremulous*. Contentment is a feeling of *imperturbable* security that comes from having one's needs met—like a purring cat on your lap. Serotonin promotes feelings of contentment in response to productive activities like exercise, sleep, and eating. Depression correlates with low neurotransmitter levels, creating a positive-feedback loop. This leaves sufferers feeling *phlegmatic* and *indifferent* to activities that normally stimulate them.

NEW WORDS

taut
tôt

banal
bə - nal

tremulous
trem - yū - ləs

imperturbable
im - pėr - tėrb - ə - bəl

phlegmatic
fleg - mat - ik

indifferent
in - dif - ə - rənt

Notable Roots: treme = shake; turbu = unrest; phlegm = illness; differ = oppose

Sample Sentences: Use the new words in the following sentences.

1. Wealthy children can find a life free from economic anxiety________________ and dull.
2. Only in dangerous situations do some otherwise ________________ people feel truly alive.
3. As Ortiz awaited Rivera's pitch, the atmosphere was ________________ with excitement.
4. The witness described the robbery with a ________________ voice.
5. Some people are utterly ________________ to the suffering of others.
6. Dr. Torres felt herself completely ________________ during surgery.

Definitions: Match the new words with their meanings.

7. taut	________	a.	obvious and dull
8. banal	________	b.	lacking energy
9. tremulous	________	c.	uncaring
10. imperturbable	________	d.	tense; poised
11. phlegmatic	________	e.	filled with fear
12. indifferent	________	f.	calm and confident

CHEMICAL INTERVENTION

The belief that luminaries like Jean-Michel Basquiat or Annie Leibowitz came out of the womb making great art is enough to make *fretful* aspiring* artists so *squeamish* that they drop their brushes and run at the first setback. Great artists only become that way by honing their craft exhaustively. Someone with a bit of creative flair but a *languid* disposition will naturally have a *lackluster* career. Avoiding a *blasé* attitude and laboring at a profession diligently is essential. So is the intestinal fortitude to not allow setback and failure to *stunt* one's development.

NEW WORDS

fretful
fret - fəl

squeamish
skwē - mish

languid
lang - wid

lackluster
lak - lust - ər

blasé
blä - zā

stunt (v.)
stunt

Notable Roots: fret = worry; luster = shine; stunt = short

Sample Sentences: Use the new words in the following sentences.

1. Many hall-of-fame caliber athletes have had _______________ playoff performances.
2. At tree line, conifers have the _______________ appearance of shrubs.
3. A _______________ doctor has no future working with sick or injured patients.
4. The _______________ Field Marshal von Moltke failed to make the adjustments that could have saved the German army's campaign in 1914.
5. It sounds sophomoric* and artificial to be so _______________ at such a young age.
6. My aunt is so _______________ that she must be sedated before flying.

Definitions: Match the new words with their meanings.

7. fretful	________	a. bored; jaded
8. squeamish	________	b. dull; unimpressive
9. languid	________	c. lacking energy; listless
10. lackluster	________	d. to impede; to inhibit
11. blasé	________	e. worrisome
12. stunt	________	f. easily affected by unpleasantness

GROUP REVIEW

Matching

Directions: Match the 24 words with their meanings. Write the letter that stands for the definition in the appropriate answer space.

	REVIEW WORDS		DEFINITIONS
______	**1.** aloof	**a.**	internal restraint on action or expression
______	**2.** apathy	**b.**	lacking energy (1)
______	**3.** banal	**c.**	worrisome
______	**4.** blasé	**d.**	unapproachable
______	**5.** cynical	**e.**	easily affected by unpleasantness
______	**6.** drudgery	**f.**	messy; uncared for
______	**7.** fretful	**g.**	obvious and dull
______	**8.** imperturbable	**h.**	lacking energy (2)
______	**9.** indifferent	**i.**	a state of numbness or insensibility
______	**10.** inhibition	**j.**	fearful
______	**11.** lackluster	**k.**	lack of concern; indifference
______	**12.** languid	**l.**	uncaring
______	**13.** lassitude	**m.**	dull; unimpressive
______	**14.** lax	**n.**	tense; poised
______	**15.** lethargic	**o.**	weariness
______	**16.** phlegmatic	**p.**	filled with fear
______	**17.** sedentary	**q.**	characterized by immobility
______	**18.** squeamish	**r.**	loosely regulated
______	**19.** stunt	**s.**	bored; jaded
______	**20.** stupor	**t.**	lacking energy; listless
______	**21.** taut	**u.**	calm and confident
______	**22.** timorous	**v.**	to impede; to inhibit
______	**23.** tremulous	**w.**	skeptical of human nature
______	**24.** unkempt	**x.**	tedious work

Wordsearch

Directions: Using the clues listed below, fill in each blank in the following story with one of the new words you learned this week.

Clues

3rd Day

2nd Day

2nd Day

1st Day

1st Day

3rd Day

4th Day

4th Day

1st Day

Hair Today . . .

Most citizens are ___________ to the fact that a hair salon can charge $60 for a woman's shampoo and haircut but only $20 for the same services for a man. Not so to one city's Department of Human Rights, which claimed that such a disparity is discriminatory. Commissioner Sophia Rodriguez has targeted gender-based pricing as a violation of city law.

Salon owners argue that many men are typically ___________ in their hair care routine, preferring a stylish but somewhat ___________ look. Female clientele, they further explain, usually do not have the same ___________; as such, it takes much longer to cut a woman's hair and requires the use of additional products. But a spokesperson for the Department of Consumer Affairs said that beauty parlor owners have adopted a dishonest and ___________ attitude toward their customers: that an injustice once normalized can become ___________ enough to escape scrutiny.

"I know that women are fighting for equality," said one ___________ owner of a chain of unisex hair salons, "but this threatens our livelihood. We cut a man's hair in no time, but we have to get more money from our female customers because their styling and cutting takes so much longer."

Many officials privately believe that in a city so beset by problems, enforcement of such an ordinance will be ___________ at best. The police are likely to consider responding to salon discrimination claims pure ___________ at the bottom of their list of priorities. A simpler solution, they argue, would be for stylists to charge by the minute instead of by the service.

FROM A TO Z

Ellis Sloane, a science teacher at a large metropolitan high school, thought it curious that his two biology classes were so disparate in their performance. In most schools, classes are alphabetically *arbitrary*, with names running the gamut from Adams to Zilch. This happens largely because of *vicissitudes* of group dynamics: in the *interim* between school years, teachers discuss combinations that *agitate* poor behavior and split them up to prevent undue *ferment*. Sloane's classes, however, had simply been split up by name. Biology 121 had the A–M students and Biology 128 had N–Z. Sloane noticed other differences: while their reading scores and IQs were roughly analogous, Biology 128 was replete with *desultory* students, while Biology 121, in the main, was not. He had unwittingly stumbled upon a sociological principle.

NEW WORDS

arbitrary
är - bə - tre - rē

vicissitudes
vi - sis - i - tūdz

interim
in - tər - əm

agitate
aj - ə - tāt

ferment (n.)
fėr - ment

desultory
des - ult - ə - rē

Notable Roots:
arbiter = judge;
inter = between;
agi = drive forward;
ferv = boil; sali = jump

Sample Sentences: Use the new words in the following sentences.

1. After noticing its _______________ drifting, mariners found the *Mary Celeste* abandoned.
2. The Boston Massacre occurred because the ________________ of a mob became unstable.
3. Remember, to those living at the time, the 1920s was not an ________________ between World Wars but a postwar period.
4. The ________________ of the president's mood could be wildly unpredictable.
5. Frederick Douglass ________________ as hard for equality as he had done for abolitionism.
6. The name *tank* was an ________________ epithet to keep its development a military secret.

Definitions: Match the new words with their meanings.

7.	arbitrary	________	a.	aimless
8.	vicissitudes	________	b.	anger; discontent
9.	interim	________	c.	to stir up
10.	agitate	________	d.	sudden changes
11.	ferment	________	e.	based on random choice
12.	desultory	________	f.	time in between events

WHAT'S IN A NAME?

At first Mr. Sloane regarded the conjecture* that last name correlated with academic performance as *tenuous*, at best. He realized that the *capricious* assortment of students in his two classes might have produced a greater concentration of temperamentally *inert* or *vacillating* students in Biology 128 by chance. Then he discovered the work of Dr. Trevor Weston of the British Medical Association. Dr. Weston found that people whose names began with letters ranging from S–Z lived an average of 12 years less than the rest of the population and more frequently suffered from stress-related maladies. *Whimsical* or not, "alphabetical predestiny" was no laughing matter and Sloane felt he would be *derelict* in his role as an educator to ignore it further.

NEW WORDS

tenuous
ten - yū - əs

capricious
kə - prē - shəs

inert
in - ėrt

vacillate
vas - ə - lāt

whimsical
wim - zik - əl

derelict
der - ə - likt

Notable Roots:
ten = hold, maintain;
cap = head; art = skill;
relic = keep

Sample Sentences: Use the new words in the following sentences. Two are interchangeable.

1. The noble gases, which bond with nothing, are chemically ________________.
2. The moments that bring couples together often have a ________________ quality.
3. A court martial decided the fate of the ________________ soldier who slept on guard duty.
4. An intelligent commander who ________________ can be defeated by a decisive foe.
5. The truce was so ________________ that neither army demobilized.
6. To be truly great, an artist must embrace the ________________ side of her creativity.

Definitions: Match the new words with their meanings. Two are interchangeable.

7. tenuous	________	a.	to waver in one's views
8. capricious	________	b.	weak or fragile
9. inert	________	c.	abandoned; negligent
10. vacillate	________	d.	spontaneous; carefree
11. whimsical	________	e.	lacking will or energy
12. derelict	________	f.	unpredictable

THE PERILS OF THE ALPHABET

Dr. Weston is convinced that teachers are responsible. Since teachers often seat their pupils in alphabetical order, the S to Z child is usually the last to receive his test marks, the last to give a presentation—frustrated because what she had to say has already been said. School age children are highly *malleable* in their personality and self-esteem. Constant waiting causes many in this group to become *mercurial*, even *volatile* in temperament. Others consider themselves inferior to those at the top of the alphabet. Of course, the good doctor suggests *amnesty* for our educators. Teachers work very hard, and their mistake has been an honest one. It is, instead, the tyranny of the alphabetical system that must be *jettisoned*. Teachers need to *extemporize* when seating and calling upon students.

NEW WORDS

malleable
mal - ē - ə - bəl

mercurial
mėr - kyur - ē - əl

volatile
vol - ə - tīl **or**
vol - ə - təl

amnesty
am - nes - tē

jettison
jet - ə - sən

extemporize
eks - temp - ôr - īz

Notable Roots:
malleus = hammer; mercury = fast; vol = flight; amnes = forget; temp = time

Sample Sentences: Use the new words in the following sentences.

1. Woodes Rogers ended piracy in the Bahamas with ________________, not war.
2. Marzipan is ________________ enough to form candies of any shape.
3. The failing conglomerate ________________ unsuccessful divisions to save money.
4. Freestyle hip-hop requires creativity and the ability to ________________ rhymes on the fly.
5. Many nitrates are highly ________________ compounds that require great care.
6. Gaston, while a great chef, is far too ________________ for the business of running a restaurant to hold his interest.

Definitions: Match the new words with their meanings.

7. malleable	________	a.	quickly changing
8. mercurial	________	b.	able to be molded
9. volatile	________	c.	to improvise
10. amnesty	________	d.	unstable
11. jettison	________	e.	a pardon
12. extemporize	________	f.	to abandon

IN THE NATURE OF EDUCATIONAL REFORM

Mr. Sloane underwent a *metamorphosis*. He began with a *provisional* system of reversing the seating in his classes. The grades of students in Biology 128 stopped *fluctuating* within a month. Worried this might be a *transient* development, he felt vindicated after a semester, so he badgered the school administration to bring about such changes throughout the building. He addressed the concern that the new system simply shifted the burden to different students. Sloane argued that reverse seating was an *ephemeral* but necessary measure to neutralize the catastrophic effects of years of the traditional policy. The adoption of non-alphabetic seating in elementary school would make reverse seating an *evanescent* step on the way to uniformly well-adjusted students.

NEW WORDS

metamorphosis
me - tə - môrf - ə - sis

provisional
prō - vizh - ən - əl

fluctuate
fluk - shū - āt

transient
tranz - ē - ənt

ephemeral
ef - em - ėr - əl

evanescent
ev - ən - es - ent

Notable Roots:
meta = between; morph = shape; pro = forward; vis = see; flux = flow

Sample Sentences: Use the new words in the following sentences.

1. Weather ________________, while climate has more stable patterns.
2. Jefferson cautioned against revolution for ________________ reasons.
3. The ________________ instant of "daylight" when lightning strikes at night is thrilling.
4. Both parts of *Henry IV* really deal with Prince Hal's________________ from hard-drinking ruffian to the future king, Henry V.
5. The era of the battleship was far more ________________ than any admiral predicted; brand new in 1914, battleships were mere targets for submarines and carrier planes by 1941.
6. The ________________ Kerensky government was overthrown by Bolsheviks within months.

Definitions: Match the new words with their meanings.

7. metamorphosis	________	a.	to rise and fall unpredictably
8. provisional	________	b.	quickly forgotten
9. fluctuate	________	c.	impermanent
10. transient	________	d.	very brief
11. ephemeral	________	e.	temporary
12. evanescent	________	f.	a significant change in form

GROUP REVIEW

You may not know the alphabet from *aardvark* to *zymurgy*, but you can certainly cope with *agitate* to *whimsical*.

Matching

Directions: Match the 24 words with their meanings. Write the letter that stands for the definition in the appropriate answer space.

REVIEW WORDS		DEFINITIONS
________	1. agitate	a. lacking will or energy
________	2. amnesty	b. to improvise
________	3. arbitrary	c. abandoned; negligent
________	4. capricious	d. to rise and fall unpredictably
________	5. derelict	e. able to be molded
________	6. desultory	f. impermanent
________	7. ephemeral	g. anger; discontent
________	8. evanescent	h. quickly changing
________	9. extemporize	i. sudden changes
________	10. ferment	j. a significant change in form
________	11. fluctuate	k. time in between events
________	12. inert	l. unstable
________	13. interim	m. quickly forgotten
________	14. jettison	n. to abandon
________	15. malleable	o. unpredictable
________	16. mercurial	p. very brief
________	17. metamorphosis	q. to waver in one's views
________	18. provisional	r. based on random choice
________	19. tenuous	s. aimless
________	20. transient	t. spontaneous; carefree
________	21. vacillate	u. temporary
________	22. vicissitudes	v. weak or fragile
________	23. volatile	w. to stir up
________	24. whimsical	x. a pardon

Wordsearch

Directions: Using the clues listed below, fill in each blank in the following story with one of the new words you learned this week.

Clues

4th day

3rd day

4th day

1st day

2nd day

Microsociety: An Antidote for School Boredom

Money, taxes, employment, legislation—these are topics that we associate with the adult world. George Richmond, Yale graduate and Manhattan educator, felt that elementary students could also be interested in such issues. He experimented in his own classes with the *Microsociety*, in which basic instruction still takes place but is reinforced by practical experience. Students operate businesses, draft a constitution, pass laws, seek redress within their own judicial system, buy, and so on. Leaders must contend with ___________ public opinion or risk being ___________ by the group as a whole.

Richmond's book on the *Microsociety* came to the attention of the school board in Lowell, Massachusetts, and their members decided to give it a try in 1981. Implemented on a ___________ basis, the results were quite remarkable: students exceeded the norm in reading and math, eighth graders passed college level exams, school attendance went up to 96%, and the dropout rate took a nosedive in Lowell.

In *Microsociety* classes, mornings cover the traditional curriculum. In the afternoon, the students apply what they learned in activities that involve auditing, banking, manufacturing, and commerce. Such learning is not acquired on a disjointed, ___________ basis, but rather integrated into a cumulative effort to create a working community.

Other school systems have since adopted George Richmond's innovative ideas. "*Microsociety*," said a Yonkers, New York, principal, "gets kids to role-play life! They enter adulthood with more than a ___________ grasp on how to cope with the wider world."

Synonym Shout-Out

Any effective educator, talented teacher, or perspicacious* pedagogue* will tell you there's more than one way to say almost anything. Synonyms give variety to language and keep it from being so terribly boring!

Directions: Here are ten sets of near or close synonyms from weeks 18–23. Match each word with the answer, or answers, that are synonymous. The number of answers is indicated.

1. tremulous ______________(2)
2. clandestine ______________
3. whimsical ______________(2)
4. disparage ______________(3)
5. lethargic ______________(3)
6. regal ______________
7. ephemeral ______________(2)
8. physiognomy ______________(4)
9. nebulous ______________
10. abstruse ______________

a. deride
b. transient
c. august
d. surreptitious
e. phlegmatic
f. deprecate
g. capricious
h. mien
i. timorous
j. impenetrable
k. languid
l. mercurial
m. veneer
n. demeanor
o. evanescent
p. countenance
q. ambiguous
r. denigrate
s. sedentary
t. squeamish

ROMAN RELIGIOSITY

The ancient Romans believed in a *pantheon* of major gods and minor deities. They *venerated* pre-Roman deities of Italian origin such as Dis Pater and Bona Dea and Gods adapted from the Greeks, such as Jupiter, Venus, and Mars (counterparts of Zeus, Aphrodite, and Ares). Over time, the Romans added deities whose *adherents* they conquered. Sometimes mystery cults from faraway lands would find new *proselytes* in Rome, such as the cult of Sol Invictus, the unconquered sun. As the Republic gave way to the Empire, the emperors themselves were also *deified*, notably Julius and Augustus Caesar. The "divine Augustus" and even his wife, Livia Augusta, had their own temples and *devout* followers.

NEW WORDS

pantheon
pan - thē - on

venerate
ven - ə - rāt

adherent
ad - hēr - ənt

proselyte
pros - ə - līt

deify
dē - ə - fī

devout
də - vout

Notable Roots:
pan = all; theo = god; vener = love; here = stick; dei = god

Sample Sentences: Now use your new words in the following sentences.

1. _______________ of the Quaker religion forsake violence and abstain from wars.
2. Monument Park at Yankee Stadium represents a _______________ of some of the greatest baseball players in the history of the game.
3. The truly _______________ tend to prefer private prayer to ostentatious displays of piety.
4. The artist known as Cat Stevens became a _______________ of Islam after nearly drowning.
5. Many cultures _______________ their elders and deceased ancestors.
6. It is unhealthy for society to _______________ celebrities, many of whom lack modesty, virtue, and talent.

Definitions: If you have studied the reading selection and the sample sentences, now try your hand at matching your new words with their definitions.

7. pantheon	________	a.	someone converted to a belief
8. venerate	________	b.	to treat someone as a god
9. adherent	________	c.	to worship; to respect
10. proselyte	________	d.	deeply committed to a faith
11. deify	________	e.	a follower
12. devout	________	f.	a collection of gods or highly respected figures

RITES, RITUALS, AND SACRIFICES

Unlike the Greeks, whose religion was deeply influenced by the philosophies of thinkers like the *stoics* and Socratics, the Romans were more *dogmatic*, concerned with ritual and mystery. The *sacrosanct* Vestal Virgins—even touching one was a *taboo*—kept alight the sacred flame that the Romans believed ensured their security. The doors to the temple of Janus were opened when war was declared and closed with the return of peace. The *zealous* Romans also sacrificed animals, whose blood was intended as payment for answered prayers. A whole class of charlatans *duped* believers of their gold by overcharging for the performance of these rites.

NEW WORDS

stoic
stō - ik

dogmatic
dôg - mat - ik

sacrosanct
sak - rō - senkt

taboo (n.)
ta - bū

zealous
zel - əs

dupe
dūp

Notable Roots: sacre = holy; sanct = holy; zeal = ardor

Sample Sentences: Has the context in which your new words appear given you clues to their meaning? Try now to use them in these sample sentences.

1. Converts are often noted as more ________________ than those born into a religious group.
2. Before the 22nd Amendment, a third term as president was merely a ________________.
3. Because they can be easily ________________, children can't legally sign contracts.
4. A professional athlete is expected to be a ________________ in the face of losing.
5. To Muslims, the city of Mecca is considered ________________ in its entirety.
6. A ________________ belief in democracy can lull citizens into passivity in its defense.

Definitions: Match the new words with their meanings.

7.	stoic	________	a.	full of enthusiasm
8.	dogmatic	________	b.	to trick
9.	sacrosanct	________	c.	one who doesn't show emotion
10.	taboo	________	d.	regarding beliefs as not open to question
11.	zealous	________	e.	custom forbidding a particular practice
12.	dupe	________	f.	of utmost sanctity or importance

MONOTHEISTIC COMPETITION

Rome's tendency to adopt aspects of new faiths they found appealing while exporting the worship of their own gods encouraged *ardent* believers of other faiths to feel invested in the Roman Empire. Rome's relationship with Judaism, however, proved an irreconcilable *schism*. *Staunch* monotheists, the Jews would not adopt Roman deities and rejected as *idolatry* the presence of statues of the emperors in Jewish temples. The Jews were also accustomed to a much more *ascetic* lifestyle and declaimed against Roman cultural practices they saw as *hedonistic*.

NEW WORDS

ardent
âr - dənt

schism
skiz - əm

staunch
stônch

idolatry
ī - dol - ə - trē

ascetic
ə - se - tik

hedonism
hē - dən - izm

Notable Roots:
ard = burning;
idol = image of a deity

Sample Sentences: Keep up the good work by using your new words in the following sentences.

1. The ________________ of 1054 split the Catholic and Orthodox branches of Christianity.
2. Because ________________ former Dodgers and Giants fans could not embrace the Yankees, the Mets were created.
3. Some adopt an ______________ lifestyle for spiritual reasons, others for health purposes.
4. Medieval Islamic art made use of geometric patterns because many clerics considered the depiction of living figures to be ____________.
5. While disciples of Apollo prized reason, acolytes of Dionysus celebrated ________________.
6. Many ________________ believers adopt a monastic life of prayer and service.

Definitions: Match your new words with their meanings.

7. ardent ________	a.	the worship of objects, usually images of a deity
8. schism ________	b.	characterized by avoidance of comfort or pleasure
9. staunch ________	c.	a philosophy or lifestyle devoted to pleasure
10. idolatry ________	d.	passionately committed
11. ascetic ________	e.	a rift caused by a disagreement on principles
12. hedonism ________	f.	dedicated

FROM MARTYRS TO MASTERS

During Rome's rise, it was *canon* that the republican system was divine and eternal. By the third century, although few had openly *recanted* this *credo*, none believed it. The emperor had usurped* the powers of the Senate. Slavery had ruined the plebes. It's not surprising, then, that average Romans became *agnostic* toward the old religion and receptive to Christianity's promises of salvation. Attempts to stamp out the new faith only created *martyrs* that strengthened Christian *fervor*. The deathbed conversion of Constantine the Great signaled the end for the old ways.

NEW WORDS

canon
kan - ən

recant
rē - kant

credo
krēdo

agnostic
ag - nos - tik

martyr
mâr - tər

fervor
fėr - vər

Notable Roots: cant = sing, chant; cred = belief; gno = know; ferv = boil

Sample Sentences: Use these new words in the following sentences.

1. Despite quantum theory's often bizarre findings, few physicists are still quantum ________________.
2. Secessionist ________________ after Lincoln's election was strongest in South Carolina.
3. Punting on fourth and long is a rarely questioned precept of football ________________.
4. Galileo, faced with death, ________________ heliocentrism.
5. Thomas More became a ________________ after refusing to acknowledge Henry VIII's supremacy over religious affairs in England.
6. Facebook has come under fire for its ________________: "Move fast and break things."

Definitions: Match the new words with their meanings.

7.	canon	________	a.	deep commitment
8.	recant	________	b.	someone who is killed for a belief
9.	credo	________	c.	belief that the truth of a disputed matter is unknowable; skeptic
10.	agnostic	________	d.	to publicly withdraw a statement of belief
11.	martyr	________	e.	a belief; a statement of belief
12.	fervor	________	f.	a generally accepted set of principles, rules, or facts

GROUP REVIEW

It's time to strengthen your word knowledge again. You've noticed, of course, that the matching definitions are not always the definitions you may have been familiar with. This is the way language works. It is impossible to provide a one-word synonym or simple definition for a word that you will always be able to substitute for it. Therefore, in our weekly review we hope not only to check your learning, but also to teach you closely related meanings.

Matching

Directions: Match the best possible definition with the word you studied. Write the letter that stands for that definition in the appropriate answer space.

REVIEW WORDS		DEFINITIONS	
_______	**1.** adherent	**a.**	a collection of gods or highly respected figures
_______	**2.** agnostic	**b.**	of utmost sanctity or importance
_______	**3.** ardent	**c.**	passionately committed
_______	**4.** ascetic	**d.**	to treat someone as a god
_______	**5.** canon	**e.**	dedicated
_______	**6.** credo	**f.**	deeply committed to a faith
_______	**7.** deify	**g.**	a follower
_______	**8.** devout	**h.**	someone who is killed for a belief
_______	**9.** dogmatic	**i.**	characterized by avoidance of comfort or pleasure
_______	**10.** dupe	**j.**	a rift caused by a disagreement on principles
_______	**11.** fervor	**k.**	to publicly withdraw a statement of belief
_______	**12.** hedonism	**l.**	full of enthusiasm
_______	**13.** idolatry	**m.**	deep commitment
_______	**14.** martyr	**n.**	one who doesn't show emotion
_______	**15.** pantheon	**o.**	a belief; a statement of belief
_______	**16.** proselyte	**p.**	custom forbidding a particular practice
_______	**17.** recant	**q.**	a generally accepted set of principles, rules, or facts
_______	**18.** sacrosanct	**r.**	a philosophy or lifestyle devoted to pleasure
_______	**19.** schism	**s.**	to trick
_______	**20.** staunch	**t.**	regarding beliefs as not open to question
_______	**21.** stoic	**u.**	someone converted to a belief
_______	**22.** taboo	**v.**	believer that the truth of a disputed matter is unknowable; skeptic
_______	**23.** venerate	**w.**	to worship; to respect
_______	**24.** zealous	**x.**	the worship of objects, usually images of a deity

Adjective Leaders and Noun Followers

Directions: Write the letter corresponding to the vocabulary word in the space provided for the noun that it is most likely to precede.

________ **1.** monk	**a.** sacrosanct	**k.** evanescent
________ **2.** guest	**b.** arbitrary	**l.** nebulous
________ **3.** walk	**c.** aloof	**m.** malleable
________ **4.** clay	**d.** staunch	**n.** ascetic
________ **5.** cloud	**e.** lax	**o.** opaque
________ **6.** decision	**f.** clandestine	
________ **7.** pilgrim	**g.** desultory	
________ **8.** window	**h.** inert	
________ **9.** tree	**i.** stunted	
________ **10.** advocate	**j.** devout	

Wordsearch

Directions: Using the clues listed below, fill in each blank in the following story with one of the new words you learned this week.

Clues

2nd Day

2nd Day

3rd Day

2nd Day

2nd Day

4th Day

1st Day

Mapmakers at Work

We are all caught up in the events that change history and the shape of the countries in Asia, Africa, and the Middle East. Each time a country changes its name or its borders, there are some people who have their work cut out for them. They are the mapmakers—the cartographers. These skilled artists are not ___________ into believing that this year's borders will remain fixed. Has there ever been a ___________ border?

Looking through an atlas of just a few years back, we realize that political ___________, brought on by ___________ diplomats, have a tendency to change the world that we're used to. The mapmaker must be a ___________, unmoved by developments that constantly render his work obsolete.

Countless trees have become ___________ for the cause of maintaining current paper maps. For this reason, mapmakers have been eager ___________ of the use of digital technology in mapmaking. Digital maps are no more permanent than the printed variety, but at least they can be updated quickly without wasting paper!

THE EXPLOSION OF KRAKATOA

There are few natural events that are so *insurgent* to the notion of human control as the eruption of a volcano. These titans of nature have the capacity to *obliterate* our artificial worlds. Perhaps the greatest volcanic event of modern times took place in 1883 when the volcanic island of Krakatoa in Indonesia unleashed *havoc*. Whole villages were *razed* in the *conflagration* caused by the blast, and an enormous tidal wave covered the nearby coasts of Java and Sumatra in a *deluge*. The explosion, which could be heard in Australia, is considered the loudest sound unleashed on Earth's surface in human history.

Sample Sentences: Relying on the contextual clues in the paragraph above, use the new words in the following sentences.

1. Heavy winds whipped the fire into a ________________ and hampered suppression efforts.
2. The ________________ that followed the fall of an ancient city rivaled battlefield carnage.
3. Water's great weight explains the destructive capacity of a ________________.
4. Many Iraqi soldiers joined the ________________ movement after the fall of the regime.
5. Although the fire of 1666 ________________ London, it also marked the end of the Bubonic plague in that city.
6. World War I ________________ whole forests, leaving only scattered tree trunks behind.

Definition: Now take the final step in learning the new words.

7.	insurgent	________	a.	chaos; destruction
8.	obliterate	________	b.	a massive fire
9.	havoc	________	c.	to wipe out utterly
10.	raze	________	d.	a large flood
11.	conflagration	________	e.	rebellious
12.	deluge	________	f.	to leave nothing standing

NEW WORDS

insurgent
in - sėr - jənt

obliterate
ə - blit - ər - āt

havoc
hav - ək

raze
rāz

conflagration
kon - flə - grā - shən

deluge
del - yūj

Notable Roots: ob = against; lit = letters; flagra = fire; delu/dilu = flood

THE END OF INNOCENCE

Read the literature of the 1890s, and you will be painfully aware of a significant *rift* between the worldview of that time and our own. The fin-de-siècle self-assuredness that marks works by H. G. Wells, Oscar Wilde, and even Bram Stoker has been *eradicated*. Few living at the end of the nineteenth century believed that *strife* had been *nullified*, but there was a tacit belief that the march of human progress had permanently gained the upper hand against the forces of chaos. The *gauntlet* of the twentieth century would quickly disabuse* people of such notions. In one *fractious* century, people learned that the wonders of our imaginations could become the stuff of nightmares.

NEW WORDS

rift
rift

eradicate
ē - rad - ə - kāt

strife
strīf

nullify
nul - ə - fī

gauntlet
gônt - lət

fractious
frak - shəs

Notable Roots:
riv = rip; radix = root; null = nothing; fract = break

Sample Sentences: Complete the sentences by filling in the blanks.

1. The *Mercury 7* astronauts were put through a ________________ of difficult tests.
2. The ________________ atmosphere in Paris grew lethal when war came in 1792.
3. It's natural for children of divorce to wish away the ________________ between parents.
4. Smallpox was the first human scourge ________________ by vaccination.
5. During the 1830s, some Southern states asserted the right to ________________ federal laws.
6. Henry VI, a weak and languid* monarch, presided over decades of ________________ before he was finally deposed.

Definitions: Match the new words with their meanings.

7. rift ________ a. a series of challenges
8. eradicate ________ b. to cancel out
9. strife ________ c. unruly; rebellious
10. nullify ________ d. to completely remove
11. gauntlet ________ e. unrest; anger
12. fractious ________ f. physical gap; estrangement

SANS CULOTTES

When Louis XIV proclaimed, "I am the state," he summed up the relationship between monarch and commoner that had existed in much of the world since the fall of Rome. Within a matter of decades, however, philosophers like Locke, Rousseau, and Voltaire had the temerity* to suggest that government exists to safeguard the people's rights and yet the commoners were instead *fettered* by a feudal system that *impeded* the progress and prosperity of society. The opening *skirmish* came in America, where the unruly colonists *wrested* control over their affairs. France entered the *fray* in 1789 when representatives of the Third Estate declared that the common folk were the state now. Unlike in America, however, the statesmen did not have the final say. The lowest French classes, called "sans culottes" because they did not wear the knee-breeches of the rich, were in an *inclement* mood and would not be placated* with a few legal reforms.

NEW WORDS

fetter
fet - ər

impede
im - pēd

skirmish
skėr - mish

wrest
rest

fray (n.)
frā

inclement
in - klem - ənt

Notable Roots: pede = foot; clemen = forgiveness

Sample Sentences: Here's your opportunity to use your new words.

1. Scrooge asked Jacob Marley why he was ________________ by heavy chains.
2. Romeo is banished after the ________________ that claims the lives of Mercutio and Tybalt.
3. Heavy fines are assessed on those who ________________ traffic by "blocking the box."
4. ________________ between police and protestors flared up all night.
5. The referees postponed the game due to ________________ weather.
6. I don't know how I ________________ the remote control from my big brother.

Definitions: Match the new words with their meanings. Remember, words may have many synonyms.

7. fetter	________	a.	a small clash with few casualties
8. impede	________	b.	a fight
9. skirmish	________	c.	to physically burden or restrain
10. wrest	________	d.	merciless; immoderate
11. fray	________	e.	to block or inhibit the progress of something
12. inclement	________	f.	to seize

PANDORA'S BOX

In 1792, the monarchies of Europe, seeking to *deter* revolt in their own lands, marched on France to end the *fracas*. The invaders publicly vowed to restore Louis XVI to his full powers and to crush all further revolutionary *dissent*. This manifesto had a far more *deleterious* effect than any royalist could have imagined. To the immediate *detriment* of their cause, the defiant French imprisoned the king and abolished the monarchy. More importantly, the people, from merchants to peasant farmers, rose up en masse to fight. Within months, a motley army of raw recruits and career soldiers halted the invasion. In the immediate aftermath, the political situation in Europe was greatly *exacerbated*. In the long term, by swamping the professional armies of their enemies, which fought only for gold, the French showed the world the raw power of nationalism for the first time. To this day, we live with the consequences of 1792.

NEW WORDS

deter
dē - tər

fracas
frak - əs

dissent (n.)
dis - ent

deleterious
dil - ə - tēr - ē - əs

detriment
de - trə - mənt

exacerbate
əg - zas - ėr - bāt

Notable Roots:
ter = turn; sens = feel, think; delete = destroy; acer = sharp, bitter

Sample Sentences: Use the new words in these sentences.

1. Selfish, individual performers can be a ________________ to the chemistry of any team.
2. The strain of the war greatly ________________ Roosevelt's heart condition.
3. A talented writer need not be ________________ by the lack of a university education.
4. A scandal is highly ________________ to the public image of any company.
5. A midnight ________________ on the streets below won't even wake most city dwellers.
6. When Supreme Court justices oppose the will of the majority, they are free to explain their ________________ in an essay published alongside the group decision.

Definitions: Match the new words with their meanings.

7.	deter	________	a.	a loud disturbance
8.	fracas	________	b.	general disagreement
9.	dissent	________	c.	to worsen
10.	deleterious	________	d.	to discourage
11.	detriment	________	e.	harmful
12.	exacerbate	________	f.	that which causes damage

GROUP REVIEW

Week by week, your word power is being built. It's like putting money in the bank. Remember, in English there may be many synonyms and related meanings for each word. Knowing one synonym is good, but you will reap greater benefits from knowing several.

Directions: Match the words for this week with their meanings.

REVIEW WORDS		DEFINITIONS
________	**1.** conflagration	**a.** to wipe out utterly
________	**2.** deleterious	**b.** a fight
________	**3.** deluge	**c.** chaos; destruction
________	**4.** deter	**d.** to cancel out
________	**5.** detriment	**e.** that which causes damage
________	**6.** dissent	**f.** a large flood
________	**7.** eradicate	**g.** a small clash with few casualties
________	**8.** exacerbate	**h.** general disagreement
________	**9.** fetter	**i.** rebellious
________	**10.** fracas	**j.** to discourage
________	**11.** fractious	**k.** merciless; immoderate
________	**12.** fray	**l.** to leave nothing standing
________	**13.** gauntlet	**m.** a loud disturbance
________	**14.** havoc	**n.** harmful
________	**15.** impede	**o.** to worsen
________	**16.** inclement	**p.** to physically burden or restrain
________	**17.** insurgent	**q.** unrest; anger
________	**18.** nullify	**r.** to block or inhibit the progress of something
________	**19.** obliterate	**s.** physical gap; estrangement
________	**20.** raze	**t.** to completely remove
________	**21.** rift	**u.** a massive fire
________	**22.** skirmish	**v.** unruly; rebellious
________	**23.** strife	**w.** to seize
________	**24.** wrest	**x.** a series of challenges

Wordsearch

Directions: Using the clues listed below, fill in each blank in the following story with one of the new words you learned this week.

Clues

3rd Day	1st Day
3rd Day	2nd Day
1st Day	1st Day
3rd Day	3rd Day
2nd Day	1st Day
3rd Day	1st Day
4th Day	

The Engine with No Off Switch

The military victories of Napoleon Bonaparte were fueled by nationalism. Republican France had raised huge armies and reformed society to support the war effort. The enemy kingdoms were too inflexible to make such sweeping changes. Their generals were similarly ___________ by this rigidity. Because the republican ethos allowed men of talent to rise, Napoleon was surrounded by gifted subordinates. Allied generals, meanwhile, were ___________ with incompetent officers, often aristocrats who owed their positions to nepotism.*

For two decades, Napoleon's legions caused ___________ wherever they went. The Grand Armée defeated one coalition of enemies after another. His conquests put an end to both the Republic of Venice and the Holy Roman Empire. He consolidated dozens of German and Italian states, providing the impetus for unification movements in both lands.

Bonaparte's downfall was inevitable, however, because the forces that the Revolution unleashed could not be turned off. France had acquired a taste for plundering, so the emperor sought fresh conquests until he overreached, nearly losing his army in 1812 to the ___________ Russian winter. After that defeat, his enemies pounced, crushing the French at Leipzig in 1813 and Waterloo in 1815.

Despite Bonaparte's failures, the worldwide growth of nationalist movements inspired by France, could not be stopped. The rest of the nineteenth century was marked by revolutionary ___________ as republicans, Marxists, and anarchists sought to ___________ power from Europe's autocrats. The repression of reactionary governments only ___________ nationalist fervor* by creating martyrs.* Multinational states such as the Austrian and Ottoman Empires, moreover, were nearly torn apart by the ___________ ambitions of the various ethnic groups. The ___________ between the various nationalities made coherent government impossible.

Unsurprisingly, the ___________ that engulfed the world in 1914 began because of nationalist violence. A group of Serbian patriots seeking to liberate Bosnia assassinated the heir to the Austrian Empire. The murder of one nobleman triggered a series of alliances that had to be honored because public opinion demanded it. The soldiers of each nation were eager for the ___________, not knowing the horror that was to come. Even after two, then three, then four years that saw whole cities ___________ and a generation of young men ___________, nationalistic fervor* would still not allow either side to sue for a compromise of peace. After all, such sacrifices could not have been in vain.

THE FIRST CELEBRITY IN HISTORY

A 5,000-year-old tablet found in Iraq bears the inscription "29,086 measures barley 37 months *Kushim*." This prosaic record is an *epistle* from the first person to conquer oblivion: Kushim is the first person—ever—whose name we know. As much as the works of Shakespeare, this *succinct missive* underscores the awesome power of writing. Humans have left behind *vestiges* of our existence for perhaps 100,000 years. Vibrant cave paintings of charging beasts made 17,000 years ago *attest* to our creativity. The flowers and shell necklaces unearthed in prehistoric graves are enduring *eulogies* that demonstrate one of our most profound human values. Our prehistoric ancestors were clearly like us, but not until Kushim's tablet did they learn to speak to us directly.

NEW WORDS

epistle
ə - pis - əl

succinct
suh - sinkt

missive
mis - iv

vestige
ves - tij

attest
ə - test

eulogy
yū - lōj - ē

Notable Roots: miss = message; test = witness; eu = good; logos = words

Sample Sentences: Based upon your understanding of the new words as discovered from the context, place them in the spaces provided.

1. The line outside the door ________________ to the quality of the diner's breakfast options.
2. The cost per additional word made telegrams a ________________ form of communication.
3. The ________________ of St. Paul, named for their recipients, comprise a substantial portion of the New Testament.
4. Ted Kennedy's quavering voice gave his ________________ for RFK incredible poignance.
5. ________________ of the last ice age can be found in boulders strewn throughout the north.
6. Many celebrities have ruined their careers with ill-considered ________________ on Twitter.

Definitions: Matching words and definitions will prove you've learned them.

7. epistle	________	a. to bear witness
8. succinct	________	b. a formal letter
9. missive	________	c. a tribute, often for someone who has died
10. vestige	________	d. to the point
11. attest	________	e. a short, often informal communication
12. eulogy	________	f. a remnant

COLLECTIVE MEMORY

Before writing, knowledge *reverberated* through generations orally. There are important differences between oral and written histories. Given the limitations of memory, oral histories recount great events rather than personal *anecdotes* or *memoirs*. Similarly, a simple but dramatic style of storytelling distinguishes oral history from *prolix* academic writing. Despite these differences, oral history is crucial to historiography. Native Americans, for example, provide an oral record of the waves of diseases and migrating herds of horses that were outriders of European arrival in the New World. This knowledge was passed down so reliably that twentieth-century researchers were able to construct a historical counter-narrative to the prevailing *discourse* of the time, which either ignored Native Americans or *libeled* them.

NEW WORDS

reverberate
rē - vėr - bėr - āt

anecdote
an - ək - dōt

memoir
mem - wâr

prolix
prol - iks

discourse
dis - kôrs

libel
lī - bəl

Notable Roots:
verb = word; mem = remember; lex = words; course = run, current

Sample Sentences: Insert the new words in these sentences.

1. Isaac Newton's writing was so _______________ and abstruse* that it took the charm of Edmund Halley to promote the brilliance of Newton's work.
2. Royalties from Grant's _______________, written while he was dying, supported his widow.
3. Oscar Wilde's suit for _______________ proved disastrous when proof of his private conduct was revealed in court.
4. Political _______________ used to only deal with the public character of politicians.
5. Winston Churchill was famous for humorous _______________ from his storied career.
6. The courage of the Spartans at Thermopylae has _______________ for millennia.

Definitions: Match the new words with their meanings.

7. reverberate	________	a. public debate or discussion
8. anecdote	________	b. wordy and convoluted
9. memoir	________	c. false written attack on one's character
10. prolix	________	d. to echo through time
11. discourse	________	e. an account based on experience
12. libel	________	f. a personal story of a minor event

FROM BUSINESS TO BILL OF RIGHTS

That Kushim's famed tablet dealt with accounting matters was not coincidental. Though writing would give rise to countless *encomiums* on the beauty of nature, *treatises* on religion, or *manifestos* on human rights, the first order of business was business. Thus, the first *glyphs* represented numbers. Then followed pictographs; images of birds, women, or wheat that were meant literally. The pivotal breakthrough would be the usage of symbols to represent sounds, like pictures of a honeybee and a safe expressing the command "Be Safe!" The French linguist who *deciphered* Egyptian hieroglyphics was only able to do so by recognizing that the Egyptian *scribes* had used symbols this way.

NEW WORDS

encomium
ən - kōm - ē - um

treatise
trēt - is

manifesto
man - ə - fest - ō

glyph
glif

decipher
dē - sī - fėr

scribe
skrīb

Notable Roots: treat = deal; manu = hand; fest = attack, disturb; cipher = code; scribe = write

Sample Sentences: Insert the new words in these sentences.

1. Linear A, a script that was written in either direction, has never been _______________.
2. Native Americans of the Southwest left ornate _______________ on rocks.
3. The _______________ was a position of importance in mostly illiterate societies.
4. Rudolph Hess's saccharin _______________ about Hitler demonstrated worshipful devotion.
5. Karl Marx wrote perhaps the most controversial and notorious _______________ in history.
6. Mahan's _______________ on the role of sea power influenced most European admiralties.

Definitions: Match the new words with their meanings.

7. encomium	________	a.	a writer or keeper of records
8. treatise	________	b.	a carved symbol
9. manifesto	________	c.	to interpret symbols or a code
10. glyph	________	d.	a formal essay on a topic
11. decipher	________	e.	an expression of political beliefs or goals
12. scribe	________	f.	an expression of praise

A NATION OF LAWS

The *expository* nature of the Declaration of Independence mirrors the values of a world reevaluating the roles of sovereign and people. Jefferson expressed the idea that government exists to protect human rights; should it neglect this duty, it ought to be *relegated* to oblivion. What follows is a *citation* of the offenses of George III and the pronouncement of American independence on that basis. Though Jefferson deserves his *accolades* and the *epithet* "The Sage of Monticello," the miracle of America's founding lies in its establishment according to clear principles expressed in writing in the Declaration and in the *preamble* of the Constitution.

NEW WORDS

expository
eks - poz - ə - tôr - ē

relegate
rel - ə - gāt

citation
sī - tā - shən

accolade
ak - ə - lād

epithet
ep - ə - thet

preamble
prē - am - bəl

Notable Roots: pose = show; legat = envoy; cite = mention, quote; pre = before

Sample Sentences: A slow and thorough study is needed today.

1. Diego found that writing proper ________________ took longer than writing the paper itself.
2. The ________________ after Lincoln's death contrasted the polemics* he suffered in life.
3. Babe Ruth's ________________ came from his cherubic appearance at the time of his debut.
4. Jill could tell from the stilted ________________ of the letter that she was being laid off.
5. Woodward's ________________ works have revealed the flaws of many presidencies.
6. After abdicating, Edward VIII was ________________ to an entirely ceremonial role.

Definitions: Match the new words with their meanings.

7. expository ________	a.	quote or reference
8. relegate ________	b.	nickname
9. citation ________	c.	examining critically
10. accolade ________	d.	opening statements
11. epithet ________	e.	to demote
12. preamble ________	f.	statement of praise

GROUP REVIEW

If you've ever watched or played baseball, you know how important a base hit is to each batter. Before the game, players spend as much time as possible taking their batting practice. During the game, the batter concentrates on every pitch. In the same way, each day you are getting in your "batting practice," and the weekly review is your chance to build up your "batting average." Collect new words with the same concentration that baseball players collect base hits.

Matching

Directions: Match the terms to their meanings.

REVIEW WORDS		DEFINITIONS	
________	**1.** accolade	**a.**	a personal story of a minor event
________	**2.** anecdote	**b.**	a tribute, often for someone who has died
________	**3.** attest	**c.**	a carved symbol
________	**4.** citation	**d.**	wordy and convoluted
________	**5.** decipher	**e.**	a quote or reference
________	**6.** discourse	**f.**	to echo through time
________	**7.** encomium	**g.**	an account based on experience
________	**8.** epistle	**h.**	a writer or keeper of records
________	**9.** epithet	**i.**	a formal essay on a topic
________	**10.** eulogy	**j.**	a false written attack on one's character
________	**11.** expository	**k.**	an expression of political beliefs or goals
________	**12.** glyph	**l.**	a nickname
________	**13.** libel	**m.**	a short, often informal communication
________	**14.** manifesto	**n.**	to interpret symbols or a code
________	**15.** memoir	**o.**	to demote
________	**16.** missive	**p.**	a formal letter
________	**17.** preamble	**q.**	examining critically
________	**18.** prolix	**r.**	to the point
________	**19.** relegate	**s.**	a statement of praise
________	**20.** reverberate	**t.**	a remnant
________	**21.** scribe	**u.**	a public debate or discussion
________	**22.** succinct	**v.**	an opening statement
________	**23.** treatise	**w.**	to bear witness
________	**24.** vestige	**x.**	an expression of praise

Wordsearch

Directions: Using the clues listed below, fill in each blank in the following story with one of the new words you learned this week.

Clues

1st Day	4th Day
1st Day	2nd Day
2nd Day	1st Day
2nd Day	4th Day
4th Day	

The Wild West

History ___________ that, in a showdown in 1881, a notorious outlaw, Billy the Kid, was killed. The ___________ version, which is now public knowledge, is that Sheriff Pat Garrett cornered the Kid at Fort Sumner, New Mexico, and shot him. Garrett's published ___________, a financial flop, though an important contemporary account, has it that Billy stumbled into a darkened room where the sheriff was questioning a witness. With no time for ___________, both men grabbed for their guns, and Garrett was quicker.

William Bonney earned his ___________ "Kid" by killing as many as ten men by the age of 21. He was a participant in a New Mexico range war and then, fleeing official ___________ for crimes committed during the war, he became an outlaw. While history lists his death as having occurred in 1881, a common conspiracy theory has it that the Kid escaped and lived for many years in Texas.

Just before his death in 1950, an old rancher named Brushy Bill Roberts claimed to be Billy the Kid, seeking to correct ___________ that sullied his reputation and to claim a pardon he felt was promised him by the former governor of New Mexico. It is true that more than one ___________ passed between Bonney and the governor before 1881, which raised the possibility of a pardon in exchange for Bonney's testimony regarding the ranch war. To settle Roberts's claim, a computer was brought in to compare Roberts's face to a photo of the Kid. The computer found major structural differences between the two faces, which ___________ the controversy to the realm of debunked fraud.

Roots Roundup

Directions: Each word below is followed by the definition for another word that contains the same root. For example, if the word is *vacuous* (devoid of thought or intellect) and the clue is *a region of space empty of matter*, the answer would be *vacuum*.

1. treatise — *a medical procedure to address a condition* ________
2. discourse — *compensation or remedy for injury or injustice* ________
3. attest — *verbal evidence given under oath* ________
4. scribe — *an order for medicine given by a doctor* ________
5. missive — *to send out a payment* ________
6. reverberate — *excessively wordy* ________
7. glyph — *Egyptian pictographic symbols* ________
8. citation — *to publicly give a speech* ________

A MUSICAL WORLD

In the nineteenth century, every leading nation produced its share of great composers. There was an *alluring* array of national schools and musical styles to *entice* the once obscure musician to come into his own. At the beginning of the century, music lovers turned to *resplendent* Vienna, a city that still echoed with Mozart's *idyllic* melodies. However, many composers became *infatuated* with Paris, which excelled in operatic music. As the century progressed, Germany took center stage during the *incandescent* career of Ludwig van Beethoven.

Sample Sentences: Take command of the new words in these sentences.

1. Central Park presents the illusion of an _______________ countryside in the heart of the city.
2. If metal is heated enough it becomes _______________, giving off shades of red light.
3. Friar Laurence suspects that Romeo is merely _______________ with Rosaline.
4. There's something _______________ about the life of a writer.
5. The Empire State Building is a _______________ beacon at night.
6. Software companies offer generous compensation to _______________ talent from rivals.

Definitions: Match the new words with their meanings.

7.	alluring	________	a.	to tempt
8.	entice	________	b.	radiating light
9.	resplendent	________	c.	attractive
10.	idyllic	________	d.	temporarily fascinated by someone
11.	infatuated	________	e.	picturesque
12.	incandescent	________	f.	colorful or luxurious

NEW WORDS

alluring
ə - lur - ing

entice
in - tīs

resplendent
rē - splen - dənt

idyllic
ī - dēl - ik

infatuated
in - fach - ū - āt - əd

incandescent
in - kan - des - ənt

Notable Roots: lure = bait; splendid = shining; fatu = fool; cand = candle, shining

A GIANT COMPOSER

Beethoven, like Mozart, started out as a child prodigy.* Later, as a successful concert pianist, he became the talk of Europe. His *dapper* appearance, outfitted in the finest *raiment* but with disheveled hair, seemed the embodiment of genius. He tutored the children of many wealthy patrons and was nearly *betrothed* to an Italian noblewoman. Despite superficial similarities, however, Beethoven was no Mozart: he had an abusive father, was unlucky in love, and was secretly becoming deaf at a young age. Beethoven's brooding personality was reflected in his work, which shunned the *dulcet* melodies of Mozart's day. *Tantalized* by grand visions of music filled with the drama and passion of real life, he crafted symphonies that broke over audiences like thunderstorms. Those who preferred Mozart's light, airy *reveries* didn't like it, but for a new generation Beethoven represented the rebelliousness of the Romantic period.

NEW WORDS

dapper
dap - ėr

raiment
rā - mənt

betrothed
bē - trō - THd

dulcet
dul - sət

tantalize
tan - tə - līz

reverie
rev - ə - rē

Notable Roots: array = assembly, appearance; dulce = sweet; reve = dream

Sample Sentences: Place the new words in these sentences.

1. The ________________ of the ultra-wealthy proclaims their elevated status.
2. Megan had not expected her prom date to look so ________________ in a tuxedo.
3. Blanche DuBois's voice is meant to have the ________________ quality of a Southern belle.
4. Henry VIII's brother, Arthur, was initially ________________ to Catherine of Aragon but died before they could be married.
5. The train ride through the snowy forests of Romania was a winter ________________.
6. Before Buckner's error, the 1986 Red Sox had been ________________ by victory.

Definitions: Match the new words with their meanings.

7.	dapper	________	a.	sweet sounding; soothing
8.	raiment	________	b.	to tease with something out of reach
9.	betrothed	________	c.	a daydream
10.	dulcet	________	d.	clothing
11.	tantalize	________	e.	neat and handsome in appearance
12.	reverie	________	f.	engaged or promised in marriage

A TROUBLESOME LEGACY

German composer Richard Wagner is remembered for his operas, which had a dramatic, even *gaudy* quality. He placed great emphasis on visual *aesthetics*; in works like *Tristan and Isolde*, he sought to create an immersive experience through the use of *luminous* set designs and *comely* costumes. Wagner lived a chaotic life, marked by *amorous* affairs and bankruptcy. In death, he became an icon for German nationalists; Hitler was obsessed with Wagner's work for its *ethereal*, Romantic quality and use of elements drawn from Germanic mythology. It is unfair to hold this against the composer, however: Wagner died before Hitler was even born and, as they did with Nietzsche, the Nazis interpreted his works in subjective ways that freely ignored elements that did not agree with their ideology.

gaudy
gô - dē

aesthetic
əs - thet - ik

luminous
lūm - in - əs

comely
kum - lē

amorous
am - ər - əs

ethereal
ē - thē - rē - əl

Notable Roots:
lumin = light; amor = love; ether = vapor

Sample Sentences: Complete the following sentences with the new words.

1. The dapper* Kennedy and his ________________ young wife were a handsome pair.
2. Repelled by ________________ displays of wealth, Charles V lived like a peasant.
3. Unrequited ________________ desires have inspired many a sonnet and ode.
4. The Lighthouse of Alexandria was so ________________ it could be seen 30 miles away.
5. The Brutalist ________________ of communist architecture remains polarizing.
6. Dreams are never in HD but have an ________________ quality.

Definitions: Match the new words with their meanings.

7. gaudy	________	a.	glowing
8. aesthetic	________	b.	otherworldly
9. luminous	________	c.	relating to desire
10. comely	________	d.	related to the subject of beauty
11. amorous	________	e.	pleasing to the eye
12. ethereal	________	f.	ostentatious and ugly

THE IMPRESSIONIST

Claude Debussy grew up in a France that found her position at the center of Europe usurped* by the rise of Germany. As a composer, although he respected Wagner's operas as *sublime* visions, he felt their *limpid* aura of mysticism belonged to a past age. Debussy's music eschewed sentimentality in favor of "symphonic sketches," depicting nature's *pellucid* qualities through the use of *mellifluous* harmonies. He explored the *diaphanous* qualities of spring and nighttime, suggesting light and motion with sound the way Impressionists would do with oil paint. Listening to his most famous work, *La Mer* (the sea), one practically undulates on *translucent* waves of sound.

NEW WORDS

sublime
sə - blīm

limpid
lim - pid

pellucid
pel - ū - sid

mellifluous
mel - if - lū - əs

diaphanous
dī - af - ən - əs

translucent
tranz - lū - sənt

Notable Roots: sub = under; lim = limit; limp = fluid; lux = light; mel = honey; flu = flow

Sample Sentences: Use the new words in these sentences.

1. Swing makes use of _______________ chord progressions and rapid tempo for dancing.
2. The _______________ quality of Edith Wharton's writing evokes the rarefied atmosphere of Gilded Age high society.
3. Unlike opaque oil colors, watercolors are _______________ and can be applied in layers.
4. The air was so _______________ that day that we could see 50 miles in every direction.
5. Venetian glass, like a fine jewel, is both _______________ and colorful.
6. The sheen and lightness of silk give it a _______________ quality.

Definitions: Match the new words with their meanings.

7.	sublime	________	a.	pleasantly flowing
8.	limpid	________	b.	light, delicate, and semi-transparent
9.	pellucid	________	c.	transparent to light but not images
10.	mellifluous	________	d.	completely transparent
11.	diaphanous	________	e.	of exceptional quality
12.	translucent	________	f.	shining and reflective

GROUP REVIEW

Another week to build your vocabulary. Words stand for concepts. The more concepts you can recognize, the better able you are to deal with complexity and abstraction.

Matching

Directions: Match the words you learned this week with their meanings.

REVIEW WORDS		DEFINITIONS
________	**1.** aesthetic	**a.** otherwordly
________	**2.** alluring	**b.** picturesque
________	**3.** amorous	**c.** to tease with something out of reach
________	**4.** betrothed	**d.** glowing
________	**5.** comely	**e.** ostentatious and ugly
________	**6.** dapper	**f.** temporarily fascinated by someone
________	**7.** diaphanous	**g.** transparent to light but not images
________	**8.** dulcet	**h.** colorful or luxurious
________	**9.** entice	**i.** radiating light
________	**10.** ethereal	**j.** clothing
________	**11.** gaudy	**k.** shining and reflective
________	**12.** idyllic	**l.** attractive
________	**13.** incandescent	**m.** to tempt
________	**14.** infatuated	**n.** completely transparent
________	**15.** limpid	**o.** engaged or promised in marriage
________	**16.** luminous	**p.** of exceptional quality
________	**17.** mellifluous	**q.** pleasing to the eye
________	**18.** pellucid	**r.** relating to desire
________	**19.** raiment	**s.** a daydream
________	**20.** resplendent	**t.** pleasantly flowing
________	**21.** reverie	**u.** neat and handsome in appearance
________	**22.** sublime	**v.** related to the subject of beauty
________	**23.** tantalize	**w.** light, delicate, and semi-transparent
________	**24.** translucent	**x.** sweet sounding; soothing

Wordsearch

Directions: Using the clues listed below, fill in each blank in the following story with one of the new words you learned this week.

Clues

1st Day	2nd Day
2nd Day	4th Day
1st Day	3rd Day
1st Day	4th Day
1st Day	

Cooking on Sunshine

Like most children of the '80s, I watched *Mr. Wizard's World* growing up. One episode, in particular, presented an idea so ___________ that it stuck with me into adulthood. In the episode, Mr. Wizard, looking ___________ in his blue cardigan, cooks an entire breakfast using nothing but sunshine. Arrayed in his backyard are a series of solar cookers, ___________ with morning sunlight glinting off of their shiny surfaces. The sausages he cooks in simple solar funnels. The eggs he poaches inside a box cooker. The bread he toasts ever so carefully using a parabolic mirror to focus light rays onto a single ___________ point.

As a science geek who also loves to cook, I found the idea so ___________ that one day, as a young adult, I found a panel cooker on the Internet and within a week I was the proud owner of one. It was flimsy, but when it cooked a banana bread on my balcony in under an hour, I was ecstatic. It was to be no mere ___________: in my middle age, I still solar cook in my back yard at least twice a week, albeit with a far superior box cooker, which can heat up to 410°F on a day with truly ___________ skies.

A solar oven makes use of a basic physical principle: light can pass through glass, but heat cannot. A solar oven simply maximizes the potential of this principle. The interior is darkened to absorb the most light, reflectors increase the ___________ shining through the glass, and a layer of insulation around the box prevents heat loss. Simple though the design may be, the experience of serving guests a chicken dinner perfectly cooked in daylight is simply ___________.

THE ELDER REPUBLIC

At first, Holland seems a *sedate* and simple land—a *bucolic* setting of churning windmills and flat, handsome farmland familiar from Rembrandt's paintings. Amsterdam, riven by canals and packed with narrow, meticulously groomed *domiciles* is perfectly *juxtaposed* with the countryside, however. The city became a *citadel* of commerce after the Netherlands achieved independence from Spain. In 1594, the Dutch and refugees from Spanish Belgium, who had taken *asylum* in the newly independent republic, pooled their investments to form the first corporation on Earth, the Dutch East India Company. The fleet of merchant ships their wealth purchased launched a century-long Golden Age.

NEW WORDS

sedate
sə - dāt

bucolic
byū - kol - ik

domicile
dōm - ə - sīl

juxtapose
juks - tə - pōz

citadel
sit - ə - del

asylum
ə - sī - lum

Notable Roots: sed = sit; domus = home

Sample Sentences: Insert the new words in the sentences.

1. The concrete _______________ of Belgium were crushed by German artillery.
2. Every _______________ requires a mixture of private spaces and common areas.
3. Despite the modernity of New York City, the _______________ character of the Hudson Valley has been well preserved.
4. Had Martin Luther not gained _______________, he would have been burned as a heretic.
5. The decay of Detroit is oddly _______________ with the prosperity of Windsor, Ontario.
6. Compared with the works of the Venetians, Dutch and Flemish paintings are _______________, even gloomy.

Definitions: Match your new words to their meanings.

7.	sedate	________	a.	a fortress
8.	bucolic	________	b.	calm; serious
9.	domicile	________	c.	a sanctuary
10.	juxtapose	________	d.	positioned side by side
11.	citadel	________	e.	reminiscent of idyllic* countryside
12.	asylum	________	f.	a home or household

THE NIFTY FIFTIETH

The Hawaiian *archipelago* was created by a volcanic hotspot in the central Pacific. It is one of the most *remote* inhabited locations on Earth. As the easternmost *terminus* of Polynesian expansion, Hawaii came to be populated slowly over the last 1,500 years—long after other inhabited *locales*. Similarly, a much smaller number of plant and animal species have become *ensconced* on the islands compared with other South Pacific island chains like Indonesia. Those species that have successfully made the long journey over water have evolved to exploit the unique *niches* of this island paradise.

Sample Sentences: Place the new words in these sentences.

1. Lake George was a popular vacation ____________ in the time before long distance commercial flights.
2. The Vatican, ________________ behind high walls in Rome, is the smallest nation.
3. Istanbul was the eastern ________________ of the Orient Express.
4. A thin ________________ of islands separates the Caribbean Sea from the Atlantic Ocean.
5. While orbiting the far side of the moon, Michael Collins became the most ________________ human being in history.
6. Colorado's ________________ as a mountain, plains, and desert state is unique.

NEW WORDS

archipelago
är - kə - pel - ə - gō

remote
rē - mōt

terminus
tėr - min - əs

locale
lō - kal

ensconced
ə - skon - səd

niche
nich

Notable Roots:
archi = chief;
pelagic = abyss;
termin = end;
locus = place

Definitions: Match the new words with their meanings.

7. archipelago	________	a. a setting
8. remote	________	b. a limit or final station
9. terminus	________	c. an advantageous position
10. locale	________	d. protected by a fortification
11. ensconced	________	e. a chain of islands
12. niche	________	f. far away; disconnected

THE CENTER OF THE WORLD

Singapore has always been a trading *enclave*: the city acts as a line of *meridian* astride the corridor of water that links the Indian and Pacific oceans and straddles the shipping lanes between Africa, Asia, and Australia. Lacking an agricultural *hinterland*, the city has always made its living from the sea. It is the natural *milieu* for commercial traders to meet, and, though one of the world's most expensive cities, home to a large *expatriate* community. City planners, harnessing the wealth that streams through the city, have created an urban environment noted for its cutting-edge green architecture and futuristic *ambience*.

NEW WORDS

enclave
on - klāv

meridian
mə - rid - ē - ən

hinterland
hin - tėr - land

milieu
mil - yə

expatriate
eks - pā - trē - ət

ambience
om - bē - ons

Notable Roots: clav = key; meridi = noon; patria = country; ambi = around

Sample Sentences: Pay attention to the fine differences in meaning.

1. The ________________ of Alexandria is rich farmland irrigated by the Nile.
2. Monaco is a tax-free ________________ surrounded by the French Riviera.
3. Unlike the equator, the location of 0° longitude is an arbitrary line of ________________.
4. Budapest's thermal baths, set in columned palaces, have a sublime* ______________.
5. Marie Curie found her ________________ in the laboratories and classrooms of Paris.
6. Life as an ______________ shows that societies operating by different rules function just fine.

Definitions: Match the new words with their meanings.

7. enclave ________ a. land surrounding and supporting a city
8. meridian ________ b. a natural setting
9. hinterland ________ c. prevailing atmosphere
10. milieu ________ d. one who lives in another country
11. expatriate ________ e. a community surrounded by foreign land
12. ambience ________ f. a dividing line on Earth's surface

SAILING TO BYZANTIUM

Istanbul is the world's only intercontinental city, and, given its *propinquity* to the east-west trade routes, it has always attracted people. In the fourth century, the Romans saw in the Greek town then known as Byzantium a natural fortress, surrounded by water on three sides. They made it their capital, adding high walls and *bastions* to safeguard its landward approaches. The *berths* of the Golden Horn welcomed ships from the Black Sea and the Aegean, while goods from the *rustic* interior of Anatolia filled its markets. When Byzantine fortunes *ebbed*, the Ottoman Turks raised the city from the *extremity* of defeat to be their capital. Today, the Blue Mosque and the Hagia Sophia stand side by side looking down on the oil tankers that ply the glittering waters of the Bosphorus.

NEW WORDS

propinquity
prō - pin - kwi - tē

bastion
bas - chən

berth
bėrth

rustic
rus - tik

ebb (n. & v.)
eb

extremity
eks - trem - i - tē

Notable Roots:
rus/rur = country;
trem = layer

Sample Sentences: Fill in the blank spaces with the new words.

1. My great-grandfather spent most his savings on a ____________ aboard a steamer to America.
2. The ____________ of New Netherland to New England guaranteed conflict.
3. As Ottoman military power ________________, European fascination with Turkey grew.
4. Victims in the last ________________ of hypothermia will often strip off their clothes.
5. After artillery became part of warfare, fortresses were built with angled ____________ to deflect cannonballs.
6. Vermont's ____________ charm has a powerful and timeless quality.

Definitions: Match the new words with their meanings.

7.	propinquity	________	a.	to decline
8.	bastion	________	b.	rural in character
9.	berth	________	c.	proximity
10.	rustic	________	d.	the outer limit of something
11.	ebb	________	e.	a projecting fortification
12.	extremity	________	f.	a designated place for a ship or bed

GROUP REVIEW

You have been learning how to use many new words by seeing them in a natural situation. Each day's story is the setting in which you meet the new words. The weekly review enables you to isolate the word and its many meanings. In this way, you can reinforce your understanding and word power. At this point, you have learned almost 600 words. Keep up the good work.

Matching

Directions: Match the weekly words with their meanings.

REVIEW WORDS		DEFINITIONS
________	**1.** ambience	**a.** one who lives in another country
________	**2.** archipelago	**b.** a limit or final station
________	**3.** asylum	**c.** reminiscent of idyllic* countryside
________	**4.** bastion	**d.** the outer limit of something
________	**5.** berth	**e.** calm; serious
________	**6.** bucolic	**f.** a setting
________	**7.** citadel	**g.** a designated place for a ship or bed
________	**8.** domicile	**h.** an advantageous position
________	**9.** ebb	**i.** prevailing atmosphere
________	**10.** enclave	**j.** a chain of islands
________	**11.** ensconced	**k.** to decline
________	**12.** expatriate	**l.** positioned side by side
________	**13.** extremity	**m.** a projecting fortification
________	**14.** hinterland	**n.** a fortress
________	**15.** juxtapose	**o.** protected by a fortification
________	**16.** locale	**p.** sanctuary
________	**17.** meridian	**q.** a community surrounded by foreign land
________	**18.** milieu	**r.** a dividing line on Earth's surface
________	**19.** niche	**s.** rural in character
________	**20.** propinquity	**t.** far away; disconnected
________	**21.** remote	**u.** land surrounding and supporting a city
________	**22.** rustic	**v.** a natural setting
________	**23.** sedate	**w.** a home or household
________	**24.** terminus	**x.** proximity

Doing Double Duty

Directions: Each of the ten words below can be used as more than one part of speech. For each word, look up the alternative definition and compose a sentence using the word both ways.

1. ebb (noun and verb)
2. discourse (noun and verb)
3. sublime (adjective and verb)
4. rift (noun and verb)
5. fetter (noun and verb)
6. sedate (adjective and verb)
7. scribe (noun and verb)
8. fray (noun and verb)
9. niche (noun and adjective)
10. expatriate (noun and verb)

WEEK 28 DAY 5

Wordsearch

Directions: Fill in each blank in the story with one of the new words you learned this week.

Clues

4th Day

3rd Day

2nd Day

4th Day

2nd Day

3rd Day

2nd Day

1st Day

2nd Day

4th Day

The Edges of the World

Hawaii is the only U.S. state located in the tropics. Ka Lae, the southern tip of Hawaii is, therefore, the southernmost point in the United States. Alaska is the site of the northernmost ___________, Point Barrow, which lies north of the Arctic Circle, less than 1,300 miles from the North Pole. The ___________ of this cape is mainly characterized by tundra that spends a few months of each year in 24-hour darkness.

Alaska is also the site of the westernmost and easternmost point. Both lie in the Aleutian ___________, which extends across the North Pacific. Now, you might think the island farthest from the mainland, Attu, would be the westernmost point. This last ___________ of the United States is home to an air base and faced Japanese attack during World War II. Technically, though, Attu is not the western ___________ of the Aleutians.

The explanation for this paradox lies in the subjectivity of east and west on a circular globe. Zero degrees longitude, a line running from the North Pole through Europe and Africa to the South Pole, divides the Eastern and Western Hemispheres *on one side*. The other seam of the globe is the 180th ___________, which passes largely unnoticed through ___________ stretches of ocean. This imaginary line demarcates *west from east*.

Since the Aleutians intersect this line, if you follow the chain far enough, you'll find yourself in the easternmost reaches of the Eastern Hemisphere. Thus, the westernmost point of the United States is found on the last Aleutian east of 180° longitude, Amatignak Island. Neatly ___________ with the westernmost ___________ is its eastern counterpart, Semisopochnoi Island. The ___________ of these islands is incredible: Semisopochnoi lies only 71 miles northwest of Amatignak.

A SPORT FOR EVERYONE

Of the many highly popular sports in the United States, football must be rated at or near the top. This sport allows the *elusive* athlete to *scurry* behind the blocks of burly teammates. The skills and strengths of many are welded together so that one team may work as a unit to gain mastery over its opponent. An *acute* football fan enjoys following *frenetic* action covering many parts of the playing field at the same time. Offenses *deploy* plays practiced to perfection, while the defense swarms in a *frenzy* of effort to make one last stop.

NEW WORDS

elusive
ē - lū - siv

scurry
skur - ē

acute
ə - kyūt

frenetic
frə - net - ik

deploy
də - plôi

frenzy
fren - zē

Notable Roots: lud = to fool; cut = sharp; ploy = to play; fren = fever

Sample Sentences: Use the new words in these sentences.

1. While predators feeding on a school of fish appear to be in a state of ________________, cornering the school requires cooperation.
2. The suffragettes expertly ________________ provocative tactics of civil disobedience.
3. A kitten will chase anything that ________________ along the floor.
4. The ________________ tension of the pitcher's duel mounted with each scoreless inning.
5. While the Americans won most pitched battles, Vietnamese forces were so ________________ that winning battles seldom translated to strategic gain.
6. Beat poetry seems to share the ________________ quality of the era's jazz.

Definitions: Match the new words with their definitions.

7. elusive	________	a. to put into action
8. scurry	________	b. feverish; energetic
9. acute	________	c. state of wild behavior
10. frenetic	________	d. hard to catch
11. deploy	________	e. severe; significant
12. frenzy	________	f. to move rapidly with quick steps

12TH MAN

The *advent* of the domed stadium has given renewed importance to the home field fans. *Spontaneous* cheers from the stands often *propagate*, encouraging the crowd to cheer louder. This gives the player on the field a boost of strength and *celerity*. When the opposing team has the ball, *unabated* cheering plays an even more important role: an offensive squad backed up on their own end of the field has difficulty hearing the play. False start penalties and broken plays are a frequent result. As a home game turns into a *romp*, the noise only becomes more relentless.

NEW WORDS

advent
ad - vent

spontaneous
spon - tān - ē - əs

propagate
prop - ə - gāt

celerity
sə - ler - ə - tē

unabated
un - ə - bāt - əd

romp (n.)
romp

Notable Roots: ven = come; spon = self; celer = swift; bate = batter

Sample Sentences: Complete the sentences with the new words.

1. Serena Williams surpassed her older sister, then conquered all of women's tennis in a ________________.
2. Although far ahead, Secretariat's ________________ kept increasing through the finish.
3. The ________________ of free agency has seen player salaries spike in most sports.
4. Without government intervention, the Great Depression continued ________________.
5. A great actor's ________________ flourishes can make a scene unforgettable.
6. Social media companies face pressure to stop the ________________ of disinformation.

Definitions: Match the new words with their meanings.

7.	advent	________	**a.**	first appearance
8.	spontaneous	________	**b.**	an easy win
9.	propagate	________	**c.**	without let up
10.	celerity	________	**d.**	self-generated
11.	unabated	________	**e.**	to spread; to multiply
12.	romp	________	**f.**	speed

FOOTBALL ON YOUR PHONE

Given life's demands, few find it *expedient* to be season-ticket holders of our favorite teams. Fortunately, the digital age has allowed the sport to be *disseminated* throughout the ether on television, radio, and Internet. Those who follow their teams' *alacrity* no longer have to miss a game. Business travelers can follow their team during their *peregrinations*. On any given Sunday, a *cursory* glance at the bowed heads on the bus reveals the continued popularity of football in an era of *febrile* activity.

NEW WORDS

expedient
eks - pēd - ē - ənt

disseminate
dis - em - ən - āt

alacrity
ə - lak - rə - tē

peregrination
per - ə - grin - ā - shən

cursory
kėr - sə - rē

febrile
fē - brīl

Notable Roots:
ped = foot; semin = seeds; per = away; agro = field; cur = run

Sample Sentences: Insert the new words in the sentences.

1. There is little ________________ in Congress for the prospect of raising taxes.
2. A ________________ physical examination runs the risk of missing latent* disorders.
3. Popular web browsers can track the ________________ of rumors through popular searches.
4. The ________________ of an albatross can cover thousands of miles.
5. While ________________, routine antibiotic injections in livestock have bred superbugs.
6. Given the circulation of his newspaper, Marat was able to instigate violence through his ________________ ravings.

Definitions: Match the new words with their meanings.

7.	expedient	________	a.	routine; with little care
8.	disseminate	________	b.	enthusiasm
9.	alacrity	________	c.	fast; convenient
10.	peregrination	________	d.	nervous or anxious
11.	cursory	________	e.	to circulate widely
12.	febrile	________	f.	wandering

THE G.O.A.T. DEBATE

Tom Brady's career began with a *spate* of Super Bowl wins: three in his first four years. Although more seemed *imminent*, the next decade saw an *escalation* of the greatest quarterback debate. While Brady continued to trail Joe Montana and Terry Bradshaw (who won four championships apiece), Peyton Manning and Drew Brees won their first titles. In 2008 and 2012, meanwhile, Brady was stymied* in title bids by the New York Giants. The frustrations of these years galvanized Brady's resolve. A more patient and intuitive passer, Brady won another *flurry* of championships. A trade to Tampa Bay then *expedited* his new team's title hopes as Brady won his seventh ring. Now discussion of the greatest quarterback is merely *perfunctory*.

NEW WORDS

spate
spāt

imminent
im - ə - nənt

escalation
es - kə - lā - shən

flurry
flėr - ē

expedite
eks - pə - dīt

perfunctory
pėr - funk - tôr - ē

Notable Roots:
scale = climb; per = by; funct = function

Sample Sentences: Complete these sentences with the new words.

1. After his SAT scores were published, a ________________ of colleges recruited Omar.
2. Carmen's ________________ interview responses did not impress anyone.
3. Angelique paid to ________________ her passport application after an opening for her dream job in London became available.
4. John Brown's raid marked a dramatic ________________ in the slavery crisis.
5. A ________________ of base hits turned the tight game into a romp.*
6. When the tornado siren sounds, disaster is ________________.

Definitions: Match the new words with their meanings.

7.	spate	________	a.	sudden burst of activity
8.	imminent	________	b.	with little thought or effort
9.	escalation	________	c.	a series of similar events in quick succession
10.	flurry	________	d.	about to occur
11.	expedite	________	e.	an increase in intensity
12.	perfunctory	________	f.	to speed up

GROUP REVIEW

Sporadic study tends to disrupt the learning process. Commit to a regular study regimen!

Matching

Directions: Match the terms you learned this week with their meanings.

REVIEW WORDS		DEFINITIONS
______	1. acute	a. severe; significant
______	2. advent	b. to spread; to multiply
______	3. alacrity	c. an increase in intensity
______	4. celerity	d. wandering
______	5. cursory	e. state of wild behavior
______	6. deploy	f. hard to catch
______	7. disseminate	g. enthusiasm
______	8. elusive	h. first appearance
______	9. escalation	i. to circulate widely
______	10. expedient	j. routine; with little care
______	11. expedite	k. self-generated
______	12. febrile	l. about to occur
______	13. flurry	m. speed
______	14. frenetic	n. to speed up
______	15. frenzy	o. to put into action
______	16. imminent	p. with little thought or effort
______	17. peregrination	q. without let up
______	18. perfunctory	r. an easy win
______	19. propagate	s. sudden burst of activity
______	20. romp	t. fast; convenient
______	21. scurry	u. nervous or anxious
______	22. spate	v. feverish; energetic
______	23. spontaneous	w. a series of similar events in quick succession
______	24. unabated	x. to move rapidly with quick steps

WEEK 29 DAY 5

Wordsearch

Directions: Using the clues listed below, fill in each blank in the following story with one of the new words you learned this week.

Clues

1st Day

1st Day

4th Day

3rd Day

2nd Day

1st Day

2nd Day

2nd Day

4th Day

3rd Day

2nd Day

3rd Day

3rd Day

Each Citizen's Obligation

The United States has an ___________ problem with administering fair elections. Sometimes the problem is voter apathy—turnout during off-year elections often falls below 50%. Some say the ___________ of political campaigning each election cycle leaves concerned citizens feeling numb. The disillusioned may feel that voting has become a ___________ ritual that makes no difference in their lives. Sadly, this may be a self-fulfilling prophecy.

A ___________ review of the current political landscape reveals the consequences of low turnout. First, some candidates are able to win elections in gerrymandered districts in a ___________, often without being properly vetted. Moreover, since corporate donors rarely allow an opportunity to increase their influence ___________ by, the average citizen's views are not represented.

Decades of ___________ civic rot have led to the ___________ of politicians that no longer respect the people's verdict. When citizens vote en masse, some in power look for ways to cull opposition voters. It begins with a ___________ of fraud claims, which are often ___________ by political hacks and ___________ through social media. Every voting ___________ is then curtailed, and voter rolls are purged with great ___________. The result is, unsurprisingly, low turnout in future elections.

IN DAYS GONE BY

The man who best described the now extinct life aboard a steamer on the Mississippi River is Mark Twain. Having actually worked aboard the river boats, his writing captures both the *amenable* and *raucous* events of those days. In his book about life on the Mississippi, Twain recalls the times when men showed *reciprocal* courtesy. One chapter *extols* the races conducted between the swiftest of the boats. When a race was set, politics and the weather were forgotten, and people talked *effusively* of the coming contest. The two steamers "stripped" and got ready; every encumbrance that might slow the passage was removed. Captains went to extremes to lighten their boats. Twain *lampoons* one captain who scraped the paint from the statue that hung between the chimneys of his steamer.

NEW WORDS

amenable
ə - men - ə - bəl

raucous
rô - kəs

reciprocal
rē - sip - rə - kəl

extol
eks - tōl

effusive
ə - fyū - siv

lampoon
lam - pūn

Notable Roots:
men = lead, threaten;
fus = flow

Sample Sentences: Insert the new words in these sentences.

1. Hollywood studios used to loan out contracted actors through ________________ agreement.
2. Only a megalomaniac enjoys the ________________ praise of sycophants.
3. Boss Tweed is most famous from the Nast cartoons that ________________ him.
4. The prosecutor is ________________ to pleas from cooperative defendants.
5. ________________ block parties are a form of communal urban celebration.
6. Even the Romans ________________ the skill and daring of the Carthaginian general, Hannibal.

Definitions: Match the new words with their meanings.

7.	amenable	________	a.	to ridicule
8.	raucous	________	b.	freely flowing
9.	reciprocal	________	c.	to list virtues or achievements
10.	extol	________	d.	agreeable
11.	effusive	________	e.	boisterous
12.	lampoon	________	f.	mutually beneficial

THE *JOHN J. ROE*

Mark Twain's boat was so slow no other steamer would condescend to race with it. With the utmost *levity*, Twain comments that his boat moved with such *nonchalance*, they used to forget in which year they left port. Twain recounts *droll* anecdotes of ferryboats waiting in consternation for the *John J. Roe* to pass. Mark Twain wrote in a *jocose* manner about the races his steamer had with islands and rafts. Throughout the book, he continues to *facetiously* malign the riverboat, but it's clear he found life on the river a *winsome* experience.

NEW WORDS

levity
lev - ə - tē

nonchalance
non - shə - lons

droll
drōl

jocose
jō - kōs

facetious
fə - sē - shəs

winsome
win - sum

Notable Roots:
lev = light; joc/jov = humor; win = desire

Sample Sentences: Insert the new words in these sentences.

1. Lord Henry's _______________ is a sign of his cynicism.
2. To speak in a _______________ manner in the face of death is known as "gallows humor."
3. Jake was too oblivious to notice the _______________ smile that indicated Mary's interest.
4. Parisian salons were known for the _______________ of the conversation.
5. The _______________ pilot said the flight plan would take the passengers to Mars.
6. Calvin Coolidge would occasionally break his famous reticence to offer up _______________ remarks.

Definitions: Match the new words with their meanings.

7. levity	________	a.	amusing in a witty or dry way
8. nonchalance	________	b.	attractive
9. droll	________	c.	sarcastic regarding serious matters
10. jocose	________	d.	humor; lightness
11. facetious	________	e.	casualness
12. winsome	________	f.	humorous

THE RIVERBOAT PILOT

The riverboat pilot was a man *exalted* above all. Mark Twain was once *jubilant* to have attained that high position. Starting out as apprentice under the *beneficence* of a master pilot, he maintained dreams of the time he would become "the only unfettered and entirely independent human being that lived in the earth." Kings, parliaments, and newspaper editors, Twain comments, are hampered and restricted. The *insouciant* river pilot issued commands with the *impunity* of an absolute monarch. The pilot's skill at avoiding the reefs and sand bars that imperiled a ship made him something of an *iconoclast* with independent authority on the bridge of older, higher ranking captains.

NEW WORDS

exalted
eg - zôl - təd

jubilant
jū - bil - ənt

beneficent
be - nif - is - ənt

insouciant
in - sū - shənt

impunity
im - pyū - nit - ē

iconoclast
ī - kon - ō - klast

Notable Roots: alt = high; jubil = shout; bene = good; puni = punish; clast = destroy

Sample Sentences: Insert the new words in these sentences.

1. Diplomats in foreign lands enjoy a measure of ________________ from local laws.
2. Former presidents typically enjoy the ________________ status of elder statesmen.
3. Marshall McLuhan was the ________________ who first theorized that media forms were more influential than the messages they carry.
4. ________________ Parisians celebrated the end of four years of Nazi occupation.
5. Marie Antoinette's ________________ attitude toward their poverty alienated the French.
6. Many of New York's museums were the gift of wealthy, ________________ private donors.

Definitions: Match the new words with their meanings.

7.	exalted	________	a.	carefree
8.	jubilant	________	b.	one who transcends traditional beliefs
9.	beneficent	________	c.	rejoicing
10.	insouciant	________	d.	immunity from punishment
11.	impunity	________	e.	high in importance
12.	iconoclast	________	f.	kind; generous

THE DOUBLE CROSS

The Mississippi is a boundary between many states; thus, the riverboat, always in motion astride legal jurisdictions, had a certain *venal* atmosphere. While the *philanthropic* and philosophical might book passage, so too did droves of *libertines*. Gamblers, con men, criminals, and those seeking a more *bohemian* lifestyle than nineteenth-century America typically had to offer would often crowd the bar and card tables of a steamship. Many incidents retold by Twain involve cheats fleecing wealthy marks who had only a *facile* understanding of card play. In one case, a particularly *profligate* cardsharp attempted to swindle a gullible-seeming farmer only to lose his shirt when the would-be dupe proved a superior hustler—one who had secretly paid off all of the other players at the table!

NEW WORDS

venal
vēn - əl

philanthropic
fil - ən - throp - ik

libertine
lib - ėr - tēn

bohemian
bō - hēm - ē - ən

facile
fas - əl

profligate
prof - lig - ət

Notable Roots: ven = love; phil = love; anthro = human; facile = easy; flag = strike, swing

Sample Sentences: Insert the new words in these sentences.

1. Greenwich Village is often associated with a ________________ lifestyle.
2. Rather than freedom, an absence of moral restraint denotes a ________________.
3. Late in life, Andrew Carnegie devoted his millions to ________________ work.
4. The police in some countries are so ________________ that they explicitly pull over tourists to extort* bribes.
5. Alaska has claimed the lives of many with only a ________________ grasp of survival skills.
6. Emma Bovary becomes so ________________ in her lifestyle that she ruins her family.

Definitions: Match the new words with their meanings.

7.	venal	________	a.	having a superficial understanding
8.	philanthropic	________	b.	wasteful; immoral
9.	libertine	________	c.	corrupt
10.	bohemian	________	d.	one who acts without regard for morality
11.	facile	________	e.	associated with an artistic lifestyle
12.	profligate	________	f.	generous toward humanity

GROUP REVIEW

Because you are learning these new words in context, they will stay with you. It is the natural method for seeing new words. Your ability to master words as they appear in normal situations should carry over to learning many other words as you read.

Matching

Directions: Match the weekly words with their meanings.

REVIEW WORDS		DEFINITIONS
______	**1.** amenable	**a.** humorous
______	**2.** reciprocal	**b.** boisterous
______	**3.** beneficent	**c.** kind; generous
______	**4.** bohemian	**d.** casualness
______	**5.** droll	**e.** to list virtues or achievements
______	**6.** effusive	**f.** corrupt
______	**7.** exalted	**g.** carefree
______	**8.** extol	**h.** amusing in a witty or dry way
______	**9.** facetious	**i.** one who acts without regard for morality
______	**10.** facile	**j.** sarcastic regarding serious matters
______	**11.** iconoclast	**k.** generous toward humanity
______	**12.** impunity	**l.** wasteful; immoral
______	**13.** insouciant	**m.** immunity from punishment
______	**14.** jocose	**n.** associated with an artistic lifestyle
______	**15.** jubilant	**o.** rejoicing
______	**16.** lampoon	**p.** attractive
______	**17.** levity	**q.** freely flowing
______	**18.** libertine	**r.** one who transcends traditional beliefs
______	**19.** nonchalance	**s.** agreeable
______	**20.** philanthropic	**t.** humor; lightness
______	**21.** profligate	**u.** mutually beneficial
______	**22.** raucous	**v.** having a superficial understanding
______	**23.** venal	**w.** to ridicule
______	**24.** winsome	**x.** high in importance

Wordsearch

Directions: Using the clues listed below, fill in each blank in the following story with one of the new words you learned this week.

Clues

1st Day	1st Day
3rd Day	3rd Day
4th Day	2nd Day
2nd Day	1st Day
3rd Day	4th Day
4th Day	1st Day
3rd Day	

The White City

After the Paris Exposition of 1889 had concluded, visitors to its pavilions ___________ its marvels, particularly the Eiffel Tower, the first man-made edifice to top 1,000 feet. The Paris fair was ___________ as a spectacle not to be equaled within a lifetime. Only an upstart nation like the United States would dare attempt to outdo the ___________ wonders of the world's cultural capital a scant four years later.

Chicago embodied American ___________ in the face of challenges. In 1871, much of the city was consumed by fire, but under determined leadership, it had been rebuilt in under 20 years. In the process, Chicago architects began designing light, steel-framed buildings to "float" on top of the city's notoriously spongy soil. Thus, with typical ___________, Chicago had invented the skyscraper. It's not surprising, then, that in 1890 ___________ and civic-minded city fathers campaigned for the city to host the World's Columbian Exposition, a world's fair to celebrate the 400th anniversary of Christopher Columbus's voyages. When Chicago was chosen over New York, the city was ___________.

Fair President, Daniel Burnham, however, immediately recognized that to outstrip Paris, the fair would have to be a national effort. By nature, an ___________ man, Burnham went to work charming the nation's greatest builders into joining the effort. Frederick Law Olmstead, the ___________ landscape architect who had created New York's Central Park, was given the task of transforming Jackson Park, a forbidding patch of marsh on the lakeshore into a ___________, cultivated setting. The heart of the fair would be the Court of Honor, an artificial harbor overlooked by a statue of the goddess of the American Republic. Surrounding the court were the principal exhibition buildings. These neoclassical structures, set in a landscape of lawns, canals, and bridges, made for an image of astonishing beauty.

The grandeur of Jackson Park was offset by the ___________ atmosphere of the Midway Plaisance, a section devoted to entertainment. For the more ___________ fair goer, there were plenty of concessions offering "liquid refreshment." The most ___________ praise for any exhibition, however, was reserved for an engineering marvel. Chicago's answer to the Eiffel Tower was the brainchild of George Ferris. His wheel was 264 feet tall with a capacity of 2,000 passengers. In a time before aviation, riders could look out over the whole park and marvel at the possibilities of an exciting age.

CHOOSE YOUR SOURCE

Today, there is no *respite* from propaganda. It is not in spite of, but because of, our democratic beliefs that pressure groups are an *intrinsic* feature of our republic. *Steeped* in a culture of personal choice, Americans are not a *homogeneous* mass of humanity. Propaganda is, therefore, an important tool in the *repertoire* of those who wish to influence the course our country takes. It is such an *indigenous* feature of our public discourse that the average person faces both credible and deceptive propaganda efforts continuously without realizing it. While propaganda has the ostensible purpose of informing the public, the most fervid propagandists use methods that must be examined by the thoughtful citizen.

NEW WORDS

respite
res - pət

intrinsic
in - trin - zic

steeped
stēpt

homogeneous
hō - mō - jēn - ē – əs **or**
hə - moj - ən - əs

repertoire
rep - ėr - twär

indigenous
in - dij - ən - əs

Notable Roots:
sic/sec = nature;
homo = same;
gen = created

Sample Sentences: Use care. Some words have more than one meaning.

1. Thermal and electric conductivity are ________________ properties of metals.
2. Regime change theory assumes populations are ________________ in their values and beliefs.
3. Naval warfare was not part of the ________________ of Spartan military strengths.
4. Seasoned fighters will use a knockdown as a brief ________________ to regain energy.
5. The ________________ Maori constitute about one-sixth of New Zealand's population.
6. The Marine Corps is a fighting organization ________________ in tradition.

Definitions: Study the fine differences. Be sure you know how to use these words.

7. respite	________	a.	immersed in
8. intrinsic	________	b.	uniform in composition
9. steeped	________	c.	native population
10. homogeneous	________	d.	an array of skills
11. repertoire	________	e.	a pause or rest
12. indigenous	________	f.	essential to something

A FREE SOCIETY

The right to propagate* ideas and try to win converts is an essential *facet* of a free society. We do not look upon an idea different from ours as an anomaly that should be avoided. Nor do we permit only *mundane* or *tranquil* beliefs and forbid those we believe are spurious *cants*. In a country of competing pressures, there is a *propensity* to feel overwhelmed by a multitude of viewpoints. Some of these are merely seeking to share information, while others aim to *indoctrinate* the fatuous.*

Sample Sentences: Insert the new words in these sentences.

1. Many with the loudest ________________ about morality are hiding their own misdeeds.
2. Some ________________ of a spouse's personality take years to uncover.
3. For the immature, the ________________ is more stressful than the dramatic.
4. Miley Cyrus has a ________________ to stick out her tongue in pictures.
5. The ________________ sea made it hard for the *Titanic*'s lookout to see the iceberg.
6. Advertising uses the power to ________________ for commercial purposes.

Definitions: Match the new words with their meanings.

7.	facet	________	a.	an often hypocritical rant
8.	mundane	________	b.	instill a set of beliefs
9.	tranquil	________	c.	aspect
10.	cant	________	d.	natural tendency
11.	propensity	________	e.	peaceful
12.	indoctrinate	________	f.	ordinary; commonplace

NEW WORDS

facet
fas - ət

mundane
mun - dān

tranquil
trenk - wil

cant
kant

propensity
prō - pen - sət - ē

indoctrinate
in - dok- trin - āt

Notable Roots:
face = face; mond = world; cant = sing; doctrine = formal belief

WHO LISTENS?

The most *rudimentary* forms of propaganda directly tell us who or what to support. Messages are piped right into one's *abode* through television and radio. As such messages become more common, they also become more insistent in order to compete. An *inevitable* result of increased levels of propaganda is that the individual may form an aversion to all attempts to influence her. A more insidious form of propaganda comes from sources that are *nominally* labeled news programs. Yellow journalism has the effect of forming entrenched *cliques* of like-minded people. In this way, extreme ideas can become *tenable* when repeated by one's friends and family.

NEW WORDS

rudimentary
rūd - ə - ment - ə - rē

abode
ə - bōd

inevitable
in - ev - it - ə - bəl

nominal
nom - ə - nəl

clique
klik

tenable
ten - ə - bəl

Notable Roots:
rudi = initial training;
nom = name;
ten = grasp

Sample Sentences: Insert the new words in these sentences.

1. For most of his reign, Henry VI was merely a ________________ ruler.
2. The sea, according to Greek mythology, is Poseidon's ________________.
3. A ________________ baseball principle is to run with a full count and two outs.
4. After the loss of its fleet, Carthage's position on Sicily was no longer ________________.
5. In *Lord of the Flies,* ________________ of boys degenerate into warring parties.
6. Birth becomes ________________ once a pregnant woman's water breaks.

Definitions: Match the new words with their definitions.

7.	rudimentary	________	a.	can be maintained
8.	abode	________	b.	a close-knit group of people
9.	inevitable	________	c.	home
10.	nominal	________	d.	in name only
11.	clique	________	e.	basic
12.	tenable	________	f.	unavoidable

THE PEOPLE DECIDE

In any *extant* authoritarian regime, the role of propaganda is dramatically different. Some dictatorships will allow *inanimate* opposition parties to exist only to be trounced in fraudulent elections and have their talking points discredited by the state-run media. Totalitarian governments won't even allow that much. The *edifice* of government has one voice—that of the *incumbent* leader. Dissenters in such lands are subject to arrest, execution, or long sentences of *menial* labor in work camps. The free expression of ideas is not *compatible* with such a system of state control because allowing any public criticism can precipitate* rebellion. Many historians believe that the Soviet policy of tolerance toward criticism that followed the Chernobyl nuclear disaster presaged the dissolution of the Soviet Union itself.

NEW WORDS

extant
eks - tant

inanimate
in - an - ə - mət

edifice
ed - ə - fəs

incumbent (adj.)
in - kum - bənt

menial
mēn - ē - əl

compatible
kəm - pat - ə - bəl

Notable Roots: anima = alive; fic/fac = make/do; cum = lying down; path = feel

Sample Sentences: Insert the new words in these sentences.

1. The Romanian Parliament Building is one of the most costly ________________ ever built.
2. Most ________________ presidents do manage to win reelection.
3. Gandhi felt that sharing ________________ tasks at the ashram helped foster solidarity.
4. An emotionally ________________ couple tends to stay together more often.
5. Anger at ________________ objects is a sign that a person struggles with frustration.
6. Only about 1% of all species that have ever lived are ________________ right now.

Definitions: Always be cognizant* of the fact that words are used in the paragraphs and sentences with only one meaning. They often have many others. Look up the word *incumbent* for a good example.

7. extant	________	a.	capable of coexistence
8. inanimate	________	b.	describes work that is unskilled
9. edifice	________	c.	not living
10. incumbent	________	d.	a man-made structure
11. menial	________	e.	still in existence
12. compatible	________	f.	currently in power

GROUP REVIEW

Always keep in mind that the context of a word determines its meaning. Used as a noun, a word has a different meaning than when it is used as an adjective or a verb. First, master the words as they appear in the daily stories. Next, work on other meanings.

Matching

Directions: Match the words with their meanings.

REVIEW WORDS		DEFINITIONS	
________	**1.** abode	**a.**	basic
________	**2.** cant	**b.**	an array of skills
________	**3.** clique	**c.**	ordinary; commonplace
________	**4.** compatible	**d.**	can be maintained
________	**5.** edifice	**e.**	essential to something
________	**6.** extant	**f.**	describes work that is unskilled
________	**7.** facet	**g.**	a pause or rest
________	**8.** homogeneous	**h.**	capable of coexistence
________	**9.** inanimate	**i.**	still in existence
________	**10.** incumbent	**j.**	home
________	**11.** indigenous	**k.**	aspect
________	**12.** indoctrinate	**l.**	peaceful
________	**13.** inevitable	**m.**	unavoidable
________	**14.** intrinsic	**n.**	not living
________	**15.** menial	**o.**	instill a set of beliefs
________	**16.** mundane	**p.**	in name only
________	**17.** nominal	**q.**	natural tendency
________	**18.** propensity	**r.**	a close-knit group of people
________	**19.** repertoire	**s.**	a man-made structure
________	**20.** respite	**t.**	native population
________	**21.** rudimentary	**u.**	currently in power
________	**22.** steeped	**v.**	immersed in
________	**23.** tenable	**w.**	uniform in composition
________	**24.** tranquil	**x.**	an often hypocritical rant

Wordsearch

Directions: Using the clues listed below, fill in each blank in the following story with one of the new words you learned this week.

Clues

2nd Day
3rd Day
1st Day
2nd Day
3rd Day
4th Day
3rd Day

Toss Me a Life Line

Humans have a natural ___________ for worrying about fate. It is thus ___________ that people throughout history have been fascinated by those who say they can predict the future. Fortune tellers, with their ___________ of theatrics, continue to attract gullible customers. Horoscopes are examined daily to see if the stars have something to reveal about ___________ matters.

Palm readers believe that a long "lifeline" on the hand means the customer will enjoy longevity. While this hardly appears to be a ___________ way to predict long life, a study done in England measured lifelines of 100 corpses, and their findings were ___________ with the claim: the length of life matched the length of the line.

However, scientists argue that this apparent connection is due to a ___________ case of reverse causality. They say the lifeline of older people is longer only because the hand becomes more wrinkled with age. Length of the line is a consequence of length of life, not the reverse.

Sensible Sentences?

Directions: Underline the word that makes sense in each of the sentences below.

1. A hunting alligator can uncannily resemble an *(incumbent, inanimate)* floating log.
2. There are many antiquated but *(extant, intrinsic)* laws like bans on kissing in public.
3. Henry Tudor's claim to the throne through distant ancestors was barely *(tenable, compatible)*.
4. The houses are so *(homogeneous, indigenous)* that residents sometimes mistake their neighbors' homes for their own.
5. Joe Torre's *(menial, tranquil)* demeanor never betrayed the pressures he faced as manager.
6. LeBron James, a superstar forward, has fewer *(cliques, respites)* than his teammates.
7. Sailors crossing the equator enter the traditional *(abode, edifice)* of King Neptune.
8. Talking about *(nominal, mundane)* daily details is a surprisingly necessary relationship skill.
9. Living abroad, one is *(steeped, indoctrinated)* in a foreign culture.
10. Polonius's famous *(facet, cant)* about public virtue to Laertes belies his scheming nature.

WEEK 32 ☼ DAY 1

Size

ANYONE FOR GOOGLE?

Servers store and search engines *aggregate* an increasingly *prodigious* volume of information. Experts try to help novices separate the *pith* of ideas from the *cavalcade* of trivial details, but society is overwhelmed by a *din* of information. Machines can scan thousands of words in nanoseconds to help expedite* any research. As a result, elementary students know how to extract *caches* of information that would have taken their grandparents an eternity to produce. This wealth of facts, should not, however, be confused with any increase in human wisdom.

aggregate (v.)
ag - grə - gāt

prodigious
prō - di - jəs

pith
pith

cavalcade
kav - əl - kād

din
din

cache
kash

Notable Roots: greg = together; prodigy = omen, wonder; caval = mounted horse

Sample Sentences: Insert your new words below.

1. Even from the other end of a phone, the ________________ of Manhattan is unmistakable.
2. Amundsen left supply ________________ along his route to the South Pole for the return trip.
3. Louis XIV ________________ the French nobility in Versailles to keep an eye on them.
4. The smiling ________________ of Olympic teams belies the fierce competition to come.
5. Lincoln's speeches, though brief, struck the ________________ of a matter resoundingly.
6. Alexander Hamilton's ________________ capacity for work impressed even his foes.

Definitions: Match the new words with their meanings.

7.	aggregate	________	a.	a hidden collection of useful items
8.	prodigious	________	b.	a considerable racket
9.	pith	________	c.	impressive; considerable
10.	cavalcade	________	d.	the heart of something
11.	din	________	e.	gather together
12.	cache	________	f.	a procession

EVERYONE IS TALKING

Can anyone under the age of 40 remember a time when the *monolithic* landline telephone was the only method of voice communication over long distances? What a bizarre concept this must seem for today's youth. It has become a *cumbersome* form of personal contact. The instrument for the modern communicator is the smartphone, which has usurped* the wired model. The cell phone user can have *voluminous* conversations almost anywhere without running up a *colossal* bill. *Augmenting* the virtuosity of the smartphone, text messaging has become an increasingly popular way to send succinct messages without the commitment of a call. Competing wireless carriers offer *comprehensive* data plans for web browsing and app usage.

Did you spot usurp *as a reintroduced word? Without looking back at the New Words, do you recall its meaning?*

Sample Sentences: Insert your new words below.

1. Henry Frick's Manhattan home is now a museum with a ________________ art collection.
2. Prior to the Reformation, European Christianity was a ________________ force.
3. Muhammad Ali's comedic taunting actually ________________ his boxing skills.
4. The Broncos ________________ defeat in Super Bowl XXIV was the worst in history.
5. Nineteenth-century photography was so ________________ that no action could be captured.
6. The ________________ Hercules bomber only flew once and barely got airborne.

Definitions: Match the new words with their meanings.

7.	monolithic	_________	a.	thorough; complete
8.	cumbersome	_________	b.	to increase or expand
9.	voluminous	_________	c.	large and uniform
10.	colossal	_________	d.	awkward; unwieldy
11.	augment	_________	e.	giant-sized
12.	comprehensive	_________	f.	full and extensive

NEW WORDS

monolithic
mon - ō - lith - ik

cumbersome
kum - bėr - sum

voluminous
və - lūm - in - əs

colossal
kə - los - əl

augment
ôg - ment

comprehensive
kom - prē - hen - siv

Notable Roots: mono = one; lith = stone; cumber = obstacle; volume = expanse; hens = grasp

THE FUTURE IS HERE

The invention of the printing press represented a *gargantuan* leap in the proliferation of the written word. Before that, texts were copied by hand. Although possessing a certain *grandeur*, with *ostentatious* calligraphy and illustration, such manuscripts took years to make. Despite the tedious process of typesetting each page in a *mammoth* frame, printing allowed the creation of hundreds of identical pages at a time. The *commodious* typewriter, first mechanical and then electronic, marked the advent* of personal printing capacity. Although an improvement over handwriting, typewriting did not allow for easy revision or correction of mistakes. The personal computer and home printer have finally *amalgamated* the advances in printing that have occurred since the Gutenberg Bible.

NEW WORDS

gargantuan
gär - gan - chū - ən

grandeur
grand - jėr

ostentatious
os - ten - tā - shəs

mammoth
mam - əth

commodious
kə - mōd - ē - əs

amalgamate
ə - mal - gə - māt

Notable Roots:
grand = large, great;
osten = display;
modus = manner

Sample Sentences: Complete the sentences with the new words.

1. The *Titanic*'s first-class cabins were both _______________ and luxurious.
2. Tourists who make an _______________ display of wealth are often robbed.
3. As mounted attacks were suicidal, WWI cavalry units were _______________ with infantry.
4. Completing *Atlas Shrugged* was a _______________ task that took Rand decades.
5. The _______________ Laurentide Ice Sheet was two miles thick and covered all of Canada.
6. The _______________ of the Spit Head naval review of 1897 during Queen Victoria's 60th jubilee symbolized the apex of British power.

Definitions: Match the new words with their meanings.

7. gargantuan	_______	a.	showy
8. grandeur	_______	b.	to fuse together
9. ostentatious	_______	c.	impressively large
10. mammoth	_______	d.	bulky, roomy
11. commodious	_______	e.	impressive splendor
12. amalgamate	_______	f.	gigantic

IT'S HAPPENING NOW

The *cumulative* pace of telecommunications technology development proceeds at such a regular pace that new breakthroughs are a mundane occurrence. Don't underestimate the power of *swank*, however: advertising has the effect of *aggrandizing* every new technological marvel. Fans of the most popular smartphone find themselves *engrossed* by the latest rumors of the next model. And yet the *bulwark* never holds; the newest gadget is always *subsumed* by a flood of new features, and the FOMO effect drives customers to pick up the newest toy.

Sample Sentences: Use the new words in these sentences.

1. Dylan was so ________________ in the novel that he missed the bus.
2. Wall Street is named for a ________________ built by the Dutch to protect New Amsterdam.
3. The Flamingo was the first ________________ casino built in Las Vegas.
4. The revolution in Paris was quickly ________________ into a nationwide movement.
5. Ethics forbid using one's office to ________________ one's private interests.
6. The general succumbed to the ________________ effects of his many wounds.

Definitions: Match the new words with their meanings.

7. cumulative	_________	a.	increase the power of something
8. swank	_________	b.	absorbed
9. aggrandize	_________	c.	include or absorb in something else
10. engrossed	_________	d.	a defensive barrier
11. bulwark	_________	e.	overall
12. subsume	_________	f.	fancy and luxurious

NEW WORDS

cumulative
kūm - yū - lə - tiv

swank
swenk

aggrandize
ə - gran - dīz

engrossed
ən - grōsd

bulwark
bul - wärk

subsume
sub - sūm

Notable Roots: cumul = heap; grand = large, great; gross = large; sume = take, obtain

GROUP REVIEW

When you can analyze a sentence and determine from the context the meaning of a previously unknown word, you are functioning at the best level. These words will become a permanent part of your ever-growing vocabulary.

Matching

Directions: Match the words you learned this week with their meanings.

REVIEW WORDS		DEFINITIONS
_______	**1.** aggrandize	**a.** the heart of something
_______	**2.** aggregate	**b.** a procession
_______	**3.** amalgamate	**c.** impressive splendor
_______	**4.** augment	**d.** large and uniform
_______	**5.** bulwark	**e.** include or absorb in something else
_______	**6.** cache	**f.** giant-sized
_______	**7.** cavalcade	**g.** fancy and luxurious
_______	**8.** colossal	**h.** a considerable racket
_______	**9.** commodious	**i.** thorough; complete
_______	**10.** comprehensive	**j.** bulky, roomy
_______	**11.** cumbersome	**k.** a hidden collection of useful items
_______	**12.** cumulative	**l.** impressively large
_______	**13.** din	**m.** impressive; considerable
_______	**14.** engrossed	**n.** absorbed
_______	**15.** gargantuan	**o.** gather together
_______	**16.** grandeur	**p.** a defensive barrier
_______	**17.** mammoth	**q.** to fuse together
_______	**18.** monolithic	**r.** increase the power of something
_______	**19.** ostentatious	**s.** full and extensive
_______	**20.** pith	**t.** gigantic
_______	**21.** prodigious	**u.** overall
_______	**22.** subsume	**v.** awkward; unwieldy
_______	**23.** swank	**w.** to increase or expand
_______	**24.** voluminous	**x.** showy

Antonyms Attract

Directions: Here are 15 words taken from the last four weeks of study. Select and underline the correct antonym for each.

1. beneficent *(malevolent, impudent)*
2. cursory *(thorough, swift)*
3. swank *(sumptuous, measly)*
4. tenable *(feasible, indefensible)*
5. scurry *(plod, ponder)*
6. mundane *(menial, extraordinary)*
7. aggregate *(hoard, scatter)*
8. mammoth *(bestial, diminutive)*
9. effusive *(taciturn, saturnine)*
10. frenetic *(phlegmatic, diabolical)*
11. prodigal *(generous, frugal)*
12. winsome *(hapless, boorish)*
13. augment *(diminish, verify)*
14. alacrity *(reluctance, ambition)*
15. homogeneous *(motley, bland)*

Wordsearch

Directions: Using the clues listed below, fill in each blank in the following story with one of the new words you learned this week.

Clues

1st Day

2nd Day

2nd Day

1st Day

4th Day

A Formidable Opponent

One of the most interesting tests of a computer's ability to "think" occurred in 1992. The world's chess champion, a man of ___________ mental ability in this game, was challenged to compete against the most powerful computer programmed to play chess. The question was: could a ___________ machine usurp* a human's place as the best chess player in the world?

The match took place before hundreds of chess enthusiasts and was recorded on film. While the computer lacked the champion's experience and emotional capacity, it worked with such a ___________ memory that it could search ahead for many thousands of choices, well beyond what any human could envision. In fact, the computer had already defeated a ___________ of chess masters in preparation for the contest.

The world was ___________ in the drama of the man vs. machine contest. The result temporarily vindicated human self-esteem: the champion won fairly easily. However, there was almost total agreement that it was only a matter of time before we had an electronic chess champion, one incapable of making a blunder. By the late 1990s, computers were regularly defeating humans in chess world championship matches.

AT A LOSS

With the *paltry* sum of $10 in his pockets, Robert Lacy worried about his *waning* fortunes. No matter how frugal he was, his *negligible* funds would run out before the next day. Never *remiss* in his responsibilities, he owed $5 in debts to friends. Hunger would *vitiate* him to the point where he could not continue his search for Evelyn. There was always the *spurious* hope that a stranger would help him with money, but that still wouldn't help him find her.

NEW WORDS

paltry
päl - trē

wane
wān

negligible
neg - lij - ə - bəl

remiss
rē - mis

vitiate
vish - ē - āt

spurious
spyur - ē - əs

Notable Roots:
neg = not; leg = select; vice = fault

Sample Sentences: Use the new words in these sentences.

1. Jefferson argues that a government _______________ in its duties should be changed.
2. Tyson's punching power was _______________ by age and inactivity.
3. Megan earned _______________ wages working for a nonprofit organization.
4. It is wise to delete all _______________ emails that appear to be from financial institutions.
5. At slow speeds, wind resistance usually has a _______________ effect.
6. After failing a second time to sack Vienna, Ottoman power began to _______________.

Definitions: Match the new words with their meanings.

7. paltry ________ a. to weaken or spoil
8. wane ________ b. small enough to be ignored
9. negligible ________ c. very small
10. remiss ________ d. illegitimate
11. vitiate ________ e. to decline
12. spurious ________ f. derelict in one's duties

MAKING PLANS

Robert had arrived in New York a week earlier. He had begun by asking *innocuous* questions of Evelyn's former landlord. The landlord was *fatalistic*, and all Robert had been able to glean from the *sporadic* replies was that Evelyn had moved to a residence that catered to single women. Robert was in a hopeless situation; in this immense city, his quarry could, *hypothetically*, be hiding in one of dozens of such places. If he searched randomly, he would be *susceptible* to wasting time. He needed to *curtail* such a haphazard strategy and form a plan.

Sample Sentences: Use the new words in these sentences.

1. Countries that lack natural defenses are more ________________ to invasion.
2. Opportunistic infections are caused by germs that are normally ________________.
3. ________________ examples do little to support a term paper.
4. The artillery bombardment was too ________________ to do any real damage.
5. New penalties have been proposed to help ________________ excessive celebration.
6. The CEO was ________________ about the prospects of the proposed plan.

Definitions: Match the new words with their meanings.

7. innocuous	________	a.	occurring irregularly
8. fatalistic	________	b.	based on a hypothesis
9. sporadic	________	c.	harmless
10. hypothetical	________	d.	to stop; to cut short
11. susceptible	________	e.	doubtful; pessimistic
12. curtail	________	f.	vulnerable

NEW WORDS

innocuous
ən - ok - yū - əs

fatalistic
fā - təl - is - tik

sporadic
spôr - ad - ik

hypothetical
hī - pō - thet - ik - əl

susceptible
sə - sep - tə - bəl

curtail
kur - tāl

Notable Roots:
spora = scatter;
hypo = under;
thesis = condition

A NEWSPAPER AD

Robert held out an *intangible* hope: Evelyn knew she was being sought, so he decided to *desist* in fruitless searching and place an ad in the leading morning newspaper. He would offer a careful, *attenuated* plea for her return. The ad read, "Evelyn. Come out of hiding. I do not reproach you for *jilting* me. I expect no *ersatz* confession. Please contact. Robert." When Robert went to the paper the next morning, there was a letter for him, and with *enervated* fingers he tore it open. It contained one sentence: "If you really care about me, you will find me by midnight, Friday. Evelyn."

NEW WORDS

intangible
in - tan - jə - bəl

desist
dē - sist

attenuate
ə - ten - yū - āt

jilt
jilt

ersatz
ėr - zatz

enervate
en - ėr - vāt

Notable Roots:
tang = touch;
sist = stop; ten = grasp, stretch

Sample Sentences: Insert the new words in these sentences.

1. As the shortages worsened, _______________ products like salt and sugar substitutes proliferated.
2. Miss Havisham became embittered after she was _______________ by her fiancé.
3. Sound walls can _______________ the noise produced by major highways.
4. Montana, _______________ by his bout with the flu, wasn't sharp in the playoff loss.
5. Cody's father sent him to his room when he didn't _______________ playing with his food.
6. Momentum is one of the most powerful, yet _______________, factors in sports.

Definitions: Match the new words with their meanings.

7.	intangible	________	**a.**	to abandon
8.	desist	________	**b.**	to weaken
9.	attenuate	________	**c.**	fake; imitation
10.	jilt	________	**d.**	to stop doing something
11.	ersatz	________	**e.**	to lessen the effect of
12.	enervate	________	**f.**	difficult to perceive; abstract

AT THE BALLET

Seeking a *cessation* of their estrangement, Robert thought hard. Evelyn *eschewed* predictability: she had a propensity* for folk music and rock and, at the same time, was an avid* fan of classical ballet. At one time, she had been a fledgling* ballet dancer until a car accident left her *supine* for months. With the *encumbrance* of a leg brace, Evelyn *regressed* as a dancer. Robert headed for a theater where a venerable* ballet company was performing. Only three more days remained before the deadline set by Evelyn. And so, although he considered ballet to be *vapid* entertainment, he joined the throng in the lobby hoping to see her.

NEW WORDS

cessation
sə - sā - shən

eschew
əs - chū

supine
sū - pīn

encumbrance
ən - kum - brəns

regress
rē - gres

vapid
vap - id

Notable Roots: cease = stop; cumulu = heap; gress = go

Sample Sentences: Insert the new words in these sentences.

1. The ________________ of their kit slowed the progress of the infantry.
2. Dementia is evident when a patient ________________ in simple tasks.
3. Donald Trump often ________________ formal speeches, preferring to improvise.
4. The ________________ victim was found face-down in an overgrown field.
5. The superb cast could not overcome the ________________ dialogue they were given.
6. An armistice simply entails a ________________ of hostilities—not lasting peace.

Definitions: Match the new words with their meanings.

7.	cessation	________	a.	lacking in interest
8.	eschew	________	b.	burden
9.	supine	________	c.	to decline in ability or maturity
10.	encumbrance	________	d.	lying down
11.	regress	________	e.	a full stop
12.	vapid	________	f.	to avoid

GROUP REVIEW

While each day's story has six new words, there are many others that are repeated from previous weeks. Repetition will help guarantee that these words will be firmly fixed as part of your ever-expanding vocabulary.

Matching

Directions: Match this week's words with their meanings.

	REVIEW WORDS		DEFINITIONS
______	**1.** attenuate	**a.**	to stop doing something
______	**2.** cessation	**b.**	to decline
______	**3.** curtail	**c.**	vulnerable
______	**4.** desist	**d.**	to weaken
______	**5.** encumbrance	**e.**	very small
______	**6.** enervate	**f.**	to avoid
______	**7.** ersatz	**g.**	lacking in interest
______	**8.** eschew	**h.**	derelict in one's duties
______	**9.** fatalistic	**i.**	to abandon
______	**10.** hypothetical	**j.**	illegitimate
______	**11.** innocuous	**k.**	based on a hypothesis
______	**12.** intangible	**l.**	fake; imitation
______	**13.** jilt	**m.**	lying down
______	**14.** negligible	**n.**	to weaken or spoil
______	**15.** paltry	**o.**	occurring irregularly
______	**16.** regress	**p.**	to lessen the effect of
______	**17.** remiss	**q.**	a full stop
______	**18.** sporadic	**r.**	to stop; to cut short
______	**19.** spurious	**s.**	burden
______	**20.** supine	**t.**	doubtful; pessimistic
______	**21.** susceptible	**u.**	to decline in ability or maturity
______	**22.** vapid	**v.**	harmless
______	**23.** vitiate	**w.**	small enough to be ignored
______	**24.** wane	**x.**	difficult to perceive; abstract

Wordsearch

Directions: Using the clues listed below, fill in each blank in the following story with one of the new words you learned this week.

Clues

3rd Day

4th Day

2nd Day

3rd Day

2nd Day

Good Enough to Eat?

There seems to be universal agreement that exposure to the ultraviolet light from the sun is deleterious* to one's health. Also, except for tobacco industry spokesmen, there is no dispute about the damage done to us from cigarette smoke. What is shocking is the fact that almost everything we once regarded as either beneficial or harmless soon gets challenged by scientists. We are urged to ___________ foods that have high fat content. There go butter and cheese. Even milk has now been added to the list of foods that we must ___________.

Whatever diet we are on, we must eventually become ___________ about its nutritional value. We are left, ultimately, with the depressing thought that, sooner or later, almost everything we eat or drink may be found to ___________ human health.

Given that there are many obstacles to maintaining good health, would it be wise to embrace every new laboratory report? Let's not ___________ old, proven, sensible food habits. Also, there is always the possibility that ice cream sundaes will be found to cure baldness and that chocolate chip cookies will eliminate our cholesterol problems.

May I Borrow That Expression?

English is constantly absorbing expressions from foreign languages and neologisms from culture. Take the German expression *zeitgeist*: the root *zeit* means time, and *geist* means spirit. The expression was adopted as a pithy way of referring to the ethos of a historical era.

Directions: Below are 20 words that have been adopted. Match each with its meaning and back story.

REVIEW WORDS		ORIGINS
________	**1.** ersatz	**a.** the verb *I believe* in Latin
________	**2.** aficionado	**b.** the Roman temple dedicated to all gods
________	**3.** supine	**c.** the French expression for *easy*
________	**4.** nuance	**d.** formed from the French verb *to hide*
________	**5.** clique	**e.** Latin word formed from two religious root words
________	**6.** grandeur	**f.** a Sanskrit word roughly referring to escape from life's suffering
________	**7.** cache	**g.** French verb *to cut*; also refers to illegal seizures of power
________	**8.** cognizance	**h.** a Spanish term referring to a devoted expert of a pursuit
________	**9.** credo	**i.** name of a rancher who lost cattle by not branding them
________	**10.** stoic	**j.** the German word for *replacement*
________	**11.** tantalize	**k.** French term for a fortified tower
________	**12.** reverie	**l.** from the Greek figure *Tantalus*, doomed to stand in water he cannot drink
________	**13.** bastion	**m.** means *middle place* in French
________	**14.** milieu	**n.** French noun meaning *greatness*
________	**15.** sacrosanct	**o.** Greek philosophers who did not show emotions
________	**16.** pantheon	**p.** from Latin verb *to know* by way of French word for *awareness*
________	**17.** coup	**q.** French expression for a subtle distinction
________	**18.** maverick	**r.** a noun formed from the French word for *dream*
________	**19.** nirvana	**s.** the Latin word that refers to lying down
________	**20.** facile	**t.** in French it refers to a door closing (on a secret meeting)

ANOTHER PLAN

Robert *bristled* as he waited in the lobby for almost an hour after the performance had begun. His *somber* appearance stood out as he attracted several stares. *Disgruntled*, he quit the site of his vigil. He had to face the *doleful* truth that he was making no tangible progress. Tomorrow he would telephone several apartment buildings. It was an *ineffectual* way of going about his search, but it was all that he could think of at the moment. He had no *qualms* about interrogating desk clerks, and perhaps he might uncover a pertinent clue to Evelyn's whereabouts.

NEW WORDS

bristle
bris - əl

somber
som - bėr

disgruntled
dis - grun - təld

doleful
dōl - fəl

ineffectual
in - əf - ek - shū - əl

qualms
kwâlmz

Notable Roots: sombre = shade; dole = sad; fac = make/do

Sample Sentences: Insert the new words in these sentences.

1. *Music for the Funeral of Queen Mary* is one of the most ____________ pieces ever written.
2. Before the mutiny, Captain Anderson was oblivious to the ____________ state of his crew.
3. Many voters ________________ at the offensive rhetoric of some politicians.
4. While brilliant, Dr. Trask was an ________________ disciplinarian with a chaotic class.
5. No one knows why minor chords have a more ________________ sound.
6. During Prohibition, few had any ________________ about drinking illegal liquor.

Definitions: Match the new words with their meanings.

7.	bristle	________	a.	not producing a desired effect
8.	somber	________	b.	full of sadness
9.	disgruntled	________	c.	react with anger
10.	doleful	________	d.	sober or serious
11.	ineffectual	________	e.	misgivings
12.	qualms	________	f.	visibly disappointed

A HOPE DASHED

The next day, Wednesday, saw Robert become more *fraught*. He would fluctuate between high hopes of finding Evelyn and *foreboding*. The phone calls had elicited almost nothing. A *neurotic* wreck, Robert had rushed to one residence when the clerk described a girl who might just be Evelyn. Robert waited in the lobby on a drab and *forlorn*-looking sofa. He watched from a discreet* distance as she came down the stairs. One look at her *sullen* face and *disheveled* hair and Robert knew it was not his impeccable Evelyn.

NEW WORDS

fraught
frôt

foreboding
fôr - bōd - ing

neurotic
nə - rot - ik

forlorn
fôr - lôrn

sullen
sul - ən

disheveled
də - shev - əld

Notable Roots:
bode = signal, message; neuro = nerve; lorn = lost; chevel = hair

Sample Sentences: Insert the new words in these sentences.

1. It's long been said that the intelligent are less happy and more ________________.
2. The two teens could not hide their ________________ appearance from their parents.
3. Rounding Cape Horn has always been ________________ with danger.
4. Few in Vienna paid much mind to the ________________ young Hitler.
5. Longstreet's sense of ________________ could not stop the doomed Pickett's Charge.
6. The ________________ kitten in the rain evoked pity in Mr. Shen, who took it in.

Definitions: Match the new words with their meanings.

7.	fraught	________	a.	seemingly doomed
8.	foreboding	________	b.	carelessly groomed
9.	neurotic	________	c.	grumpy or moody
10.	forlorn	________	d.	imperiled
11.	sullen	________	e.	unusually sensitive or anxious
12.	disheveled	________	f.	dejected; unloved

WEEK 34 DAY 3

TO THE POLICE

Robert felt utterly *hapless*. Thursday was his penultimate day; he had followed up every lead to no avail. Now he felt *lachrymose* and was in *deplorable* physical condition. In desperation, he turned to the police. They asked many questions and requested that he not leave anything out, although some of their queries seemed *inane*. When they inquired about his relationship to the missing girl, he replied with a grimace, "Fiancé." It was an *ignominious* admission: the woman he loved had jilted* him in a fit of *ennui*. He bristled* when they suggested she might be hiding in a part of the city known for low characters, but he had to admit that searching everywhere else had proven fruitless.*

NEW WORDS

hapless
hap - ləs

lachrymose
lak - rə - mōs

deplorable
də - plôr - ə - bəl

inane
in - ān

ignominious
ig - nō - min - ē - əs

ennui
ən - wē

Notable Roots: hap = luck; lagrima = cry; plore = cry, rain; ig = ill; nomen = name

Sample Sentences: Insert the new words in these sentences.

1. Bettors wager on which player will earn the ________________ distinction of last selection in the NFL Draft.
2. ________________ is typically the complaint of intellectuals, artists, and wealthy heirs.
3. Serena Williams once defeated an opponent so ________________ she failed to win a game.
4. After imbibing their share of rum, the old sailors sang ________________ sea shanties.
5. The Sanitary Commission fought against ________________ Civil War camp conditions.
6. Ron's ________________ chatter repelled many a would-be companion.

Definitions: Match the new words with their meanings.

7.	hapless	________	a.	disgraceful
8.	lachrymose	________	b.	silly
9.	deplorable	________	c.	listless boredom
10.	inane	________	d.	in terrible condition
11.	ignominious	________	e.	unlucky
12.	ennui	________	f.	tearful

EVELYN DISCOVERED

Robert was hopeless: his mind veered toward *macabre* visions involving her grisly demise at the hands of the *dregs* of the urban populace. What if some *nonentity* with a gun or knife attacked her? He steadied himself; it was now Friday. An impulse brought him to an unfamiliar, decrepit section of the city. Always fastidious* about proper dress and behavior, he felt like an *interloper*. A moment later, he saw her! Evelyn! She was *bedraggled*, sitting at a table in a coffee shop, surrounded by the most noisome* individuals he had ever seen. So this was her milieu*! At that instant, Robert knew he had lost her. He walked away, a *melancholy* figure with his head down.

NEW WORDS

macabre
mə - kob - rə

dregs
dregz

nonentity
non - en - tit - ē

interloper
in - tėr - lōp - ėr

bedraggled
bē - drag - əld

melancholy
mel - ən - kol - ē

Notable Roots: inter = between; lope = leap; choler = rage

Sample Sentences: Insert the new words in these sentences.

1. In a small town, an _______________ feels most out place.
2. President Garfield was shot by a _______________ who demanded a diplomatic post.
3. The _______________ acts of the real Vlad Dracula have redounded through the ages.
4. Depression is more than mere _______________; it is a form of emotional paralysis.
5. The lawless Western Frontier attracted the _______________ of Eastern society.
6. George Bailey surmises from Mr. Gower's _______________ appearance that he has suffered a terrible blow.

Definitions: Match the new words with their meanings.

7. macabre	________	**a.**	abiding sadness
8. dregs	________	**b.**	dirty and messy in appearance
9. nonentity	________	**c.**	an outsider or meddler
10. interloper	________	**d.**	the most worthless part of something
11. bedraggled	________	**e.**	related to death or horror
12. melancholy	________	**f.**	a person with no notable qualities

GROUP REVIEW

Learning by context is the most natural and effective way. However, there is work and self-discipline, too. Keep at it!

Matching

Direction: Match the new words you learned this week with their meanings.

REVIEW WORDS		DEFINITIONS
________	**1.** bedraggled	**a.** in terrible condition
________	**2.** bristle	**b.** sober or serious
________	**3.** deplorable	**c.** grumpy or moody
________	**4.** disgruntled	**d.** visibly disappointed
________	**5.** disheveled	**e.** silly
________	**6.** doleful	**f.** dirty and messy in appearance
________	**7.** dregs	**g.** carelessly groomed
________	**8.** ennui	**h.** listless boredom
________	**9.** foreboding	**i.** the most worthless part of something
________	**10.** forlorn	**j.** unusually sensitive or anxious
________	**11.** fraught	**k.** abiding sadness
________	**12.** hapless	**l.** a person with no notable qualities
________	**13.** ignominious	**m.** misgivings
________	**14.** inane	**n.** imperiled
________	**15.** ineffectual	**o.** an outsider or meddler
________	**16.** interloper	**p.** not producing a desired effect
________	**17.** lachrymose	**q.** disgraceful
________	**18.** macabre	**r.** react with anger
________	**19.** melancholy	**s.** seemingly doomed
________	**20.** neurotic	**t.** unlucky
________	**21.** nonentity	**u.** dejected; unloved
________	**22.** qualms	**v.** related to death or horror
________	**23.** somber	**w.** full of sadness
________	**24.** sullen	**x.** tearful

Wordsearch

Directions: Using the clues listed below, fill in each blank in the following story with one of the new words you learned this week.

Clues

2nd Day

3rd Day

3rd Day

1st Day

3rd Day

3rd Day

4th Day

1st Day

Women in the Ring

Boxing, as well as Ultimate Fighting and wrestling, has become a sport popular with men and women. Once viewed as a pursuit ___________ with brutality, boxing has been transformed in gymnasiums across the country into the latest form of workout, weight reduction, and energy stimulator.

In the twenty-first century, women have proven themselves to be adept* soldiers, serving in military organizations the world over. Given that they have stood up to the rigors of combat, the suggestion that women should not expose themselves to the blows of boxing is ___________ at best and ___________ sexist at worst. Certainly, the women of the professional boxing circuit, like Ronda Rousey and Laila Ali, ___________ at the notion that fighting is too dangerous for them.

The tennis world well remembers when the ___________ Bobby Riggs met with ___________ defeat at the hands of Billie Jean King. Women have made a name for themselves in other sports, like horse-racing and NASCAR, where Danica Patrick has proven herself no mere ___________. Given these welcome advances in equality, society should have no ___________ about tough and highly trained female pugilists entering the brass ring.

WEEK 35 DAY 1

A MODERN AESOP

The telling of a *pithy* story with an inherently important message is an art form. The *parable* may be found teaching a moral lesson in the Bible. Aesop is the undisputed master of the fable. This story form has revived under the modern Aesop, James Thurber. His *concise* tales lampoon* the strange behavior of his fellow men. Thurber seems *flabbergasted* by the notions that permeate our society. He is most *skeptical* of sanctimonious* *paeans* and the inevitability of good triumphing over evil.

NEW WORDS

pithy
pith - ē

parable
pa - rə - bəl

concise
kən - sīs

flabbergasted
flab - ėr - gas - təd

skeptical
skep - tik - əl

paean
pē - ən

Notable Roots: pith = core; con = together; cis = cut

Sample Sentences: Note that some words do not have a one-word definition. Frequently, several words or an entire sentence is required.

1. George III was _______________ when he learned Washington resigned his commission.
2. Gordon Gekko's _______________ to greed reverberates* in business culture to this day.
3. The letter from Princeton was so _______________ Tyler already knew it was a rejection.
4. The _______________ of the Good Samaritan is one of the most famous of Jesus's teachings.
5. An investment banker's job requires being _______________ of far-fetched business ideas.
6. Boss Murphy spoke in _______________ epithets; his protege, Al Smith, gave speeches.

Definitions: Match 'em up!

7. pithy	________	**a.**	long-winded praise
8. parable	________	**b.**	using an economy of words
9. concise	________	**c.**	astonished
10. flabbergasted	________	**d.**	expressive in few words
11. skeptical	________	**e.**	dubious
12. paean	________	**f.**	a fable

MODERNIZING A PARABLE*

Thurber punctures the *sophistry* accepted by everyone. In one tale, a tortoise beats a hare in a race. The *laconic* old tortoise hunted for a hare and soon found one. "Do you have the effrontery to challenge me?" asked the hare *demurely*. "You are a nonentity,*" *averred* the tortoise. A course of 50 feet was set out. The other animals created a *clamor* with their excitement. At the sound of the gun, they were off. When the hare crossed the finish line, the flabbergasted* tortoise had gone approximately eight and three-quarter inches. The moral Thurber draws from this debacle is a *curt* one: a new broom may sweep clean, but never trust an old saw.

NEW WORDS

sophistry
sof - əs - trē

laconic
lə - kon - ik

demure
də - myur

aver
ə - ver

clamor
klam - ər

curt
kėrt

Notable Roots: soph = wisdom; ver = truth; clamo = cry out

Sample Sentences: Insert the new words in these sentences.

1. Brett's sullen mood and ________________ replies didn't endear him to his hosts.
2. The ________________ surrounding the president's announcement was unfounded.
3. Roosevelt ________________ he would not run for president again and instantly regretted it.
4. Card sharks know that when a novice seems ________________, he has a good hand.
5. Wallach's gritty "Tuco" earns the respect of the ________________ "man with no name."
6. No amount of ________________ or clever phrases can save Little Finger from justice.

Definitions: Match the new words with their meanings.

7. sophistry	________	a.	modest; unassuming
8. laconic	________	b.	to openly declare
9. demure	________	c.	the use of language to deceive or impress
10. aver	________	d.	not talkative
11. clamor	________	e.	short to the point of rudeness
12. curt	________	f.	uproar

WEEK 35 ⚙ DAY 3

THINGS HAVE CHANGED

Thurber modernizes a story most children know *verbatim*. It begins in the forest with a *dissembling* wolf engaging in conversation with a little girl traveling to her grandmother's cottage. With alacrity,* this *loquacious* youngster told the wolf the address to which she was going. The hungry wolf rushed to the house. When the girl arrived and entered, she saw a figure dressed like her grandmother. She quickly surmised* that it didn't look like her grandmother. The girl greeted her hairy "grandma"; from the wolf's *utterance* of reply and *garbled* speech, the girl became cognizant* of the wolf's deception. Thurber *explicates* his moral: it is not so easy to fool little girls nowadays.

NEW WORDS

verbatim
vėr - bā - tim

dissemble
dis - em - bəl

loquacious
lō - kwā - shəs

utterance
ut - ėr - əns

garble
gär - bəl

explicate
eks - plik - āt

Notable Roots:
verb = word; semble = appearance; loq = talk; plik = fold

Sample Sentences: Insert the new words in these sentences.

1. With his every ____________, Iago sought to play on Othello's jealousy.
2. When the suspects' stories matched _____________, Detective Diaz suspected collusion.
3. Messages over the first transatlantic cable came through hopelessly _____________.
4. Incredibly, it took centuries for physicists to ____________ why night is dark.
5. To Shakespeare, few villains are capable of ____________ to the point that corruption will not show on their faces.
6. Propaganda posters warned that a single ____________ soldier could doom the mission.

Definitions: Match the new words with their meanings.

7.	verbatim	________	a.	to hide one's thoughts or feelings
8.	dissemble	________	b.	distort the sound of something
9.	loquacious	________	c.	to explain in detail
10.	utterance	________	d.	word for word
11.	garble	________	e.	short spoken word or sound
12.	explicate	________	f.	talkative

ANOTHER SURPRISE

Thurber's stories read like the tales of a *garrulous* storyteller without being *verbose*. At the same time, they hint at some *ineffable* truths. He tells of some builders who left a pane of glass standing upright at their work site. A hapless* goldfinch then strikes the glass. He rushes back and *divulges* to his friends that the air had crystallized. The only bird who believes him is the swallow. The other birds deride* him for his *gaffe*. The goldfinch challenges them to follow the same path he had flown: only the swallow demurs. The large bird strikes the glass and is knocked into a stupor. Thurber *tersely* observes that he who hesitates is sometimes saved.

NEW WORDS

garrulous
gar - ə - ləs

verbose
vėr - bōs

ineffable
in - ef - ə - bəl

divulge
dī - vulj

gaffe
gaf

terse
tėrs

Notable Roots:
verb = word; di = apart; vulg = common

Sample Sentences: Insert the new words in these sentences.

1. Throughout his career, President Biden has been prone to verbal ________________.
2. Many call Edward Snowden a hero, others a traitor, for ____________ classified information.
3. Music and visual arts are ways of communicating what is ________________ in words.
4. The ________________ Rickey Henderson was one of the most quotable athletes of his era.
5. It is perfectly normal to give ________________ replies while concentrating.
6. Critics consider Roger Waters's later work with Pink Floyd too________________ for music.

Definitions: Match the new words with their meanings.

7. garrulous	________	a. wordy
8. verbose	________	b. employing few words
9. ineffable	________	c. a mistake (often spoken)
10. divulge	________	d. chatty
11. gaffe	________	e. to reveal often sensitive information
12. terse	________	f. cannot be expressed

GROUP REVIEW

To strengthen your word power, keep adding words from all the sources you use during the day. Textbooks, news articles, and the like should all give you the opportunity to augment* the work you're doing in this book. Guess the meaning of unknown words before looking them up.

Matching

Directions: Match the weekly words with their meanings.

	REVIEW WORDS		DEFINITIONS
________	**1.** aver	**a.**	talkative
________	**2.** clamor	**b.**	astonished
________	**3.** concise	**c.**	using an economy of words
________	**4.** curt	**d.**	expressive in few words
________	**5.** demure	**e.**	to explain in detail
________	**6.** dissemble	**f.**	short spoken word or sound
________	**7.** divulge	**g.**	a fable
________	**8.** explicate	**h.**	chatty
________	**9.** flabbergasted	**i.**	cannot be expressed
________	**10.** gaffe	**j.**	a mistake (often spoken)
________	**11.** garble	**k.**	to reveal often sensitive information
________	**12.** garrulous	**l.**	not talkative
________	**13.** ineffable	**m.**	uproar
________	**14.** laconic	**n.**	long-winded praise
________	**15.** loquacious	**o.**	wordy
________	**16.** paean	**p.**	to openly declare
________	**17.** parable	**q.**	modest; unassuming
________	**18.** pithy	**r.**	distort the sound of something
________	**19.** skeptical	**s.**	dubious
________	**20.** sophistry	**t.**	short to the point of rudeness
________	**21.** terse	**u.**	word for word
________	**22.** utterance	**v.**	employing few words
________	**23.** verbatim	**w.**	to hide one's thoughts or feelings
________	**24.** verbose	**x.**	the use of language to deceive or impress

Wordsearch

Directions: Using the clues listed below, fill in each blank in the following story with one of the new words you learned this week.

Clues

1st Day	2nd Day
3rd Day	1st Day
2nd Day	1st Day
2nd Day	3rd Day
3rd Day	4th Day
3rd Day	4th Day

Latin Lives!

Everyone knows the _____________ truism that Latin is a "dead language." If so, exactly when and how did it die? _____________ the answer to these questions is no mean feat. From the outset, let's_____________ a few facts. The language of the ancient Romans was spoken throughout much of Europe from the third century BCE when Rome completed the conquest of Italy to the fifth century CE when the Western Roman Empire was overthrown by those surly and _____________ Goths. At Rome's height, Latin was the *lingua franca* of its day: non-Romans used its _____________ as a way to communicate with Romans and other foreigners in matters of business and diplomacy.

Some _____________ philosopher might argue that Latin simply died of old age alongside the empire, but there are problems with this piece of _____________. First, Latin remains the official language of the Catholic Church. Vatican City retains Latin as its official language, and the Pope's encyclicals—_____________ on spiritual matters–are written in Latin. Second, other ancient languages are still spoken today. China has existed for millennia, and the Chinese would be _____________ if they heard Mandarin or Cantonese pronounced as "dead" simply because no one speaks like the courtiers of Emperor Qin anymore. Other ancient languages have also managed to survive the fall of their parent cultures: Egyptian hieroglyphics were deciphered because a variant of ancient Egyptian is still spoken by the country's Coptic minority.

In truth, Latin's death has been greatly exaggerated. Try this: look up a video of someone speaking English as it sounded 1,000 years ago. That once-standard form of English has become so _____________ by accumulated changes in spelling, grammar, and pronunciation that it is no more intelligible to the untrained American or British ear than Swahili or Aramaic. The language of the Romans has simply morphed into Romance languages like Spanish and Portuguese. So the next time you hear something as _____________ as an Italian weather report or as _____________ as a French discourse on fine wine, remember that the venerable language of Virgil and Cicero is alive and well!

A TALE FROM THE MOORS

One of the most powerful and *disconcerting* novels ever written is the only exhibition of the writing *legerdemain* of Emily Brontë. Emily came from a family with a *disparate* measure of talent: her sisters, Charlotte and Anne, also published literary classics. The setting of her novel, *Wuthering Heights*, is the windswept Yorkshire region. The narrator, Mr. Lockwood, is the tenant of Thrushcross Grange, a handsome estate neighboring the *incongruous* Wuthering Heights, the home of his *enigmatic* landlord, Heathcliff. During a visit to the dilapidated Heights, Lockwood encounters a brutish young man, a haughty young girl, and the sullen,* middle-aged Heathcliff. Forced by a blizzard to spend the night, Lockwood falls asleep in a small bedroom reading a diary from decades ago. Suddenly, he awakens to an *incoherent* vision of Catherine, the diary's author, begging entry at his window! He informs Heathcliff of this apparent nightmare, and the latter becomes greatly disturbed.

NEW WORDS

disconcerting
dis - kən - ser - ting

legerdemain
leg - ėr - də - mān

disparate
dis - par - ət

incongruous
in - kən - grū - əs

enigmatic
en - ig - mat - ik

incoherent
in - kō - hēr - ənt

Notable Roots:
cert = agreement;
par = equal; gru = grow;
here = stick

Sample Sentences: Insert the new words in these sentences.

1. Richard Nixon, a flawed man of prodigious talent, was an _______________ president.
2. Rodney's paper was so _______________ its main thesis was hard to divine.
3. Humor was a powerful tool in Casey Stengel's managerial _______________.
4. There is no more _______________ image than that of violence on one's own streets.
5. The fraternal twins were so _______________ in appearance as to seem unrelated.
6. Baseball struggles with woefully _______________ payrolls among its teams.

Definitions: Match the new words with their meanings.

7. disconcerting	________	a.	puzzling; mysterious
8. legerdemain	________	b.	incomprehensible
9. disparate	________	c.	not matching
10. incongruous	________	d.	dexterity; collection of skills
11. enigmatic	________	e.	uneven
12. incoherent	________	f.	unsettling

THE NEW ARRIVAL

Lockwood finds his experience so *anomalous* that he determines to find out the history of the two estates. He asks Nelly, his housekeeper, who grew up at Wuthering Heights before becoming a servant herself. Her tale begins on the night 30 years earlier that Mr. Earnshaw returned from a trip with a scruffy, dark-haired boy he names Heathcliff. Without explaining the boy's *cryptic* origins, he declares that Heathcliff is to be raised alongside his own children. Heathcliff's relationships with the Earnshaw children are quite *divergent*. Catherine and Heathcliff, who are the same age, become inseparable. Hindley, however, Catherine's older brother, develops a jealousy *tinged* with hatred for his adoptive brother. Mr. Earnshaw's *indiscriminate* affection for Heathcliff only serves to further *contort* his firstborn son with rage.

NEW WORDS

anomalous
ə - nom - ə - ləs

cryptic
krip - tik

divergent
dī - vėr - jənt

tinge
tinj

indiscriminate
in - də - skrim - ə - nət

contort
kən - tôrt

Notable Roots:
a = not; crypt = hidden; di = two; verg = turn; crimin = separate; tort = twist

Sample Sentences: Insert the new words in these sentences.

1. World War II bombers caused_______________ damage to military and civilian targets.
2. Welsh's voice was _______________ with disgust when he rebuked McCarthy's indecency.
3. Stonehenge's _______________ origins remain mysterious to this day.
4. History reveals that bipartisanship is more _______________ than habitual.
5. After the map dried out, its pages were still _______________ and warped.
6. The _______________ goals of the chairman and CEO led to the latter's dismissal.

Definitions: Match the new words with their meanings.

7. anomalous	________	a. branching in different directions
8. cryptic	________	b. out of the ordinary
9. divergent	________	c. to bend out of shape
10. tinge	________	d. ambiguous
11. indiscriminate	________	e. without special consideration
12. contort	________	f. to color or corrupt

WEEK 36 ⚙ DAY 3

HINDLEY TAKES CHARGE

Heathcliff's life became easier when Hindley is sent off for a formal education. This proves to be an *atypical* respite,* however, and due to *extrinsic* factors, it could not last. Mr. Earnshaw's sudden death makes Hindley master of Wuthering Heights. He returns, along with his young wife, and demotes Heathcliff to the role of servant. Though they are now *heterogeneous* in station, Catherine and Heathcliff remain close. One night, they sneak onto Thrushcross Grange, home of the Linton family, but are soon caught. Heathcliff, with his disheveled* appearance and *maladjusted* temperament, is driven off. The Linton's bulldog catches Catherine, however, wounding her leg, and she is taken in to heal. While Catherine stays with the Lintons, she is struck by the *dichotomy* between the fine *baroque* style of their home and the plainness of Wuthering Heights. She is similarly charmed by their gentile manners. Edgar, the Linton's son, is, for his part, captivated by Catherine's beauty and spirited nature.

NEW WORDS

atypical
ā - tip - ik - əl

extrinsic
eks - trin - zik

heterogeneous
het - ər - ō - jēn - ē - əs

maladjusted
mal - ə - just - əd

dichotomy
dī - kot - ə - mē

baroque
bə - rōk

Notable Roots: hetero = different; gen = create; mal = bad

Sample Sentences: Insert the new words in these sentences.

1. While social creatures, it is _______________ of cats to hunt in groups.
2. Some quip that a salad, not a melting pot, better symbolizes a country as _______________ as the United States.
3. The _____________ between the ideas of Locke and Rousseau still divides intellectuals.
4. Preference for _______________ design was partly a reaction against Puritan simplicity.
5. Court protocols were relaxed in an attempt to help the _______________ princess.
6. When examining Rome's fall, _______________ factors should not be ignored.

Definitions: Match the new words with their meanings.

7. atypical	_________	a.	unable to properly cope
8. extrinsic	_________	b.	characterized by ornate design
9. heterogeneous	_________	c.	a sharp contrast
10. maladjusted	_________	d.	unusual
11. dichotomy	_________	e.	unessential
12. baroque	_________	f.	mixed in composition

CULTURE CLASH

Upon Catherine's return to Wuthering Heights, the Earnshaws invite Edgar and Isabella Linton for dinner. Hindley uses the evening as part of his *perverse* plan to humiliate Heathcliff. Hindley bars him from partaking in the *pungent* feast and joins in with Edgar in insulting him. To Catherine, who aspires to be more ladylike after her time with the Lintons, the *discrepancy* between Edgar and Heathcliff cannot be more stark. Soon after, Hindley's wife dies after giving birth; Hindley is crippled by grief and becomes increasingly *dissolute*. Despite Hindley's increasingly *aberrant* behavior, Edgar continues to court Catherine. One night, Catherine confides to Nelly that she has agreed to marry Edgar as she cannot marry Heathcliff in his *degenerate* state. Heathcliff overhears this and runs away—just before Catherine admits that her love for Heathcliff runs far deeper than her affection for Edgar.

NEW WORDS

perverse
pėr - vėrs

pungent
pun - jənt

discrepancy
dis - krep - ən - sē

dissolute
dis - ə - lūt

aberrant
ab - ər - ənt

degenerate
də - jen - ər - ət

Notable Roots: vers = turn; crep = crack; err = mistake; gener = create

Sample Sentences: Insert the new words in these sentences.

1. Truffles are so ________________ that too much can overpower any dish.
2. George III's ________________ behavior eventually rendered him unfit to rule.
3. From a young age, Joy had a ________________ interest in grisly murder stories.
4. The corrupt accountant could not explain the ________________ in his clients' financials.
5. ________________ organs like the tiny human tailbone are viewed as evidence of evolution.
6. Eleanor was the daughter of Theodore Roosevelt's ________________ brother, Eliot, who died young from alcoholism.

Definitions: Match the new words with their meanings.

7. perverse	________	a.	given to self-destructive living
8. pungent	________	b.	contrary to normal standards
9. discrepancy	________	c.	ill-formed; degraded
10. dissolute	________	d.	different from expectations
11. aberrant	________	e.	strong in flavor or aroma
12. degenerate	________	f.	a contradiction

GROUP REVIEW

Whether you read a classic novel or a modern one, the one thing they have in common is their use of a rather extensive vocabulary. Don't be handicapped in your reading—increase your vocabulary by constant study and review.

Matching

Directions: Match the words you learned this week with their meanings.

REVIEW WORDS		DEFINITIONS
________	**1.** aberrant	**a.** unsettling
________	**2.** anomalous	**b.** strong in flavor or aroma
________	**3.** atypical	**c.** dexterity; collection of skills
________	**4.** baroque	**d.** unusual
________	**5.** contort	**e.** to color or corrupt
________	**6.** cryptic	**f.** incomprehensible
________	**7.** degenerate	**g.** unable to properly cope
________	**8.** dichotomy	**h.** given to self-destructive living
________	**9.** disconcerting	**i.** contrary to normal standards
________	**10.** discrepancy	**j.** characterized by ornate design
________	**11.** disparate	**k.** a contradiction
________	**12.** dissolute	**l.** ambiguous
________	**13.** divergent	**m.** uneven
________	**14.** enigmatic	**n.** out of the ordinary
________	**15.** extrinsic	**o.** a sharp contrast
________	**16.** heterogeneous	**p.** different from expectations
________	**17.** incoherent	**q.** to bend out of shape
________	**18.** incongruous	**r.** mixed in composition
________	**19.** indiscriminate	**s.** branching in different directions
________	**20.** legerdemain	**t.** without special consideration
________	**21.** maladjusted	**u.** puzzling; mysterious
________	**22.** perverse	**v.** unessential
________	**23.** pungent	**w.** ill-formed; degraded
________	**24.** tinge	**x.** not matching

Sensible Sentences?

Directions: Underline the word that makes sense in each of the sentences below.

1. Maddie's appearance of sweetness was her way to *(dissemble, divulge)* her vindictiveness.
2. Many lovers of theater find reality television *(vapid, supine)* and uninspiring.
3. The queen looked out from her high *(milieu, bastion)* upon the siege to her capital.
4. Malik quickly found himself lost in the *(reverie, grandeur)* of Mardi Gras celebration.
5. Dolores's love of kittens is *(disconcerting, incongruous)* with her penchant* for cruelty.
6. So many setbacks made the wedding a highly *(inane, fraught)* affair.
7. Velma found her sources often became more *(laconic, loquacious)* after a few drinks.
8. The *(macabre, maudlin)* ending of *Reservoir Dogs* sees every major character die.
9. A(n) *(extrinsic, cryptic)* inscription on a tree is the only clue the Roanoke settlers left behind.
10. Ashton was so stricken by *(ennui, qualms)* that he no longer delighted in Paris.

Wordsearch

Directions: Using the clues listed below, fill in each blank in the following story with one of the new words you learned this week.

Clues

3rd Day	2nd Day
4th Day	4th Day
2nd Day	3rd Day
4th Day	3rd Day
2nd Day	

The Antihero

As the plot of *Wuthering Heights* progresses, it's clear that Heathcliff is the protagonist. Heathcliff does possess some desirable attributes: he is strong, handsome, and successful; he is also cunning and determined. At the same time, his flaws form quite a _____________ with these qualities. At a glance, he is surly in the extreme: Heathcliff's ____________ behavior shocks Lockwood, a stranger. His attitude toward nearly every other character is _____________ by malice.

Sometimes heroes who are wronged, like the Count of Monte Cristo, can be terrible in their quest for justice. Can this be said of Heathcliff? As the plot of *Wuthering Heights* unfolds, it becomes clear Heathcliff's vengeance has a ___________ quality. He is cruel and so implacable that his revenge doesn't end even when his victims die. Moreover, Heathcliff is rather ___________ in terms of whom he is willing to harm. In short, Heathcliff is no hero.

And yet we root for him! First, Heathcliff's undying love for Catherine Earnshaw humanizes him. Additionally, he is an underdog. Heathcliff's rise to wealth and power is ____________ in a society obsessed with class and etiquette. His two rivals, the one a ____________ wreck and the other a sickly snob, are not sympathetic characters. They only triumph over Heathcliff when he's young and poor. Once Heathcliff becomes a man with wealth, strength, and good looks, all ____________ advantages Hindley and Edgar once possessed are gone. On a level playing field, Heathcliff, despite his ____________ background, completely overmatches both men through cunning and force of personality.

HEATHCLIFF RETURNS

Heathcliff is away for three years. During his absence, Catherine and Edgar are married and living at Thrushcross Grange where Edgar is now master. Hindley's drinking and *irascible* behavior have worsened, while his son Hareton is neglected. Heathcliff's return causes delight and *vexation*. He's somehow acquired a fortune and is now a social equal to the inhabitants of both households. Upon his first visit to Thrushcross Grange, Catherine is delighted to see him but feels *consternation* to learn that he's living at Wuthering Heights given the *asperity* of Hindley and Heathcliff's relationship. Edgar allows Heathcliff's visits but has misgivings. Isabella Linton, meanwhile, young and unmarried, is *inexorably* drawn to Heathcliff, who is confident and handsome. She *badgers* Catherine to allow her presence when Heathcliff visits.

NEW WORDS

irascible
ə - ras - ə - bəl

vexation
veks - ā - shən

consternation
kon - stėr - nā - shən

asperity
ə - sper - ə - tē

inexorable
in - eks - ôr - ə - bəl

badger
baj - ər

Notable Roots: ire = anger; asper = rough; exort = move, motivate

Sample Sentences: Insert the new words in these sentences.

1. My parents' _______________ with my grades led them to ground me.
2. The estranged brothers couldn't converse without _______________ in their voices.
3. John Adams was so _______________ that he even quarreled with Ben Franklin.
4. Doctors felt _______________ at the discovery that Covid-19 could be spread by the asymptomatic.
5. Micah's cat would often _______________ her for extra food at night.
6. Big box retailers have been in _______________ decline for some time.

Definitions: Match the new words with their definitions.

7. irascible	________	a. annoyance
8. vexation	________	b. harshness
9. consternation	________	c. to pester
10. asperity	________	d. worried astonishment
11. inexorable	________	e. unstoppable; unavoidable
12. badger	________	f. easily angered

THE CLASH

Catherine tries to warn Isabella about Heathcliff's *belligerent* nature but is *reproached* as selfish by her sister-in-law for the attempt. Catherine retaliates by revealing Isabella's feelings to Heathcliff, who decides to use Edgar's sister to exact revenge on his rival. After catching Heathcliff kissing Isabella, Catherine *accosts* him, knowing his feelings for Isabella are not genuine. Heathcliff replies that Catherine should not *begrudge* him the budding relationship since she chose Edgar over him. Nelly informs Edgar about this "argument" and, *irate*, he orders Heathcliff off his property. After a humiliating confrontation in which Catherine sides with Heathcliff, Edgar bars him from Thrushcross Grange. In short order, Edgar's peaceful household erupts in *internecine* fighting.

NEW WORDS

belligerent
bel - lij - ər - ənt

reproach
rē - prō - ch

accost
ə - kôst

begrudge
bē - gruj

irate
ī - rāt

internecine
in - tėr - nes - ēn

Notable Roots:
belli = war; ire = anger; nec = kill

Sample Sentences: Insert the new words in these sentences.

1. The Thirty Years' War was the most ________________ religious conflict in Europe's history.
2. After a two hour delay, an ________________ passenger demanded to be let off the airplane.
3. Politicians complain about being ________________ in public for their policy positions.
4. In the 1930s, Germany's ________________ attitude toward other nations was obvious.
5. Duelists would not often ________________ one another certain courtesies before combat.
6. Some public figures deserve ________________ for their misdeeds, not ostracism.

Definitions: Match the new words with their meanings.

7.	belligerent	_________	a.	enraged
8.	reproach	_________	b.	to verbally attack
9.	accost	_________	c.	to deny someone something
10.	begrudge	_________	d.	warlike
11.	irate	_________	e.	destructive; deadly
12.	internecine	_________	f.	to scold

TRAGEDY STRIKES

Catherine's *paroxysm* of anger leads to a wasting sickness, which is complicated by the fact that she's pregnant. With Edgar distracted, Isabella elopes with Heathcliff whose coldness and cruelty toward her soon confirm Catherine's warnings. Regarding her a substitute for her brother, he subjects Isabella to verbal *diatribes* during which he *rails* against Edgar. Learning of Catherine's condition, Heathcliff compels Nelly to arrange a reunion with Catherine. After Edgar bursts in, however, Catherine collapses and dies that night shortly after giving birth. Standing vigil outside, a distraught Heathcliff *inveighs* at Catherine's spirit to haunt him. On the night of the funeral, Isabella *nettles* Heathcliff by mocking his grief. *Livid*, he attacks her. She flees to the seaside where she later gives birth to a son. Soon after, Hindley dies, having mortgaged Wuthering Heights to Heathcliff. This leaves Hareton a servant to his father's greatest enemy.

NEW WORDS

paroxysm
pə - roks - izm

diatribe
dī - ə - trīb

rail
rāl

inveigh
in - vā

nettle
net - əl

livid
liv - id

Notable Roots:
oxy = sharpen;
veher = carry on;
livid = bluish, pale

Sample Sentences: Insert the new words in these sentences.

1. Cicero's many ________________ against Mark Antony eventually led to his own execution.
2. Alexander the Great was so ________________ by insulting remarks at his father's marriage to a new wife that he risked execution or banishment as retaliation.
3. Northerners were so ________________ after Fort Sumter that many joined the Union army.
4. Many entitled actors have been reproached for their temperamental ________________.
5. Carrie Nation is known for ________________ at "demon rum" and trashing saloons.
6. Douglass ________________ against the exclusion of African Americans from the army.

Definitions: Match the new words with their meanings.

7.	paroxysm	________	a.	to bother or unsettle
8.	diatribe	________	b.	furious
9.	rail	________	c.	to protest or complain about
10.	inveigh	________	d.	a violent emotional response
11.	nettle	________	e.	to denounce
12.	livid	________	f.	an angry speech

THE FINAL REVENGE

Over the next decade, Edgar dotes on his daughter, Cathy, who is beautiful but less *pugnacious* than her mother. Isabella spoils her sickly son, Linton, while Hareton becomes brutish and prone to the *invectives* he has learned from Heathcliff. After Isabella dies, Heathcliff seizes custody of his son. A few years later, Cathy encounters Heathcliff, who brings her to see Linton. Cathy, who does not know her uncle's true nature, *rebukes* Nelly for keeping Linton's whereabouts secret. Spurred on by Heathcliff, Linton sends love letters to his cousin and asks that they be allowed to see one another. Edgar, who is now dying of consumption, allows the relationship, hoping that Linton will take care of Cathy. Subjected to his father's *vitriolic* abuse, Linton presses Cathy to marry him. Linton, however, is also sick, so Heathcliff imprisons Cathy and forces their marriage. After she *vituperates* against him for this treachery, he strikes her in a fit of *pique*. In short order, first Edgar dies and then Linton, and, thus, Heathcliff inherits Thrushcross Grange. Cathy, like Hareton, is now at the mercy of her father's enemy.

NEW WORDS

pugnacious
pug - nā - shəs

invective
in - vek - tiv

rebuke (v.)
rē - byūk

vitriolic
vi - trē - ol - ik

vituperate
vī - tū - pėr - āt

pique (n.)
pēk

Notable Roots:
pugna = fight;
veher = to carry away;
vitre = glass

Sample Sentences: Insert the new words in these sentences.

1. Kayleigh ________________ her husband for his neglect of their son.
2. ________________ language is so common that most online debates are overly fraught.*
3. Ron's ears turn red every time he feels a spasm of ________________.
4. Honey badgers are so ________________ that they will attack lions.
5. Shrewd politicians know that ________________ against the press won't change their stories.
6. Silas was fired after he accidentally sent an email full of ________________ about the board.

Definitions: Match the new words with their meanings.

7. pugnacious	________	a.	critical language
8. invective	________	b.	to reproach sternly
9. rebuke	________	c.	harshly critical
10. vitriolic	________	d.	combative
11. vituperate	________	e.	sudden anger
12. pique	________	f.	strongly blame or insult

GROUP REVIEW

Wuthering Heights is a novel that defies expectations given the genteel era in which it was written. It can be difficult to find words to describe characters that do despicable things and yet are sympathetic and compelling. The words from weeks 36 and 37 can help.

Matching

Directions: Match the words with their meanings.

	REVIEW WORDS		DEFINITIONS
________	**1.** accost	**a.**	to reproach sternly
________	**2.** asperity	**b.**	an angry speech
________	**3.** badger	**c.**	harshly critical
________	**4.** begrudge	**d.**	unstoppable; unavoidable
________	**5.** belligerent	**e.**	strongly blame or insult
________	**6.** consternation	**f.**	warlike
________	**7.** diatribe	**g.**	enraged
________	**8.** inexorable	**h.**	easily angered
________	**9.** internecine	**i.**	to scold
________	**10.** invective	**j.**	to bother or unsettle
________	**11.** inveigh	**k.**	to verbally attack
________	**12.** irascible	**l.**	harshness
________	**13.** irate	**m.**	annoyance
________	**14.** livid	**n.**	destructive; deadly
________	**15.** nettle	**o.**	worried astonishment
________	**16.** paroxysm	**p.**	to protest or complain about
________	**17.** pique	**q.**	to deny someone something
________	**18.** pugnacious	**r.**	combative
________	**19.** rail	**s.**	a violent emotional response
________	**20.** rebuke	**t.**	to pester
________	**21.** reproach	**u.**	to denounce
________	**22.** vexation	**v.**	sudden anger
________	**23.** vitriolic	**w.**	furious
________	**24.** vituperate	**x.**	critical language

Wordsearch

Directions: Using the clues listed below, fill in each blank in the following story with one of the new words you learned this week.

Clues

1st Day	1st Day	1st Day
2nd Day	4th Day	4th Day
3rd Day	4th Day	3rd Day
3rd Day	2nd Day	3rd Day
1st Day	1st Day	2nd Day

In This Life and the Next

With Heathcliff's revenge complete, Nelly's tale has come to end. In the final chapters, Lockwood leaves Thrushcross Grange, but when he sees Nelly again eight months later, she provides a surprising epilogue. Not long after Lockwood's departure, Heathcliff's behavior became increasingly peculiar. His _________ and _________ nature changed completely. He became unable to look at Cathy, _________ by her resemblance to her mother. He shunned all company and took to spending his nights on the moors, denying himself both food and rest. Not long after, he was found dead in Catherine's bedroom with a rapturous expression on his face, as though he had been overcome by a __________ of joy.

With his death, ownership of the two houses reverted to the last descendants of both families. Hareton was the only one who felt __________ at Heathcliff's death. He also sought to befriend his cousin. Cathy at first felt __________ by his efforts, but eventually loneliness compelled the girl to take on the project of civilizing him. Romance ensued, and the two become engaged. Nelly concludes that locals have claimed to see the spirits of Heathcliff and Catherine walking the moors.

Upon finishing *Wuthering* Heights many readers are left with the question, how could so singular a novel have been written in the early Victorian age, especially by so inexperienced an author? While it was her first novel, Emily Brontë was, first off, extremely well-read. She would have known the works of Romantic poets like William Blake and Lord Byron that explored subjective human experience and the natural world. Mary Shelly's *Frankenstein*, a novel with a protagonist destroyed by his unnatural pursuits, is also an implicit ________ of Enlightenment values like faith in science and reason. Like Dr. Frankenstein, Heathcliff holds a __________ attitude toward basic standards of human conduct. He __________ the dead their peace, __________ in his vengeance against Hindley long after his death and calling on Catherine to haunt him.

To create Heathcliff, the author also drew upon personal experience. Emily's home on the moors, a place both beautiful and desolate, proved a perfect setting for Heathcliff, like a wild garden menaced by the __________ presence of a wolf. It also is generally believed that Emily's brother, Bramwell, who died young from alcoholism, was a model. Bramwell's descent into madness, marked by fits of _________ and unhinged __________, was an experience that haunted Emily and her sisters throughout their lives.

Ironically, *Wuthering Heights* is enhanced by the fact that it proved to be the author's only novel. Like many of her characters, consumption claimed Emily's life at a young age. *Wuthering Heights* has a singular, eerie quality *because* its author was dying. Rather than ________ against the unfairness of mortality, Emily saw wonder in her tenuous* existence. She described it as the dividing line between this world and the next becoming blurred. In *Wuthering Heights*, the supernatural is always suggested: we never know whether the ghosts that _________ the living are real or hallucinations.

WEEK 38 DAY 1

SELF-EVIDENT TRUTHS

In the 1770s, John Adams described the new nation he envisioned as "a republic of laws, not men." He envisioned a society first in which the rights of all were *inviolable* because they were not a gift from princes but from God. Other thinkers defined the concept in *secular* terms: the preconditions necessary for the pursuit of happiness based on human nature itself. Jefferson's justification for independence was that government could not rightly *mandate* that which is destructive to these rights or *proscribe* that which safeguards them. In the case that king or parliament *flout* this compact, the right of rebellion *supersedes* allegiance to the crown. Thus, the people are free to choose a new system in which the law is made by and applies to all citizens.

inviolable
in - vī - ō - lə - bəl

secular
sek - yū - lär

mandate
man - dāt

proscribe
prō - skrīb

flout
flout

supersede
sū - pėr - sēd

Notable Roots:
viola = force; man = hand; scribe = write; super = over

Sample Sentences: Insert the new words in these sentences.

1. 1930s bank robbers were an FBI priority because they so publicly ______________ the law.
2. Insider trading is ________________ because otherwise private investors would be saddled with the consequences of company mistakes.
3. Federal law always ________________ state law when the two conflict.
4. ________________ marriages are often performed by local officials or judges.
5. Respecting embassies is the one ________________ principle of diplomacy.
6. The judge ________________ that Mr. Brown pay a fair amount of child support.

Definitions: Match the new words with their meanings.

7. inviolable	________		**a.**	to take the place of
8. secular	________		**b.**	cannot be broken
9. mandate	________		**c.**	to openly violate
10. proscribe	________		**d.**	to order
11. flout	________		**e.**	unrelated to religion
12. supersede	________		**f.**	to prohibit

SEPARATION OF POWERS

When the framers of the Constitution met in Philadelphia, it was uppermost in everyone's mind to create a government that was non-tyrannical. The framers held as *doctrine* the idea that there are three overarching functions of government: making law, executing law, and *adjudicating* disputes. In autocracies, these powers were invested in a single individual who ruled by *fiat*. In such a system, there is no mechanism to stop the *transgressions* of a tyrant. The Virginia plan, presented by James Madison, addressed this shortcoming by creating three branches of government for each of the three functions. Each branch was given the power to *sanction* or put into *abeyance* any abuses of the other two.

NEW WORDS

doctrine
dok - trin

adjudicate
ə - jūd - ə - kāt

fiat
fē - ot

transgression
tranz - gresh - ən

sanction
senk - shən

abeyance
ə - bā - ins

Notable Roots: doct = teacher; jud = judge; gress = pass; sanc = decree

Sample Sentences: Insert the new words in these sentences.

1. The defendant was charged with over 80 distinct ________________.
2. An ________________ of the Olympic Games was held during both World Wars.
3. Heretics are defined as those who promote teachings contrary to religious ________________.
4. King Joffrey never learned his ________________ meant nothing without others to enforce it.
5. Many recalcitrant nations have withstood UN ________________ for years.
6. The Pope helped ________________ the territorial dispute between Spain and Portugal.

Definitions: Match the new words with their meanings.

7. doctrine	________	a.	suspension
8. adjudicate	________	b.	a unilateral action
9. fiat	________	c.	a crime
10. transgression	________	d.	to assess a penalty; to approve
11. sanction	________	e.	a set of formal principles
12. abeyance	________	f.	to settle

WEEK 38 DAY 3

NEW JERSEY OBJECTS

New Jersey is the only state with a nationwide *prohibition* on motorists pumping their own gas. It, therefore, seems fitting that the principal objection to the Virginia plan was raised by an *emissary* from the Garden State, William Paterson. Paterson argued that a congress composed of a single chamber of delegates elected by population would be *manifestly* unfair to small states. At the nation's founding, each state considered the national government a voluntary *accord* between sovereign countries. Paterson asserted that states like New Jersey would be unwilling to give up autonomy only to have populous states *dictate* national policy. The solution arrived at was to add a second house, the Senate, where each state would have equal voice. According to this new *protocol*, both houses would need to assent to any law.

NEW WORDS

prohibition
prō - hib - ish - ən

emissary
em - ə - ser - ē

manifest
ma - nə - fest

accord
ə - kôrd

dictate
dik - tāt

protocol
prō - tō - kôl

Notable Roots:
hibit = hold, restrain; man = hand; fest = catch; cord = agree; dict = say

Sample Sentences: Insert the new words in these sentences.

1. Churchill wrote volumes of history by _______________ text to typists.
2. Wars have begun over breeches of etiquette committed by _______________.
3. Cheryl's qualifications were so _______________ that her interview was a mere formality.
4. Roman _______________ gave the people's tribunes veto power over Senate motions.
5. The _______________ of gambling seems to be rolling back without debate.
6. Italy viewed its _______________ with the Central Powers to be defensive only.

Definitions: Match the new words with their meanings.

7.	prohibition	________	a.	obvious
8.	emissary	________	b.	rules or accepted procedures
9.	manifest	________	c.	agreement or treaty
10.	accord	________	d.	ban
11.	dictate	________	e.	to command; to speak out loud
12.	protocol	________	f.	a representative

IMPLIED POWERS

The Constitutional Convention was called because our first national government lacked the *requisite* power to be effective. Thus, one *criterion* for a new compact was fashioning a system with authority to meet all crises. After ratification, Federalists like Alexander Hamilton argued that government held all powers not forbidden to it. The implied powers argument can be seen in the doctrine* of Judicial Review, which has given Supreme Court *precedent* the force of law. Some question the *propriety* of this since the justices are not elected. Court fans assert that as seasoned* jurists with life tenure, the justices are truly impartial. Advocates point out the *decorum* of justices *abstaining* from cases they had once argued before joining the court.

NEW WORDS

requisite
rek - wiz - ət

criterion
crī - tēr - ē - on

precedent
pres - ə - dent

propriety
prō - prī - ə - tē

decorum
də - kôr - um

abstain
ab - stān

Notable Roots:
quire = seek; ced = go, yield; decor = grace

Sample Sentences: Insert the new words in these sentences.

1. Teachers socializing with students raises issues of academic _______________.
2. Facing the Royal Navy offshore, New York _______________ from the July 2nd vote.
3. Providing relevant evidence is a _______________ for any effective argument.
4. Dora lacked the _______________ calm an ER doctor needs to be effective.
5. Rick broke _______________ by having his first drink with customers.
6. Breaches of _______________ are actually common in the House of Commons.

Definitions: Match the new words with their meanings.

7. requisite	________	a.	an action that sets a standard
8. criterion	________	b.	conforming to accepted norms
9. precedent	________	c.	a requirement
10. propriety	________	d.	etiquette
11. decorum	________	e.	to withdraw or not participate
12. abstain	________	f.	necessary

GROUP REVIEW

No matter what the fashion in dress, the fashion in education is an extensive vocabulary. Keep up with the fashion; build your vocabulary wardrobe.

Matching

Directions: Match the words to their meanings.

REVIEW WORDS		DEFINITIONS
________	**1.** abeyance	**a.** unrelated to religion
________	**2.** abstain	**b.** ban
________	**3.** accord	**c.** etiquette
________	**4.** adjudicate	**d.** obvious
________	**5.** criterion	**e.** to withdraw or not participate
________	**6.** decorum	**f.** to settle
________	**7.** dictate	**g.** to take the place of
________	**8.** doctrine	**h.** a unilateral action
________	**9.** emissary	**i.** to openly violate
________	**10.** fiat	**j.** a set of formal principles
________	**11.** flout	**k.** an action that sets a standard
________	**12.** inviolable	**l.** necessary
________	**13.** mandate	**m.** to command; to speak out loud
________	**14.** manifest	**n.** to order
________	**15.** precedent	**o.** to prohibit
________	**16.** prohibition	**p.** rules or accepted procedures
________	**17.** propriety	**q.** conforming to accepted norms
________	**18.** proscribe	**r.** agreement or treaty
________	**19.** protocol	**s.** a crime
________	**20.** requisite	**t.** suspension
________	**21.** sanction	**u.** to assess a penalty; to approve
________	**22.** secular	**v.** cannot be broken
________	**23.** supersede	**w.** a representative
________	**24.** transgression	**x.** a requirement

Wordsearch

Directions: Using the clues listed below, fill in each blank in the following story with one of the new words you learned this week.

Clues

2nd Day	1st Day	4th Day	2nd Day
4th Day	3rd Day	3rd Day	1st Day
2nd Day	2nd Day	3rd Day	
3rd Day	4th Day	2nd Day	
4th Day	3rd Day	1st Day	

The Power of Expertise

It's taught to school children that there are three branches of government, and yet many of the __________ that affect our lives are the work of what many consider a fourth branch. Most Americans agree this cohort of power is a ___________ for maintaining a complex society. The controversy lies in its size, power, and accountability—or lack of it—to the electorate. Many a diatribe* has been written about independent federal regulatory agencies encroaching upon civil liberties and stifling economic growth.

The members of the House of Representatives are the federal officers most directly responsible to the people. Elected every two years to represent a specific congressional district from their home state, they must have the __________ of their neighbors to keep power. At the same time, a congresswoman is no more qualified to write a prescription, fly an airplane, or determine safe levels of chemicals in drinking water than any other layperson. All elected officials need experts to inform them about technical matters. An apt analogy can be found in war. The president has the ultimate power to __________ military objectives. At the same time, very few chief executives have ever been senior military commanders, and they rightly ___________ from micromanaging the logistics of carrying out what they have ___________.

The _________ between experts and government becomes more complicated in areas where technical expertise is essential to set _________ as well as carry it out. In such cases, the well-established __________ is to create an agency using executive authority. For example, the Food and Drug Administration, an agency whose creation led to the _________ of untried and potentially poisonous patent medicines, is empowered to approve medical treatments. The ________ of this is _________: patients cannot judge for themselves which medicines are safe.

Unfortunately, many private citizens have claimed that _________ from agencies they did not elect are _________ against their _________ rights. The courts have had to ________ disputes between the Bureau of Land Management and ranchers over the grazing of animals on federal lands. Industry leaders inveigh* against the impact of EPA regulations on their businesses. One reason for government is the clash of interests in society. Whose interests should _________ whose will never be an easy question.

WEEK 39 DAY 1

Strength

OUR FINEST HOUR

An unforgettable saga of World War II has to do with the small French coastal town of Dunkirk. There, in 1940, thousands of British troops made a belated escape from the *domineering* German armed forces. They were removed by naval vessels *reinforced* by a fleet of private boats, from huge yachts to decrepit fishing boats. Of their own volition, the *redoubtable* skippers came close to the shore, seemingly *impervious* to the German bombers overhead. When their vessels were loaded, they dashed back to England. Once unloaded, the *flotilla* returned to rescue more men. The actions of these private citizens, like Churchill's pugnacious* speeches, helped to *fortify* the spirits of the British nation during one of its darkest hours.

Sample Sentences: Insert the new words in these sentences.

1. Cleopatra's _______________ was destroyed by the Roman fleet at Actium.
2. Grant was _______________: he might fail but would never panic.
3. Many cereals are artificially _______________ with vitamins and minerals.
4. Children of _______________ parents can become anxious or passive adults.
5. Teflon is the only material so _______________ it can contain the strongest acids.
6. Concrete is much stronger when _______________ with steel.

Definitions: Match the new words with their meanings.

7.	domineering	________	a.	overbearing
8.	reinforce	________	b.	unable to be penetrated
9.	redoubtable	________	c.	a fleet of ships
10.	impervious	________	d.	to strengthen
11.	flotilla	________	e.	to defend; to augment
12.	fortify	________	f.	difficult to defeat

NEW WORDS

domineering
dom - ə - nēr - ing

reinforce
rē - in - fôrs

redoubtable
rē - dou - tə - bəl

impervious
im - per - vē - əs

flotilla
flō - til - ə

fortify
fôr - tə - fī

Notable Roots:
domin = master;
redoubt = outpost;
permea = slip through;
fort = strong

SYMPATHY FOR THE DEVIL

The key to any great action or adventure story is the villain. The Romans knew this: accounts of their most *steadfast* adversary, Hannibal, were written by the Romans themselves. One might rightly question the fairness of a biography written by one's enemies, but Polybius and Tacitus went out of their way to describe what a *dynamic* commander Hannibal was, how *virile* his Carthaginian troops were, and what *behemoths* were his elephants. The reasoning for their praise is simple: the greatest glory for the *strapping* Roman heroes of old requires victory in the most *titanic* struggle against the deadliest enemy.

NEW WORDS

steadfast
sted - fast

dynamic
dī - nam - ik

virile
və - rīl

behemoth
bə - hē - məth

strapping
strap - ing

titanic
tī - tan - ik

Notable Roots: dyna = power; vir = man; titan = giant

Sample Sentences: Insert the new words in these sentences.

1. Compared with all other countries, Russia is a geographic ________________.
2. Through his writings about hunting, fishing, and bullfighting, Hemingway cultivated a ________________ public persona.
3. A ________________ effort by dozens of scientists realized the Manhattan Project.
4. By harnessing the talents of ambitious rivals, Lincoln fashioned a ________________ cabinet.
5. Theodore Roosevelt, while progressive, was a ________________ and combative imperialist.
6. Compared with his sickly cousin, Hareton was a ________________ young man.

Definitions: Match the new words with their meanings.

7.	steadfast	________	a.	strong and handsome
8.	dynamic	________	b.	a giant or monster
9.	virile	________	c.	unwavering
10.	behemoth	________	d.	gigantic
11.	strapping	________	e.	manly
12.	titanic	________	f.	versatile and energetic

A FAMOUS MUTINY

One of the most repugnant* names in popular legend is that of William Bligh, the captain of the HMS *Bounty*. The 1789 mutiny that erupted aboard that ship was the basis for a film in which Charles Laughton portrayed Bligh as an unmitigated *ruffian*. Anyone who challenged his *hegemony* was subjected to mental and physical torture. A *junta* formed among the crew with such an aversion* to Bligh's command that they plotted a takeover of the ship. Led by Fletcher Christian, a cohort of *hale* and *sinewy* sailors overthrew the captain's *supremacy*, setting him and 17 shipmates adrift in a lifeboat in the South Pacific. The ship continued on to the Pitcairn Islands where the crew remained to live with the islanders.

NEW WORDS

ruffian
ruf - ē - ən

hegemony
hə - jem - ō - nē

junta
hun - tə

hale
hāl

sinewy
sin - yū - ē

supremacy
sū - prem - ə - sē

Notable Roots:
sinew = muscle;
super = above

Sample Sentences: Insert the new words in these sentences.

1. The ruling ________________ is notorious for brutality and corruption.
2. British ________________ had given way to American dominance by World War II.
3. The wolf is a slender but ________________ creature that is both fast and strong.
4. In a fascist society, the worst ________________ tend to rise to the top.
5. The ________________ of modern humans over Neanderthals has come into question.
6. John Adams remained ________________ and vital into his 80s.

Definitions: Match the new words with their meanings.

7. ruffian	________	a.	power of one group over others
8. hegemony	________	b.	healthy and energetic
9. junta	________	c.	a thug or bully
10. hale	________	d.	superiority over others
11. sinewy	________	e.	an undemocratic regime
12. supremacy	________	f.	strong and wiry

THE LAST PLANTAGENET

The House of Plantagenet ruled England continuously until the deposition of Richard II in 1399. The War of the Roses followed, during which rival Plantagenet branches fought for the throne until 1471 when King Edward IV, a *brawny* and *vigorous* ruler, won final victory. Edward's war and subsequent reign were *undergirded* by the support of his brother, Richard, the future King Richard III. Richard III is best remembered as a hunchbacked villain, largely thanks to Shakespeare's histories. While some facts *buttress* this assessment, the popular image is hardly *invulnerable*. Edward trusted Richard enough to name him protector of the realm until his own sons came of age. Richard immediately faced a *robust* threat from the queen's family, who sought power at the expense of Edward IV's blood relatives. Swift action stymied* the coup.* However, Richard went far beyond that, deposing his nephew and claiming the throne. The disappearance of the boy-king and his brother in the Tower was likely Richard's doing.

NEW WORDS

brawny
brô - nē

vigorous
vig - ôr - əs

undergird
un - dėr - gėrd

buttress (v.)
but - tres

invulnerable
in - vul - nėr - ə - bəl

robust
rō - bust

Notable Roots:
vigor = life; gird = hold up; vulner = wound

Sample Sentences: Insert the new words in these sentences.

1. Earth's dense, liquid mantle ________________ the crust of continents and the seafloor.
2. The hard-shelled ankylosaurus was practically ________________ to attack.
3. Even ________________ cleaning could not remove radioactivity from the ships contaminated in the Baker tests.
4. Despite a ________________ colonial defense, the British ultimately captured Bunker Hill.
5. The ________________ Jess Willard was pummeled by the small and lithe* Jack Dempsey.
6. Using external arches to ________________ the outer walls allowed for taller cathedrals.

Definitions: Match the new words with their meanings.

7. brawny	________	a.	to strengthen
8. vigorous	________	b.	powerful; sturdy
9. undergird	________	c.	strong and energetic
10. buttress	________	d.	large; muscular
11. invulnerable	________	e.	to support from below
12. robust	________	f.	cannot be harmed

GROUP REVIEW

Our British cousins have a vocabulary that differs from ours in many ways. Isn't it fortunate that we have to be responsible for the American version of this language only?

Directions: Match the weekly words to their definitions.

REVIEW WORDS		DEFINITIONS	
________	**1.** behemoth	**a.**	powerful; sturdy
________	**2.** brawny	**b.**	to defend; to augment
________	**3.** buttress	**c.**	to strengthen
________	**4.** domineering	**d.**	power of one group over others
________	**5.** dynamic	**e.**	unable to be penetrated
________	**6.** flotilla	**f.**	healthy and energetic
________	**7.** fortify	**g.**	superiority over others
________	**8.** hale	**h.**	strong and handsome
________	**9.** hegemony	**i.**	cannot be harmed
________	**10.** impervious	**j.**	overbearing
________	**11.** invulnerable	**k.**	a fleet of ships
________	**12.** junta	**l.**	strong and energetic
________	**13.** redoubtable	**m.**	versatile and energetic
________	**14.** reinforce	**n.**	gigantic
________	**15.** robust	**o.**	to strengthen
________	**16.** ruffian	**p.**	difficult to defeat
________	**17.** sinewy	**q.**	to support from below
________	**18.** steadfast	**r.**	an undemocratic regime
________	**19.** strapping	**s.**	a giant or monster
________	**20.** supremacy	**t.**	manly
________	**21.** titanic	**u.**	strong and wiry
________	**22.** undergird	**v.**	large; muscular
________	**23.** vigorous	**w.**	a thug or bully
________	**24.** virile	**x.**	unwavering

Wordsearch

Directions: Using the clues listed below, fill in each blank in the following story with one of the new words you learned this week.

Clues

3rd Day	2nd Day
2nd Day	3rd Day
2nd Day	4th Day
1st Day	3rd Day
4th Day	1st Day
1st Day	3rd Day

Droughts and Curses

The NFL is known for parity among teams with a near constant turnover of the league's elite. Sharing revenue, playing fewer games, and having a high injury rate prevent any one team from maintaining lasting ___________. Major League Baseball teams, on the other hand, can go decades—even lifetimes—without winning it all. When the World Series debuted in 1903, there were 16 total teams. It was not until 1980 that the last of these, the ___________ but long-suffering Philadelphia Phillies, finally won its first title. Baseball has seen worse. From 1903 to 1920, the Boston Red Sox, Chicago White Sox, and Chicago Cubs were some of the sport's most ___________ teams, with at least two rings apiece. None would win again during the twentieth century!

The Boston Red Sox were a ___________ team during the 1910s, winning four titles. At decade's end, however, owner Harry Frazee sold off the contracts of his best players—including the ___________ Babe Ruth—to finance musicals. Most of his stars were bought out by the New York Yankees, an American League team that had never been to a World Series. In 1923, however, the Yankees opened their own stadium and, ___________ by former Red Sox, won their first title. In the subsequent decades, the Yankees would become a ___________, winning 27 rings in 40 trips to the Series. On the occasions Boston did break through, they lost, usually in tragic and unlikely ways. The ___________ of the Yankees seemed ___________ until, in 2004, the Red Sox did something unprecedented: coming back from down three games to none to beat New York en route to their first championship in 86 years.

The true capital of baseball misery, however, is Chicago. In 1906, the Cubs won 116 games and advanced to the World Series against the White Sox in the only all-Chicago series to date. Though heavy underdogs, the ___________ White Sox pulled over the upset behind the pitching of "Big Ed" Walsh. The ___________ Cubs, however, rebounded, winning in 1907 and 1908. The White Sox won a second title in 1917 and seemed poised to win a third in 1919, but gamblers bribed a number of players to "throw" the series. When these ___________ were banned from the sport, it doomed the team to a generation of failure. The White Sox wouldn't win again until 2005. The Cubs, meanwhile, endured a record 108-year drought that finally ended in 2016.

WEEK 40 DAY 1

TEMPUS FUGIT

In one of his most famous skits, comedian George Carlin commented on the central *paradox* of the way humans perceive time: although stretching *interminably* into the past and future, time is nothing more than a collection of fleeting moments.

"Do you have the time?"
"When?"
"Just now."
"I think you mean just then."

Time also *elapses* in ways that are completely subjective. An arduous* *regimen* of tasks at the office seem to take years, but a week-long vacation feels *truncated* down to five minutes. Always, in *retrospect*, it all went by so quickly.

NEW WORDS

paradox
par - ə - doks

interminable
in - tėr - min - ə - bəl

elapse
ē - laps

regimen
rej - ə - men

truncate
trun - kāt

retrospect
ret - rō - spekt

Notable Roots: termin = finish; lapse = expire; retro = backward; spec = vision

Sample Sentences: Insert the new words in these sentences.

1. If a certain amount of time _______________ with the president ignoring a bill, it expires.
2. Some find a _______________ that never varies to be comforting.
3. Cold Harbor was the only battle Grant regretted in _______________.
4. Since no snow days were used, the school year was _______________.
5. Many lottery winners bemoan the _______________ of becoming miserable millionaires.
6. After an _______________ delay, the flight was cleared for takeoff.

Definitions: Match the new words with their meanings.

7. paradox	________	a.	never-ending
8. interminable	________	b.	to shorten
9. elapse	________	c.	an inherent contradiction
10. regimen	________	d.	a routine
11. truncate	________	e.	in hindsight
12. retrospect	________	f.	to pass; to expire

TIME BEFORE TIME

The *annals* of history go back no further than roughly 5,000 years because historiography requires the invention of writing. Prehistory, which may go back 100,000 years, is no mere *prelude* to the wars and king lists of the Bronze Age, however. Do we know nothing of this *defunct* world? Of course not. A *trove* of physical evidence has survived detailing the lives of humans in remote *antiquity*: their diet, dress, art, and social habits. We have also been able to re-create *obsolete* technologies, which reveal the surprising level of innovation of which our ancestors were capable. In fact, when history "began," people were already farming, trading, and drinking beer in complex cities ruled by kings.

NEW WORDS

annals
an - nəls

prelude
prā - lūd

defunct
dē - funkt

trove
trōv

antiquity
an - tik - wit - ē

obsolete
ob - sō - lēt

Notable Roots: clud = avoid; func = work; antique = old

Sample Sentences: Insert the new words in these sentences.

1. People alive during ________________ held very different values and beliefs.
2. The thawing of Siberian permafrost has revealed ________________ of ancient artifacts.
3. Because of their ingenuity and flaws, ________________ mechanical devices are fascinating.
4. Violence over the status of slavery in Kansas was a ________________ to wider conflict.
5. The products of many ________________ manufacturers are still sold secondhand online.
6. "Luminiferous ether," a proposed medium in which light waves propagate, has joined the ________________ of discarded scientific theories.

Definitions: Match the new words with their meanings.

7.	annals	________	a.	ancient times
8.	prelude	________	b.	no longer functioning
9.	defunct	________	c.	out of date
10.	trove	________	d.	archives
11.	antiquity	________	e.	a hidden treasure
12.	obsolete	________	f.	an opening move

THE GOOD OLD DAYS

Nostalgia is a well-known psychological phenomenon. *Pining* for the days of our ancestors when things were "simpler" has become a passion of history lovers. However, no amount of dress-up can bring back the *zeitgeist* of a past era when notions like belief in unfettered progress or repugnant* racial theories were widely accepted. *Reminiscing* about lost youth is a favorite pastime of curmudgeons,* right up there with dominoes. Even when the days of one's youth were marked by deprivation, instead of having gratitude for present abundance, we *rue* the loss of thriftiness. Frustration with *antiquated* technologies is transformed into maudlin* affection for their quaintness.

Once more, your keen eye and memory were being tested. Did you recognize curmudgeon *as being from an earlier lesson?*

NEW WORDS

nostalgia
nō - stal - jə

pine (v.)
pīn

zeitgeist
zīt - gīst

reminisce
rem - ə - nəs

rue
rū

antiquated
an - ti - kwāt - əd

Notable Roots: zeit = times; geist = spirit; antique = old

Sample Sentences: Insert the new words in these sentences.

1. The ________________ of the medieval era held that death was always imminent.*
2. Rail transport only becomes ________________ if we fail to invest in its improvement.
3. A judge must consider whether a convict ________________ his action or getting caught.
4. For team owners, the economic attractiveness of Los Angeles outweighed ________________ for the Dodgers' years in Brooklyn.
5. Romeo's ________________ for Rosaline is quickly forgotten when he meets Juliet.
6. Animosity forgotten, elderly Union and Confederate veterans would ________________ about their wartime experiences.

Definitions: Match the new words with their meanings.

7.	nostalgia	________	a.	the defining spirit of an era
8.	pine	________	b.	to remember fondly
9.	zeitgeist	________	c.	behind the times
10.	reminisce	________	d.	to regret
11.	rue	________	e.	sentimental attachment to the past
12.	antiquated	________	f.	to long for

TOO LATE

The Galveston Hurricane of 1900 underscores the dangers of *belated* warnings. The U.S. Weather Bureau ignored *prognostications* from Cuban meteorologists that a storm passing into the Gulf of Mexico would grow monstrous and strike the Texas coast. U.S. experts *procrastinated* until the day the storm arrived before issuing a warning for Galveston. This came about not due to *clairvoyance*, but because ships encountering the storm reported its uncommon ferocity. Unfortunately, few in the city were *prescient* enough to evacuate; some even considered fine weather that morning to be an *auspice*. The result of this lack of foresight was the largest death toll of any disaster in U.S. history when the storm surge inundated the entire island city.

NEW WORDS

belated
bē - lāt - əd

prognosticate
prog - nos - tik - āt

procrastinate
prō - kras - tin - āt

clairvoyant
klar - vôi - ənt

prescient
pre - shənt

auspice
ô - spis

Notable Roots: gnostic = know; pro = forward; cras = tomorrow; voir = see; scient = know

Sample Sentences: Insert the new words in these sentences.

1. A few ________________ leaders saw the Treaty of Versailles as a mere 20-year armistice.
2. An eagle with a serpent in its talons was considered a high ______________ to the Greeks.
3. An adult realizes that to ________________ is to cause more anxiety than it relieves.
4. Sansa's ________________ thanks does little to thaw relations with the queen.
5. Con men research their marks, learning enough to appear truly ________________.
6. As late as 1928, many economists continued to ________________ an endless boom.

Definitions: Match the new words with their meanings.

7. belated _________ a. to postpone
8. prognosticate _________ b. able to foresee future events supernaturally
9. procrastinate _________ c. a sign of good fortune
10. clairvoyant _________ d. to predict
11. prescient _________ e. tardy
12. auspice _________ f. able to predict based on present facts

GROUP REVIEW

Chaos theory posits that in systems with many variables—like the weather—you can never know enough to offer accurate predictions beyond the immediate future. However, prediction improves with data—like the prediction that vocabulary knowledge grows with diligent studying!

Matching

Directions: Match the words with their meanings.

	REVIEW WORDS		DEFINITIONS
________	**1.** annals	**a.**	a routine
________	**2.** antiquated	**b.**	to regret
________	**3.** antiquity	**c.**	tardy
________	**4.** auspice	**d.**	to pass; to expire
________	**5.** belated	**e.**	to shorten
________	**6.** clairvoyant	**f.**	to long for
________	**7.** defunct	**g.**	a sign of good fortune
________	**8.** elapse	**h.**	to postpone
________	**9.** interminable	**i.**	archives
________	**10.** nostalgia	**j.**	sentimental attachment to the past
________	**11.** obsolete	**k.**	able to predict based on present facts
________	**12.** paradox	**l.**	behind the times
________	**13.** pine	**m.**	no longer functioning
________	**14.** prelude	**n.**	ancient times
________	**15.** prescient	**o.**	a hidden treasure
________	**16.** procrastinate	**p.**	out of date
________	**17.** prognosticate	**q.**	never-ending
________	**18.** regimen	**r.**	an inherent contradiction
________	**19.** reminisce	**s.**	to predict
________	**20.** retrospect	**t.**	to remember fondly
________	**21.** rue	**u.**	in hindsight
________	**22.** trove	**v.**	the defining spirit of an era
________	**23.** truncate	**w.**	an opening move
________	**24.** zeitgeist	**x.**	able to foresee future events supernaturally

Hapless Headlines

Directions: Choose the best words to complete each of the newspaper headlines.

a. aberrant
b. accost
c. belligerent
d. dissolution
e. elapse
f. emissary
g. extrinsic
h. flotilla
i. hegemony
j. incoherent
k. inexorable
l. invulnerable
m. junta
n. paradox
o. prelude
p. prohibition
q. protocol
r. rail
s. sanction
t. trove

1. Allied __________ Closes in on Iwo Jima
2. Alcohol __________ a "Total Failure" Says Smith
3. Rebels Target Headquarters of Ruling __________
4. __________ of Spanish Gold Found in Caribbean
5. CEO Considers Slide Toward Bankruptcy __________
6. FAA Rules __________ Factors, Not Design, Cause of Crash
7. Senator __________ by Critics at Restaurant
8. Russian Mobilization a "__________ to War" Says Germany
9. Budget Deadline __________ without Deal
10. __________ Weather More Common as Climate Warms

Wordsearch

Directions: Using the clues listed below, fill in each blank in the following story with one of the new words you learned this week.

Clues

1st Day	1st Day
3rd Day	3rd Day
3rd Day	4th Day
2nd Day	2nd Day
4th Day	3rd Day

Butterfly Effects

Time travel is a staple device of science fiction. One consistent feature of time travel plots is the ___________ that arise when people travel back and interfere with causality. In many a film, a well-meaning protagonist, driven by ___________ for the past or the desire to obviate* some ___________ tragedy discovers just how complex and delicate a chain of events leads from past to present.

In some stories, the ___________ of history are inadvertently altered, creating a new, often dystopian, present. In others, an unscrupulous, "___________" visitor from the future uses their foreknowledge for profit, becoming a tyrant by means of fraud. Sometimes a time traveler becomes stuck in another era, facing an ___________ stay in a space-time entrepôt where the ___________ makes it very uncomfortable for a voyager with modern sensibilities.

In the happier films, however, all works out well. The plucky hero ___________ but successfully repairs the damage. Immersion in a ___________ world grants the protagonist new respect for our predecessors. ___________ for her own time, moreover, teaches appreciation of each moment.

STANDING OUT FROM THE CROWD

Fungible products are those that are practically interchangeable. Many of the products we *imbibe* fall under this heading. Manufacturers are forever *afflicted* with the fear that a successful product will soon appear old and *spartan*, so they come out with "new and improved" versions. Sometimes it is only a box or package that has been changed—perhaps a colorful photo of a succulent meal on a frozen dinner box. Some products peddle an image. For example, shaving cream makers project an image of their users as strapping* and *ruddy*, while those that use "the other brand" are *gaunt* bookworms with *atrophied* muscles.

NEW WORDS

imbibe
im - bīb

afflict
ə - flikt

spartan
spär - tən

ruddy
rud - ē

gaunt
gônt

atrophy
a - trō - fē

Notable Roots:
bib = drink; rud = red; troph = grow

Sample Sentences: Insert the new words in these sentences.

1. Romeo ________________ poison just before Juliet wakes up.
2. The cold air made Beverly's cheeks so ________________ the portrait was ruined.
3. Some talents may ________________ from disuse but never really desert us.
4. Before receiving a transfusion, Nadia's face had a ________________ look.
5. The cheapest youth hostels have decidedly ________________ accommodations.
6. Those in the tropics are often ________________ by mosquito-borne diseases.

Definitions: Match the new words with their meanings.

7.	imbibe	________	a.	to trouble or cause pain
8.	afflict	________	b.	bare; uncomfortable
9.	spartan	________	c.	drink or consume
10.	ruddy	________	d.	pale and sickly
11.	gaunt	________	e.	weaken by disuse
12.	atrophy	________	f.	red-faced

PHARMACEUTICAL HALLUCINATIONS

If you watch enough commercials by major drug-makers, it almost seems as if those suffering terrible *maladies* are being offered a life better than the one they had before getting sick. No matter whether the drug in question *palliates* suffering from rheumatism or offers a few extra months of *longevity* to those suffering *malignant* tumors. The shop-worn visual clichés in drug commercials of running through fields of flowers or playing softball with grandkids promise a *panacea*—regardless of which drug is being peddled. The juxtaposition of a voiceover detailing potentially debilitating side effects underscores the inauthenticity of this style of advertising.

NEW WORDS

malady
mal - ə - dē

palliate
pal - ē - āt

longevity
lon - jev - ə - tē

malignant
mə - lig - nənt

panacea
pan - ə - sē - ə

debilitate
dē - bil - ə - tāt

Notable Roots: mal = bad; pall = shadow; pan = all

Sample Sentences: Insert the new words in these sentences.

1. Quinine was a tragic ________________, so effective at treating malaria that it opened up Africa to conquest.
2. Finding a medicine to ________________ migraines can change the lives of sufferers.
3. Although ________________ by abdominal cancer, Matisse created vibrant "cut-out" artworks.
4. Ty Cobb's ________________ personality may explain why his team failed to win a title.
5. Queen Elizabeth's ________________ has made her the icon of an age.
6. Genetic ________________, though incurable, are now increasingly treatable.

Definitions: Match the new words with their definitions.

7. malady	________	a. to soothe without curing
8. palliate	________	b. destructive; harmful
9. longevity	________	c. a sickness
10. malignant	________	d. to handicap
11. panacea	________	e. length of life
12. debilitate	________	f. a cure-all

"TRIED AND TRUE"

At one time, before the advent of radio, products were advertised on the merits of their "tried and true" qualities. Such advertising assumed pragmatic consumers, *abstemious* in consumption, *repose* dictated by the cycle of night and day. They were usually in fine *fettle*, though *masticating* with poor teeth and subject to *virulent* pathogens. Manufacturers did not presume to tell such stolid* folk what they should want, but catered to what they needed: cereal grains for nourishment, wool for warmth, and gauze for *lacerations*. The inventory of the grocer was carefully limited to meet demand. Advertising reversed this relationship, enticing increased demand to meet the dizzying volume of goods supplied by an industrial economy.

Sample Sentences: Insert the new words in these sentences.

1. The most ________________ germs are those that are most novel to our systems.
2. War allows little ________________ for soldiers who must remain vigilant.
3. Without antibiotics, every ________________ is potentially fatal.
4. Clementine's horses were in such poor ________________ that she rested them for days.
5. Cows are famous for their long, patient ________________ of fibrous grasses.
6. Churchill, a drinker and smoker who lived to be 90, defied the maxim that only the ________________ enjoy longevity.

Definitions: Match the new words with their meanings.

7.	abstemious	________	a.	to chew
8.	repose	________	b.	a cut
9.	fettle	________	c.	rest
10.	masticate	________	d.	moderate in consumption
11.	virulent	________	e.	condition or health
12.	laceration	________	f.	powerful; deadly

NEW WORDS

abstemious
ab - stēm - ē - əs

repose
rē - pōz

fettle
fet - əl

masticate
mas - tik - āt

virulent
vir - ə - lənt

laceration
las - ər - ā - shən

Notable Roots: temer = daring; vir = man; lacer = sharp

WHAT'S IN A NAME?

Supermarkets often carry their own products to compete with the national brands. These "house" brands are in an *adverse* position because they cannot be advertised widely. Supermarkets overcome this *deficiency* by making these brands less expensive. Many people believe the aphorism "You get what you pay for," and they purchase items on the premise* that the quality is *degraded* at lower price points. Are the *gallant* boasts of nationally advertised brands bogus? How can one bread company prove its product is more *salubrious* than another? As there is no incontrovertible evidence, the more expensive bread (or coffee, etc.) must compensate* by making inordinate claims to convince the *austere* consumer to switch.

NEW WORDS

adverse
ad - vers

deficiency
də - fish - ən - sē

degrade
də - grād

gallant
gal - ənt

salubrious
sə - lūb - rē - əs

austere
ô - stēr

Notable Roots:
ad = away; vers = turn;
fac/fic = make/do;
salu = health

Sample Sentences: Insert the new words in these sentences.

1. The Mediterranean diet has been touted for its _______________ effects.
2. Unlike the mud-covered infantry, WWI pilots were celebrated as _______________ heroes.
3. Candidates employ strategists to handle _______________ publicity.
4. Protestant churches of the seventeenth century were highly _______________, a reaction to the baroque* character of Renaissance Catholic churches.
5. Recognizing his _______________ as a leader, Tommy preferred to be a loner.
6. After a century under water, the *Titanic* has _______________ to the point of dissolution.

Definitions: Match the new words with their meanings.

7.	adverse	_______	a.	flaw; shortcoming
8.	deficiency	_______	b.	healthy
9.	degrade	_______	c.	unfavorable
10.	gallant	_______	d.	severe; plain
11.	salubrious	_______	e.	to break down; to humiliate
12.	austere	_______	f.	brave and daring

GROUP REVIEW

You can be sure of a balanced language if you are well acquainted with all the products (words) available in your supermarket (vocabulary).

Matching

Directions: Match this week's words with their meanings.

	REVIEW WORDS	DEFINITIONS
______	**1.** abstemious	**a.** rest
______	**2.** adverse	**b.** to handicap
______	**3.** afflict	**c.** a cut
______	**4.** atrophy	**d.** powerful; deadly
______	**5.** austere	**e.** destructive; harmful
______	**6.** debilitate	**f.** red-faced
______	**7.** deficiency	**g.** healthy
______	**8.** degrade	**h.** unfavorable
______	**9.** fettle	**i.** pale and sickly
______	**10.** gallant	**j.** moderate in consumption
______	**11.** gaunt	**k.** brave and daring
______	**12.** imbibe	**l.** bare; uncomfortable
______	**13.** laceration	**m.** to soothe without curing
______	**14.** longevity	**n.** a sickness
______	**15.** malady	**o.** weaken by disuse
______	**16.** malignant	**p.** to break down; to humiliate
______	**17.** masticate	**q.** to chew
______	**18.** palliate	**r.** a cure-all
______	**19.** panacea	**s.** drink or consume
______	**20.** repose	**t.** condition or health
______	**21.** ruddy	**u.** to trouble or cause pain
______	**22.** salubrious	**v.** length of life
______	**23.** spartan	**w.** severe; plain
______	**24.** virulent	**x.** flaw; shortcoming

Wordsearch

Directions: Using the clues listed below, fill in each blank in the following story with one of the new words you learned this week.

Clues

2nd Day
4th Day
2nd Day
4th Day
1st Day
4th Day
1st Day
3rd Day
1st Day

Age Discrimination

One of the most ___________ forms of discrimination is that based upon age. We have become aware through publicity and education that bias and discrimination based upon race, color, creed, and gender are not to be accepted. Through laws passed by the Congress of the United States and by individual states, we agree that using these criteria for hiring, promoting, or firing in the workplace is a ___________ and undemocratic excuse. Many lawsuits have supported this most basic right to "life, liberty, and the pursuit of happiness" protected by our Constitution.

Why is it, then, that so few question the practice of preventing some from getting positions or promotions based on their ___________? Advanced age leads to ___________ conditions, such as the firing of such employees and their replacement with ___________-cheeked younger applicants. Is there any evidence that the young are more ___________ while older workers are inherently___________? Many workers over 60 are, in fact, in fine ___________ with minds that have not ___________ but remained active. Therefore, such discrimination is unwarranted.

YOU CAN'T HELP BUT WATCH

The consumer is in a quandary* *discerning* the best selection among the array of products. The advertisers must *convert* the consumer to their brand, and often they do it in the most crass and *overt* ways. Manufacturers have *ascertained* that television is the most effective way to reach a mass audience; therefore, consumer messaging *permeates* television. Through their studies *delving* into the human psyche, advertisers are able to craft messages that are both persuasive and difficult to ignore.

NEW WORDS

discern
dis - ėrn

convert (v.)
kən - vėrt

overt
ō - vėrt

ascertain
as - ėr - tān

permeate
pėr - mē - āt

delve
delv

Notable Roots: vers = turn; ouvre = open; perme = pass through

Sample Sentences: Insert the new words in these sentences.

1. If banks _______________ a prospective borrower might default, they don't offer a loan.
2. Republics persist as long as _______________ unconstitutional acts are resisted.
3. Dissatisfaction _______________ the team culture until the coach lost all control.
4. Humans have _______________ the ocean deeps less than the reaches of space.
5. A camouflaged warship is harder to _______________ on the horizon.
6. A zealot is rarely someone who has been _______________ to a faith by force.

Definitions: Match the new words with their meanings.

7. discern	_________	a.	open; obvious
8. convert	_________	b.	perceive the difference
9. overt	_________	c.	spread throughout
10. ascertain	_________	d.	cause to change; win over
11. permeate	_________	e.	to dive deeply
12. delve	_________	f.	figure out

BUREAU OF PUBLIC INFORMATION

The power of advertising was discovered when the United States government set its collective mind to *eliciting* public support for the First World War. After the U.S. entered the fray* in the spring of 1917, President Woodrow Wilson immediately realized he had an image problem: his 1916 reelection campaign had *candidly* boasted that he had kept the country out of war! To overcome, he named George Creel, a man who was the *epitome* of *cogent* and persuasive messaging, the Director of Public Information. Soon posters like the famous portrait of Uncle Sam with the *glib* slogan "I want you for the U.S. army!" were everywhere. Creel also conceived of the "Four Minute Men," community leaders who would give four-minute speeches during movie intermissions about why the war was *germane* to American lives.

NEW WORDS

elicit
ē - lis - it

candid
kan - did

epitome
ə - pit - ō - mē

cogent
kō - jənt

glib
glib

germane
jėr - mān

Notable Roots: licit = lure; cand = shine; tomo = cut

Sample Sentences: Insert the new words in these sentences.

1. In a time when people want authenticity, a _______________ campaign slogan will fail.
2. In the 1960s, Steve McQueen, tough and flinty, was the _______________ of cool.
3. Pundits quash scandal by bringing up misdeeds not _______________ to the controversy.
4. To _______________ meaningful class participation, avoid yes or no questions.
5. Suspects without counsel are advised not to be too _______________ with detectives.
6. A sophist is an expert at presenting a _______________ defense of an absurd position.

Definitions: Match the new words with their meanings.

7.	elicit	________	a.	clear and persuasive
8.	candid	________	b.	articulate but insincere
9.	epitome	________	c.	relevant
10.	cogent	________	d.	open and honest
11.	glib	________	e.	the ideal example
12.	germane	________	f.	to encourage a response

THE PROPAGANDA COUP

Creel's campaign was so effective at convincing the public that the rationale for the war was *incontrovertible* that the army was soon awash in volunteers. Unfortunately, with such passions aroused, many *construed* the call to action as permission to badger* German-Americans. Later, when the draft was instituted, Creel created newsreels from which people *gleaned* the false notion that the "selective service" program *denoted* another form of volunteering. When more foodstuffs were needed for the army, Creel's messaging never *enunciated* the word "rationing," instead encouraging the home front to regard participation in "Meatless Mondays" and "Wheatless Wednesdays" as *pertinent* ways of fighting the war.

NEW WORDS

incontrovertible
in - kon - trə - vėr - tə - bəl

construe
kən - strū

glean
glēn

denote
də - nōt

enunciate
ə - nuns - ē - āt

pertinent
pėr - tə - nənt

Notable Roots: contra = against; stru = build; nunce = announce

Sample Sentences: Insert the new words in these sentences.

1. It's not necessary to ________________ every syllable clearly in a song.
2. Sherlock Holmes ________________ far more data from a crime scene than the police.
3. Joan's skills turned out to be highly ________________ to her success in the competition.
4. Conspiracists ________________ nefarious* plots in chains of loosely connected events.
5. The number of stars ________________ a general's rank.
6. Negatives can't be proven, thus denial of the supernatural is not technically ______________.

Definitions: Match the new words with their meanings.

7.	incontrovertible	________	a.	to indicate
8.	construe	________	b.	related; appropriate
9.	glean	________	c.	to announce; to speak clearly
10.	denote	________	d.	to perceive from limited information
11.	enunciate	________	e.	cannot be disproven
12.	pertinent	________	f.	gain information or understanding

PERFECTING THE MACHINE

After the successes of the BPI, the same methods were employed after the U.S. entered World War II. Everyone got the *gist* of why we were fighting Japan—*alluding* to the name Pearl Harbor was sufficient to rouse passions. A pressing need was to *elucidate* the reasons for fighting Germany. Some of America's best filmmakers, like Frank Capra and John Huston, created propaganda films *delineating* the horrors of the Nazi regime. Waging a worldwide conflict also meant *reinvigorating* an economy shuttered since the Depression for the production of armaments. The image of Rosie the Riveter is an enduring legacy of the propaganda effort on the home front. Posters, events, and short films on the need for rationing and investing in war bonds were also wildly successful. The success of the postwar economy was *derived* from the savings Americans—habitual consumers—accumulated by following the directives of wartime propaganda.

NEW WORDS

gist
jist

allude
ə - lūd

elucidate
ə - lūs - ə - dāt

delineate
də - lin - ē - āt

reinvigorate
rē - in - vig - ər - āt

derive
də - rīv

Notable Roots: lud = play; lucid = clear, bright; line = draw lines; vigor = strength; rive = flow

Sample Sentences: Insert the new words in these sentences.

1. The time-out served to ________________ the defense, which forced a game-saving fumble.
2. Mark Antony's funeral oration ________________ the reasoning behind Caesar's actions so successfully that the Optimates who killed the dictator fled in terror.
3. The poems of T. S. Eliot ________________ to so many classical references that they are best read with an encyclopedia at one's side.
4. Preserving slavery was the true ________________ of the Confederate cause.
5. Jefferson argues government power is ________________ from the consent of the governed.
6. Daniel Burnham would ________________ in words what Root's blueprints could not.

Definitions: Match the new words with their meanings.

7.	gist	_________	a.	to arise from
8.	allude	_________	b.	to express precisely
9.	elucidate	_________	c.	to give new life
10.	delineate	_________	d.	the substance of something
11.	reinvigorate	_________	e.	to make clear
12.	derive	_________	f.	to make reference to

GROUP REVIEW

As you watch your next television commercial, try to imagine what questions were asked by the research people as they interviewed the possible consumers. Advertisers have to select their words carefully. You can select words only when you have large numbers at your command.

Matching

Directions: Match this week's words with their meanings.

REVIEW WORDS		DEFINITIONS
________	**1.** allude	**a.** gain information or understanding
________	**2.** ascertain	**b.** cause to change; win over
________	**3.** candid	**c.** to make reference to
________	**4.** cogent	**d.** to announce; to speak clearly
________	**5.** construe	**e.** articulate but insincere
________	**6.** convert	**f.** relevant
________	**7.** delineate	**g.** perceive the difference
________	**8.** delve	**h.** the substance of something
________	**9.** denote	**i.** to make clear
________	**10.** derive	**j.** to indicate
________	**11.** discern	**k.** to perceive from limited information
________	**12.** elicit	**l.** to express precisely
________	**13.** elucidate	**m.** to encourage a response
________	**14.** enunciate	**n.** open and honest
________	**15.** epitome	**o.** related; appropriate
________	**16.** germane	**p.** to give new life
________	**17.** gist	**q.** spread throughout
________	**18.** glean	**r.** open; obvious
________	**19.** glib	**s.** cannot be disproven
________	**20.** incontrovertible	**t.** figure out
________	**21.** overt	**u.** the ideal example
________	**22.** permeate	**v.** to arise from
________	**23.** pertinent	**w.** to dive deeply
________	**24.** reinvigorate	**x.** clear and persuasive

Wordsearch

Directions: Using the clues listed below, fill in each blank in the following story with one of the new words you learned this week.

Clues

1st Day	2nd Day
1st Day	4th Day
1st Day	1st Day
3rd Day	2nd Day
2nd Day	2nd Day

Peacetime Propaganda

In the beginning, there was only word of mouth. Advertising began in earnest with the advent of print media. The combination of printing and widespread literacy gave manufacturers a way to ___________ readers into customers. As the Industrial Revolution spawned a multiplicity of products, however, merchants could ___________ the limits of print advertising. Many still could not read. Those that could might choose to read one periodical over another or simply ignore the small blurbs of advertising. It was not until the invention of radio that advertising could truly ___________ every home. The effectiveness of radio advertising was ___________: clumsy radio ads generated more business than the most ___________ print messages.

Advertising did not truly come into its own until after World War II, however. Breakthroughs in psychology had shown propagandists how to ___________ desired behaviors. After the war, the advertising industry sought to ___________ demand using many of the same methods. One such technique was selling the consumer an image of who they wanted to be—a VIP, a mountaineer, a fashion model, or a movie star—and then encouraging the consumer to ___________ associate the product with the image. Through advertising, Americans were encouraged to see certain brands as the ___________ of identity and status. Through techniques like "___________" celebrity endorsements and product placement, advertising gained new levels of influence during the golden age of television. Teenagers became the prime consumers of music during the rise of rock 'n' roll. Children's programming not only encouraged kids to plead for the latest toys, but also began the process of inculcating the ethos of consumerism.

LIGHT IS NOT ENOUGH

When the speed of light was first computed, scientists recognized it to be a velocity *inordinate* to that of any known object. Einstein later proved that light speed is *ubiquitous*, unaffected by the motion of the source from which it is *emanating*. His mathematics also demonstrated light speed to be an unreachable limit. Due to an *array* of discoveries, astronomers simultaneously began to comprehend the vastness of space. Edwin Hubble discovered that our nearest galactic neighbor, Andromeda, is two million light-years away. Since that time, scientists have dealt with a paradox*: the universe *abounds* with objects too far to reach, while our world is *saturated* with light that has taken eons to arrive.

NEW WORDS

inordinate
in - ôr - də - nət

ubiquitous
yū - bik - wit - əs

emanate
em - ən - āt

array
ə - rā

abound
ə - bound

saturate
sach - ə - rāt

Notable Roots: ordinal = order, degree; ubiqui = everywhere; emana = flow; bound = limit

Sample Sentences: Insert the new words in these sentences.

1. By adolescence, Mozart had already composed an impressive ________________ of music.
2. Rumors that America ________________ with gold proved to be unfounded.
3. Prices crash when the market is ________________ with supply.
4. Punitive damages may seem ________________ but are meant to deter future crimes.
5. The sounds that ________________ from a laboring person can be unearthly.
6. Cell towers are ________________ on the coasts but rarer in the rural interior.

Definitions: Match the new words with their meanings.

7. inordinate	________		**a.**	an impressive display
8. ubiquitous	________		**b.**	occur in large quantity
9. emanate	________		**c.**	out of proportion
10. array	________		**d.**	fill beyond capacity
11. abound	________		**e.**	to flow from
12. saturate	________		**f.**	to be found everywhere

LIFE ABOUNDS*

Earth is so *inundated* with life that life forms have altered the planet. Photosynthesis is so effective that the *extraneous* oxygen has changed the composition of the atmosphere. Before this change, iron-rich rocks did not rust, and the dominant species were anaerobic bacteria. The *concomitant* binding of atmospheric carbon in living tissues proved to be an *unmitigated* loss of a crucial greenhouse gas, beginning a cycle of wild climatic swings. Thanks to genetic mutation and natural selection, however, life has proven a *consummate* survivor of climate fluctuation. Since the Cambrian explosion, *myriad* forms of life have arisen to exploit the opportunities that have followed mass extinction events.

NEW WORDS

inundate
in - un - dāt

extraneous
eks - trān - ē - əs

concomitant
kon - kom - ə - tənt

unmitigated
un - mit - ə - gāt - əd

consummate
kon - sə - mət

myriad
mēr - ē - ad

Notable Roots: inundat = flood; extra = beyond; comit = companion; summa = peak

Sample Sentences: Insert the new words in these sentences.

1. The Ford Edsel proved to be an _______________ disaster.
2. Army-Navy stores sell _______________ supplies not required by the armed forces.
3. Egyptian farmers once relied on the Nile to annually _______________ their fields.
4. Charles Lindbergh ultimately rued* the fame _______________ with his achievement.
5. Teachers hear _______________ excuses from their students for late assignments.
6. Christy Mathewson was such a _______________ gentlemen that his death was mourned by all of baseball.

Definitions: Match the new words with their meanings.

7. inundate	________	a.	without compensation; total
8. extraneous	________	b.	extremely skilled; perfect
9. concomitant	________	c.	more than necessary
10. unmitigated	________	d.	great in number
11. consummate	________	e.	accompanying
12. myriad	________	f.	to flood

FEEDING THE MASSES

The rise of cities, with their *manifold* benefits and drawbacks, began with food surpluses. When each person was needed to farm in order for a whole community to survive, there was little time to do anything else. Once crop yields were so *bounteous* that extra farmhands were *superfluous*, however, it allowed for the development of specialist workers like craftsmen and artisans. Yields that were truly *copious* allowed for trade with neighboring communities for *succulent* delicacies and *epicurean* luxuries. Thus, economics was born.

Sample Sentences: Insert the new words in these sentences.

1. Many creatures produce ________________ eggs to ensure survival of some offspring.
2. College is an environment with ________________ distractions.
3. A slow-roasted steak is a truly ________________ entrée.
4. Roman conservatives like Cato lamented the adoption of ________________ tastes in the city.
5. Even a superficial head wound is usually accompanied by ________________ bleeding.
6. This year's Thanksgiving feast was so ________________ that dessert was barely touched.

Definitions: Match the new words with their definitions.

7.	manifold	________	a.	surplus
8.	bounteous	________	b.	abundant
9.	superfluous	________	c.	tender and juicy
10.	copious	________	d.	pleasure-loving
11.	succulent	________	e.	in generous quantity
12.	epicurean	________	f.	numerous

NEW WORDS

manifold
man - ə - fōld

bounteous
boun - tē - əs

superfluous
sū - pėr - flū - əs

copious
kō - pē - əs

succulent
suk - yū - lənt

epicurean
ep - ə - kyur - ē - ən

Notable Roots:
mani = many; bound = limit; super = over; fluous = flow

MARKETPLACE OF CIVILIZATION

Trade *enhances* both the space and time of the urban environment. In Turkey, a land at the intersection of trade routes, every town is *replete* with an open-air market, which serves as the climax to every week. In fact, the Turkish name for Sunday, *pazar*, means "market day." In Istanbul, not only does each neighborhood hold its own bazaar, but there's also a *plethora* of permanent institutions. The Spice Bazaar, located on the opposite end of the city's busiest bridge, is *redolent* with the smells of Turkey's most treasured trade goods: pistachios, dried apricots, figs, tea, and cumin. A mile away lies the Grand Bazaar, a warren of passageways *rife* with trade. Here merchants and shoppers engage, with *profuse* swearing and gesturing, in the time-honored ritual of haggling over everything from hookahs and tea sets to leather purses and engagement rings.

NEW WORDS

enhance
in - hans

replete
rə - plēt

plethora
pleth - ôr - ə

redolent
red - ə - lənt

rife
rīf

profuse
prō - fyūs

Notable Roots: plere = fill; olea = oil, essence; fuse = flow

Sample Sentences: Insert the new words in these sentences.

1. The interior of my father's work van was _______________ with nostalgic* smells.
2. The wealthiest, most _______________ donors have inordinate* political influence.
3. The young couple's bridal purse was _______________ with generous gifts.
4. With modern software, the once-grainy image had been greatly _______________.
5. Small children often feel overwhelmed when presented with a _______________ of options.
6. New York society was _______________ with gossip after the murder of Stanford White.

Definitions: Match the new words with their meanings.

7.	enhance	________	a.	plentiful amount
8.	replete	________	b.	filled with the odor of something
9.	plethora	________	c.	prevalent; common
10.	redolent	________	d.	overflowing with
11.	rife	________	e.	to improve or refine
12.	profuse	________	f.	equipped with

GROUP REVIEW

It's been said that societies have the greatest abundance of words for the subjects that most occupy people's minds. The English language is saturated* with words related to both trade and language. Thus, your supply of synonyms on these topics should never run dry.

Matching

Directions: Match the words you learned this week with their meanings.

REVIEW WORDS		DEFINITIONS
________	**1.** abound	**a.** filled with the odor of something
________	**2.** array	**b.** fill beyond capacity
________	**3.** bounteous	**c.** overflowing with
________	**4.** concomitant	**d.** to flood
________	**5.** consummate	**e.** to flow from
________	**6.** copious	**f.** abundant
________	**7.** emanate	**g.** without compensation; total
________	**8.** enhance	**h.** out of proportion
________	**9.** epicurean	**i.** extremely skilled; perfect
________	**10.** extraneous	**j.** prevalent; common
________	**11.** inordinate	**k.** numerous
________	**12.** inundate	**l.** in generous quantity
________	**13.** manifold	**m.** pleasure-loving
________	**14.** myriad	**n.** plentiful amount
________	**15.** plethora	**o.** accompanying
________	**16.** profuse	**p.** to be found everywhere
________	**17.** redolent	**q.** more than necessary
________	**18.** replete	**r.** surplus
________	**19.** rife	**s.** great in number
________	**20.** saturate	**t.** occur in large quantity
________	**21.** succulent	**u.** tender and juicy
________	**22.** superfluous	**v.** an impressive display
________	**23.** ubiquitous	**w.** equipped with
________	**24.** unmitigated	**x.** to improve or refine

Wordsearch

Directions: Using the clues listed below, fill in each blank in the following story with one of the new words you learned this week.

Clues

4th Day

2nd Day

2nd Day

1st Day

1st Day

1st Day

2nd Day

1st Day

2nd Day

4th Day

Whistle Blowing

How much loyalty do employees owe to their employers? Many industries are ___________ with companies that go out of their way to encourage employees to make suggestions that will improve the way they operate. A ___________ ethicist will not reprimand an employee who points out ___________ problems that are harming the business. In fact, it should be in the bosses' interest that the secrets the whistleblower unearths ___________ to upper management.

However, there seems to be a ___________ problem in business of whistleblowers facing harsh punishment for calling attention to unethical actions. The whistleblower soon faces an ___________ of problems. He or she is ostracized at the workplace, often ___________ with abuse. The informer might face ___________ punishment for some minor error—real or invented. Such punishment carries with it ___________ damage to reputation, and soon enough the whistleblower either is fired or quits. As a result, the employees go back to "business as usual" without any change. The annals* of business and government are unfortunately ___________ with such stories.

HAVE WE MASTERED OUR ENVIRONMENT?

Natural disasters tend to leave the best efforts of mankind in *disarray*. It is as though *tumultuous* forces are contemptuous* of our proud achievements. Hurricanes, arising from *turbulent* air on the other side of the Atlantic, unleash *pandemonium* along our coasts. Those living along fault lines face the *conundrum* of when the next earthquake will strike. A more patient *phenomenon*, drought, is an implacable enemy of agriculture as well as the fuel for conflagrations.*

NEW WORDS

disarray
dis - ər - ā

tumultuous
tû - mul - chū - əs

turbulent
tər - byū - lənt

pandemonium
pan - də - mō - nē - ûm

conundrum
kə - nûn - drûm

phenomenon
fə - nom - ə - non

Notable Roots: array = impressive display; tumult = disturbance; turbu = disorder; pan = all

Sample Sentences: Insert the new words in these sentences.

1. Fenway Park was in a state of ________________ after Fisk's famous World Series home run.
2. A total eclipse is the most astounding astronomical ________________ one can witness.
3. Passage of the Civil Rights Act was one of the most ________________ acts of legislation in congressional history.
4. Fort Ticonderoga was in such ________________ it could not repel an attack.
5. FDR faced the ________________ of preparing a nation with an isolationist people for war.
6. The ________________ cultural rift* that opened in the 1960s has never fully healed.

Definitions: Match the new words with their meanings.

7.	disarray	________	a.	unsteady; violent
8.	tumultuous	________	b.	ruin; disorder
9.	turbulent	________	c.	singular occurrence
10.	pandemonium	________	d.	dilemma
11.	conundrum	________	e.	full of uproar
12.	phenomenon	________	f.	total chaos

WHO CAN YOU TRUST?

Societies go *awry* when sources of trustworthy information are discredited. Documents leaked during the Vietnam War showed that top officials were offering rosy prognostications* to the press long after privately admitting the conflict was a fiasco. Later, President Nixon's recorded conversations revealed that he had lied about his knowledge of the Watergate break-in. Scientists have lent their credentials to *tortuous* studies denying the harm of tobacco use. Media have prioritized sensationalism—*impromptu* scandals or celebrity gossip—over dry, often *unwieldy*, policy concerns. It's no wonder, then, that people have turned to the Internet in an attempt to access unfiltered information. Unfortunately, the web is a *cacophony* of voices, and many are lured by the loudest or those that tell them what they want to hear. A society in which each person feels entitled to their own facts is a *bedlam* in which nothing is certain.

NEW WORDS

awry
ə - rī

tortuous
tôr - tū - əs

impromptu
im - promp - tū

unwieldy
un - wēl - dē

cacophony
kə - kof - ən - ē

bedlam
bed - ləm

Notable Roots: wry = twisted; tort = twist; prompt = cue; phon = sound

Sample Sentences: Insert the new words in these sentences.

1. Unlike the mellifluous* harmonies of Beethoven's Ninth, ___________ denotes* sonic discord.
2. _______________ would be one way to describe a sword too heavy to be swung.
3. Without its prefix, the root of _______________ describes an ironic smile.
4. _______________, a word that better describes mountain roads, has nothing to do with pain.
5. An _______________ speech, given without electronic cues, can be refreshingly candid.*
6. The noun _______________ has no roots but refers to a notorious London lunatic asylum.

Definitions: Study these carefully for the fine differences in meaning.

7. awry	________	a.	awkward; heavy
8. tortuous	________	b.	madness
9. impromptu	________	c.	off kilter
10. unwieldy	________	d.	full of twists and turns
11. cacophony	________	e.	spontaneous
12. bedlam	________	f.	unpleasant noise

EVIDENCE OF ABSENCE

Believers in the *occult* need never fear disillusionment because of one simple principle: absence of evidence is not evidence of absence. In practical terms, it means that proving that something does not exist, no matter how *absurd*, is next to impossible. *Apocryphal* sightings of the Loch Ness Monster will never stop *hoodwinking* the credulous unless we are willing to drain the 263 million cubic feet of water in the Scottish lake. Even that probably would not do it. However *jarring* it may seem in a scientific world, belief in the fantastic is a common *peccadillo*. Some people would just rather live in a world where monsters could exist.

NEW WORDS

occult
ə - kult

absurd
əb - surd

apocryphal
ə - pok - rif - əl

hoodwink
hud - wink

jarring
jär - ing

peccadillo
pek - ə - dil - ō

Notable Roots:
occlu = cover, hide;
pecado = sin

Sample Sentences: Insert the new words in these sentences.

1. Awakening from intubation is a _______________ experience.
2. During the demonstration, the pickpocket _______________ a dozen FBI trainees.
3. Abstract art uses _______________ images to convey dreams, movement, or emotions.
4. Interest in the _______________ arose concomitantly* with scientific advancement.
5. Criminals are sometimes tracked because of _______________ like tearing up matchbooks.
6. _______________ tales, like the legend of the *Flying Dutchman*, are part of sea lore.

Definitions: Match the new words with their meanings.

7. occult	________	a.	illogical
8. absurd	________	b.	unnerving
9. apocryphal	________	c.	a minor fault
10. hoodwink	________	d.	the supernatural
11. jarring	________	e.	of doubtful origin
12. peccadillo	________	f.	to trick

THE POWER OF LAUGHTER

Charlie Chaplin's "The Great Dictator" was a devastating *satire* that invited audiences to laugh at the ridiculousness of fascist dictators. The absurdity* of Hitler and Mussolini's theatrics had hitherto been *occluded* by the fear they inspired. Chaplin's *mordant* wit, however, transformed them into clowns, in the process inspiring resistance to their tyranny.* In this way, humor often constitutes the earliest, *inchoate* phase of rebellion. The *acerbic* pens of Voltaire, Mencken, and Wilde were frontline weapons aimed at the pretensions of would-be strongmen. The shrill laugh, a defiant battle cry rising above the *welter* of shouts proclaiming "you may take our lives, but we will never take you seriously!"

NEW WORDS

satire
sat - īr

occlude
ə - klūd

mordant
môr - dənt

inchoate
in - kō - āt

acerbic
ə - sėr - bik

welter
wel - tėr

Notable Roots:
occlu = cover, hide;
acer = sharp

Sample Sentences: Insert the new words in these sentences.

1. The ________________ solar system had many protoplanets that were destroyed or ejected.
2. Ben's self-esteem was destroyed by years of his father's ________________ comments.
3. *Calvin and Hobbes*'s ________________ humor is best recognized by parents.
4. A fumble is always followed by a ________________ of strong bodies grasping for a ball.
5. Compared with slapstick comedy, ________________ is characterized by subtle wordplay.
6. Recent studies suggest that the star Betelgeuse was ________________ by a gas cloud.

Definitions: Match the new words with their meanings.

7. satire	_________	a.	a mass of confusion
8. occlude	_________	b.	barely formed
9. mordant	_________	c.	a form of humor that ridicules
10. inchoate	_________	d.	to hide or block
11. acerbic	_________	e.	humorously critical
12. welter	_________	f.	cutting

GROUP REVIEW

The history, or derivation, of words is called *etymology*. This is a fascinating study, and it gives insight into the background of words, such as *canary* and thousands of others. Knowing the history of a word helps you remember it.

Matching

Directions: Match the words with their meanings.

	REVIEW WORDS		DEFINITIONS
______	**1.** absurd	**a.**	humorously critical
______	**2.** acerbic	**b.**	to trick
______	**3.** apocryphal	**c.**	awkward; heavy
______	**4.** awry	**d.**	barely formed
______	**5.** bedlam	**e.**	unsteady; violent
______	**6.** cacophony	**f.**	a minor fault
______	**7.** conundrum	**g.**	to hide or block
______	**8.** disarray	**h.**	total chaos
______	**9.** hoodwink	**i.**	a form of humor that ridicules
______	**10.** impromptu	**j.**	the supernatural
______	**11.** inchoate	**k.**	cutting
______	**12.** jarring	**l.**	off kilter
______	**13.** mordant	**m.**	of doubtful origin
______	**14.** occlude	**n.**	spontaneous
______	**15.** occult	**o.**	dilemma
______	**16.** pandemonium	**p.**	full of uproar
______	**17.** peccadillo	**q.**	madness
______	**18.** phenomenon	**r.**	singular occurrence
______	**19.** satire	**s.**	ruin; disorder
______	**20.** tortuous	**t.**	a mass of confusion
______	**21.** tumultuous	**u.**	illogical
______	**22.** turbulent	**v.**	full of twists and turns
______	**23.** unweildy	**w.**	unpleasant noise
______	**24.** welter	**x.**	unnerving

Sensible Sentences?

Directions: Underline the word that makes sense in each of the sentences below.

1. The downpour was so *(consummate, copious)* that the canal flooded its banks.
2. For many, Leonardo is the *(gist, epitome)* of the Renaissance Man.
3. The team faced such *(gaunt, adverse)* conditions that the trip to the summit was postponed.
4. Regardless of their veracity, *(occult, satire)* topics can be fascinating.
5. Trade wars can occur when countries *(abound, saturate)* foreign markets with cheap goods.
6. Fine art can command prices *(inordinate, redolent)* to those of other luxuries.
7. The Tunguska incident is a *(peccadillo, phenomenon)* that has never been properly explained.
8. The *(salubrious, ruddy)* effects of desert air can help improve lung function.
9. The real Northwest Passage is a *(turbulent, tortuous)* journey through many ice-choked straits.
10. Napoleon was quick to *(discern, allude)* the strength of enemy forces.

Wordsearch

Directions: Using the clues listed below, fill in each blank in the following story with one of the new words you learned this week.

Clues

1st Day
1st Day
4th Day
1st Day
1st Day
3rd Day
2nd Day
3rd Day

Reprieve for Wolves

One of the most difficult ___________ to resolve has to do with the conflicting interests of environmentalists and profit-making businesses. Examples of this dilemma—and the resulting ___________—seem to abound.* While a dispute about cutting down a forest to preserve owls was in the news, there appeared another ___________ in Alaska. Hoping to increase the number of tourists who seek to hunt deer and caribou, the state ordered the killing of wolves that prey on those animals.

This resulted in a ___________ struggle waged by letter and article condemning the ___________ that would result from the anti-wolf policy. The environmentalists maintain that the natural balance should not be interfered with. The Alaskan tourist industry, which wants to attract hunters to increase state revenue, considers this position ___________. After a ___________ of protest, Alaska brought the plan to a ___________ halt.

COLLUSION WITH THE ENEMY

Cooperation is so vital to society that it persists even in the most competitive endeavors. Belligerent* armies during a siege *tacitly* agree not to attack during mealtimes since having one's own feast disturbed by retaliation negates any *material* benefit from the original assault. Military necessity is, at times, *subservient* to the physical and spiritual needs of the soldiers. On Christmas Eve in 1914, units along the western front of World War I engaged in a ceasefire of their own *volition* in honor of the holiday. Commanders on both sides did not *condone* such fraternization and punished many responsible. However, the event is celebrated today as an example of the spirit of brotherhood that *galvanizes* all honorable warriors. It explains why veterans from opposite sides of a conflict are often able to become fast friends years later.

NEW WORDS

tacit
ta - kit

material (adj.)
mə - tēr - ē - əl

subservient
sûb - sėr - vē - ənt

volition
və - lish - ən

condone
kən - dōn

galvanize
gal - və - nīz

Notable Roots: tacit = silent; mat = matter; sub = under; serv = slave, servant; vol = want

Sample Sentences: Insert the new words in these sentences.

1. Moral decisions are those made by _______________ and not under compulsion.
2. Martyrs have a way of _______________ adherents to a cause more powerfully than rhetoric.
3. Monks of any faith regard _______________ attachments as distractions from the spiritual.
4. Old partners, Scrooge and Marley could communicate by mere _______________ looks.
5. No one knows if Montcalm _______________ attacking the British who had surrendered.
6. Douglass notes that Mrs. Auld was initially uncomfortable with the _______________ demeanor of her husband's servants.

Definitions: Match the new words with their definitions.

7.	tacit	________	a.	to allow; to offer unspoken approval
8.	material	________	b.	unspoken
9.	subservient	________	c.	actions of one's own will
10.	volition	________	d.	obedient
11.	condone	________	e.	to unify; to harden
12.	galvanize	________	f.	of concrete value

THE CORPORATE POINT OF VIEW

The concept of the corporation is, at first, a hard one to *rationalize*. Some consider such entities to represent nothing more than *coteries* of magnates who despoil all weaker competition. Those who *advocate* for corporations counter that, taken to an extreme, competition can be destructive to everyone. During the nineteenth century, John D. Rockefeller observed that when oil reservoirs are drained by too many competing wells, pressure is lost and more oil is left in the ground. He also saw that too much oil on the market leads to prices too low to justify its extraction. Rockefeller's solution was Standard Oil, a corporation that made partners of small drillers under the *aegis* of a single banner. Standard Oil's success *vindicated* Rockefeller's vision and, before long, corporations were in *vogue* throughout American business.

NEW WORDS

rationalize
rash - ən - ə - līz

coterie
kō - tə - rē

advocate (v.)
ad - vō - kāt

aegis
ē - jis

vindicate
vin - də - kāt

vogue
vōg

Notable Roots:
ratio = calculation;
ad = to, for; voc = voice;
vinc = conquer

Sample Sentences: Insert the new words in these sentences.

1. For decades, a _______________ of baseball owners kept wages low by barring free agency.
2. Robespierre _______________ many executions as "necessary to preserve the Revolution."
3. Madison argued that the states are stronger under the _______________ of one nation.
4. Fashions that are in _______________ to one generation can appear ridiculous to posterity.
5. The right of conquest claims that victory at arms _______________ the winner's position.
6. To maintain position, one should minimize _______________ for ideas that have fallen into disfavor with the regime.

Definitions: Match the new words with their meanings.

7.	rationalize	________	a.	to uphold
8.	coterie	________	b.	the latest fashion
9.	advocate	________	c.	to justify what one desires
10.	aegis	________	d.	an inner circle
11.	vindicate	________	e.	to argue for a person or position
12.	vogue	________	f.	a unifying banner or standard

THE *CODEDUELLO*

Dueling is the defunct practice by which gentlemen settled disputes involving personal honor. The "code" of dueling demanded that the parties would first try to *concur* on a peaceful resolution. If both remained *adamant*, however, they would agree on a time, place, and weapon with which to conduct an "interview." Each combatant's *entourage* of "seconds" would then settle the details. On the day of the contest, each duelist's closest *confidant* would inspect the weapons and dueling ground before the fight commenced. Victory in such contests was an *ancillary* concern compared with upholding one's reputation as a *paragon* of honor and courage. The objective was usually to draw first blood, but many lives were still claimed by such affairs.

NEW WORDS

concur
kən - kur

adamant
ad - ə - mənt

entourage
on - tər - oj

confidant
kon - fə - dont

ancillary
an - sə - ler - ē

paragon
par - ə - gon

Notable Roots:
con = together; cur = run; adaman = hard; fidel = faith

Sample Sentences: Insert the new words in these sentences.

1. The War of 1812 was an ________________ contest of the Napoleonic Wars.
2. The position of *consiglieri* is held by the closest ________________ of a mafioso.
3. To prevent accidents, two officers must ________________ before a nuclear weapon is fired.
4. To the Ancient Greeks, Hercules was the ________________ of strength.
5. Stars that avoid having an ________________ tend to remain grounded and practical.
6. Despite his ________________ disapproval of Stalin, Churchill hated Hitler more.

Definitions: Match the new words with their meanings.

7.	concur	_________	a.	secondary; supplemental
8.	adamant	_________	b.	a trustworthy friend
9.	entourage	_________	c.	a perfect example
10.	confidant	_________	d.	to agree
11.	ancillary	_________	e.	a circle of followers
12.	paragon	_________	f.	set on a point of view

HONOR AMONG THIEVES

The Golden Age of Piracy began during the sixteenth century when the English and Dutch found it *conducive* to their interests to authorize privateers. The successes of buccaneers like Henry Morgan raiding the Spanish certainly *corroborated* this view but it also set an awful precedent.* Sailors who enjoyed the wealth and freedom of privateering were loath* to live any other way when the wars ended. Thus, the unintended *progeny* of this system were men of a different *ilk* who fought under their own flags. They elected as captains their most able leaders. The result of this perverse* meritocracy was men like Blackbeard, who spent years *substantiating* reputations for cunning and ruthlessness. With towns like Nassau as *havens*, the pirates became a scourge to all transatlantic commerce.

NEW WORDS

conducive
kən - dū - siv

corroborate
kə - rob - ər - āt

progeny
pro - jən - ē

ilk
ilk

substantiate
sub - stan - chē - āt

haven
hā - vin

Notable Roots: duc = lead; robo = strengthen; gen = create; stan = stance

Sample Sentences: Insert the new words in these sentences.

1. Associating with the _______________ of bootleggers and gangsters harms Gatsby's respectability.
2. Switzerland was a well-armed _______________ during both world wars.
3. Multiple independent witnesses _______________ the prosecutor's charges.
4. Parents in industrial societies have fewer _______________ than in pre-industrial times.
5. The Zimmerman Telegram _______________ Wilson's case that Germany had to be stopped.
6. Offering free alcohol has proven quite _______________ to casino profits.

Definitions: Match the new words with their meanings.

7.	conducive	________	a.	to provide material* evidence
8.	corroborate	________	b.	enabling
9.	progeny	________	c.	to support another's testimony
10.	ilk	________	d.	sanctuary
11.	substantiate	________	e.	offspring
12.	haven	________	f.	similar people

GROUP REVIEW

English is the first language with over one million words in its vocabulary. Erudite individuals make new words part of their vocabulary as quickly as they come into accepted use.

Matching

Directions: Match the words with their meanings.

	REVIEW WORDS		DEFINITIONS
______	**1.** adamant	**a.**	to argue for a person or position
______	**2.** advocate	**b.**	to uphold
______	**3.** aegis	**c.**	to provide material* evidence
______	**4.** ancillary	**d.**	of concrete value
______	**5.** concur	**e.**	sanctuary
______	**6.** condone	**f.**	unspoken
______	**7.** conducive	**g.**	a circle of followers
______	**8.** confidant	**h.**	a unifying banner or standard
______	**9.** corroborate	**i.**	to agree
______	**10.** coterie	**j.**	actions of one's own will
______	**11.** entourage	**k.**	to allow; to offer unspoken approval
______	**12.** galvanize	**l.**	to unify; to harden
______	**13.** haven	**m.**	a trustworthy friend
______	**14.** ilk	**n.**	similar people
______	**15.** material	**o.**	obedient
______	**16.** paragon	**p.**	set on a point of view
______	**17.** progeny	**q.**	secondary; supplemental
______	**18.** rationalize	**r.**	the latest fashion
______	**19.** subservient	**s.**	enabling
______	**20.** substantiate	**t.**	to justify what one desires
______	**21.** tacit	**u.**	an inner circle
______	**22.** vindicate	**v.**	a perfect example
______	**23.** vogue	**w.**	to support another's testimony
______	**24.** volition	**x.**	offspring

Wordsearch

Directions: Using the clues listed below, fill in each blank in the following story with one of the new words you learned this week.

Clues

4th Day	4th Day	3rd Day
3rd Day	1st Day	1st Day
3rd Day	4th Day	2nd Day
4th Day	2nd Day	
2nd Day	2nd Day	

Henry VIII and British History

The brevity of the existence of the United States is ___________ to knowing its history well. Students in Great Britain would certainly ___________, for their history goes back some 1,000 years! In that time, England has had rulers. Some were ___________ of responsible stewardship. Other less virtuous examples of royal ___________ have also held power. Perhaps the most fascinating is Henry VIII.

When his first wife could not bear him a son, he ___________ his divorce by claiming their marriage to have been illegitimate. When the Pope refused to ___________ this charge, Henry VIII renounced Catholicism. He founded the Church of England and filled his treasury by selling off Church property. This act ___________ Protestants, who stood to lose their new lands if Catholicism ever returned. It also ensured over a century of religious strife.*

Henry then married Anne Boleyn, whom he later had executed on a charge of adultery that was never ___________. His third wife ___________ herself in Henry's eyes by giving birth to a son, but she died in the process. He divorced a fourth wife, whom he never met. His fifth, Katherine Howard, was beheaded after evidence surfaced that she was having an affair with one of her ___________. Only his sixth wife, who was more of a ___________, was neither discarded nor executed. Although his contemporaries could only offer ___________ condemnation of Henry's behavior, history has more vociferously ___________ against him.

ANCIENT EMPIRES OF THE "NEW" WORLD

One of the anomalies* of our approach to history is the propensity* to look only to Europe for *exemplars* of great and *charismatic* societies. Despite living in the Western Hemisphere, Americans fall under the same spell. That the Incan Empire began four millennia ago and lasted until the sixteenth century ought to instill some *humility* in European ethnocentrists. Although their empire is gone, descendants of the Incas can take *solace* in wonders that have survived. Cusco and Machu Picchu, Incan ruins poised high in the Andes, are *poignant* reminders that the inhabitants of this half of the world were just as capable as their Greco-Roman counterparts. Similarly, we owe *deference* to the Mayans, one of only a handful of civilizations on Earth to independently invent a system of writing.

NEW WORDS

exemplar
eg - zemp - lär

charisma
kə - riz - mə

humility
hyū - mil - ə - tē

solace
sol - əs

poignant
poi - nyənt

deference
def - ər - əns

Notable Roots: exem/exam = sample; humus = soil; sole = soothe

Sample Sentences: Insert the new words in these sentences.

1. How many ideas have been lost because their thinkers lacked ________________?
2. The most intense competitors take little ________________ in moral victories.
3. In Greek tragedy, lack of ________________ is a flaw of many figures punished by the gods.
4. Jon Snow considers his father to be an ________________ of honesty.
5. Jefferson made it a point to show equal ________________ to all foreign dignitaries.
6. *Dido's Lament* is the ________________ valedictory speech of a spurned queen.

Definitions: Match the new words with their meanings.

7. exemplar	________	a. comfort
8. charisma	________	b. respect
9. humility	________	c. moving
10. solace	________	d. perfect specimen
11. poignant	________	e. charm
12. deference	________	f. meekness

WEEK 46 ⚙ DAY 2

Virtue

A BATTLE FOR POWER

It's often been said that the projection of strength is the most important attribute of a wartime leader. Certainly, many a *demagogue* has cultivated an image of machismo by strutting in uniform. However, during its three worst wars, the United States was led by a lawyer, a college professor, and an *affable* socialite in a wheelchair. All three had a *virtuosity* as war leaders that was not readily apparent. Abraham Lincoln was by all accounts physically strong—he could hold an axe at arm's length for one minute—but was by nature a *congenial*, yarn-spinning country lawyer. Woodrow Wilson, the first PhD elected president, had a sense of personal *rectitude* one might expect from a preacher. FDR, after losing the use of his legs to polio, gained strength as a *philanthropist* running a hot springs resort for fellow sufferers. All three possessed a strength of purpose that served them better than the martial fortitude of generals and knights.

NEW WORDS

demagogue
dem - ə - gog

affable
af - ə - bəl

virtuosity
vėr - chū - os - ə - tē

congenial
kən - jēn - ē - əl

rectitude
rek - tə - tūd

philanthropist
fil - an - thrō - pist

Notable Roots: deme = people; gen = create, nature; rect = upright; phil = love; anthro = people

Sample Sentences: Insert the new words in these sentences.

1. Edmond Dantes was ________________ company for the Abbé Faria.
2. Many great museums were endowed by nineteenth century ________________.
3. Greatness is not always accompanied by personal ________________.
4. A ________________ arouses the passions of the masses for selfish ends.
5. No other element can match the ________________ of carbon in forming compounds.
6. Long John Silver proves a more ________________ leader than Captain Flint.

Definitions: Match the new words with their meanings.

7.	demagogue	________	a.	like-minded
8.	affable	________	b.	a leader who appeals to people's emotions
9.	virtuosity	________	c.	pleasant and friendly
10.	congenial	________	d.	benefactor
11.	rectitude	________	e.	versatility
12.	philanthropist	________	f.	righteousness

SUPERMAN

In 1943, Ayn Rand published a novel noteworthy for the unconventionality of its hero. Howard Roark, the protagonist of *The Fountainhead*, is an architect with *impeccable* manners, but who makes no effort to be *amiable*. He lives *frugally* because he has no desire to impress. Devoted to his inner vision, he constructs buildings that flaunt their modernity, with no *conciliatory* nods to the neoclassical designs then in vogue.* In time, independent-minded individuals come to love his buildings and *congregate* around him because of his devotion to excellence. In the end, he designs a housing project—not to be *altruistic*, but because he enjoys solving its technical challenges. When his design is changed without his permission, he destroys the building and successfully defends his right to do so in court, arguing that creators offer their best efforts on their own terms and expect the same in exchange from others.

NEW WORDS

impeccable
im - pek - ə - bəl

amiable
ā - mē - ə - bəl

frugal
frū - gəl

conciliatory
kən - sil - ē - ə - tôr - ē

congregate
kon - grə - gāt

altruistic
al - trū - is - tik

Notable Roots: pecca = flaw; ami = friend; concil = counsel, soothe; greg = social; alt = other

Sample Sentences: Insert the new words in these sentences.

1. The Trojans thought the wooden horse on their beach to be a ________________ gesture.
2. A rare few are so ________________ that they give their lives to helping the downtrodden.
3. Children during the Great Depression grew up to be naturally ________________ adults.
4. The forgery was so ________________ that it went unnoticed by experts for years.
5. People ________________ around televisions on the afternoon that JFK was assassinated.
6. A teacher cannot be so ________________ that she passes students who haven't earned it.

Definitions: Match the new words with their meanings.

7. impeccable	_________	a.	careful with money
8. amiable	_________	b.	to gather together
9. frugal	_________	c.	concerned about others
10. conciliatory	_________	d.	likeable
11. congregate	_________	e.	without mistakes
12. altruistic	_________	f.	offering peace

THE IMPORTANCE OF BEING NICE

It used to be a maxim of polite society that it never hurts to be *amicable.* When Aaron Burr met Alexander Hamilton on the dueling ground of Weehawken, the too old rivals were unfailingly *cordial* to the very end. In fact, just before shooting him, Burr allowed Hamilton to retrieve his glasses! The moral, if there is one, is that people can show *equanimity* toward everyone—even enemies. Humans are naturally *gregarious* creatures. Studies have shown that it is actually stressful to not return a smile or greeting. Giving in to the *convivial* spirit can improve one's mood and may lead to a *benevolent* disposition simply by habit.

NEW WORDS

amicable
am - ik - ə - bəl

cordial
kôr - jəl

equanimity
ek - wə - nim - ə - tē

gregarious
grə - gar - ē - əs

convivial
kən - viv - ē - əl

benevolent
bə - nev - ō - lənt

Notable Roots:
ami = friend; equa = equal; greg = social; viv = life; bene = good; vol = desire

Sample Sentences: Insert the new words in these sentences.

1. Jesse Owens's ________________ endeared him to his fellow Olympians from all nations.
2. Bill Clinton and George Bush, naturally ________________ men, became friends after office.
3. Such a ________________ invitation is hard to refuse.
4. Bipartisanship relies on an ________________, if not friendly, atmosphere in Congress.
5. Prince Hans's ________________ personality soon evaporated, revealing his selfishness.
6. The ________________ feeling between families allowed friendships to form among in-laws.

Definitions: Match the new words with their meanings.

7.	amicable	________	**a.**	outgoing
8.	cordial	________	**b.**	kind; generous
9.	equanimity	________	**c.**	not outwardly hostile
10.	gregarious	________	**d.**	evenness of temper
11.	convivial	________	**e.**	gracious; polite
12.	benevolent	________	**f.**	friendly; jovial

GROUP REVIEW

This is your *last* week. At this point, you have worked with over 1100 of the most useful words in our language. The final review test will give you some idea of how well you have mastered them. From time to time, you should reread sections of this book to refresh your memory. Remember, keep learning new words at every opportunity!

Matching

Directions: Match the words you learned this week with their meanings.

	REVIEW WORDS		DEFINITIONS
________	**1.** affable	**a.**	gracious; polite
________	**2.** altruistic	**b.**	offering peace
________	**3.** amiable	**c.**	benefactor
________	**4.** amicable	**d.**	friendly; jovial
________	**5.** benevolent	**e.**	moving
________	**6.** charisma	**f.**	versatility
________	**7.** conciliatory	**g.**	a leader who appeals to people's emotions
________	**8.** congenial	**h.**	careful with money
________	**9.** congregate	**i.**	charm
________	**10.** convivial	**j.**	to gather together
________	**11.** cordial	**k.**	comfort
________	**12.** deference	**l.**	meekness
________	**13.** demagogue	**m.**	respect
________	**14.** equanimity	**n.**	outgoing
________	**15.** exemplar	**o.**	righteousness
________	**16.** frugal	**p.**	concerned about others
________	**17.** gregarious	**q.**	without mistakes
________	**18.** humility	**r.**	kind; generous
________	**19.** impeccable	**s.**	not outwardly hostile
________	**20.** philanthropist	**t.**	evenness of temper
________	**21.** poignant	**u.**	perfect specimen
________	**22.** rectitude	**v.**	likeable
________	**23.** solace	**w.**	like-minded
________	**24.** virtuosity	**x.**	pleasant and friendly

Which Word Comes to Mind?

Directions: Write the letter of the vocabulary word in the space adjacent to the headline or sentence that brings it to mind.

a. charisma
b. condone
c. subservient
d. rationalize
e. gregarious
f. humility
g. confidant
h. frugal
i. amicable
j. benevolent
k. progeny
l. amiable
m. conducive
n. substantiate
o. exemplar
p. corroborate

_________ **1.** Mayor Says Nothing in Wake of Attack
_________ **2.** Best in Show
_________ **3.** "Remember, thou are mortal."
_________ **4.** Rabbits are good at multiplication.
_________ **5.** The Velvet Divorce: The Peaceful Breakup of Czechoslovakia
_________ **6.** How to Save on Your Electric Bill
_________ **7.** Madison: Jefferson's Closest Adviser
_________ **8.** Eclipse Observations Confirm Einstein's Theory
_________ **9.** Blanche relies on "the kindness of strangers."
_________ **10.** He's a hard man not to like.

Wordsearch

Directions: Using the clues listed below, fill in each blank in the following story with one of the new words you learned this week.

Clues

1st Day
2nd Day
1st Day
1st Day
1st Day

1st Day
1st Day
3rd Day
4th Day
2nd Day

2nd Day
4th Day
3rd Day

Words, Words, Words

Your vocabulary is now 1100 words larger. If you've sojourned this far, take pride in being an ___________ of fortitude. Hopefully you've shown ___________ in using these words in your speech and writing. Perhaps you've noticed how an apt* turn of phrase can enhance your personal ___________.

A person with ___________ will recall that no one knows every word. Moreover, it's important to show ___________ to their power. Used judiciously, words make for ___________ expressions of sentiment. Words of ___________ can comfort those suffering from loss. ___________ words can heal rifts* between former friends. ___________ words can make those we love feel treasured.

Beware, however: an ___________ person is not one who flaunts ostentatious* erudition in order to show superiority. In the mouth of a ___________, words can be weapons that destroy the ___________ spirit that allows society to flourish. So just remember, when you ___________ with others, choose your words carefully!

Appendix

Answer Key

Index

ANSWER KEY

Week 1, Day 1

1. probity
2. acuity
3. prudence
4. astute
5. proffered
6. surmised
7. e
8. a
9. f
10. b
11. c
12. d

Week 1, Day 2

1. concocted
2. apprised
3. cognizant
4. pedantic
5. circumspect
6. peruse
7. d
8. f
9. b
10. e
11. a
12. c

Week 1, Day 3

1. incisive
2. politic
3. ruminate
4. cogent
5. introspective
6. canny
7. e
8. c
9. a
10. b
11. f
12. d

Week 1, Day 4

1. trenchant
2. pensive
3. pedagogue
4. pragmatic
5. perspicacious
6. stipulated
7. d
8. f
9. e
10. c
11. a
12. b

Week 1, Day 5

Matching

1. t
2. u
3. r
4. e
5. l
6. h
7. a
8. w
9. k
10. x
11. j
12. n
13. d
14. g
15. s
16. q
17. b
18. f
19. v
20. p
21. c
22. o
23. i
24. m

Exploring Roots

1. h
2. g
3. e
4. f
5. d
6. a
7. b
8. c

Wordsearch

1. canny
2. concocted
3. astute
4. stipulated
5. probity

Week 2, Day 1

1. infamous
2. dilatory
3. impish
4. unsavory
5. iniquities
6. egotist
7. b
8. f
9. d
10. e
11. a
12. c

Week 2, Day 2

1. slovenly
2. brigands
3. miscreants
4. scurrilous
5. asinine
6. untoward
7. d
8. f
9. a
10. e
11. c
12. b

Week 2, Day 3

1. dilettante
2. obsequious
3. callow
4. sinister
5. pathological
6. megalomania
7. d
8. f
9. a
10. e
11. b
12. c

Week 2, Day 4

1. bias
2. servile
3. callous
4. sordid
5. nefarious
6. lurid
7. d
8. a
9. f
10. b
11. c
12. e

Week 2, Day 5

Matching

1. g
2. o
3. e
4. i
5. x
6. q
7. k
8. w
9. p
10. l
11. t
12. a
13. b
14. d
15. r
16. n
17. v
18. h
19. c
20. m
21. f
22. u
23. s
24. j

Exploring Roots

1. f
2. h
3. a
4. g
5. c
6. d
7. b
8. e

Wordsearch

1. pathological
2. slovenly
3. callous
4. obsequious
5. asinine

Week 3, Day 1

1. feasible
2. zenith
3. prestigious
4. sally
5. prolific
6. acclaim
7. e
8. f
9. b
10. a
11. d
12. c

Week 3, Day 2

1. pinnacle
2. ebullient
3. acme
4. prodigy
5. fortuitous
6. plaudits
7. e
8. f
9. b
10. d
11. a
12. c

Week 3, Day 3

1. viable
2. nirvana
3. anointed
4. ascend
5. sanguine
6. efficacy
7. b
8. e
9. a
10. f
11. d
12. c

Week 3, Day 4

1. burgeoning
2. felicitous
3. laudable
4. halcyon
5. propitious
6. auspicious
7. f
8. a
9. e
10. b
11. c
12. d

Week 3, Day 5

Matching

1. u
2. t
3. i
4. a
5. e
6. s
7. q
8. n
9. j
10. b
11. p
12. h
13. l
14. v
15. x
16. w
17. g
18. f
19. o
20. d
21. r
22. m
23. k
24. c

Wordsearch

1. acclaim
2. zenith
3. viable
4. fortuitous
5. sanguine

Synonym Shout-Out

1. l
2. o
3. g

4. i
5. b, e, p
6. s
7. h, n
8. f, k, m, q
9. d
10. a
11. t
12. c, j, r

Week 4, Day 1

1. ominous
2. debacle
3. harbinger
4. carnage
5. incapacitated
6. succumb
7. d
8. a
9. f
10. b
11. c
12. e

Week 4, Day 2

1. forestalled
2. moribund
3. balked
4. nadir
5. ramifications
6. abortive
7. d
8. f
9. b
10. a
11. c
12. e

Week 4, Day 3

1. repulse
2. catastrophic
3. besieged
4. fiasco
5. fruitless
6. capitulate
7. c
8. f
9. a
10. e
11. d
12. b

Week 4, Day 4

1. thwarted/stymied
2. plight
3. quandary
4. falter
5. impasse
6. stymie/thwart
7. d
8. a
9. e
10. f
11. c
12. b

Week 4, Day 5

Matching

1. u
2. o
3. x
4. v
5. t
6. l
7. h
8. k
9. s
10. b
11. a
12. w
13. r
14. d
15. i
16. f
17. j
18. n
19. c
20. m
21. e
22. p
23. q
24. g

Sensible Sentences?

1. incapacitated
2. harbinger
3. plight
4. fruitless
5. moribund
6. nadir
7. fiasco
8. thwarted
9. abortive
10. faltered

Antonyms Attract

1. b, h
2. k, o
3. e
4. a
5. g, j
6. c
7. d, l
8. n
9. f, q, s
10. m
11. i, p
12. r

Wordsearch

1. impasse
2. plight
3. debacle
4. carnage
5. balk

Week 5, Day 1

1. subterfuge
2. absconded
3. dupe
4. chicanery
5. duplicity
6. perfidious
7. c
8. e
9. f
10. a
11. d
12. b

Week 5, Day 2

1. cabal
2. duress
3. fabricate
4. mendacious
5. foisted
6. charlatan
7. e
8. d

9. f
10. c
11. a
12. b

Week 5, Day 3

1. guile
2. prevarication
3. usurped
4. fulsome
5. artifice
6. fawning
7. c
8. f
9. e
10. a
11. d
12. b

Week 5, Day 4

1. repress
2. canard
3. factitious
4. feinting
5. fallacious
6. guise
7. d
8. e
9. a
10. b
11. f
12. c

Week 5, Day 5

Matching

1. g
2. v
3. e
4. x
5. w
6. s
7. n
8. u
9. l
10. q
11. o
12. f
13. a
14. p
15. t
16. r
17. m
18. i
19. d
20. h
21. b
22. c
23. k
24. j

Wordsearch

1. canards
2. guile
3. artifice
4. duress
5. repress

Exploring Roots

1. d
2. g
3. a
4. h
5. b
6. c
7. e
8. f

Week 6, Day 1

1. lucrative
2. underwrite
3. mercenary
4. glut
5. pecuniary
6. surfeit
7. c
8. d
9. e
10. a
11. f
12. b

Week 6, Day 2

1. largess
2. compensation
3. hoards
4. affluent
5. copious
6. avarice
7. e
8. d
9. b
10. a
11. f
12. c

Week 6, Day 3

1. sinecures
2. fiscal
3. sumptuous
4. voracious
5. remuneration
6. covet
7. b
8. e
9. a
10. f
11. c
12. d

Week 6, Day 4

1. palatial
2. cupidity
3. rapacious
4. bountiful
5. opulence
6. munificent
7. c
8. e
9. f
10. b
11. a
12. d

Week 6, Day 5

Matching

1. p
2. g
3. b
4. c
5. h
6. o
7. w
8. u
9. q
10. t
11. m
12. i
13. e
14. n
15. j
16. s

17. v
18. x
19. a
20. l
21. d
22. r
23. k
24. f

Wordsearch

1. surfeit
2. lucrative
3. pecuniary
4. fiscal
5. opulence

Sensible Sentences?

1. hoards
2. sinecure
3. mercenary
4. rapacious
5. largess
6. underwrite
7. sumptuous
8. affluent
9. opulence
10. fiscal

Week 7, Day 1

1. futile
2. liquidation
3. bereft
4. destitution
5. insolvent
6. pittance
7. e
8. f
9. b
10. d
11. c
12. a

Week 7, Day 2

1. barren
2. alms
3. meager
4. dearth
5. supplicant
6. penniless
7. d
8. e
9. b
10. f
11. c
12. a

Week 7, Day 3

1. pauper
2. privation
3. scanty
4. indigent
5. piteous
6. penury
7. d
8. a
9. e
10. f
11. b
12. c

Week 7, Day 4

1. miserly
2. paucity
3. mendicant
4. extortion
5. abjection
6. parsimonious
7. d
8. f
9. e
10. c
11. a
12. b

Week 7, Day 5

Matching

1. m
2. p
3. a
4. f
5. t
6. b
7. u
8. w
9. g
10. k
11. s
12. c
13. h
14. e
15. o
16. r
17. l
18. v
19. i
20. j
21. q
22. x
23. d
24. n

Wordsearch

1. penury
2. privation
3. destitution
4. supplicants
5. miserly

Synonym Shout-Out

1. j
2. g
3. f
4. h
5. b
6. d
7. i
8. e
9. a
10. c

Week 8, Day 1

1. impetuous
2. incipient
3. neophyte
4. fledgling
5. nascent
6. indolence
7. c
8. f
9. d
10. e
11. b
12. a

Week 8, Day 2

1. dabbler
2. juvenile
3. ingenuous

4. utopian
5. artless
6. quixotic
7. d
8. e
9. f
10. a
11. c
12. b

Week 8, Day 3

1. scion
2. puerile
3. dilatory
4. jejune
5. imprudent
6. fatuous
7. d
8. f
9. b
10. a
11. c
12. e

Week 8, Day 4

1. mawkish
2. maudlin
3. sophomoric
4. infantile
5. pretentious
6. tyros
7. f
8. e
9. a
10. c
11. d
12. b

Week 8, Day 5

Matching

1. v
2. a
3. x
4. e
5. q
6. p
7. w
8. t
9. n
10. g
11. c
12. i
13. b
14. o
15. r
16. f
17. h
18. j
19. s
20. m
21. k
22. d
23. u
24. l

Sensible Sentences?

1. mawkish
2. quixotic
3. fledgling
4. incipient
5. indolent
6. scion
7. artless
8. utopian
9. impetuous
10. sophomoric
11. jejune

Parts of Speech

1. g
2. f
3. l
4. a
5. e
6. d
7. m
8. h
9. c
10. o
11. j
12. b
13. n
14. k

Wordsearch

1. dilatory
2. nascent
3. indolent
4. imprudent
5. dabblers

Week 9, Day 1

1. inveterate
2. eminent
3. perennial
4. inured
5. curmudgeon
6. seasoned
7. b
8. e
9. a
10. f
11. d
12. c

Week 9, Day 2

1. urbane
2. enfeebled
3. erudite
4. revere
5. sage
6. prosaic
7. d
8. e
9. b
10. f
11. a
12. c

Week 9, Day 3

1. decrepit
2. unaffected
3. trite
4. patriarch
5. archaic
6. venerable
7. c
8. f
9. a
10. e
11. b
12. d

Week 9, Day 4

1. recondite
2. stagnant
3. doddering
4. passé
5. pedestrian
6. immutable

7. f
8. e
9. a
10. c
11. d
12. b

Week 9, Day 5

Matching

1. d
2. k
3. m
4. i
5. s
6. u
7. o
8. j
9. w
10. q
11. g
12. c
13. t
14. f
15. r
16. v
17. n
18. e
19. p
20. l
21. h
22. a
23. b
24. x

Wordsearch

1. pedestrian
2. inured
3. perennial
4. doddering
5. enfeebled

Sensible Sentences?

1. patriarch
2. seasoned
3. erudite
4. immutable
5. perennial
6. urbane
7. trite
8. venerable
9. archaic
10. enfeebled

Week 10, Day 1

1. recoils
2. repugnant
3. grotesque
4. heinous
5. insidious
6. pernicious
7. b
8. f
9. e
10. d
11. a
12. c

Week 10, Day 2

1. abhorrent
2. malevolent
3. mortified
4. appalled
5. trepidation
6. aversion
7. d
8. e
9. a
10. f
11. b
12. c

Week 10, Day 3

1. unctuous
2. anathema
3. acrimonious
4. antipathy
5. repulsed
6. odious
7. d
8. f
9. a
10. e
11. c
12. b

Week 10, Day 4

1. loath
2. internecine
3. noisome
4. antithesis
5. loathed
6. reviled
7. c
8. e
9. d
10. a
11. f
12. b

Week 10, Day 5

Matching

1. a
2. d
3. l
4. k
5. b
6. t
7. c
8. o
9. s
10. m
11. h
12. p
13. j
14. i
15. w
16. e
17. r
18. q
19. u
20. v
21. g
22. n
23. f
24. x

Wordsearch

1. appalled
2. recoil
3. trepidation
4. aversion
5. antithesis

First and 10

1. b, i
2. f, m
3. g, o
4. e, t
5. d, s
6. j, q
7. p, r

8. c, k
9. a, l
10. h, n

Week 11, Day 1

1. hyperbole
2. adorned
3. vivid
4. enthralling
5. embellish
6. florid
7. d
8. e
9. b
10. f
11. c
12. a

Week 11, Day 2

1. excruciating
2. panoply
3. archetype
4. pall
5. histrionic
6. deliverance
7. f
8. d
9. a
10. b
11. c
12. e

Week 11, Day 3

1. entrancing
2. flamboyant
3. climactic
4. grandiloquent
5. pageantry
6. rhetoric
7. d
8. f
9. e
10. c
11. b
12. a

Week 11, Day 4

1. rousing
2. salient
3. resolution
4. extenuating
5. sanctimonious
6. denouement
7. f
8. d
9. c
10. a
11. e
12. b

Week 11, Day 5

Matching

1. k
2. h
3. w
4. v
5. u
6. t
7. o
8. m
9. e
10. b
11. s
12. i
13. g
14. x
15. a
16. q
17. p
18. r
19. c
20. d
21. j
22. f
23. l
24. n

Wordsearch

1. florid
2. sanctimonious
3. hyperbole
4. grandiloquent
5. entrancing

Sensible Sentences?

1. panoply
2. excruciating
3. vivid
4. salient
5. deliverance
6. histrionic
7. flamboyant
8. denouement
9. adorned
10. archetype

Exploring Roots

1. e
2. g
3. h
4. a
5. b
6. c
7. d
8. f

Week 12, Day 1

1. savvy
2. apt
3. versatile
4. chimerical
5. aptitude
6. utilitarian
7. e
8. d
9. c
10. f
11. b
12. a

Week 12, Day 2

1. agile
2. adept
3. obliging
4. impresario
5. acumen
6. proficient
7. e
8. d
9. a
10. f
11. b
12. c

Week 12, Day 3

1. dexterity
2. lithe
3. aficionado
4. emulate

5. apposite
6. precocious
7. b
8. d
9. a
10. e
11. f
12. c

Week 12, Day 4

1. aplomb
2. adroit
3. connoisseur
4. protean
5. mavericks
6. arbiter
7. c
8. e
9. d
10. b
11. f
12. a

Week 12, Day 5

Matching

1. q
2. n
3. o
4. x
5. l
6. p
7. i
8. s
9. u
10. c
11. h
12. f
13. g
14. k
15. d
16. v
17. a
18. t
19. b
20. m
21. r
22. j
23. w
24. e

Sensible Sentences?

1. precocious
2. lithe
3. maverick
4. chimerical
5. prestigious
6. aplomb
7. protean
8. agile
9. arbiter
10. apt
11. dexterity

Wordsearch

1. proficiency
2. adroit
3. lithe
4. precocious
5. savvy
6. acumen
7. maverick
8. chimerical

Week 13, Day 1

1. precludes
2. reactionary
3. forthwith
4. inciting
5. tantamount
6. induce
7. c
8. e
9. f
10. b
11. a
12. d

Week 13, Day 2

1. culmination
2. premise
3. eventuates
4. catalyst
5. precursor
6. perpetuating
7. e
8. f
9. a
10. b
11. d
12. c

Week 13, Day 3

1. contingencies
2. inadvertently
3. fomenting
4. engendered
5. consummation
6. analogous
7. f
8. d
9. e
10. a
11. c
12. b

Week 13, Day 4

1. extrapolating
2. substrate
3. obviated
4. precipitated
5. antecedent
6. promulgated
7. e
8. d
9. f
10. c
11. a
12. b

Week 13, Day 5

Matching

1. r
2. q
3. j
4. l
5. x
6. i
7. g
8. a
9. v
10. n
11. h
12. c
13. m
14. s

15. d
16. t
17. b
18. k
19. f
20. w
21. o
22. p
23. e
24. u

Wordsearch

1. induced
2. precipitates
3. precursor
4. incited
5. reactionary

Exploring Roots

1. d
2. f
3. h
4. e
5. c
6. a
7. b
8. g

Week 14, Day 1

1. intransigence
2. imperious
3. indomitable
4. affront
5. intrepid
6. poise
7. d
8. c
9. f
10. b
11. a
12. e

Week 14, Day 2

1. effrontery
2. stalwart
3. formidable
4. brazen
5. temerity
6. undaunted
7. c
8. f
9. a
10. e
11. b
12. d

Weeks 14, Day 3

1. stolid
2. recalcitrant
3. braggadocio
4. brash
5. audacity
6. obdurate
7. d
8. a
9. e
10. c
11. f
12. b

Week 14, Day 4

1. gravitas
2. pluck
3. stentorian
4. bravado
5. intractable
6. haughty
7. f
8. c
9. e
10. b
11. a
12. d

Week 14, Day 5

Matching

1. r
2. i
3. m
4. w
5. p
6. f
7. j
8. v
9. l
10. b
11. h
12. k
13. o
14. s
15. g
16. c
17. e
18. x
19. a
20. u
21. d
22. t
23. q
24. n

Wordsearch

1. affront
2. brazen
3. poise
4. effrontery
5. stalwart

Too Much of a Good Thing?

1. pluck
2. tyro
3. glut
4. patriarch
5. intrepid
6. fomented
7. grandiloquent
8. circumspect
9. guile
10. dilettante

Week 15, Day 1

1. accomplices
2. egregious
3. alleged
4. unconscionable
5. culpable
6. perpetrator
7. d
8. f
9. b
10. e
11. c
12. a

Week 15, Day 2

1. infraction
2. rampant

3. jeopardize
4. abrogated
5. expurgated
6. blatant
7. e
8. a
9. d
10. b
11. f
12. c

Week 15, Day 3

1. reprimanded
2. heresy
3. tainted
4. admonished
5. empirical
6. indicted
7. f
8. a
9. e
10. b
11. c
12. d

Week 15, Day 4

1. nepotism
2. redress
3. flagrant
4. castigated
5. culprit
6. unrepentant
7. c
8. e
9. a
10. b
11. f
12. d

Week 15, Day 5

1. e
2. r
3. a
4. m
5. c
6. j
7. q
8. p
9. x
10. t
11. u
12. n
13. v
14. d
15. i
16. o
17. g
18. w
19. k
20. b
21. s
22. h
23. f
24. l

Wordsearch

1. blatantly
2. castigated
3. abrogate
4. flagrant
5. reprimand
6. redress
7. culpable
8. egregious

Week 16, Day 1

1. persevere
2. resourceful
3. industrious
4. automatons
5. vigilant
6. punctilious
7. b
8. d
9. f
10. c
11. a
12. e

Week 16, Day 2

1. unstinting
2. thrifty
3. prompt
4. meticulous
5. unflagging
6. attentive
7. e
8. a
9. d
10. f
11. c
12. b

Week 16, Day 3

1. foraged
2. scrupulous
3. arduous
4. assiduously
5. chary
6. indefatigable
7. d
8. e
9. f
10. c
11. a
12. b

Week 16, Day 4

1. solicit
2. resolved
3. aspiring
4. tenacious
5. fastidious
6. laborious
7. c
8. e
9. d
10. b
11. f
12. a

Week 16, Day 5

Matching

1. k
2. l
3. d
4. q
5. x
6. b
7. w
8. s
9. j
10. u
11. o
12. p
13. a
14. m
15. e
16. c

17. h
18. f
19. r
20. n
21. v
22. i
23. t
24. g

Wordsearch

1. thrifty
2. fastidious
3. aspiring
4. scrupulous
5. persevered

Exploring Roots

1. d
2. g
3. h
4. a
5. c
6. b
7. e
8. f

Week 17, Day 1

1. credentials
2. accommodate
3. alleviate
4. cajole
5. ingratiate
6. ameliorate
7. f
8. d
9. a
10. e
11. b
12. c

Week 17, Day 2

1. assuaged
2. propitiate
3. inconsolable
4. allay
5. entreaties
6. wheedling
7. c
8. e
9. a
10. f
11. d
12. b

Week 17, Day 3

1. blandishments
2. quell
3. condolences
4. petitioner
5. importuned
6. placated
7. c
8. e
9. a
10. b
11. f
12. d

Week 17, Day 4

1. implored
2. mollify
3. deflect
4. coerced
5. insatiable
6. pacify
7. d
8. a
9. f
10. e
11. b
12. c

Week 17, Day 5

Matching

1. e
2. p
3. d
4. l
5. x
6. b
7. h
8. v
9. r
10. c
11. q
12. m
13. f
14. u
15. a
16. g
17. n
18. w
19. j
20. t
21. i
22. k
23. s
24. o

Wordsearch

1. accommodated
2. petitioner
3. entreaties
4. deflected
5. wheedling

Sensible Sentences?

1. placated
2. cajoled
3. credentials
4. alleviate
5. ingratiated
6. allay
7. implores
8. propitiated
9. accommodated
10. inconsolable

Week 18, Day 1

1. gesticulated
2. demonstrative
3. lexicon
4. hail
5. evoked
6. impart
7. c
8. e
9. f
10. a
11. d
12. b

Week 18, Day 2

1. evinced
2. vivacious
3. emotive
4. veneer
5. grimace
6. countenance
7. d
8. a
9. f

10. e
11. b
12. c

Week 18, Day 3

1. winced
2. innate
3. mien
4. tableau
5. diminutive
6. avid
7. c
8. d
9. a
10. f
11. b
12. e

Week 18, Day 4

1. facades
2. chagrin
3. penchant
4. demeanor
5. physiognomy
6. nondescript
7. b
8. a
9. f
10. e
11. d
12. c

Week 18, Day 5

Matching

1. p
2. l
3. g
4. u
5. a
6. x
7. m
8. q
9. c
10. d
11. o
12. e
13. n
14. j
15. b
16. w
17. f
18. h
19. v
20. t
21. k
22. i
23. r
24. s

Wordsearch

1. wince
2. vivacious
3. nondescript
4. countenance
5. mien
6. tableau
7. emotive
8. innately
9. physiognomy
10. demeanor

Week 19, Day 1

1. tyranny
2. legion
3. coups
4. infallible
5. despot
6. omnipotent
7. c
8. e
9. f
10. a
11. d
12. b

Week 19, Day 2

1. officious
2. disinterested
3. august
4. abjure
5. prerogative
6. paramount
7. d
8. e
9. a
10. f
11. b
12. c

Week 19, Day 3

1. impregnable
2. potentates
3. subjugated
4. miscarried
5. puissant
6. abstruse
7. e
8. d
9. a
10. f
11. c
12. b

Week 19, Day 4

1. imperative
2. abdicated
3. regal
4. effigies
5. peremptory
6. foiled
7. c
8. e
9. a
10. f
11. b
12. d

Week 19, Day 5

Matching

1. v
2. j
3. o
4. m
5. h
6. g
7. c
8. q
9. w
10. n
11. r
12. f
13. p
14. k
15. a
16. d
17. l
18. e
19. x
20. t
21. u

22. s
23. i
24. b

Wordsearch

1. abdicate
2. regal
3. impregnable
4. tyranny
5. legion
6. prerogatives
7. august
8. paramount
9. subjugated
10. potentate

Week 20, Day 1

1. defamatory
2. polemics
3. denigrated
4. stigmatized
5. opprobrium
6. vilified
7. d
8. f
9. a
10. b
11. c
12. e

Week 20, Day 2

1. condescend
2. calumny
3. besmirched
4. umbrage
5. derided
6. excoriated
7. e
8. f
9. b
10. a
11. c
12. d

Week 20, Day 3

1. scoffed
2. retort
3. risible
4. disdain
5. belittle
6. quipped
7. c
8. f
9. d
10. b
11. a
12. e

Week 20, Day 4

1. deprecate
2. contemptuous
3. caustic
4. repudiated
5. repulsive
6. disparaged
7. f
8. a
9. d
10. b
11. e
12. c

Week 20, Day 5

Matching

1. e
2. g
3. p
4. n
5. s
6. v
7. a
8. c
9. t
10. x
11. r
12. o
13. h
14. i
15. w
16. u
17. m
18. k
19. j
20. l
21. b
22. d
23. q
24. f

Hapless Headlines

1. k
2. w
3. s
4. m, q, x
5. u
6. c
7. a, b, h, i, j, l, x
8. h, i, j, k, q
9. r
10. n

Wordsearch

1. defamatory
2. besmirching
3. polemics
4. denigrate
5. vilified
6. opprobrium
7. deprecating
8. risible
9. stigmatize
10. umbrage

Week 21, Day 1

1. deluding
2. conjecture
3. latent
4. nuances
5. dubious
6. imperceptible
7. d
8. f
9. e
10. a
11. b
12. c

Week 21, Day 2

1. opaque
2. inscrutable
3. euphemism
4. dormant
5. disabuse
6. reticent
7. c
8. e
9. a
10. f
11. b
12. d

Week 21, Day 3

1. furtive
2. nebulous
3. discreet
4. ostensible
5. esoteric
6. circuitous
7. b
8. d
9. f
10. a
11. e
12. c

Week 21, Day 4

1. ambiguous
2. clandestine
3. reputed
4. specious
5. surreptitious
6. impenetrable
7. c
8. a
9. f
10. e
11. d
12. b

Week 21, Day 5

Matching

1. s
2. p
3. o
4. h
5. x
6. n
7. d
8. i
9. f
10. u
11. a
12. t
13. k
14. e
15. g
16. w
17. r
18. c
19. v
20. b
21. q
22. l
23. j
24. m

Wordsearch

1. euphemism
2. dubious
3. nebulous
4. discreet
5. deluded
6. dormant
7. nuances
8. latent
9. esoteric
10. reputed
11. conjecture

Week 22, Day 1

1. aloof
2. cynical
3. apathy
4. lethargic
5. drudgery
6. timorous
7. d
8. f
9. e
10. a
11. c
12. b

Week 22, Day 2

1. unkempt
2. stupor
3. sedentary
4. lax
5. lassitude
6. inhibition
7. e
8. a
9. d
10. f
11. b
12. c

Week 22, Day 3

1. banal
2. phlegmatic
3. taut
4. tremulous
5. indifferent
6. imperturbable
7. d
8. a
9. e
10. f
11. b
12. c

Week 22, Day 4

1. lackluster
2. stunted
3. squeamish
4. languid
5. blasé
6. fretful
7. e
8. f
9. c
10. b
11. a
12. d

Week 22, Day 5

Matching

1. d
2. k
3. g
4. s
5. w
6. x
7. c
8. u
9. l
10. a
11. m
12. t
13. o
14. r
15. b
16. h
17. q
18. e
19. v
20. i

21. n
22. p
23. j
24. f

Wordsearch

1. indifferent
2. lax
3. unkempt
4. apathy
5. cynical
6. banal
7. fretful
8. lackluster
9. drudgery

Week 23, Day 1

1. desultory
2. ferment
3. interim
4. vicissitudes
5. agitated
6. arbitrary
7. e
8. d
9. f
10. c
11. b
12. a

Week 23, Day 2

1. inert
2. whimsical
3. derelict
4. vacillates
5. tenuous
6. capricious
7. b
8. f
9. e
10. a
11. d
12. c

Week 23, Day 3

1. amnesty
2. malleable
3. jettisoned
4. extemporize
5. volatile
6. mercurial
7. b
8. a
9. d
10. e
11. f
12. c

Week 23, Day 4

1. fluctuates
2. transient
3. ephemeral
4. metamorphosis
5. evanescent
6. provisional
7. f
8. c
9. a
10. e
11. d
12. b

Week 23, Day 5

Matching

1. w
2. x
3. r
4. o
5. c
6. s
7. p
8. m
9. b
10. g
11. d
12. a
13. k
14. n
15. e
16. h
17. j
18. u
19. v
20. f
21. q
22. i
23. l
24. t

Wordsearch

1. fluctuating
2. jettisoned
3. provisional
4. arbitrary
5. tenuous

Synonym Shout-Out

1. i, t
2. d
3. g, i
4. a, f, r
5. e, k, s
6. c
7. b, o
8. h, m, n, p
9. q
10. j

Week 24, Day 1

1. adherents
2. pantheon
3. devout
4. proselyte
5. venerate
6. deify
7. f
8. c
9. e
10. a
11. b
12. d

Week 24, Day 2

1. zealous
2. taboo
3. duped
4. stoic
5. sacrosanct
6. dogmatic
7. c
8. d
9. f
10. e
11. a
12. b

Week 24, Day 3

1. schism
2. staunch
3. ascetic
4. idolatry
5. hedonism

6. ardent
7. d
8. e
9. f
10. a
11. b
12. c

Week 24, Day 4

1. agnostics
2. fervor
3. canon
4. recanted
5. martyr
6. credo
7. f
8. d
9. e
10. c
11. b
12. a

Week 24, Day 5

Matching

1. g
2. v
3. c
4. i
5. q
6. o
7. d
8. f
9. t
10. s
11. m
12. r
13. x
14. h
15. a
16. u
17. k
18. b
19. j
20. e
21. n
22. p
23. w
24. l

Adjective Leaders and Noun Followers

1. n
2. c
3. g
4. m
5. l
6. b
7. j
8. o
9. i
10. d

Wordsearch

1. duped
2. sacrosanct
3. schisms
4. zealous
5. stoic
6. martyrs
7. proselytes

Week 25, Day 1

1. conflagration
2. havoc
3. deluge
4. insurgent
5. razed
6. obliterated
7. e
8. c
9. a
10. f
11. b
12. d

Week 25, Day 2

1. gauntlet
2. fractious
3. rift
4. eradicated
5. nullify
6. strife
7. f
8. d
9. e
10. b
11. a
12. c

Week 25, Day 3

1. fettered
2. fray
3. impede
4. skirmishes
5. inclement
6. wrested
7. c
8. e
9. a
10. f
11. b
12. d

Week 25, Day 4

1. detriment
2. exacerbated
3. deterred
4. deleterious
5. fracas
6. dissent
7. d
8. a
9. b
10. e
11. f
12. c

Week 25, Day 5

Matching

1. u
2. n
3. f
4. j
5. e
6. h
7. t
8. o
9. p
10. m
11. v
12. b
13. x
14. c
15. r
16. k
17. i
18. d
19. a
20. l

21. s
22. g
23. q
24. w

Wordsearch

1. impeded
2. fettered
3. havoc
4. inclement
5. strife
6. wrest
7. exacerbated
8. insurgent
9. rift
10. conflagration
11. fray
12. razed
13. obliterated

Week 26, Day 1

1. attested
2. succinct
3. epistles
4. eulogy
5. vestiges
6. missives
7. b
8. d
9. e
10. f
11. a
12. c

Week 26, Day 2

1. prolix
2. memoir
3. libel
4. discourse
5. anecdotes
6. reverberated
7. d
8. f
9. e
10. b
11. a
12. c

Week 26, Day 3

1. deciphered
2. glyphs
3. scribe
4. encomiums
5. manifesto
6. treatise
7. f
8. d
9. e
10. b
11. c
12. a

Week 26, Day 4

1. citations
2. accolades
3. epithet
4. preamble
5. expository
6. relegated
7. c
8. e
9. a
10. f
11. b
12. d

Week 26, Day 5

Matching

1. s
2. a
3. w
4. e
5. n
6. u
7. x
8. p
9. l
10. b
11. q
12. c
13. j
14. k
15. g
16. m
17. v
18. d
19. o
20. f
21. h
22. r
23. i
24. t

Wordsearch

1. attests
2. succinct
3. memoir
4. discourse
5. epithet
6. citation
7. libels
8. epistle
9. relegated

Roots Roundup

1. treatment
2. recourse
3. testimony
4. prescription
5. remit
6. verbose
7. hieroglyphics
8. recite

Week 27, Day 1

1. idyllic
2. incandescent
3. infatuated
4. alluring
5. resplendent
6. entice
7. c
8. a
9. f
10. e
11. d
12. b

Week 27, Day 2

1. raiment
2. dapper
3. dulcet
4. betrothed
5. reverie
6. tantalized
7. e
8. d
9. f
10. a
11. b
12. c

Week 27, Day 3

1. comely
2. gaudy
3. amorous
4. luminous
5. aesthetic
6. ethereal
7. f
8. d
9. a
10. e
11. c
12. b

Week 27, Day 4

1. mellifluous
2. sublime
3. translucent
4. limpid
5. pellucid
6. diaphanous
7. e
8. d
9. f
10. a
11. b
12. c

Week 27, Day 5

Matching

1. v
2. l
3. r
4. o
5. q
6. u
7. w
8. x
9. m
10. a
11. e
12. b
13. i
14. f
15. n
16. d
17. t
18. k
19. j
20. h
21. s
22. p
23. c
24. g

Wordsearch

1. alluring
2. dapper
3. resplendent
4. incandescent
5. enticing
6. reverie
7. limpid
8. luminosity
9. sublime

Week 28, Day 1

1. citadels
2. domicile
3. bucolic
4. asylum
5. juxtaposed
6. sedate
7. b
8. e
9. f
10. d
11. a
12. c

Week 28, Day 2

1. locale
2. ensconced
3. terminus
4. archipelago
5. remote
6. niche
7. e
8. f
9. b
10. a
11. d
12. c

Week 28, Day 3

1. hinterland
2. enclave
3. meridian
4. ambience
5. milieu
6. expatriate
7. e
8. f
9. a
10. b
11. d
12. c

Week 28, Day 4

1. berth
2. propinquity
3. ebbed
4. extremity
5. bastions
6. rustic
7. c
8. e
9. f
10. b
11. a
12. d

Week 28, Day 5

Matching

1. i
2. j
3. p
4. m
5. g
6. c
7. n
8. w
9. k
10. q
11. o
12. a
13. d
14. u
15. l
16. f
17. r
18. v
19. h
20. x
21. t
22. s
23. e
24. b

Doing Double Duty

Answers will vary.

Wordsearch

1. extremity
2. hinterland
3. archipelago
4. bastion
5. terminus
6. meridian
7. remote
8. juxtaposed
9. locale
10. propinquity

Week 29, Day 1

1. frenzy
2. deployed
3. scurries
4. acute
5. elusive
6. frenetic
7. d
8. f
9. e
10. b
11. a
12. c

Week 29, Day 2

1. romp
2. celerity
3. advent
4. unabated
5. spontaneous
6. propagation
7. a
8. d
9. e
10. f
11. c
12. b

Week 29, Day 3

1. alacrity
2. cursory
3. dissemination
4. peregrination
5. expedient
6. febrile
7. c
8. e
9. b
10. f
11. a
12. d

Week 29, Day 4

1. spate
2. perfunctory
3. expedite
4. escalation
5. flurry
6. imminent
7. c
8. d
9. e
10. a
11. f
12. b

Week 29, Day 5

Matching

1. a
2. h
3. g
4. m
5. j
6. o
7. i
8. f
9. c
10. t
11. n
12. u
13. s
14. v
15. e
16. l
17. d
18. p
19. b
20. r
21. x
22. w
23. k
24. q

Wordsearch

1. acute
2. frenzy
3. perfunctory
4. cursory
5. romp
6. scurry
7. unabated
8. advent
9. flurry
10. disseminated
11. propagated
12. expedience
13. alacrity

Week 30, Day 1

1. reciprocal
2. effusive
3. lampooned
4. amenable
5. raucous
6. extolled
7. d
8. e
9. f
10. c
11. b
12. a

Week 30, Day 2

1. nonchalance
2. facetious
3. winsome
4. levity
5. jocose
6. droll
7. d
8. e
9. a
10. f
11. c
12. b

Week 30, Day 3

1. impunity
2. exalted
3. iconoclast
4. jubilant
5. insouciant
6. beneficent
7. e
8. c

9. f
10. a
11. d
12. b

Week 30, Day 4

1. bohemian
2. libertine
3. philanthropic
4. venal
5. facile
6. profligate
7. c
8. f
9. d
10. e
11. a
12. b

Week 30, Day 5

Matching

1. s
2. u
3. c
4. n
5. h
6. q
7. x
8. e
9. j
10. v
11. r
12. m
13. g
14. a
15. o
16. w
17. t
18. i
19. d
20. k
21. l
22. b
23. f
24. p

Wordsearch

1. extolled
2. exalted
3. bohemian
4. nonchalance
5. insouciance
6. philanthropists
7. jubilant
8. amenable
9. iconoclastic
10. winsome
11. raucous
12. libertine
13. effusive

Week 31, Day 1

1. intrinsic
2. homogeneous
3. repertoire
4. respite
5. indigenous
6. steeped
7. e
8. f
9. a
10. b
11. d
12. c

Week 31, Day 2

1. cants
2. facets
3. mundane
4. propensity
5. tranquil
6. indoctrinate
7. c
8. f
9. e
10. a
11. d
12. b

Week 31, Day 3

1. nominal
2. abode
3. rudimentary
4. tenable
5. cliques
6. inevitable
7. e
8. c
9. f
10. d
11. b
12. a

Week 31, Day 4

1. edifices
2. incumbent
3. menial
4. compatible
5. inanimate
6. extant
7. e
8. c
9. d
10. f
11. b
12. a

Week 31, Day 5

Matching

1. j
2. x
3. r
4. h
5. s
6. i
7. k
8. w
9. n
10. u
11. t
12. o
13. m
14. e
15. f
16. c
17. p
18. q
19. b
20. g
21. a
22. v
23. d
24. l

Wordsearch

1. propensity
2. inevitable
3. repertoire
4. mundane
5. tenable

6. compatible
7. rudimentary

Sensible Sentences?

1. inanimate
2. extant
3. tenable
4. homogeneous
5. tranquil
6. respites
7. abode
8. mundane
9. steeped
10. cant

Week 32, Day 1

1. din
2. caches
3. aggregated
4. cavalcade
5. pith
6. prodigious
7. e
8. c
9. d
10. f
11. b
12. a

Week 32, Day 2

1. voluminous
2. monolithic
3. augmented
4. comprehensive
5. cumbersome
6. colossal
7. c
8. d
9. f
10. e
11. b
12. a

Week 32, Day 3

1. commodious
2. ostentatious
3. amalgamated
4. mammoth
5. gargantuan
6. grandeur
7. f
8. e
9. a
10. c
11. d
12. b

Week 32, Day 4

1. engrossed
2. bulwark
3. swank
4. subsumed
5. aggrandize
6. cumulative
7. e
8. f
9. a
10. b
11. d
12. c

Week 32, Day 5

Matching

1. r
2. o
3. q
4. w
5. p
6. k
7. b
8. f
9. j
10. i
11. v
12. u
13. h
14. n
15. t
16. c
17. l
18. d
19. x
20. a
21. m
22. e
23. g
24. s

Antonyms Attract

1. malevolent
2. thorough
3. measly
4. indefensible
5. plod
6. extraordinary
7. scatter
8. diminutive
9. taciturn
10. phlegmatic
11. frugal
12. boorish
13. diminish
14. reluctance
15. motley

Wordsearch

1. prodigious
2. cumbersome
3. voluminous
4. cavalcade
5. engrossed

Week 33, Day 1

1. remiss
2. vitiated
3. paltry
4. spurious
5. negligible
6. wane
7. c
8. e
9. b
10. f
11. a
12. d

Week 33, Day 2

1. susceptible
2. innocuous
3. hypothetical
4. sporadic
5. curtail
6. fatalistic
7. c
8. e
9. a
10. b
11. f
12. d

Week 33, Day 3

1. ersatz
2. jilted

3. attenuate
4. enervated
5. desist
6. intangible
7. f
8. d
9. e
10. a
11. c
12. b

Week 33, Day 4

1. encumbrance
2. regresses
3. eschewed
4. supine
5. vapid
6. cessation
7. e
8. f
9. d
10. b
11. c
12. a

Week 33, Day 5

Matching

1. p
2. q
3. r
4. a
5. s
6. d
7. l
8. f
9. t
10. k
11. v
12. x
13. i
14. w
15. e
16. u
17. h
18. o
19. j
20. m
21. c
22. g
23. n
24. b

Wordsearch

1. jilt
2. eschew
3. fatalistic
4. enervate
5. curtail

May I Borrow That Expression?

1. j
2. h
3. s
4. q
5. t
6. n
7. d
8. p
9. a
10. o
11. l
12. r
13. k
14. m
15. e
16. b
17. g
18. i
19. f
20. c

Week 34, Day 1

1. somber
2. disgruntled
3. bristle
4. ineffectual
5. doleful
6. qualms
7. c
8. d
9. f
10. b
11. a
12. e

Week 34, Day 2

1. neurotic
2. disheveled
3. fraught
4. sullen
5. foreboding
6. forlorn
7. d
8. a
9. e
10. f
11. c
12. b

Week 34, Day 3

1. ignominious
2. ennui
3. hapless
4. lachrymose
5. deplorable
6. inane
7. e
8. f
9. d
10. b
11. a
12. c

Week 34, Day 4

1. interloper
2. nonentity
3. macabre
4. melancholy
5. dregs
6. bedraggled
7. e
8. d
9. f
10. c
11. b
12. a

Week 34, Day 5

Matching

1. f
2. r
3. a
4. d
5. g
6. w
7. i
8. h
9. s
10. u

11. n
12. t
13. q
14. e
15. p
16. o
17. x
18. v
19. k
20. j
21. l
22. m
23. b
24. c

Wordsearch

1. fraught
2. inane
3. deplorably
4. bristle
5. hapless
6. ignominious
7. interloper
8. qualms

Week 35, Day 1

1. flabbergasted
2. paean
3. concise
4. parable
5. skeptical
6. pithy
7. d
8. f
9. b
10. c
11. e
12. a

Week 35, Day 2

1. curt
2. clamor
3. averred
4. demure
5. laconic
6. sophistry
7. c
8. d
9. a
10. b
11. f
12. e

Week 35, Day 3

1. utterance
2. verbatim
3. garbled
4. explicate
5. dissembling
6. loquacious
7. d
8. a
9. f
10. e
11. b
12. c

Week 35, Day 4

1. gaffes
2. divulging
3. ineffable
4. garrulous
5. terse
6. verbose
7. d
8. a
9. f
10. e
11. c
12. b

Week 35, Day 5

Matching

1. p
2. m
3. c
4. t
5. q
6. w
7. k
8. e
9. b
10. j
11. r
12. a
13. i
14. l
15. h
16. n
17. g
18. d
19. s
20. x
21. v
22. f
23. u
24. o

Wordsearch

1. pithy
2. explicating
3. aver
4. laconic
5. utterances
6. loquacious
7. sophistry
8. paeans
9. flabbergasted
10. garbled
11. terse
12. verbose

Week 36, Day 1

1. enigmatic
2. incoherent
3. legerdemain
4. disconcerting
5. incongruous
6. disparate
7. f
8. d
9. e
10. c
11. a
12. b

Week 36, Day 2

1. indiscriminate
2. tinged
3. cryptic
4. anomalous
5. contorted
6. divergent
7. b
8. d
9. a
10. f
11. e
12. c

Week 36, Day 3

1. atypical
2. heterogeneous
3. dichotomy
4. baroque
5. maladjusted
6. extrinsic
7. d
8. e
9. f
10. a
11. c
12. b

Week 36, Day 4

1. pungent
2. aberrant
3. perverse
4. discrepancy
5. degenerate
6. dissolute
7. b
8. e
9. f
10. a
11. d
12. c

Week 36, Day 5

Matching

1. p
2. n
3. d
4. j
5. q
6. l
7. w
8. o
9. a
10. k
11. m
12. h
13. s
14. u
15. v
16. r
17. f
18. x
19. t
20. c
21. g
22. i
23. b
24. e

Sensible Sentences?

1. dissemble
2. vapid
3. bastion
4. reverie
5. incongruous
6. fraught
7. loquacious
8. macabre
9. cryptic
10. ennui

Wordsearch

1. dichotomy
2. aberrant
3. tinged
4. perverse
5. indiscriminate
6. anomalous
7. dissolute
8. extrinsic
9. atypical

Week 37, Day 1

1. vexation
2. asperity
3. irascible
4. consternation
5. badger
6. inexorable
7. f
8. a
9. d
10. b
11. e
12. c

Week 37, Day 2

1. internecine
2. irate
3. accosted
4. belligerent
5. begrudge
6. reproach
7. d
8. f
9. b
10. c
11. a
12. e

Week 37, Day 3

1. diatribes
2. nettled
3. livid
4. paroxysms
5. railing
6. inveighed
7. d
8. f
9. e
10. c
11. a
12. b

Week 37, Day 4

1. rebuked
2. vitriolic
3. pique
4. pugnacious
5. vituperating
6. invectives
7. d
8. a
9. b
10. c
11. f
12. e

Week 37, Day 5

Matching

1. k
2. l
3. t
4. q
5. f
6. o
7. b
8. d
9. n
10. x
11. p

12. h
13. g
14. w
15. j
16. s
17. v
18. r
19. u
20. a
21. i
22. m
23. c
24. e

Wordsearch

1. irascible
2. belligerent
3. nettled
4. paroxysm
5. consternation
6. badgered
7. rebuke
8. pugnacious
9. begrudges
10. inexorable
11. vexatious
12. pique
13. diatribes
14. railing
15. accost

Week 38, Day 1

1. flouted
2. proscribed
3. supersedes
4. secular
5. inviolable
6. mandated
7. b
8. e
9. d
10. f
11. c
12. a

Week 38, Day 2

1. transgressions
2. abeyance
3. doctrine
4. fiat
5. sanctions
6. adjudicate
7. e
8. f
9. b
10. c
11. d
12. a

Week 38, Day 3

1. dictating
2. emissaries
3. manifest
4. protocol
5. prohibition
6. accord
7. d
8. f
9. a
10. c
11. e
12. b

Week 38, Day 4

1. propriety
2. abstained
3. criterion
4. requisite
5. precedent
6. decorum
7. f
8. c
9. a
10. b
11. d
12. e

Week 38, Day 5

Matching

1. t
2. e
3. r
4. f
5. x
6. c
7. m
8. j
9. w
10. h
11. i
12. v
13. n
14. d
15. k
16. b
17. q
18. o
19. p
20. l
21. u
22. a
23. g
24. s

Wordsearch

1. fiats
2. requisite
3. sanction
4. dictate
5. abstain
6. mandated
7. accord
8. doctrine
9. precedent
10. prohibition
11. propriety
12. manifest
13. emissaries
14. transgressing
15. inviolable
16. adjudicate
17. supersede

Week 39, Day 1

1. flotilla
2. redoubtable
3. fortified
4. domineering
5. impervious
6. reinforced
7. a
8. d
9. f
10. b
11. c
12. e

Week 39, Day 2

1. behemoth
2. virile
3. titanic
4. dynamic
5. steadfast
6. strapping
7. c
8. f
9. e
10. b
11. a
12. d

Week 39, Day 3

1. junta
2. hegemony
3. sinewy
4. ruffians
5. supremacy
6. hale
7. c
8. a
9. e
10. b
11. f
12. d

Week 39, Day 4

1. undergirds
2. invulnerable
3. vigorous
4. robust
5. brawny
6. buttress
7. d
8. c
9. e
10. a
11. f
12. b

Week 39, Day 5

Matching

1. s
2. v
3. o
4. j
5. m
6. k
7. b
8. f
9. d
10. e
11. i
12. r
13. p
14. c
15. a
16. w
17. u
18. x
19. h
20. g
21. n
22. q
23. l
24. t

Wordsearch

1. hegemony
2. steadfast
3. dynamic
4. domineering
5. brawny
6. reinforced
7. behemoth
8. supremacy
9. invulnerable
10. sinewy
11. redoubtable
12. ruffians

Week 40, Day 1

1. elapses
2. regimen
3. retrospect
4. truncated
5. paradox
6. interminable
7. c
8. a
9. f
10. d
11. b
12. e

Week 40, Day 2

1. antiquity
2. troves
3. obsolete
4. prelude
5. defunct
6. annals
7. d
8. f
9. b
10. e
11. a
12. c

Week 40, Day 3

1. zeitgeist
2. antiquated
3. rues
4. nostalgia
5. pining
6. reminisce
7. e
8. f
9. a
10. b
11. d
12. c

Week 40, Day 4

1. prescient
2. auspice
3. procrastinate
4. belated
5. clairvoyant
6. prognosticate
7. e
8. d
9. a
10. b
11. f
12. c

Week 40, Day 5

Matching

1. i
2. l
3. n
4. g
5. c
6. x

7. m
8. d
9. q
10. j
11. p
12. r
13. f
14. w
15. k
16. h
17. s
18. a
19. t
20. u
21. b
22. o
23. e
24. v

Hapless Headlines

1. h
2. p
3. m
4. t
5. k
6. g
7. b
8. o
9. e
10. a

Wordsearch

1. paradoxes
2. nostalgia
3. rued
4. annals
5. clairvoyant
6. interminable
7. zeitgeist
8. belatedly
9. defunct
10. pining

Week 41, Day 1

1. imbibes
2. ruddy
3. atrophy
4. gaunt
5. spartan
6. afflicted
7. c
8. a
9. b
10. f
11. d
12. e

Week 41, Day 2

1. panacea
2. palliate
3. debilitated
4. malignant
5. longevity
6. maladies
7. c
8. a
9. e
10. b
11. f
12. d

Week 41, Day 3

1. virulent
2. repose
3. laceration
4. fettle
5. mastication
6. abstemious
7. d
8. c
9. e
10. a
11. f
12. b

Week 41, Day 4

1. salubrious
2. gallant
3. adverse
4. austere
5. deficiency
6. degraded
7. c
8. a
9. e
10. f
11. b
12. d

Week 41, Day 5

Matching

1. j
2. h
3. u
4. o
5. w
6. b
7. x
8. p
9. t
10. k
11. i
12. s
13. c
14. v
15. n
16. e
17. q
18. m
19. r
20. a
21. f
22. g
23. l
24. d

Wordsearch

1. malignant
2. deficient
3. longevity
4. adverse
5. ruddy
6. salubrious
7. gaunt
8. fettle
9. atrophied

Week 42, Day 1

1. ascertain
2. overt
3. permeated
4. delved
5. discern
6. converted
7. b
8. d
9. a
10. f
11. c
12. e

Week 42, Day 2

1. glib
2. epitome
3. germane
4. elicit
5. candid
6. cogent
7. f
8. d
9. e
10. a
11. b
12. c

Week 42, Day 3

1. enunciate
2. gleaned
3. pertinent
4. construed
5. denotes
6. incontrovertible
7. e
8. d
9. f
10. a
11. c
12. b

Week 42, Day 4

1. reinvigorate
2. delineated
3. allude
4. gist
5. derived
6. elucidate
7. d
8. f
9. e
10. b
11. c
12. a

Week 42, Day 5

Matching

1. c
2. t
3. n
4. x
5. k
6. b
7. l
8. w
9. j
10. v
11. g
12. m
13. i
14. d
15. u
16. f
17. h
18. a
19. e
20. s
21. r
22. q
23. o
24. p

Wordsearch

1. convert
2. discern
3. permeate
4. incontrovertible
5. cogent
6. elicit
7. reinvigorate
8. overtly
9. epitome
10. candid

Week 43, Day 1

1. array
2. abounded
3. saturated
4. inordinate
5. emanate
6. ubiquitous
7. c
8. f
9. e
10. a
11. b
12. d

Week 43, Day 2

1. unmitigated
2. extraneous
3. inundate
4. concomitant
5. myriad
6. consummate
7. f
8. c
9. e
10. a
11. b
12. d

Week 43, Day 3

1. superfluous
2. manifold
3. succulent
4. epicurean
5. copious
6. bounteous
7. f
8. e
9. a
10. b
11. c
12. d

Week 43, Day 4

1. redolent
2. profuse
3. replete
4. enhanced
5. plethora
6. rife
7. e
8. f
9. a
10. b
11. c
12. d

Week 43, Day 5

Matching

1. t
2. v
3. l
4. o
5. i
6. f
7. e
8. x
9. m
10. q

11. h
12. d
13. k
14. s
15. n
16. c
17. a
18. w
19. j
20. b
21. u
22. r
23. p
24. g

Wordsearch

1. replete
2. consummate
3. unmitigated
4. emanate
5. ubiquitous
6. array
7. inundated
8. inordinate
9. unmitigated
10. rife

Week 44, Day 1

1. pandemonium
2. phenomenon
3. tumultuous
4. disarray
5. conundrum
6. turbulent
7. b
8. e
9. a
10. f
11. d
12. c

Week 44, Day 2

1. cacophony
2. unwieldy
3. awry
4. tortuous
5. impromptu
6. bedlam
7. c
8. d
9. e
10. a
11. f
12. b

Week 44, Day 3

1. jarring
2. hoodwinked
3. absurd
4. occult
5. peccadilloes
6. apocryphal
7. d
8. a
9. e
10. f
11. b
12. c

Week 44, Day 4

1. inchoate
2. acerbic
3. mordant
4. welter
5. satire
6. occluded
7. c
8. d
9. e
10. b
11. f
12. a

Week 44, Day 5

Matching

1. u
2. k
3. m
4. l
5. q
6. w
7. o
8. s
9. b
10. n
11. d
12. x
13. a
14. g
15. j
16. h
17. f
18. r
19. i
20. v
21. p
22. e
23. c
24. t

Sensible Sentences?

1. copious
2. epitome
3. adverse
4. occult
5. saturate
6. inordinate
7. phenomenon
8. salubrious
9. tortuous
10. discern

Wordsearch

1. conundrums
2. pandemonium
3. welter
4. tumultuous
5. disarray
6. absurd
7. cacophony
8. jarring

Week 45, Day 1

1. volition
2. galvanizing
3. material
4. tacit
5. condoned
6. subservient
7. b
8. f
9. d
10. c
11. a
12. e

Week 45, Day 2

1. coterie
2. rationalized
3. aegis
4. vogue
5. vindicates
6. advocating
7. c
8. d
9. e
10. f
11. a
12. b

Week 45, Day 3

1. ancillary
2. confidant
3. concur
4. paragon
5. entourage
6. adamant
7. d
8. f
9. e
10. b
11. a
12. c

Week 45, Day 4

1. ilk
2. haven
3. corroborated
4. progeny
5. substantiated
6. conducive
7. b
8. c
9. e
10. f
11. a
12. d

Week 45, Day 5

Matching

1. p
2. a
3. h
4. q
5. i
6. k
7. s
8. m
9. w
10. u
11. g
12. l
13. e
14. n
15. d
16. v
17. x
18. t
19. o
20. c
21. f
22. b
23. r
24. j

Wordsearch

1. conducive
2. concur
3. paragons
4. progeny
5. rationalized
6. corroborate
7. galvanized
8. substantiated
9. vindicated
10. coterie
11. confidant
12. tacit
13. advocated

Week 46, Day 1

1. charisma
2. solace
3. humility
4. exemplar
5. deference
6. poignant
7. d
8. e
9. f
10. a
11. c
12. b

Week 46, Day 2

1. congenial
2. philanthropists
3. rectitude
4. demagogue
5. virtuosity
6. affable
7. b
8. c
9. e
10. a
11. f
12. d

Week 46, Day 3

1. conciliatory
2. altruistic
3. frugal
4. impeccable
5. congregated
6. amiable
7. e
8. d
9. a
10. f
11. b
12. c

Week 46, Day 4

1. equanimity
2. gregarious
3. cordial
4. amicable
5. benevolent
6. convivial
7. c
8. e
9. d
10. a
11. f
12. b

Week 46, Day 5

Matching

1. x
2. p
3. v
4. s
5. r
6. i

7. b
8. w
9. j
10. d
11. a
12. m
13. g
14. t
15. u
16. h
17. n
18. l
19. q
20. c
21. e
22. o
23. k
24. f

Which Word Comes to Mind?

1. b
2. o
3. f
4. k
5. i
6. h
7. g
8. n
9. j
10. a

Wordsearch

1. exemplar
2. virtuosity
3. charisma
4. humility
5. deference
6. poignant
7. solace
8. conciliatory
9. benevolent
10. affable
11. demagogue
12. convivial
13. congregate

INDEX

A

Abdicate, 130, 131
Aberrant, 241, 242, 269
Abeyance, 253, 256
Abhorrent, 67, 70
Abjection, 47, 48
Abjure, 128, 131
Abode, 207, 209, 211
Abortive, 23, 26, 27, 121
Abound, 283, 284, 287, 294
Abrogate (abrogated), 102, 105
Abscond (absconding), 30, 34
Abstain (abstaining), 160, 255, 256
Abstemious, 273, 275
Abstruse, 129, 131, 159, 174
Absurd (absurdity), 278, 291, 292, 293
Acclaim, 15, 19, 21
Accolade, 176, 177
Accommodate (accommodated), 114, 118, 120, 121
Accomplice, 101, 105
Accord, 254, 256
Accost, 246, 249, 269
Acerbic, 292, 293
Acme, 16, 19, 21, 28
Acrimonious, 68, 70
Acuity, 1, 5
Acumen, 81, 84, 85
Acute, 193, 197
Adamant, 43, 297, 299
Adept, 81, 84, 115, 231
Adherent, 160, 164, 295
Adjudicate (adjudicating), 253, 256
Admonish (admonished), 103, 105
Adorn (adorned), 73, 77, 79
Adroit (adroitly), 83, 84, 85
Advent, 194, 197, 214, 273, 282
Adverse, 274, 275, 294
Advocate, 296, 299
Aegis, 296, 299
Aesthetic, 182, 184
Affable, 302, 305
Afflict, 271, 275
Affluent, 38, 41, 43, 57
Affront, 94, 98
Aficionado, 82, 84, 85, 123, 225
Aggrandize (aggrandized) (aggrandizing), 79, 215, 216
Aggregate, 212, 216, 217
Agile, 81, 84, 85
Agitate, 153, 157
Agnostic, 163, 164
Alacrity, 195, 197, 217, 234
Allay, 115, 118, 120
Alleged, 101, 104, 105
Alleviate, 114, 118, 120
Allude (alluding), 280, 281, 294
Alluring, 180, 184
Alms, 45, 48
Aloof, 147, 151, 165
Altruistic, 303, 305
Amalgamate (amalgamated), 214, 216
Ambience, 188, 190
Ambiguous, 144, 145, 159, 239, 242
Ameliorate (ameliorated), 114, 118, 120
Amenable, 199, 203
Amiable, 303, 305, 306
Amicable, 304, 305, 306
Amnesty, 155, 157
Amorous, 182, 184
Analogous, 89, 91, 123, 153
Anathema, 68, 70
Ancillary, 297, 299
Anecdote, 174, 177, 200
Annals, 265, 268, 288
Anoint (anointed), 17, 19
Anomalous, 239, 242
Antecedent, 90, 91
Antipathy, 68, 70
Antiquated, 211, 266, 268
Antiquity, 265, 268
Antithesis, 69, 70
Apathy, 13, 147, 151, 198
Aplomb, 83, 84, 85
Apocryphal, 291, 293
Appalled, 67, 70
Apposite, 82, 84
Apprise (apprised), 2, 5
Apt (aptly), 80, 84, 85, 257, 307
Aptitude, 80, 84, 85
Arbiter, 83, 84, 85
Arbitrary, 153, 157, 165, 188
Archaic, 61, 63, 65
Archetype, 74, 77, 79
Archipelago, 187, 190
Ardent, 162, 164
Arduous, 109, 111, 264
Array, 283, 287
Artifice, 32, 34, 50, 72
Artless, 52, 55, 56, 57
Ascend (ascended), 17, 19, 51, 89
Ascertain (ascertained), 277, 281
Ascetic, 143, 162, 164, 165
Asinine, 9, 12, 28
Asperity, 245, 249
Aspire, 94, 110, 111, 241
Assiduous, 109, 111
Assuage (assuaged), 115, 118, 120
Astute, 1, 3, 5, 14, 21, 28, 72
Asylum, 186, 190, 290
Atrophy (atrophied), 271, 275
Attentive, 108, 111, 113
Attenuate (attenuated), 221, 223
Attest, 173, 177, 179
Atypical, 240, 242
Audacity, 96, 98
Augment (augmenting), 213, 216, 217, 236, 258, 262
August, 128, 131, 159
Auspice, 267, 268
Auspicious, 18, 19, 21, 28
Austere, 274, 275
Automaton, 107, 111
Avarice, 38, 41, 43, 50, 57
Aver (averred), 233, 236
Aversion, 67, 70, 207, 260
Avid (avidly), 123, 125, 222
Awry, 290, 293

B

Badger, 116, 118, 245, 249, 279
Balk (balked), 23, 26, 35, 130
Banal, 149, 151
Baroque, 240, 242, 274
Barren, 45, 47, 48
Bastion, 189, 190, 225, 243
Bedlam, 290, 293
Bedraggled, 229, 230
Begrudge, 246, 249
Behemoth, 259, 262
Belated, 258, 267, 268
Belittle, 136, 138, 139
Belligerent, 246, 249, 269, 295
Beneficent, 201, 203
Benevolent, 304, 305, 306
Bereft, 44, 48, 57, 72
Berth, 189, 190
Besieged, 24, 26, 27, 52, 66
Besmirch (besmirched), 135, 138, 139
Betrothed, 181, 184
Bias, 11, 12, 93, 97, 276
Blandishment, 116, 118
Blasé, 150, 151
Blatant (blatantly), 102, 105
Bohemian, 202, 203
Bounteous, 285, 287
Bountiful, 40, 41, 43, 50
Braggadocio, 96, 98
Brash, 96, 98, 100
Bravado, 97, 98
Brawny, 261, 262
Brazen, 95, 98
Brigand, 9, 12, 21
Bristle (bristled), 226, 228, 230
Bucolic, 186, 190
Bulwark, 129, 215, 216
Burgeon (burgeoning), 18, 19, 40, 57
Buttress, 261, 262

C

Cabal, 31, 34
Cache, 109, 212, 216, 225
Cacophony, 290, 293
Cajole (cajoled), 114, 118, 120
Callous (callously), 11, 12, 28
Callow, 10, 12, 28
Calumny, 135, 138, 139
Canard, 33, 34
Candid (candidly), 278, 281, 290
Canny, 3, 5, 21
Canon, 163, 164
Cant, 206, 209, 211
Capitulate (capitulated), 24, 26, 28, 72, 93
Capricious, 154, 157, 159
Carnage, 22, 26, 167
Castigate (castigating), 104, 105
Catalyst, 88, 91, 146
Catastrophic, 22, 24, 26, 27, 156
Caustic (caustically), 15, 137, 138, 139
Cavalcade, 212, 216
Celerity, 194, 197
Cessation, 222, 223
Chagrin, 124, 125, 127
Charisma (charismatic), 54, 146, 301, 305, 306
Charlatan, 31, 34, 161
Chary, 109, 111
Chicanery, 30, 34, 50
Chimerical, 80, 84, 85
Circuitous, 143, 145
Circumspect, 2, 5, 16, 21, 100
Citadel, 186, 190
Citation, 176, 177, 179
Clairvoyant (clairvoyance), 267, 268
Clamor, 233, 236

Clandestine, 144, 145, 159, 165
Climactic, 75, 77, 79
Clique, 207, 209, 211, 225
Coerce (coerced), 74, 117, 118, 120
Cogent, 3, 5, 278, 281
Cognizant, 2, 5, 100, 208, 234
Colossal, 213, 216
Comely, 182, 184
Commodious, 214, 216
Compatible, 208, 209, 211
Compensation, 38, 39, 41, 76, 104, 105, 179, 180, 284, 287
Comprehensive, 213, 216
Conciliatory, 303, 305
Concise, 232, 236
Concoct (concocted) (concocting), 2, 5, 114, 138
Concomitant (concomitantly), 284, 287, 291
Concur, 297, 299
Condescend, 135, 138, 139, 200
Condolence, 116, 118
Condone, 295, 299, 306
Conducive, 298, 299, 306
Confidant, 297, 299, 306
Conflagration, 167, 171, 289
Congenial, 302, 305
Congregate, 303, 305
Conjecture, 141, 145, 154
Connoisseur, 83, 84
Consternation, 200, 245, 249
Construe (construed), 279, 281
Consummate, 284, 287, 294
Consummation (consummating), 89, 91
Contemptuous, 137, 138, 139, 289
Contingency, 89, 91
Contort, 239, 242
Conundrum, 289, 293
Convert, 79, 277, 281
Convivial, 304, 305
Copious, 38, 41, 43, 50, 285, 287, 294
Cordial, 304, 305
Corroborate (corroborated), 298, 299, 306
Coterie, 296, 299
Countenance, 122, 125, 159
Coup, 127, 131, 225, 261, 279
Covet (coveted), 39, 41, 57
Credentials, 114, 118, 120, 290
Credo, 163, 164, 225
Criterion, 255, 256
Cryptic, 90, 239, 242, 243
Culmination, 88, 91
Culpable, 101, 105
Culprit, 104, 105
Cumbersome, 213, 216
Cumulative, 158, 215, 216
Cupidity, 40, 41, 43, 50, 72, 112
Curmudgeon, 59, 61, 62, 63, 65, 100, 266
Cursory, 107, 195, 197, 217
Curt, 233, 236
Curtail, 220, 223
Cynical, 147, 151

D

Dabbler, 52, 55
Dapper, 181, 182, 184
Dearth, 45, 48
Debacle, 22, 26, 27, 57, 233
Debilitate (debilitating), 272, 275
Decipher (deciphered), 175, 177, 237
Decorum, 255, 256
Decrepit, 61, 63, 65, 229, 258
Defamatory, 134, 138, 139
Deference, 301, 305
Deficiency, 274, 275
Deflect (deflected), 117, 118, 120, 189
Defunct, 265, 268, 297
Degenerate, 207, 241, 242
Degrade (degraded), 241, 242, 274, 275
Deify (deified), 160, 164
Deleterious, 170, 171, 224
Delineate (delineating), 280, 281
Deliverance, 74, 77, 79
Delude (deluded), 141, 145
Deluge, 167, 171
Delve (delving), 277, 281
Demagogue, 74, 302, 305
Demeanor, 124, 125, 130, 131, 159, 211, 295
Demonstrative, 121, 125
Demure (demurely), 233
Denigrate, 134, 138, 139, 159
Denote (denoted), 57, 202, 279, 281, 290
Denouement, 76, 77, 79
Deplorable, 228, 230
Deploy, 193, 197
Deprecate, 137, 138, 139, 159
Derelict, 154, 157, 219, 223
Deride, 135, 138, 139, 159, 235
Derive (derived), 280, 281
Desist, 221, 223
Despot, 127, 131
Destitution, 44, 48, 50, 142
Desultory, 153, 157, 165
Deter, 170, 171
Detriment, 170, 171
Devout, 160, 164, 165
Dexterity, 82, 84, 85, 238, 242
Diaphanous, 183, 184
Diatribe, 247, 249, 257
Dichotomy, 240, 242
Dictate, 254, 256
Dilatory, 8, 12, 53, 55, 56, 72
Dilettante, 10, 12, 100
Diminutive, 123, 125, 217
Din, 212, 216
Disabused (disabuse), 142, 145, 168
Disarray, 289, 293
Discern (discerning), 277, 281, 294
Disconcerting, 238, 242, 243
Discourse, 174, 177, 179, 191, 205, 237
Discreet, 143, 145, 227
Discrepancy, 241, 242
Disdain, 136, 138, 139
Disgruntled, 226, 230
Disheveled, 181, 227, 230, 240
Disinterested, 128, 131
Disparage, 137, 138, 139, 159
Disparate, 153, 238, 242
Dissemble (dissembling), 234, 236, 243
Disseminate (disseminated), 195, 197
Dissent, 170, 171
Dissolute, 241, 242
Divergent, 239, 242
Divulge, 235, 236
Doctrine, 253, 255, 256
Doddering, 62, 63, 65
Dogmatic, 161, 164
Doleful, 226, 230
Domicile, 186, 190
Domineering, 258, 262
Dormant, 142, 145
Dregs, 229, 230
Droll, 200, 203
Drudgery, 147, 151
Dubious, 141, 145, 232, 236
Dulcet, 181, 184
Dupe (duped), 30, 34, 161, 164, 202
Duplicity, 30, 34, 57, 100
Duress, 31, 34
Dynamic, 259, 262

E

Ebb (ebbed), 189, 190, 191
Ebullient, 16, 19, 21, 28, 121
Edifice, 208, 209, 211
Efficacy, 17, 19
Effigy, 130, 131
Effrontery, 95, 98, 233
Effusive (effusively), 199, 203, 217
Egotist, 8, 12
Egregious, 101, 105
Elapse, 264, 268, 269
Elicit (eliciting), 121, 125, 278, 281
Elucidate, 280, 281
Elusive, 103, 193, 197
Emanate (emanating), 283, 287
Embellish (embellished), 73, 77, 79
Eminent, 59, 63, 65
Emissary, 254, 256
Emotive, 122, 125
Empirical, 103, 105
Emulate (emulating), 82, 84
Enclave, 188, 190
Encomium, 175, 177
Encumbrance, 199, 222, 223
Enervate (enervated), 221, 223
Enfeebled, 60, 63, 65
Engender (engendered), 89, 91
Engrossed, 215, 216
Enhance, 121, 286, 287, 307
Enigmatic, 238, 242
Ennui, 228, 230, 243
Ensconced, 187, 190
Enthralling (enthralled), 73, 77
Entice, 180, 184
Entourage, 297, 299
Entrancing (entranced), 75, 77
Entreaty (entreaties), 115, 118, 120
Enunciate (enunciated), 279, 281
Ephemeral, 156, 157, 159
Epicurean, 285, 287
Epistle, 173, 177
Epithet, 138, 153, 176, 177, 232
Epitome, 278, 281, 294
Equanimity, 304, 305
Eradicate (eradicated), 6, 168, 171
Ersatz, 221, 223, 225
Erudite, 60, 63, 65, 299
Escalation, 196, 197
Eschew (eschewed), 183, 222, 223
Esoteric, 143, 145
Ethereal, 182, 184
Eulogy (eulogies), 3, 85, 173, 177
Euphemism, 142, 145
Evanescent, 156, 157, 159, 165
Eventuate, 88, 91
Evince, 122, 125
Evoke (evoking), 46, 48, 121, 125, 183

Exacerbate (exacerbated), 65, 170, 171
Exalted, 201, 203
Excoriate, 135, 138, 139
Excruciating, 74, 77, 79
Exemplar, 301, 305, 306
Expatriate, 128, 188, 190, 191
Expedient, 195, 197
Expedite (expedited), 196, 197, 212
Explicate, 234, 236
Expository, 176, 177
Expurgate, 102, 105
Extant, 136, 208, 209, 211
Extemporize, 155, 157
Extenuating, 76, 77, 79
Extol, 199, 203
Extortion, 47, 48, 59
Extraneous, 284, 287
Extrapolate (extrapolated), 90, 91
Extremity, 148, 189, 190
Extrinsic, 240, 242, 243, 269

F

Fabricate (fabricated), 34, 36, 103, 126
Facade, 124, 125
Facet, 206, 209, 211
Facetious (facetiously), 200, 203
Facile, 202, 203, 225
Factitious, 33, 34
Fallacious, 33, 34
Falter (faltered), 25, 26, 27, 28
Fastidious (fastidiously), 110, 111
Fatalistic, 220, 223
Fatuous, 53, 55, 56, 206
Fawning, 32, 34
Feasible, 15, 19, 21, 28, 57, 217
Febrile, 195, 197
Feint (feinting), 33, 34
Felicitous, 18, 19, 21
Ferment, 153, 157
Fervor, 163, 164, 172
Fetter (fettered), 103, 169, 171, 191
Fettle, 273, 275
Fiasco, 24, 26, 27, 290
Fiat, 253, 256
Fiscal, 39, 41, 43, 50, 103
Flabbergasted, 232, 233, 236
Flagrant, 67, 104, 105
Flamboyant, 54, 75, 77, 79, 85
Fledgling, 51, 55, 56, 66, 222
Florid, 73, 77, 79
Flotilla, 258, 262, 269
Flout, 252, 256
Fluctuate (fluctuating), 156, 157, 227
Flurry, 196, 197
Foil, 130, 131
Foist (foisted), 31, 34
Foment (fomented), 89, 91, 100
Forage, 109, 111
Foreboding, 227, 230
Forestall (forestalled), 23, 26, 27
Forlorn, 227, 230
Formidable, 95, 98, 218
Forthwith, 87, 91, 102
Fortify, 258, 262
Fortuitous, 16, 19, 21, 88
Fracas, 170, 171
Fractious, 83, 168, 171
Fraught, 129, 227, 230, 243, 248
Fray, 169, 171, 191, 278
Frenetic, 193, 197, 217
Frenzy, 193, 197
Fretful, 150, 151
Frugal (frugally), 108, 217, 219, 303, 305, 306
Fruitless, 24, 26, 27, 28, 73, 221, 228
Fulsome, 32, 34, 141
Furtive (furtively), 143, 145
Futile, 24, 26, 44, 48

G

Gaffe, 235, 236
Gallant, 274, 275
Galvanize, 295, 299
Garble (garbled), 234, 236
Gargantuan, 214, 216
Garrulous, 235, 236
Gaudy, 182, 184
Gaunt, 271, 275, 294
Gauntlet, 168, 171
Germane, 278, 281
Gesticulate (gesticulations), 121, 125
Gist, 280, 281, 294
Glean (gleaned), 279, 281
Glib, 278, 281
Glut, 37, 41, 43, 50, 100
Glyph, 175, 177, 179
Grandeur, 204, 214, 216, 225, 243
Grandiloquent, 75, 77, 100
Gravitas, 97, 98
Gregarious, 121, 304, 305, 306
Grimace, 122, 125, 228
Grotesque, 66, 70
Guile, 32, 34, 57, 100
Guise, 33, 34

H

Hail (hailing), 121, 125, 132
Halcyon, 18, 19
Hale, 260, 262
Hapless, 217, 228, 230, 235, 269
Harbinger, 22, 26, 27, 53, 58
Haughty, 97, 98, 238
Haven, 87, 298, 299
Havoc, 167, 171
Hedonism (hedonistic), 162, 164
Hegemony, 260, 262, 269
Heinous, 66, 70
Heresy, 103, 105
Heterogeneous, 240, 242
Hinterland, 188, 190
Histrionic, 74, 77, 79
Hoard, 38, 41, 43, 217
Homogeneous, 205, 209, 211, 217
Hoodwink (hoodwinking), 291, 293
Humility, 301, 305
Hyperbole, 73, 77
Hypothetical (hypothetically), 220, 223

I

Iconoclast, 201, 203
Idolatry, 162, 164
Idyllic, 180, 184, 186, 190
Ignominious, 228, 230
Ilk, 298, 299
Imbibe, 271, 275
Imminent, 196, 197, 266
Immutable, 62, 63, 65
Impart, 121, 125
Impasse, 25, 26, 27
Impeccable, 115, 227, 303, 305
Impede (impeded), 150, 151, 169, 171
Impenetrable, 144, 145, 159
Imperative, 130, 131
Imperceptible, 141, 145
Imperious, 94, 98
Imperturbable, 149, 151
Impervious, 258, 262
Impetuous, 51, 55, 56
Impish (impishly), 8, 12, 72
Implore, 117, 118, 120
Importune (importuned), 116, 118, 120
Impregnable, 129, 131
Impresario, 59, 81, 84, 85
Impromptu, 82, 290, 293
Imprudent, 53, 55, 56
Impunity, 201, 203
Inadvertent (inadvertently), 89, 91, 270
Inane, 228, 230, 243
Inanimate, 208, 209, 211
Incandescent, 180, 184
Incapacitate (incapacitated), 22, 26, 27
Inchoate, 292, 293
Incipient, 51, 55, 56, 66
Incisive, 3, 5, 21, 57
Incite (incited), 87, 91
Inclement, 169, 171
Incoherent, 238, 242, 269
Incongruous, 238, 242, 243
Inconsolable, 115, 118, 120
Incontrovertible, 279, 281
Incumbent, 208, 209, 211
Indefatigable, 109, 111
Indict (indictment), 103, 105
Indifferent, 136, 149, 151
Indigenous, 107, 205, 209, 211
Indigent, 46, 48, 72
Indiscriminate, 1, 239, 242
Indoctrinate (indoctrinated), 141, 206, 209, 211
Indolence (indolent), 51, 55, 56
Indomitable, 94, 98
Induce, 87, 91
Industrious, 107, 111, 128
Ineffable, 235, 236
Ineffectual, 66, 95, 226, 230
Inert, 154, 157, 165
Inevitable, 207, 209
Inexorable (inexorably), 245, 249, 269
Infallible, 36, 127, 131
Infamous, 8, 12, 21, 28, 95
Infantile, 54, 55, 56
Infatuated, 180, 184
Infraction, 102, 105
Ingenuous, 52, 55, 56, 72
Ingratiate (ingratiated), 114, 118, 120
Inhibition, 148, 151
Iniquity, 8, 12, 28
Innate, 121, 123, 125
Innocuous, 220, 223
Inordinate, 274, 283, 286, 287, 294
Insatiable, 57, 117, 118, 120
Inscrutable, 142, 145

Insidious, 66, 70, 207
Insolvent, 44, 48
Insouciant, 201, 203
Insurgent, 167, 171
Intangible, 221, 223
Interim, 153, 157
Interloper, 229, 230
Interminable (interminably), 264, 268
Internecine, 69, 70, 246, 249
Intractable, 97, 98
Intransigence, 94, 98
Intrepid, 8, 94, 98, 100
Intrinsic, 205, 209, 211
Introspective, 3, 5, 21, 28
Inundate (inundated), 73, 267, 284, 287
Inured, 59, 63, 72
Invective, 248, 249
Inveigh, 247, 249, 257
Inveterate, 59, 63
Inviolable, 252, 256
Invulnerable, 261, 262, 269
Irascible, 245, 249
Irate, 246, 249

J

Jarring, 291, 293
Jejune, 53, 55, 56
Jeopardize, 102, 105
Jettison (jettisoned), 155, 157
Jilt (jilted) (jilting), 221, 223, 229
Jocose, 200, 203
Jubilant, 201, 203
Junta, 260, 262, 269
Juvenile, 52, 55
Juxtapose (juxtaposed), 186, 190

L

Laborious, 110, 111
Laceration, 273, 275
Lachrymose, 228, 230
Lackluster, 150, 151
Laconic, 233, 236, 243
Lampoon, 199, 203, 232
Languid, 150, 151, 159, 168
Largess, 38, 41, 43
Lassitude, 148, 151
Latent, 141, 145, 195
Laudable, 18, 19, 28
Lax, 148, 151, 165
Legerdemain, 238, 242
Legion, 127, 131
Lethargic, 147, 151, 159
Levity, 200, 203
Lexicon, 121, 125
Libel (libeled), 134, 174, 177
Libertine, 202, 203
Limpid, 183, 184
Liquidation, 44, 48, 57
Lithe, 82, 84, 85, 261
Livid, 247, 249
Loath, 69, 70, 298
Loathe, 69, 70, 72
Locale, 187, 190
Longevity, 210, 271, 273, 275
Loquacious, 79, 234, 236, 243
Lucrative, 37, 41
Luminous, 182, 184
Lurid, 11, 12, 21, 28, 62, 76

M

Macabre, 229, 230, 243
Maladjusted, 240, 242
Malady (maladies), 272, 275
Malevolent, 67, 70, 217
Malignant, 53, 272, 275
Malleable, 155, 157, 165
Mammoth, 214, 216, 217
Mandate, 252, 256
Manifest (manifestly), 254, 256
Manifesto, 170, 175, 177
Manifold, 285, 287
Martyr, 163, 164, 172, 295
Masticate (masticating), 273, 275
Material, 295, 298, 299
Maudlin, 54, 55, 56, 243, 266
Maverick, 83, 84, 85, 225
Mawkish, 54, 55, 56, 72
Meager, 45, 48, 50
Megalomania, 10, 12
Melancholy, 229, 230
Mellifluous, 183, 184, 290
Memoir, 174, 177
Mendacious, 31, 34, 50
Mendicant, 47, 48, 50
Menial, 208, 209, 211, 217
Mercenary, 37, 41, 43
Mercurial, 126, 155, 157, 159
Meridian, 188, 190
Metamorphosis, 143, 156, 157
Meticulous (meticulously), 108, 111, 186
Mien, 123, 125, 159
Milieu, 188, 190, 225, 229, 243
Miscarry, 129, 131
Miscreant, 9, 12, 21, 100
Miserly, 47, 48
Missive, 173, 177, 179
Mollify (mollified), 117, 118, 120
Monolithic, 213, 216
Mordant, 292, 293
Moribund, 23, 26, 27, 28
Mortified, 67, 70
Mundane, 62, 63, 107, 206, 209, 211, 215, 217
Munificent, 40, 41, 43, 57
Myriad, 284, 287

N

Nadir, 23, 26, 27, 28, 72
Nascent, 51, 55, 56
Nebulous, 143, 145, 159, 165
Nefarious, 11, 12, 21, 279
Negligible, 219, 223
Neophyte, 51, 55
Nepotism, 104, 105, 172
Nettle, 247, 249
Neurotic, 227, 230
Niche, 187, 190, 191
Nirvana, 17, 19, 144, 225
Noisome, 69, 70, 229
Nominal (nominally), 207, 209, 211
Nonchalance, 200, 203
Nondescript, 124, 125
Nonentity, 229, 230, 233
Nostalgia (nostalgic), 266, 268, 286
Nuance, 141, 145, 225
Nullify (nullified), 168, 171

O

Obdurate, 96, 98
Obliging, 81, 84, 85
Obliterate, 167, 171
Obsequious, 10, 12, 21
Obsolete, 166, 265, 268
Obviate (obviated), 76, 90, 91, 93, 270
Occlude (occluded), 292, 293
Occult, 291, 293, 294
Odious, 68, 70, 72
Officious, 128, 131
Ominous, 22, 26, 27, 28
Omnipotent, 127, 131
Opaque, 142, 145, 165, 183
Opprobrium, 134, 138, 139
Opulence, 40, 41, 43
Ostensible, 143, 145, 205
Ostentatious, 75, 77, 83, 160, 182, 184, 214, 216, 307
Overt, 277, 281

P

Pacify (pacified), 117, 118
Paean, 232, 236
Pageantry, 42, 75, 77, 79
Palatial, 40, 41, 50
Pall, 74, 77, 79
Palliate, 272, 275
Paltry, 219, 223
Panacea, 272, 275
Pandemonium, 289, 293
Panoply, 74, 77, 79
Pantheon, 160, 164, 225
Parable, 232, 233, 236
Paradox, 192, 264, 268, 269, 283
Paragon, 297, 299
Paramount, 128, 131
Paroxysm, 247, 249
Parsimonious, 47, 48
Passé, 62, 63, 65
Pathological (pathologically), 10, 12, 30, 47
Patriarch, 61, 63, 65, 100
Paucity, 47, 48
Pauper, 46, 48
Peccadillo, 291, 293, 294
Pecuniary, 37, 41, 43, 50
Pedagogue, 4, 5, 159
Pedantic, 2, 5
Pedestrian, 62, 63, 65
Pellucid, 183, 184
Penchant, 124, 125, 243
Penniless, 45, 48
Pensive, 4, 5, 17, 21
Penury, 46, 48, 50
Peregrination, 195, 197
Peremptory, 130, 131
Perennial (perennially), 59, 63, 65
Perfidious, 30, 34, 50
Perfunctory, 196, 197
Permeate, 232, 277, 281
Pernicious, 66, 70
Perpetrator, 101, 105, 110
Perpetuate (perpetuated) (perpetuating), 61, 88, 91, 106
Persevere (persevered), 107, 111, 121
Perspicacious, 4, 5, 21, 159
Pertinent, 67, 69, 226, 279, 281
Peruse (perusal), 2, 5, 66
Perverse, 241, 242, 298
Petitioner, 116, 118
Phenomenon, 289, 293, 294
Philanthropic, 202, 203
Philanthropist, 302, 305
Phlegmatic, 149, 151, 159, 217
Physiognomy, 124, 125, 159

Pine (pining), 266, 268
Pinnacle, 16, 19, 21
Pique, 248, 249
Piteous, 46, 48
Pith, 212, 216
Pithy, 225, 232, 236
Pittance, 44, 48
Placate (placated), 116, 118, 120, 169
Plaudits, 16, 19, 21, 72
Plethora, 286, 287
Plight, 25, 26, 27, 52
Pluck (plucky), 97, 98, 100, 270
Poignant, 301, 305
Poise, 83, 84, 94, 98
Polemic, 134, 138, 139, 147, 176
Politic, 3, 5, 28
Potentate, 129, 131
Pragmatic, 4, 5, 28, 273
Preamble, 176, 177
Precedent, 255, 256, 298
Precipitate (precipitated), 90, 91, 208
Preclude, 87, 91, 147
Precocious, 82, 84, 85
Precursor, 88, 91
Prelude, 265, 268, 269
Premise, 88, 91, 274
Prerogative, 128, 131
Prescient, 267, 268
Prestigious, 15, 19, 28, 81, 85, 97
Pretentious, 54, 55, 56
Prevarication, 32, 34
Privation, 46, 48
Probity, 1, 5, 28, 72
Procrastinate (procrastinated), 267, 268
Prodigious, 85, 212, 216, 238
Prodigy, 16, 19, 100, 181
Proffer (proffered), 1, 5
Proficient, 81, 84
Profligate, 202, 203
Profuse, 286, 287
Progeny, 110, 298, 299, 306
Prognosticate (prognostications), 267, 268, 290
Prohibition, 254, 256, 269
Prolific, 15, 19
Prolix, 174, 177
Prompt (promptly), 108, 111
Promulgate (promulgated), 90, 91
Propagate, 194, 197, 206, 265
Propensity, 206, 209, 222, 301
Propinquity, 189, 190
Propitiate (propitiated), 115, 118, 120
Propitious, 18, 19, 21, 28
Propriety, 255, 256
Prosaic, 60, 63, 65, 173
Proscribe, 252, 256
Proselyte, 160, 164
Protean, 83, 84, 85
Protocol, 128, 131, 240, 254, 256, 269
Provisional, 156, 157
Prudence, 1, 5
Puerile, 53, 55, 56, 57
Pugnacious, 23, 248, 249, 258
Puissant, 129, 131
Punctilious (punctiliousness), 107, 111
Pungent, 241, 242

Q

Qualms, 226, 230, 243
Quandary, 25, 26, 27, 277
Quell (quelled), 116, 118, 120
Quip (quipped), 76, 136, 138, 139, 240
Quixotic, 52, 55, 56

R

Rail, 247, 249, 269
Raiment, 181, 184
Ramifications, 23, 26
Rampant, 43, 102, 104, 105, 127
Rapacious, 40, 41, 43
Rationalize, 296, 299, 306
Raucous, 199, 203
Raze (razed), 167, 171
Reactionary (reactionaries), 87, 91, 172
Rebuke, 248, 249
Recalcitrant (recalcitrance), 96, 98, 253
Recant (recanted), 101, 163, 164
Reciprocal, 199, 203
Recoil (recoiled), 66, 70
Recondite, 62, 63
Rectitude, 302, 305
Redolent, 135, 140, 286, 287, 294
Redoubtable, 258, 262
Redress, 104, 105, 158
Regal, 130, 131, 159
Regimen, 197, 264, 268
Regress (regressed), 222, 223
Reinforce (reinforced), 149, 158, 190, 258, 262
Reinvigorate (reinvigorating), 280, 281
Relegate (relegated), 176, 177
Reminisce, 266, 268
Remiss, 219, 223
Remote, 187, 190, 265
Remuneration, 39, 41, 81
Repertoire, 86, 205, 209
Replete, 134, 153, 286, 287
Repose, 273, 275
Repress (repressed), 33, 34
Reprimand (reprimanded), 103, 105, 288
Reproach (reproached), 221, 246, 247, 248, 249
Repudiate (repudiated), 69, 70, 137, 138, 144
Repugnant, 66, 70, 260, 266
Repulse (repulsed), 24, 26, 32, 68, 70, 95, 107
Repulsive, 137, 138, 139
Reputed, 144, 145
Requisite, 99, 255, 256
Resolution, 76, 77, 79, 297
Resolve (resolved), 92, 110, 111, 196, 294
Resourceful (resourcefulness), 46, 107, 111, 121, 138
Respite, 205, 209, 211, 240
Resplendent, 180, 184
Reticent, 142, 145
Retort (retorted), 71, 136, 138, 139
Retrospect, 97, 264, 268
Reverberate (reverberated), 174, 177, 179, 232
Revere (revered), 60, 63, 129
Reverie, 181, 184, 225, 243
Revile (reviled), 69, 70, 130
Rhetoric, 49, 52, 75, 77, 79, 226, 295
Rife, 66, 78, 130, 286, 287
Rift, 162, 164, 168, 171, 191, 289, 307
Risible, 136, 138, 139
Robust, 261, 262
Romp, 194, 196, 197
Rousing, 76, 77, 79, 100
Ruddy, 271, 275, 294
Rudimentary, 207, 209
Rue (rued), 266, 268, 284
Ruffian, 156, 260, 262
Ruminate (ruminating), 3, 5
Rustic, 189, 190

S

Sacrosanct, 79, 161, 164, 165, 225
Sage, 60, 63, 65, 176
Salient, 76, 77, 79, 126
Sally, 15, 19, 28
Salubrious, 274, 275, 294
Sanctimonious, 76, 77, 79, 232
Sanction, 253, 256, 269
Sanguine, 17, 19, 21, 72, 73
Satire, 293, 294
Saturate (saturated), 110, 283, 287, 294
Savvy, 44, 80, 84, 85
Scanty, 46, 48, 50
Schism, 162, 164
Scion, 53, 55, 56, 141
Scoff, 136, 138, 139
Scribe, 78, 175, 177, 179, 191
Scrupulous (scrupulously), 109, 111
Scurrilous, 9, 12, 25, 28, 29, 59
Scurry, 193, 197, 217
Seasoned, 52, 59, 63, 65, 146, 205, 255
Secular, 252, 256
Sedate, 186, 190, 191
Sedentary, 108, 148, 151, 159
Servile, 11, 12, 21
Sinecure, 39, 41, 43, 97
Sinewy, 260, 262
Sinister, 10, 12, 52
Skeptical, 17, 141, 145, 147, 151, 232, 236
Skirmish, 169, 171
Slovenly, 9, 12
Solace, 301, 305
Solicit (soliciting), 110, 111
Somber, 226, 230
Sophistry, 233, 236
Sophomoric, 54, 55, 56, 78, 150
Sordid, 11, 12, 21, 24, 28, 29
Spartan, 271, 275
Spate, 196, 197
Specious, 144, 145
Spontaneous, 154, 157, 194, 197, 290, 293
Sporadic, 75, 197, 220, 223
Spurious, 206, 219, 223
Squeamish, 150, 151, 159
Stagnant, 62, 63, 65
Stalwart, 95, 98
Staunch, 161, 164, 165
Steadfast, 259, 262
Steeped, 205, 209, 211
Stentorian, 97, 98
Stigmatize (stigmatized), 134, 138, 139
Stipulate, 4, 5, 57
Stoic, 33, 161, 164, 225
Stolid, 96, 98, 273
Strapping, 259, 262, 271
Strife, 103, 127, 168, 171, 300

Stunt, 150, 151
Stupor, 148, 151, 235
Stymie (stymied), 25, 26, 53, 196, 261
Subjugate, 129, 131
Sublime, 183, 184, 188, 191
Subservient, 295, 299, 306
Substantiate (substantiating), 298, 299, 306
Substrate, 90, 91
Subsume (subsumed), 215, 216
Subterfuge, 30, 34, 72, 114
Succinct, 173, 177, 213
Succulent, 271, 285, 287
Succumb (succumbed) (succumbing), 22, 26, 28, 96, 215
Sullen, 227, 230, 233, 238
Sumptuous, 39, 41, 43, 50, 143, 217
Superfluous, 285, 287
Supersede, 252, 256
Supine, 95, 222, 223, 225, 243
Supplicant, 45, 48, 50
Supremacy, 87, 163, 250, 262
Surfeit, 37, 41, 43, 50, 72
Surmise (surmised), 1, 5, 229, 234
Surreptitious, 87, 144, 145, 159
Susceptible, 220, 223
Swank, 215, 216, 217

T

Tableau, 123, 125
Taboo, 161, 164
Tacit (tacitly), 168, 295, 299
Taint (tainted), 103, 105
Tantalize (tantalized), 181, 184, 225
Tantamount, 87, 91
Taut, 149, 151
Temerity, 95, 98, 100, 112, 169
Tenable, 207, 209, 211, 217
Tenacious, 110, 111
Tenuous, 154, 157, 251
Terminus, 187, 190
Terse (tersely), 235, 236
Thrifty, 108, 111
Thwart (thwarted) (thwarting), 25, 26, 27, 53, 54, 130
Timorous, 83, 147, 151, 159
Tinge (tinged), 66, 239, 242
Titanic, 259, 262
Tortuous, 290, 293, 294
Tranquil, 206, 209, 211
Transgression, 33, 253, 256
Transient, 156, 157, 159
Translucent, 183, 184
Treatise, 175, 177, 179
Tremulous, 149, 151, 159
Trenchant, 4, 5, 21
Trepidation, 67, 70
Trite, 61, 63, 65
Trove, 112, 144, 265, 268, 269
Truncate (truncated), 264, 268
Tumultuous, 289, 293
Turbulent, 289, 293, 294
Tyranny, 127, 131, 155, 292
Tyro, 54, 55, 56, 100

U

Ubiquitous, 53, 134, 283, 287
Umbrage, 135, 138, 139
Unabated, 194, 197
Unaffected, 61, 63, 283
Unconscionable, 101, 105
Unctuous, 68, 70
Undaunted, 95, 98
Undergird (undergirded), 261, 262
Underwrite (underwritten), 37, 41, 43
Unflagging, 108, 111
Unkempt, 148, 151
Unmitigated, 260, 284, 287
Unrepentant, 104, 105
Unsavory, 8, 12, 21
Unstinting (unstintingly), 108, 111
Untoward, 9, 12, 21
Unwieldy, 213, 216, 290, 293
Urbane, 60, 61, 63, 65, 72
Usurp (usurped) (usurping), 32, 34, 146, 163, 183, 213, 218
Utilitarian, 80, 84, 85
Utopian, 52, 55, 56
Utterance, 234, 236

V

Vacillate (vacillating), 154, 157
Vapid, 222, 223, 243
Venal, 202, 203
Veneer, 122, 125, 159
Venerable, 61, 63, 65, 222, 237
Venerate (venerated), 160, 164
Verbatim, 234, 236
Verbose, 235, 236
Versatile, 80, 84, 85, 259, 262
Vestige, 173, 177
Vexation, 245, 249
Viable, 17, 19, 21, 28, 57, 93
Vicissitudes, 153, 157
Vigilant, 107, 111, 273
Vigorous, 261, 262
Vilify (vilified), 134, 138, 139
Vindicate (vindicated), 156, 218, 296, 299
Virile, 259, 262
Virtuosity, 213, 302, 305
Virulent, 65, 273, 275
Vitiate, 219, 223
Vitriolic, 248, 249
Vituperate, 248, 249
Vivacious, 122, 125
Vivid, 73, 77, 79
Vogue, 296, 299, 303
Volatile, 155, 157
Volition, 258, 295, 299
Voluminous, 213, 216
Voracious (voraciously), 39, 41, 57

W

Wane (waning), 219, 223
Welter, 292, 293
Wheedle (wheedled), 115, 118, 120
Whimsical, 154, 157, 159
Wince, 123, 125
Winsome, 200, 203, 217
Wrest (wrested), 169, 171

Z

Zealous, 161, 164
Zeitgeist, 225, 266, 268
Zenith, 15, 16, 19, 21, 28